BODY AND MIND

A HISTORY AND A DEFENSE
OF ANIMISM

BY

WILLIAM McDOUGALL, M.B., F.R.S.

FELLOW OF CORPUS CHRISTI COLLEGE, AND READER IN MENTAL PHILOSOPHY
IN THE UNIVERSITY OF OXFORD, FORMERLY FELLOW OF
ST JOHN'S COLLEGE, CAMBRIDGE

WITH THIRTEEN DIAGRAMS

THIRD EDITION

METHUEN & CO. LTD.
36 ESSEX STREET W.C.
LONDON

"Philosophy may assure us that the account of body and mind given by materialism is neither consistent nor intelligible. Yet body remains the most fundamental and all-pervading fact with which mind has got to deal, the one from which it can least easily shake itself free, the one that most complacently lends itself to every theory destructive of high endeavour."

A. J. BALFOUR

" Even the contrast between corporeal and mental existence may not be final and irreconcilable—but our present life is passed in a world where it has not yet been resolved, but yawning underlies all the relations of our thinking and acting. And, even as it will always be indispensable to life, it is, at present at least, indispensable to science. Things that appear to us incompatible, we must first establish separately each on its own foundation. If we have made ourselves acquainted with the natural growth and the ramification of each one of the groups of phenomena which we have thus discriminated, we may afterwards find it possible to speak of their common root. To try prematurely to unite them would only mean to obscure the survey of them, and to lower the value which every distinction possesses even when it may be done away with."

R. H. LOTZE

" Quant à l'idée que le corps vivant pourrait être soumis par quelque calculateur surhumain au même traitement mathématique que notre système solaire, elle est sortie peu à peu d'une certaine métaphysique qui a pris une forme plus précise depuis les découvertes physiques de Galilée, mais qui fut toujours la métaphysique naturelle de l'esprit humain. Sa clarté apparente, notre impatient désir de la trouver vraie, l'empressement avec laquelle tant d'excellents esprits l'acceptent sans preuve, toutes les séductions enfin qu'elle exerce sur notre pensée devraient nous mettre en garde contre elle."

H. BERGSON

PREFACE

IN writing this volume my primary aim has been to provide for students of psychology and philosophy, within a moderate compass, a critical survey of modern opinion and discussion upon the psycho-physical problem, the problem of the relation between body and mind. But I have tried to present my material in a manner not too dry and technical for the general reader who is prepared to grapple with a difficult subject. For I hold that men of science ought to make intelligible to the general public the course and issue of scientific discussions upon the wider questions to which their researches are directed, and that this obligation is especially strong in respect of the subject dealt with in these pages. Among the great questions debated by philosophers in every age the psycho-physical problem occupies a special position, in that it is one in which no thoughtful person can fail to be interested; for any answer to this question must have some bearing upon the fundamental doctrines of religion and upon our estimate of man's position and destiny in the world. And that interest in this question is widespread among the English-reading public, is shown by the dense stream of popular books upon it which continues to issue from the press both of this country and of the United States.

The greater part of this book is, then, occupied with a survey of modern discussions and modern theories of the psycho-physical relation; but without some knowledge of the course of development of speculation upon this topic it is impossible to understand the present state of opinion. I have written, therefore, in the earlier chapters a very brief history of the thought of preceding ages. This historical sketch makes no pretence of being a work of original research; in putting it together I have relied largely upon the standard histories of philosophy and science, especially the histories of philosophy of Ueberweg, Lewes, and Höffding, F. A. Lange's "History of Materialism," Erwin Rhode's "Psyche," Sir Michael Foster's "History of Physiology," the "History of European Thought in the Nineteenth Century" of Dr T. Merz, and the "Vitalismus als Geschichte und Lehre" of Dr Hans Driesch.

The history of thought upon the psycho-physical problem is in the main the history of the way in which Animism, the oldest and, in all previous ages, the most generally accepted answer to it, has been attacked and put more and more upon the defensive in succeeding centuries, until towards the end of the nineteenth century it was generally regarded in academic circles as finally driven from the field. I have therefore given to the historical chapters the form of a history of Animism.

The sub-title describes this book as a defense, as well as a history, of Animism. I hasten to offer some explanation of this description, lest the mere title of the book should repel a considerable number of possible readers.

The word Animism is frequently used by contemporary writers to denote what is more properly called primitive Animism, or primitive Anthropomorphism, namely, the belief that all natural objects which seem to exert any power or influence are moved or animated by "spirits," or intelligent purposive beings. It is perhaps hardly necessary to say that the Animism I defend is not of this primitive type. But this is only one variety of Animism, one which seems to have been reached by extending the essential animistic notion far beyond its original and proper sphere of application. The modern currency and usage of the word derives chiefly from Prof. Tylor's "Primitive Culture," and I use it with the general connotation given it in that celebrated treatise. The essential notion, which forms the common foundation of all varieties of Animism, is that all, or some, of those manifestations of life and mind which distinguish the living man from the corpse and from inorganic bodies are due to the operation within him of something which is of a nature different from that of the body, an animating principle generally, but not necessarily or always, conceived as an immaterial and individual being or soul.

"Primitive Animism" seems to have grown up by extension of

this notion to the explanation of all the more striking phenomena of nature. And the Animism of civilized men, which has been and is the foundation of every religious system, except the more rigid Pantheisms, is historically continuous with the primitive doctrine. But, while religion, superstition, and the hope of a life beyond the grave, have kept alive amongst us a variety of animistic beliefs, ranging in degree of refinement and subtlety from primitive Animism to that taught by Plato, Leibnitz, Lotze, William James, or Henri Bergson, modern science and philosophy have turned their backs upon Animism of every kind with constantly increasing decision; and the efforts of modern philosophy have been largely directed towards the excogitation of a view of man and of the world which shall hold fast to the primacy and efficiency of mind or spirit, while rejecting the animistic conception of human personality. My prolonged puzzling over the psycho-physical problem has inclined me to believe that these attempts cannot be successfully carried through, and that we must accept without reserve Professor Tylor's dictum that Animism "embodies the very essence of spiritualistic, as opposed to materialistic, philosophy,"[1] and that the deepest of all schisms is that which divides Animism from Materialism.[2]

The main body of this volume is therefore occupied with the presentation and examination of the reasonings which have led the great majority of philosophers and men of science to reject Animism, and of the modern attempts to render an intelligible account of the nature of man which, in spite of the rejection of Animism, shall escape Materialism. This survey leads to the conclusion that these reasonings are inconclusive and these attempts unsuccessful, and that we are therefore compelled to choose between Animism and Materialism; and, since the logical necessity of preferring the animistic horn of this dilemma cannot be in doubt, my survey constitutes a defense and justification of Animism.

I have chosen to use the word Animism rather than any other, not only because it clearly marks the historical continuity of the modern with the ancient conception, but also because no other term indicates precisely all those theories of human personality

[1] "Primitive Culture," vol. i. p. 415.   [2] *Op. cit.*, p. 502.

which have in common the notion which, as I believe, provides the only alternative to Materialism. The word "Spiritualism" as used in philosophy is ambiguous, and it has been spoilt for scientific purposes by its current usage to denote that popular belief which is more properly called Spiritism. Nor is all Animism spiritualistic; during long ages the dominant form of it was a materialistic Dualism. The term "psycho-physical dualism" accurately expresses the essential animistic notion; but it is cumbrous, and the word Dualism is apt to be taken to imply metaphysical Dualism, an implication which I am anxious to avoid; for Animism does not necessarily imply metaphysical Dualism, or indeed any metaphysical or ontological doctrine, and may logically be held in conjunction with a monistic metaphysic, or indeed with any metaphysical doctrine, Solipsism alone excepted. The expression "psycho-physical interactionism" will not serve my purpose, because (as we see in the philosophy of Leibnitz, and in that modification of the Cartesian system known as Occasionalism) Animism may be combined with the denial of psycho-physical interaction. Again, the term "soul-theory" does not cover all varieties of Animism, in illustration of which statement I may remind the reader that the late Prof. James advocated a distinctly animistic view of human personality, which he called the "transmission theory," but explicitly rejected the conception of the soul as a unitary and individual being.

The reader may perhaps be helped to grasp the long argument of the book, if I make here a summary statement of its course. The first six chapters trace in outline through the European culture-tradition, from primitive ages to the present time, the history of Animism and of the attacks upon it from the sides of metaphysic, epistemology, and the natural sciences, and they indicate the principal doctrines proposed as alternatives to it. Chapters VII., VIII., IX., and X. display the grounds on which at the present day the rejection of Animism is generally founded. It is shown that, although in former ages the psycho-physical problem has generally been regarded as one to be solved by metaphysic, it is now widely recognized that the issue must be decided by the methods of empirical science; and it is shown how the modern rejection of Animism finds its principal ground in the claim of the physical sciences that their mechanical principles of explanation must hold exclusive sway throughout the universe, a claim which I venture to characterize as "the mechanistic dogma."

Chapters XI. and XII. state, examine, and display the special difficulties of, the more important of the monistic doctrines proposed as substitutes for Animism. The least unsatisfactory of these are closely allied, and in accordance with current usage are classed together under the head of psycho-physical Parallelism. In Chapter XIII. it is shown that the choice of Parallelism or Animism is a dilemma from which we cannot escape, unless indeed we are prepared to adopt all the absurdities of thoroughgoing Materialism or of Solipsism.

Chapters XIV., XV., and XVI. examine the modern arguments against Animism, and show that no one of them, nor all of them together, logically necessitate its rejection.

Chapters XVII. to XXIV. exhibit the inadequacy of the mechanical principles to the explanation of the facts of general physiology, of biological evolution, of human and animal behaviour, and of psychology, and bring forward certain positive arguments in favour of Animism.

Chapter XXV. states my attitude towards the work of the Society for Psychical Research, and shows how, as it seems to me, the results hitherto achieved by that line of investigation strengthen the case against the "mechanistic dogma."

In the last chapter I have tried to draw together the threads of the argument, and regarding the "mechanistic dogma" (the only serious objection to Animism) as discredited, I have weighed the claims of the principal varieties of Animism in a discussion which results in favour of the hypothesis of the soul. Finally, I have endeavoured to indicate a view of the nature of the soul which shall be in harmony with all the facts established by empirical science.

I am aware that to many minds it must appear nothing short of a scandal that anyone occupying a position in an academy of learning, other than a Roman Catholic seminary, should in this twentieth century defend the old-world notion of the soul of man.

For it is matter of common knowledge that "Science" has given its verdict against the soul, has declared that the conception of the soul as a thing, or being, or substance, or mode of existence or activity, different from, distinguishable from, or in any sense or degree independent of, the body is a mere survival from primitive culture, one of the many relics of savage superstition that obstinately persist among us in defiance of the clear teachings of modern science. The greater part of the philosophic world also, mainly owing to the influence of the natural sciences, has arrived at the same conclusion. In short, it cannot be denied that, as William James told us at Oxford three years ago, "souls are out of fashion."

But I am aware also that not one in a hundred of those scientists and philosophers who confidently and even scornfully reject the notion has made any impartial and thorough attempt to think out the psycho-physical problem in the light of all the relevant data now available and of the history of previous thought on the question. And I am young enough to believe that there is amongst us a considerable number of persons who prefer the dispassionate pursuit of truth to the interests of any system, and to hope that some of them may find my book acceptable as an honest attempt to grapple once more with this central problem. And I am fortified by the knowledge that a few influential contemporary philosophers adhere to the animistic conception of human personality, or at least regard the psycho-physical question as still open, as also by certain indications that the "mechanistic dogma" no longer holds the scientific world in so close a grip as during the later part of the nineteenth century.

"Animism," writes Professor Tylor, "is, in fact, the groundwork of the Philosophy of Religion, from that of savages up to that of civilized men."[1] And, though modern Pantheisms have generally rejected Animism, the statement remains substantially correct. And it must be admitted that most of those who have defended Animism in the modern period have been openly or secretly moved by the desire to support religious doctrines

[1] "Primitive Culture," i. p. 426.

which they have accepted on other than scientific grounds. It follows that anyone who undertakes to defend the theory is liable to be suspected of a bias of this kind.

These considerations are my apology for setting down here a personal confession, which may aid the reader in judging of the nature and degree of any bias that may have affected my presentation of the arguments for and against Animism. I believe that the future of religion is intimately bound up with the fate of Animism; and especially I believe that, if science should continue to maintain the mechanistic dogma, and consequently to repudiate Animism, the belief in any form of life after the death of the body will continue rapidly to decline among all civilized peoples, and will, before many generations have passed away, become a negligible quantity. Nevertheless, I claim that the discussions of the following pages are conducted with as much impartiality as is possible for one to whom the argument seems to point strongly towards one of the rival hypotheses. For I can lay claim to no religious convictions; I am not aware of any strong desire for any continuance of my personality after death; and I could accept with equanimity a thoroughgoing Materialism, if that seemed to me the inevitable outcome of a dispassionate and critical reflection. Nevertheless, I am in sympathy with the religious attitude towards life; and I should welcome the establishment of sure empirical foundations for the belief that human personality is not wholly destroyed by death. For, as was said above, I judge that this belief can only be kept alive if a proof of it, or at least a presumption in favour of it, can be furnished by the methods of empirical science. And it seems to me highly probable that the passing away of this belief would be calamitous for our civilization. For every vigorous nation seems to have possessed this belief, and the loss of it has accompanied the decay of national vigour in many instances.

Apart from any hope of rewards or fear of punishment after death, the belief must have, it seems to me, a moralizing influence upon our thought and conduct that we can ill afford to dispense with. The admirable Stoic attitude of a Marcus Aurelius or a

Huxley may suffice for those who rise to it in the moral environment created by civilizations based upon a belief in a future life and upon other positive religious beliefs; but I gravely doubt whether whole nations could rise to the level of an austere morality, or even maintain a decent working standard of conduct, after losing those beliefs. A proof that our life does not end with death, even though we knew nothing of the nature of the life beyond the grave, would justify the belief that we have our share in a larger scheme of things than the universe described by physical science; and this conviction must add dignity, seriousness, and significance to our lives, and must thus throw a great weight into the scale against the dangers that threaten every advanced civilization. While, then, I should prefer for myself a confident anticipation of total extinction at death to a belief that I must venture anew upon a life of whose nature and conditions we have no knowledge, I desire, on impersonal grounds, to see the world-old belief in a future life established on a scientific foundation. To that extent, and to that extent only, I think, my inquiry is biassed.

Finally, I wish to state emphatically that my inquiry is not conceived as a search for metaphysical truth, but that it is rather conducted by the methods and with the aims of all empirical science; that is to say, it aims at discovering the hypotheses which will enable us best to co-ordinate the chaotic data of immediate experience by means of a conceptual system as consistent as may be, while recognizing that such conceptions must always be subject to revision with the progress of science. Of course, if the term metaphysic be taken in the older sense as implying an inquiry into that which is not physical, the theme of this work is metaphysical; but that is a usage which is no longer accepted; metaphysic is now distinguished from empirical science by its aims and methods rather than by its subject-matter. I claim, then, for the conception of the soul, advocated in the last chapter of this book, no more than that it is an hypothesis which is indispensable to science at the present time.

CONTENTS

CHAPTER I

ANIMISM IN THE ANCIENT WORLD

                                                                           PAGES

Primitive Animism or Anthropomorphism—The ghost-soul—Burial customs—Origin of ghost-soul—Ghost-soul not immaterial—Extension of original idea of soul—Survivals of ghost-soul—Hebrew Animism—Homeric Animism—The Ionian physicists—Post-Homeric Animism—Greek Materialism—Plato—Aristotle—Stoicism and Scepticism 1-27

CHAPTER II

ANIMISM IN THE MIDDLE AGES

Pneuma—Materialistic Animism of early Fathers—Spiritualisation of the soul—Neoplatonism—The Schoolmen—Averroism—Roman Materialism . . 28-38

CHAPTER III

ANIMISM AT THE TIME OF THE RENASCENCE OF LEARNING

Pomponazzi—Vives—Telesio—Bruno—Physiology founded—Vesalius and Van Helmont 39-45

CHAPTER IV

ANIMISM IN THE SEVENTEENTH CENTURY

Rise of modern Materialism—Descartes—Occasionalism—Leibnitz—Spinoza—Hobbes 46-60

CHAPTER V

ANIMISM IN THE EIGHTEENTH CENTURY

The attack on "Substance"—Locke leads the attack—His dualism—The Deists—Bishop Berkeley's idealism—Hume's scepticism—The Wolffian rationalism dominant on the Continent—French materialism of the "Enlightenment"—Kant's reconciliation of Spiritualism with Materialism—The Vitalists . 61-78

CHAPTER VI

ANIMISM IN THE NINETEENTH CENTURY

The romantic speculation—Reaction against it—The modern phase of psycho-physical discussion introduced by Fechner—Modern defenders of Animism in Germany, France, Great Britain, and America 79-86

CHAPTER VII

MODERN DEVELOPMENTS OF PHYSICAL SCIENCE ADVERSE TO ANIMISM

Solipsism unacceptable—The psycho-physical problem to be dealt with by methods of empirical science—Kinetic mechanism—The law of the conservation of energy . . . 87-93

CHAPTER VIII

THE RISE OF THE MECHANISTIC PHYSIOLOGY AND OF THE "PSYCHOLOGY WITHOUT A SOUL"

Hylozoism of the "Enlightment"—Vitalists—Mechanical explanations of vital processes confidently assumed—The search for the seat of the soul fails—The doctrine of the reflex type of all nervous process—Unconscious cerebration—The association-psychology and the law of habit—The dependence of thought on integrity of brain-functions—The law of psycho-neural correlation—The composite nature of the mind 94-118

CHAPTER IX

THE INFLUENCE OF THE DARWINIAN THEORY

Lamarckism—Neo-Darwinism—Organic adaptations mechanically explained—No need for teleology—Continuity of evolution—Interment of Animism by Tyndall 119-121

CHAPTER X

CURRENT PHILOSOPHICAL ARGUMENTS AGAINST ANIMISM

Inconceivability of psycho-physical interaction—Variants of the inconceivability argument—Immediate knowledge of consciousness, but not of the soul—*Rapprochement* of science and philosophy on basis of Monism . . 122-125

CHAPTER XI

THE AUTOMATON THEORIES

Epiphenomenalism—Its "energetic" variant—Psycho-physical Parallelism proper—Phenomenalistic Parallelism—Psychical Monism as expounded by Paulsen, Strong, Clifford, and Fechner—Fechner's "proof" of the sub-conscious—Fechner's "day-view" of nature—Continuity of evolution—Psychical Monism compatible with scientific Materialism—Its many advantages . . . 122-148

CONTENTS

CHAPTER XII

EXAMINATION OF THE AUTOMATON-THEORIES AND OF THE SPECIAL ARGUMENTS IN THEIR FAVOUR

Epiphenomenalism combines the difficulties of materialism and of interaction—Parallelism proper must go on to accept the identity hypothesis in one or other of its two forms—The "two-aspect doctrine" meaningless—Therefore "Psychical Monism" the only form of Parallelism deserving of serious consideration—The difficulty of doing without "things"—My self is not my consciousness, but rather the sum of enduring conditions which we call the structure of the mind—Difficulties of the compounding of consciousnesses—Difficulties common to all forms of Parallelism—Universal consciousness—It necessitates assumption of unconscious consciousness—Parallelism of mechanical sequences with the logical and teleological . . . 149-178

CHAPTER XIII

IS THERE ANY WAY OF ESCAPE FROM THE DILEMMA—ANIMISM OR PARALLELISM?

The acceptance of "idealism" does not absolve us from the psycho-physical problem—Kant neither resolved nor dissolved the problem—Three attitudes towards it of Post-Kantians, represented by Parallelism of Paulsen, the ambiguity of Lange, and the transubjective Idealism of Ward—The last implies Animism as hypothesis necessary to natural science . . . 179-188

CHAPTER XIV

ARGUMENTA AD HOMINEM

Proposed dualism of science and philosophy—A calculable universe—Animism does not necessarily imply metaphysical Dualism or Pluralism—Parallelism admits only pantheistic religion—Parallelism incompatible with belief in any continuance of personality after death—Fechner, Kant, and Paulsen fail to reconcile the mechanistic dogma with human immortality—High authorities for and against Animism 189-205

CHAPTER XV

EXAMINATION OF THE ARGUMENTS AGAINST ANIMISM FROM EPISTEMOLOGY, "INCONCEIVABILITY," AND THE LAW OF CONSERVATION OF ENERGY

Necessity of giving all scientific explanation the mechanical form not proved—Guidance without work—Various possibilities—Argument from conservation of energy describes a circle—Difficulty of defining the "physical"—Immediate awareness not the highest type of knowledge 206-223

CHAPTER XVI

EXAMINATION OF THE ARGUMENTS AGAINST ANIMISM DRAWN FROM PHYSIOLOGY AND GENERAL BIOLOGY

Inadequate conceptions of interaction alone give plausibility to arguments from cerebral physiology—Continuity of evolution a postulate—But, if accepted, not fatal to Animism—Statistics and teleology—Abiogenesis . . . 224-234

CHAPTER XVII

THE INADEQUACY OF MECHANICAL CONCEPTIONS IN PHYSIOLOGY

PAGES

Last half-century has done nothing to justify physiological materialism—The impossibility of mechanistic explanation of morphogenesis and heredity—Experimental embryology, restitution, and regeneration—Organisms and machines—Organisms and the degradation of energy 235-245

CHAPTER XVIII

INADEQUACY OF MECHANICAL PRINCIPLES TO EXPLAIN ORGANIC EVOLUTION

Neo-Darwinism based on mechanistic assumption in regard to heredity—Natural selection implies the struggle for existence—Difficulties of Neo-Darwinism—Diminished by "organic selection"—But this is a teleological principle—Mutations not fortuitous—Regeneration not explicable on Darwinian principles—Resuscitation of Vitalism—Appendix on organic selection . . . 246-257

CHAPTER XIX

INADEQUACY OF MECHANICAL CONCEPTIONS TO EXPLAIN ANIMAL AND HUMAN BEHAVIOUR

The "total reactions" of animalcules are not tropisms—Persistence and "trial and error" among the lowest animals—Purely instinctive actions initiated by perceptions which involve mental synthesis—Instinctive actions co-operating with intelligence imply more extensive synthesis—Meaning and purpose as factors in instinctive behaviour—Human instincts—"Meaning" is an essential link between sense-impression and reaction—Values 258-271

CHAPTER XX

THE ARGUMENT TO PSYCHO-PHYSICAL INTERACTION FROM THE "DISTRIBUTION OF CONSCIOUSNESS"

Darwinism implies the usefulness of consciousness—And not merely of infra-consciousness, but of integrated personal consciousness—True consciousness accompanies not all nervous processes, but only those which result in modification 272-280

CHAPTER XXI

THE UNITY OF CONSCIOUSNESS

Two lines of argument—The metaphysical (Lotze) valid, but not capable of convincing—The physiological—The *sensorium commune*, variously conceived—All these conceptions untenable—No physical medium of composition of effects of sense-stimuli—Some medium demanded by our intellect—Why refuse to trust it?—Fechner's doctrine of the threshold and of psycho-physical continuity—The facts of sensory "fusion" incompatible with Parallelism, however stated—Multiple personality 281-300

CONTENTS

CHAPTER XXII

THE PSYCHO-PHYSICS OF "MEANING"

The association-psychology ignored "meaning"—But without meaning "ideas" are meaningless—The doctrine of the "psychic fringe"—Spatial meanings are not identical with clusters of kinæsthetic sensations—Sensations are merely cues to meanings—And meanings are relatively independent of sensations and have no physical parallels 301-311

CHAPTER XXIII

PLEASURE, PAIN, AND CONATION

The facts of feeling-tone—Feeling has no immediate correlate among the brain-processes—Yet feeling determines the trend of thought and action—Feeling and the establishment of associations — Feeling and evolution — The peculiarities of conative process have no physical analogues 312-329

CHAPTER XXIV

MEMORY

Parallelism implies that all mental retention can be described in terms of brain-structure—The fantastic "memory-cell"—Motor-habit the type of all retention founded in brain-structure—But true memory cannot be identified with habit—The law of neural association as generally stated is false—All remembering involves co-operation of two factors, habit and true memory—Suggestion towards a theory of memory 330-346

CHAPTER XXV

THE BEARING OF THE RESULTS OF "PSYCHICAL RESEARCH" ON THE PSYCHO-PHYSICAL PROBLEM

The search for empirical evidence of survival—Telepathy seems to be established—Hypernormal control of bodily by mental processes—Post-hypnotic appreciation of time 347-354

CHAPTER XXVI

CONCLUSION

Animism preferable to Parallelism—Four varieties of Animism—The animistic "actuelle Seele"—The transmission theory of James and Bergson—The objections to the soul-theory flimsy, if psycho-physical interaction is accepted—The contentless soul—The soul a developing system of psychical dispositions—Multiple personalities are of two kinds, both consistent with the soul-theory—The vegetative functions of the soul—The soul-theory and organic evolution 355-379

INDEX 381-384

BODY AND MIND

CHAPTER I

ANIMISM IN THE ANCIENT WORLD

IT would seem that from a very remote period men of almost all races have entertained the belief that the living man differs from the corpse in that his body contains some more subtle thing or principle which determines its purposive movements, its growth and self-repair, and to which is due his capacity for sensation, thought, and feeling. For the belief in some such animating principle, or soul, is held by almost every existing race of men, no matter how lowly their grade of culture nor how limited their mental powers; and we find evidences of a similar belief among the earliest human records.

Among the more highly civilized peoples, the soul has generally been regarded by the more cultured members of each community as an immaterial being or agency; but the distinction between material and immaterial things was only achieved after long ages of discussion and by many steps of refinement of the conception of the soul. The belief most widely current among the peoples of lower culture is that each man consists, not only of the body which is constantly present among his fellows, but also of a shadowy vapour-like duplicate of his body; this shadow-like image, the animating principle of the living organism, is thought to be capable of leaving the body, of transporting itself rapidly, if not instantaneously, from place to place, and of manifesting in those places all or most of the powers that it exerts in the body during waking life. Sleep is regarded as due to its temporary withdrawal from the body; trance, coma, and other serious illness, as due to longer absence; and death is thought to imply its final departure to some distant place.

That this belief is a very real one among many peoples, is shown by their careful observance of customs in which it finds expression. Thus, among some of the peoples who entertain this belief, it is customary to avoid wakening a sleeper, lest his wandering soul should not return to him; and, if it becomes absolutely necessary to waken him, it is done as gradually as possible, in order that his soul may have time to find its way back to the body. Or again, the friends of a sick person will procure a medicine-man, who, falling into trance, will send his soul after the retreating soul, to arrest it if possible on its journey toward the land of the dead, and to lead it back to the body of the patient. And after death the friends or relatives will take all possible measures to aid the departing soul on its journey, and to promote its welfare in the land of shades, where it is believed to lead a life very much like that of its embodied state in this world.[1]

The burial customs of many peoples afford the best evidence that the disembodied soul is conceived as like in all essential respects to the living whole of soul and body. The widespread custom of killing slaves or wives on the death of a man of some importance is an expression of the belief that the souls of the victims will accompany his soul and will continue to serve it as they served him before death. And the even more widely spread custom of burying or burning with the body of the dead man his most valued possessions, especially weapons and ornaments, is due to the belief that even these things have their shadowy duplicates or ghost-souls, which can be carried away by the departing soul and used by it as the real objects were used by the living man.

Professor E. B. Tylor first clearly expounded this primitive conception of the ghost-soul, showed its wide distribution in space and time, and illustrated with a wealth of detail its many variations, in his celebrated chapters on Animism;[2] and there can be no reasonable doubt that he has given the true account of its origin, in attributing it in the main to reflection upon the experiences of dreams and visions, in conjunction with the objectively observed facts of sleep, trance, and death. In sleep, while the body lies at rest, the sleeper remains unconscious of the surroundings of his body; he seems to himself to visit other scenes, to meet and converse with other persons, and to have the use in these dream-adventures of his dress and weapons. In visions and

---

[1] Among the Kayans of Borneo, for example, it is the custom for an elderly person learned in such matters to sit beside the corpse, where the soul is supposed to hover for some days after death, and to impart to the latter minute directions for its journey to the land of the dead.

[2] "Primitive Culture," first edition, London, 1871; especially chap. xi.

in dreams he sees, too, the shadowy forms of dead friends. Since, then, most savages regard their dream-experiences as equally real with those of waking life, they naturally and inevitably arrive at the theory that the ghost-self, which in dreams can appear in distant places, leaving the deserted body in death-like stillness, is identical with the animating principle.

It is sometimes said that primitive man conceives the ghost-soul as material; while Professor Tylor describes it as a spiritualistic conception. But to describe the primitive ghost-soul as either matter or spirit is misleading; if these terms are to be applied to it, we must describe it as a material spirit. This is, of course, a contradiction in terms, which we can only resolve by recognizing that the peoples who believe in the ghost-soul have not achieved the comparatively modern distinction between material and immaterial or spiritual existents. It is clear that the ghost-soul is generally conceived as having many of the properties of matter, and as having the same needs as the embodied soul, as subject to the pains of cold and heat, of hunger and thirst, and as being bound, though less strictly than the body, by conditions of space and matter. This quasi-materiality of the ghost-soul is well illustrated by the custom, observed among many peoples, of making a hole in the roof or wall of the death-chamber for the exit of the departing soul, or by that of sinking a bamboo tube through the earth above the buried corpse in order to allow the soul to revisit it.

Two things seem chiefly to have determined the form of the primitive belief as to the substance of the ghost-soul, namely, the shadow and the breath. Each man's shadow is an impalpable something which has a certain likeness to the man, and which accompanies him when actively employed, but which disappears when he lies down in sleep or death. And the breath that comes and goes from his nostrils seems bound up with his life, and disappears at death. In some regions the new-born babe is held to the mouth of a dying person, in order to receive his escaping soul or breath. And language clearly shows the important part played by the ideas of the shadow and of the breath in such words as manes and shade, spirit, *spiritus*, *anima*, *animus*, *pneuma*, and in similar words of many other languages.

The conception of the ghost-soul cannot be better defined than in the following words of Professor Tylor, from whose classical account the foregoing brief description has been condensed. He writes: "It is a thin, unsubstantial human image, in its nature a sort of vapour, film, or shadow; the cause of life and thought in the individual it animates; independently possessing the personal consciousness and volition of its corporeal owner, past or present; capable of leaving the body far behind, to flash swiftly from place to place; mostly impalpable and invisible, yet also manifesting physical power, and especially appearing to men waking or asleep as a phantasm separate from the body of which it bears the likeness; continuing to exist and appear to men after the death of that body; able to enter into, possess, and act in the bodies of other men, of animals, and even of things."[1]

Since the publication of "Primitive Culture," the origin of Animism has been the subject of much discussion and controversy; but in their main outlines Dr Tylor's account of the ghost-soul, and his theory of the genesis of the idea, seem to remain unshaken. Mr Andrew Lang has urged that waking hallucinations or apparitions (in common phrase, the seeing of ghosts) may have played an important part in developing the idea. Mr R. R. Marett[2] and others have attempted to describe a pre-animistic conception, which attributed an ill-defined power or virtue to all things that evoked awe in the mind of primitive man; it is suggested that this notion was the common matrix from which ideas of the souls of men, animals, and plants, anthropomorphic conceptions of natural forces, the ideas of gods and demons, in fact, all ideas of spiritual existences, have been differentiated. These are interesting suggestions which, in so far as they are accepted (and to me a strong case seems to be made out for both views), are to be regarded as supplementing Dr Tylor's doctrine, rather than as conflicting with it.[3]

---

[1] "Primitive Culture," third edition, vol. i. p. 429.
[2] "The Threshold of Religion," London, 1908.
[3] More recently Mr A. E. Crawley has published a work ("The Idea of the Soul") in which he claims to have completely refuted Dr Tylor's theory of the origin of the ghost-soul, and to have established a rival. To my mind the weight of the arguments brought forward against Dr Tylor's view is a negligible quantity, and the hypothesis proposed as an alternative seems highly improbable. Mr Crawley maintains that the visual images of waking life are the source from which primitive man derived his ideas of the souls of men and things. Though this view cannot be seriously entertained as a substitute for Dr Tylor's theory, it may, I think, be regarded as supplementing it, by drawing attention to a factor which may have played some considerable part in the genesis of the ghost-soul, and which, perhaps, has not been sufficiently taken into account. The tendency to visualize our dead friends, when we think

The ascription by primitive men of ghost-souls to animals, plants, and inert objects, is probably regarded as an extension of the theory first arrived at by reflection on the problem of human life. Such extension was rendered almost inevitable by the fact that persons met in dreams and visions, as well as the dreamer himself, seem to have about them their dogs, their weapons, their dress, and other material objects. It seems probable also that the ghost-soul of man was the first definite conception of personal intelligent powers, living and working in detachment from ordinary solid matter and all the narrow limitations of embodied existence. If so, the developments of ideas of other powers of a similar, but non-human, nature, demons, gods, spirits good and evil of all sorts, must have been in large degree merely extensions and differentiations of this fundamental notion of the human ghost-soul.[1]

In various ages and places many variants of this primitive conception of the ghost-soul have been held; some savages, for example, agree with certain philosophers of classical antiquity in assigning to each man two, three, or even four souls of different functions. But the diversities of the opinions of uncultured peoples on this great subject are far less striking than the uniformities; and the theory of the ghost-soul is so widely distributed throughout all regions of the world, and gives so natural and satisfactory explanations of so many facts that force themselves upon the attention of men of every grade of culture, that we may suppose it to have been independently reached by many peoples. So concordant is it with the way of thinking of unsophisticated mankind, that it has lived on up to the present day in the popularly accepted traditions of almost all the peoples of the world; and every feature of the primitive conception is illustrated by practices and beliefs still current among the most highly civilized peoples of Europe. Even the belief in the materiality of the soul still finds expression in the custom of opening the door or window of the death-chamber to give free egress to the departing soul,[2] and in the German superstition[3]

---

of them, is strong in most of us, and perhaps stronger in the men of primitive culture than in others. And this tendency may well have facilitated the development of the notion of the ghost-soul by reflection upon the facts of sleep, dream, trance, and death.

[1] This is the view forcibly defended by Prof. W. Wundt in his *Völker-psychologie* (second edition, vol. iv. part i.), Leipzig, 1910.

[2] " Primitive Culture," vol. i. p. 454.   [3] *Ibid.*, vol. i. p. 455.

that the ghost-soul of a mother who dies in child-birth will return to suckle the infant and will leave the impress of its weight upon the bed.

The history of Animism throughout the course of the development of European civilization affords one of the most striking illustrations of the law that, in every civilized community, two streams of tradition, two strata of belief and custom, persist side by side, influencing one another, but never fusing: namely, the stream of popular tradition and the literary tradition of the cultured few.

Throughout the development of European civilization, popular beliefs regarding the nature and destiny of the human soul have remained vague, diversified, and fluctuating. Although, amid all changes, the primitive conception of the ghost-soul has persisted in the popular mind, for just the same reasons as have led to its independent adoption by so many savage peoples; it has been modified in various ways, and partially overlaid and obscured, by the teachings of the leaders of religious, philosophical, and scientific thought. The elements taken up by the popular tradition from these sources have been for the most part logically incompatible with the theory of the ghost-soul; and this incompatibility has no doubt played a principal part in preventing, within the stream of popular tradition, the formation of any definite and generally accepted notion, and in maintaining in every age among large numbers of the people a sceptical or negative attitude towards the doctrine of a future life.

The further civilization has progressed, the more chaotic has the state of popular opinion upon this great question become; until, at the present time, there is current among us almost every variety of opinion and belief that the foregoing generations have excogitated.

To attempt to trace the devious and many-branched course of the muddy stream of popular tradition would be a hopeless task. In the following pages I am concerned only with the history of Animism in the culture-tradition. I have to attempt to show how, starting with primitive Animism, the culture-tradition has successively modified it and refined it; until at the present day the venerable doctrine seems to be on the point of being finally dismissed to the anthropologists' museum of curiosities.

The principal influences that differentiated the Animism of

the culture-tradition from primitive Animism, and set it upon its long and troubled course, were: (1) the teachings of the Hebrew prophets; (2) the speculations of the theologians and philosophers of ancient Greece; and (3) the efforts of the Christian fathers, influenced by the culture-tradition of the ancient Greek world as well as by that of the Hebrews, to set up a consistent and generally acceptable doctrine of the soul among the dogmas of the Church. The operation of these influences will be briefly traced in the present and in the following chapter.

The primitive Hebrew conception of the soul was essentially the same as the ghost-soul of so many other peoples. As the Rev. Prof. Charles points out,[1] we must distinguish the earlier from the later view expressed in the Old Testament. According to the earlier view, "man consists of two elements, spirit or soul and body"; "the soul is the seat of feeling and desire, and, in a secondary degree, of the intelligence, and is identified with the personality"; the soul leaves the body at death (though, as by so many other peoples, it was thought of as hovering in its neighbourhood for some time after death) to pass to the dark underworld of the souls of the dead, Sheol. "The relations and customs of earth were reproduced in Sheol. Thus the prophet was distinguished by his mantle, kings by their crowns and thrones, the uncircumcised by his foreskin. Each nation also preserved its individuality, and no doubt its national garb and customs. . . . Indeed the departed were regarded as reproducing exactly the same features as marked them at the moment of death." And the ghost-souls of ancestors were believed to have knowledge of their descendants and to benefit from their ministrations. Under the teaching of the prophets and the development of Monotheism, the spirit began to be distinguished from the soul; and, while the soul remained as the vital principle of the body and as the seat of all the mental activities, it was not conceived as surviving the death of the body —"in death the soul is extinguished and only the spirit survives. But since the spirit is only the impersonal force of life common to men and brutes, it returns to the Fount of all life, and thus all personal existence ceases at death." "In the above threefold division of man's personality the spirit and soul are distinct alike

[1] "A Critical History of the Doctrine of a Future Life in Israel, in Judaism, and in Christianity," by R. H. Charles, D.D.

in essence and origin. The former is the impersonal basis of life coming from God, and returning on death to God. The latter, which is the personal factor in man, is simply the supreme function of the quickened body, and perishes on the withdrawal of the spirit." Hence, according to this later view, the soul is annihilated at the death of the body, and " Sheol, the abode of the souls, became a synonym of Abaddon or destruction." But, says Prof. Charles, "this doctrine never succeeded in dispossessing the older and rival doctrine; their conflicting views of soul and spirit were current together"[1]; that is to say, the primitive conception of the ghost-soul lived on among the Hebrews alongside the later developed and, doubtless, less popular, because more difficult, conception.

Just as among the Hebrews the notion of the ghost-soul continued to be widely entertained, in spite of the teaching by the prophets of a more difficult conception of human personality; so also among the Greeks the ghost-soul retained its place in popular belief, while the philosophers developed a literary tradition in which the conception of the soul underwent many changes, and in which almost every phase of later speculation upon this topic was either foreshadowed or definitely taught.

The pages of Homer show clearly enough that the Greeks of the Homeric age believed in the ghost-soul. But their conception differed markedly in certain respects from the typical ghost-soul of primitive Animism and of so many savage and barbarous peoples in all ages. The typical ghost-soul enjoys all the powers, both bodily and mental, of the living man, and differs from the man chiefly in being less substantial and less strictly subject to limitations of time and space; but the ghost-soul of the Homeric Greeks, the eidolon (εἴδωλον) or psyche (ψυχή), was not conceived as the bearer of the mental faculties, or at least not as enjoying the whole of the mental faculties of the living man. It was rather a shadowy image merely, which leaves the body of the dying man by way of the mouth or gaping wound; and this shadow or shade, descending to Hades, enjoyed but the shadow of its former life and powers. The strength and will, the intellect and mental powers in general, were supposed to reside in the region of the diaphragm and to be dissolved or annihilated at the death of the body. Disembodied minds were unknown to the Greeks of this age; even their gods lived upon the earth, and were fully incarnate in bodies which differed from those of men only in that they were subject to neither disease nor death.

The shades, once banished to Hades, were strictly imprisoned there; and thus the Homeric world was freed from the terror of ghosts that has haunted, and still haunts, almost all other peoples. And the cult of the dead had no recognized place in that world; for the dead were incapable of influencing the living for good or ill.

It is clear, then, that the Homeric Greeks had departed widely from primitive Animism; that they had modified it in a way natural to their vigorous, joyous, and but little religious disposition, in a period of national expansion and victorious self-assertion.

There is no reason to doubt that at an earlier period Animism of the more usual kind had been current among them; traces of this, and of the cult of the dead appropriate to it, survive in the story of Achilles and Patroclus and of the funeral sacrifices of wine, sheep, oxen, horses, and Trojan youths. These seem to have been but ceremonial survivals of a cult of souls that had prevailed in an earlier age, when souls were dreaded for their active powers of intervention in human life.[1]

There appears in the Homeric writings a foretaste of that tendency to the reification of abstractions which was to play so great a part in the philosophy of later ages. The psyche is sometimes identified with life; and the mental powers, regarded as resident in the region of the diaphragm, are sometimes attributed to the θυμός, or βουλή, entities which, though belonging to the body, are not identified with any bodily organs.

The continuance of the ghost-soul in Hades did not constitute a survival of personality; for to the Greeks of this age the body was an essential part of personality. Nevertheless there appears in Homer, possibly as a late addition, the belief in the immortality of a favoured few. This immortality was not an immortality of the soul alone, but rather of the whole person, who was conceived as transported bodily by the favour of some divinity to "the isles of the blest," or to "the Elysian fields," a distant region of the earth which might yet be discovered by the daring voyager. This notion, probably a poetic invention, was given a permanent place in popular belief by its embodiment in the Homeric poems;

---

[1] In this brief account of the Homeric and post-Homeric beliefs I follow Erwin Rhode's "Psyche," second edition, Leipzig, 1906.

it was a natural supplement to the peculiar form that Greek Animism had assumed.

The Homeric beliefs continued to be generally held up to the sixth century B.C.; but a new class of immortals arose, men who, like the dwellers in the Happy Isles, had not known death, but who, by the power of some god, were engulfed in some deep chasm or cave, swallowed by earthquake, or struck but not killed by the bolt of Zeus; and these heroes became in many cases the centres of local cults. It was probably under the influence of this belief and of these cults that the pre-Homeric belief in the survival of the personality after death was revived. Hesiod's doctrine of the Golden Age seems to have played a considerable part in restoring this belief. For he taught that, though the men of the Golden Age had died, their souls were raised by the will of Zeus to a life even fuller and richer than that they had enjoyed in the body; and these souls, partaking of the immortal nature of the gods, and known like them as Dæmons, were regarded by him as wandering invisible among men, seeing their good and their evil deeds.

There can be little doubt that these influences played a considerable part in bringing into prominence in the religious life of post-Homeric Greece a new cult of the dead. Not all men were held to survive the death of the body, but only great leaders, men who in life had bulked large in the eyes of their fellows. At this time earth-burial had replaced the funeral pyre of the Homeric age, and the soul of the dead hero was believed to hover in the neighbourhood of the tomb where his bones were laid. Since these surviving souls were held to be capable of affecting the welfare of men, especially of their own descendants, they became the objects of local and family cults and of propitiatory rites. Wine, honey, oil, and burnt sheep were offered to the dead hero; and the whole cult implied the belief that the dead man lived on among his people but little changed by death. This survival did not imply immortality of the soul; rather the continuance of the soul depended upon the maintenance of the cult by the friends, especially the family, of the dead hero.

The hero attained this life after death by the favour of some god, generally announced by the Delphic oracle; but the process became easier and more frequent, and the heroes multiplied rapidly, until it was customary to regard as surviving in this way all that fell in glorious battle.

A still wider gate to the life after death was opened by the Eleusinian Mysteries. These were derived from the cult of Demeter and Persephone of Eleusis, the local divinities of the underworld. The cult was adopted by Athens, and became ever more widely open; until even slaves were admitted to initiation Those initiated to participation in this cult were held to be assured of a future life less shadowy and unreal than the life of the dim underworld of shades, which still was all that the uninitiated could look forward to. Thus the hope of a future life became possible to all men; but still there was no general acceptance of a belief in the immortality of the soul.

This first appeared in Greece with the Dionysiac cult, whose central feature was a mystic union of the worshipper with the god. In the original form of the cult as practised in Thrace, the worshippers gave themselves up to a wild dance. In the excitement of the dance they attained an ecstatic exaltation which they believed to imply their possession by the bull-god; the soul of the ecstatic was supposed to depart from his body and to wander in distant scenes, holding communion with gods and dæmons.

From Thrace this cult spread throughout all Greece, fusing with the cult of Apollo. Under its influence the populace became familiar with the notion that the soul, with all the mental faculties, is separable from the body; and under the same influence there sprang up the belief that the soul is formed for a higher destiny than its life in the body, that it is clogged and held down by its association with the body, and that it must be freed from this degrading influence by purificatory and ascetic rites.

In the Orphic cult these ideas were further developed, until the soul was regarded as having its true life among the gods, its life in the body being a temporary banishment from this true or higher life. The soul at death goes to judgment in the underworld. Thence it returns to be reincarnated again and again, until it is wholly purified; when it is set free to live for ever with the gods. In fact, under the influence of the Dionysiac and Orphic cults, the soul came to be regarded as a god imprisoned in the body.[1] But immortality had always been the most fundamental attribute of the gods, and thus the human soul, by assimilation to the gods, became immortal.

While Animism was developing towards the theory of human

[1] Rhode, *op. cit.*, II. S. 133.

immortality of the Orphic theologians, the philosophers known as the Ionian physicists initiated, in the sixth century B.C., that prolonged effort to learn by pure unprejudiced reasoning the ultimate nature of things which we call European philosophy. It was their principal aim to exhibit the whole world as the manifestation of some fundamental and primary mode of being. And this aim led them to reject from the outset both the Animism of popular opinion and that of the theologians. For them the soul of man was but one mode of manifestation of the power which moves and works in all things, without which the world would be dead and motionless and unchanging. The *psyche* of these philosophers had nothing in common with the *psyche* of the Homeric traditions. The word was used by them to denote the powers of thinking, feeling, willing (and the untranslatable θυμός), which, according to the Homeric tradition, were bodily functions resident about the diaphragm. Nor was their *psyche* an individual immortal being like that of the Animism of the Orphic priesthood. The question as to personal immortality seemed meaningless to these philosophers; nevertheless, since the soul is the working in man of the power that moves all things, the universal life itself, it is, in a sense, imperishable and immortal. So conceived, "the soul acquired a new dignity; in another sense than that of the mystics and the theologians, it could be claimed as divine; in the sense, namely, that it is a partial manifestation of the one power which builds and guides the universe. Not a single dæmon is it, but the divine power itself."[1]

The principal Ionian physicists adopted different views of the nature of that which they sought as the foundation and origin of all things. Thales (B.C. 636), the first of them, held that the fundamental element is water; Anaximenes, that it is the universal air. "Diogenes adopted the tenet of Anaximenes respecting Air as the origin of things; but he gave a wider and deeper significance to the tenet by pointing out the analogy of air with the soul (or life). . . . The air is a soul; therefore it is living and intelligent. But this Force of Intelligence is a higher thing than the air through which it manifests itself; it must consequently be prior in point of time; it must be the ἀρχή philosophers have sought. The Universe is a living being, spontaneously evolving itself, deriving its transformations from its own vitality."[2] Thus air was for Diogenes but the symbol of mind.

[1] Rhode, *op. cit.*, II. S. 143. [2] Lewes' "History of Philosophy," vol. i. p. 11.

Heraclitus (503 B.C.), who belongs to this group of thinkers, elaborated this type of speculation on the basis of the assumption that fire is the principle of life and action which works in the perpetual flux of things. "Whatever in the manifold of phenomena partakes of the nature of the divine fire is for Heraclitus soul, and soul is fire. Fire and soul are interchangeable notions, and so the soul of man also is fire, a part of the universal vital fire which envelops it, and through the inbreathing of which the soul maintains itself alive, a part of the universal reason, by participation in which the soul itself is reasonable. In man lives the god. Not that, as in the doctrine of the theologians, he descends as a closed individuality into the form of a single human being; but, as a unity, he envelops mankind, permeating men as with tongues of fire. A part of the all-wisdom lives in the soul of man; ... the soul is such a part of the universal fire which, absorbed into the flux of existing forms, is bound up and interwoven with the bodily functions."[1] The fire which is the soul perpetually converts itself into the water and earth of which the body is composed, and thus builds up the body; while it renews itself by drafts from the universal fire. The soul, being thus constantly in process of conversion into the lower elements and constantly renewed, is no enduring self-identical entity. "So long as the soul renews itself from the enveloping world-fire, the individual lives. Separation from the source of all life, the universal fire, would be death. Now and then, in sleep and dreams, the individual soul loses its life-giving connexion with the universal fire and is for a time shut up in its own world, and this is a partial death. ... There comes a moment at which the soul of man can no longer make good what it loses in the process of metabolism, and then comes death." Thus the individual dies, but the universal fire is eternal. "The question as to individual immortality, or even the continuance of the individual soul, has scarcely any meaning for Heraclitus. ... The individual as a separate being has no value and significance; the perpetuation of this separate existence (if it were possible) would seem to him an absurdity. For him only the fire as a whole is eternal; not its separate manifestations in individuals, but only the universal energy which transmutes itself into all things and reabsorbs all things into itself."[2]

[1] Rhode, *op. cit.*, II. S. 146.
[2] *Op. cit.*, II., S. 154.

For the Ionian philosophers of nature, the soul was, then, a part of nature, and psychology a part of natural science. There was for them no distinction between the physical and the psychical; rather, all things, including life and mind, were manifestations of one universal energy.[1]

Though philosophy had thus begun its course by the rejection of Animism, it was not long before the popular doctrine found a powerful defender among the philosophers. Pythagoras founded his school and acquired a great influence, hardly a generation after Thales appeared as the first of the philosophers. The Ionian philosophy, contemplating the whole of nature, had wellnigh overlooked man, regarding him as but an insignificant fragment of the whole. Pythagoras restored man and the problems of human nature to their position of prime and central importance, giving the soul of man a central position in his doctrine.

The human soul was conceived as in the Animism then current in the dominant religious sect, namely, as the double of the visible body and as a dæmon, *i.e.* a godlike and immortal being fallen from the divine heights in which is its true home, and shut up in the body for punishment. The soul was distinguished from the body as something opposed to nature, rather than a part of it. Even during its sojourn in the body it has no organic relation to it, but maintains uncontaminated its peculiar nature. It does not constitute the personality of the man, for any soul may inhabit any body; and after death it tarries in Hades, whence it returns again and again to earth, seeking each time a new body for its abode. So it wanders during long ages, inhabiting in turn many human and animal bodies; its fate at each incarnation being determined by its actions during its preceding periods of embodied life. But it is immortal, and in its essence an unchanging individual being. Its ultimate destiny is to be freed from the bonds of the natural life of the body, and to return to dwell for ever in the supernatural realm of pure souls whence it came. The practical aspect and ultimate aim of the Pythagorean philosophy was to learn how to hasten this return of the soul to its divine home by means of ascetic and purificatory rites.

---

[1] The conception of energy current at the present day was of course unknown to the ancients; but if, in the teachings of Heraclitus, we substitute energy for fire, we shall realize that he was striving after the modern conception, and that he foreshadowed the modern doctrine of the conservation of energy and the view, upheld at the present time by some distinguished physicists, according to which both mind and matter are but manifestations of the universal energy.

Thus, at the very dawn of philosophy, we find the leading thinkers arrayed in the opposed camps of naturalistic Monism and animistic Pluralism.

Another very influential philosopher, Empedocles (B.C. 444), gave to the soul a position very similar to that which it occupied in the Pythagorean doctrine. His teaching differed from the latter in that he attempted the impossible task of combining a wide-ranging Animism, similar to the Pythagorean, with a thoroughgoing Hylozoism like that of the Ionian school. The soul was for him "of a divine order, too noble for this visible world, only on release from which it will attain its full and true life. Banished to the body, it leads there its separate existence; not everyday perception and feeling is its part, nor even reasoning, which is the function of the heart's blood; but in the 'higher' modes of thought and in ecstatic 'exaltation' only is it active; to it belongs the philosophical insight which, penetrating beyond the apprehension of the narrow range of sensory experience, knows the totality of the world's being according to its true nature."[1]

About the same time that Empedocles thus formulated anew the animistic philosophy, Anaxagoras and Democritus took up again the way of thought of the Ionian school, and the latter especially carried it to a more definite issue than had been reached by any of his predecessors.

Anaxagoras occupies a middle position between the animists and the naturalists. For him the universal power that moves and orders all things is Reason (νοῦς). Wherever in the world life and movement appear, there this universal power is active. Its activity within an animated being constitutes the soul of that being. At death, therefore, the individual soul ceases to exist, but the supreme power remains. Yet so uncertain still was the distinction between matter and spirit that, according to Lewes, the supreme energy "was only the abstract form of the vital principle animating animals and plants," and "was simply one among the numerous agents, material like the rest, and only differing from them in being pure"; and Grote says of it that "it is one substance or form of matter among the rest, but thinner than all of them, thinner even than fire or air."

Democritus (B.C. 460) gave the speculations of the Ionian school a more modern and definitely materialistic form by reducing all things to material atoms and their movements.

[1] Rhode, *op. cit.*, II. S. 185.

The atom was an indivisible unit constantly in motion, and by impact with others constantly imparting and receiving motion. The soul, that which animates living beings, consists also of atoms, which are peculiar only in being finer, smoother, more rounded, and therefore more mobile, than any others; these finest atoms permeate the whole body and produce the phenomena of life. These soul atoms are drawn in with the breath, and, when they are no longer breathed in, death ensues. Democritus is assigned by Rhode the distinction of being the first Greek thinker explicitly to deny that the individual may in any sense survive the death of the body.

Democritus' conception of the soul was thus very different from the primitive ghost-soul; nevertheless this latter conception seems to have been familiar to him and to have been used by him in a novel manner; he first proposed a theory of perception, teaching that, when we see solid objects, it is because these objects throw off shadow-like images of themselves (εἴδωλα) which enter the eye and pass through it into the soul. As Professor Tylor[1] has pointed out, there is good reason to believe that these εἴδωλα were the ghost-souls of popular belief adapted to serve a new purpose; in this changed capacity the ghost-soul survived for long ages in the literary tradition.

Protagoras, the pupil of Democritus, developed into a thoroughgoing sensationalism his master's doctrine that thought and sensation are identical, and thus provided the mental atomism which has always been the necessary supplement of metaphysical materialism.

The pre-Socratic philosophy thus culminated in a thoroughgoing Materialism. The doctrine of the Ionian philosophers was not properly Materialism, for the distinction between matter and spirit had not yet been clearly drawn. It is impossible to say that their universal principles (*e.g.* the air of Diogenes, the fire of Heraclitus) were more nearly allied to the spiritual or to the physical, as conceived by later thought. Nor did the conception of the soul entertained by the animistic philosophers imply any clear distinction between the material or physical and the spiritual or mental, such as has been commonly maintained in later ages. For them it seems to have retained something of the nature of the dæmon of the theologians from which it derived, and this in turn was but the ghost-soul of primitive Animism, glorified by

[1] "Primitive Culture," vol. i. p. 497.

assimilation to the nature of the gods, but still, like them, incompletely dematerialized.

That the distinction was not clearly drawn by the Pythagoreans appears from the fact that they saw in the motes, which dance in the sunbeam with apparently spontaneous movement, discarnate souls seeking new bodies, in which to take up again their earth-life. And that Empedocles also failed to achieve this distinction is shown by his assigning to the body all the mental functions, save only those which he regarded as of the most exalted kind and alone worthy of the soul, namely, processes of ecstatic vision and philosophic intuition.

Democritus, by giving greater definition to the notion of matter and by describing the universe as composed wholly of atoms of matter in motion, sharpened the issue between Materialism and Animism, and prepared the way for the clearer distinction between matter and spirit which Plato established in the literary tradition of Europe, and to the abolition of which the efforts of modern philosophers have been so largely directed.

Plato's teaching in regard to the soul and its relation to the body is scattered through a number of the dialogues, which were written at considerable intervals of time; and during the long course of his philosophic activity his views seem to have undergone considerable changes. Partly for this reason, and partly because much of what he wrote of the soul took the form of symbolism in the myths, whose aim was moral and æsthetic rather than strictly scientific, it is impossible to summarize his doctrine in any clear-cut and entirely consistent statement.

The view of the soul expressed in the earlier dialogues is part of an ontological scheme whose nature was largely determined by ethical considerations. Two realms of being are distinguished; on the one hand the realm of intelligible and true Being, consisting of the timeless unchanging Ideas; on the other hand the realm of Becoming, to which belong all objects of sense-perception (including, of course, the human body).

Souls are existences of a third class, whose function it is to mediate between these two realms. Their position in this ontological scheme is peculiar. They belong in a sense to both realms, for they are active in both. Souls have affinity to or kinship with the Ideas, and it is in virtue only of their kinship that they are able to contemplate and know the Ideas. Like the Ideas, they are wholly immaterial and wholly real; yet they are necessarily different from them, if only because they know them, and because they are subject to change in their intercourse with the realm of becoming. But the soul differs still more widely from the body, with whose nature it has nothing in common. The soul's activities are of two principal kinds, knowing and moving or causing movement. The cognitive activity is exercised in two very different ways: on the one hand, by immediate contemplation of the Ideas the soul attains true knowledge; on the other hand, by the aid of the bodily faculties, it becomes aware of the objects of the sensible world; and these stir up within it imperfect reminiscences of the Ideas of which they are the symbols or shadows. These two modes of cognitive activity, distinguished as Reason (νοῦς) and Sense (αἴσθησις), and sometimes referred to by Plato as functions of different parts of the soul, were regarded as yielding two kinds of knowledge of very different value, true knowledge and mere opinion respectively.

In regard to the soul's function as a principle of movement, it is to be noted that, whereas earlier philosophers had generally regarded the soul (or soul-atoms) as moving spontaneously in space and as capable of imparting its motion to other things, Plato regarded the soul, not as itself in movement, but as that which initiates or generates all movement. This at least seems to be his meaning, if we consider his remarks on this head in the light of the rest of his teaching; though Aristotle attributes to him the older view, and undertakes an elaborate refutation of it.

This position of the soul intermediate between the two realms of existence, that of the Ideas and that of sensible things, is so unsatisfactory that some interpreters[1] have maintained that in this earlier period Plato, starting with the two realms of existence, had failed to grasp, or at any rate to offer, any satisfactory solution of the problem of the soul's position in his ontological scheme; and they hold that his later doctrine of the soul involved a fundamental change of position. The soul of man, instead of appearing as an appendage to the ontological scheme, added by an afterthought, acquires a

---

[1] Thus e.g. Mr E. J. Roberts, in his article, "Plato's View of the Soul," *Mind* N.S., vol. xiv.

position of primary importance; it, or the world-soul from which it was said to derive its being, becomes the supreme reality on which the Ideas are dependent.

So far did this change go that some recent interpreters have forcibly argued that the Ideas were for Plato, not, as most others, following Aristotle, have maintained, separate things or realities subsisting independently of mind, but the logical concepts of the mind, by aid of which it brings order and intelligibility into the chaos of sense-experience, and that this was Plato's meaning throughout the earlier as well as the later Dialogues.[1]

Whatever may be the truth as to Plato's view of the relation of the soul to the Ideas, his teaching as to the purely immaterial and immortal nature of the soul is clear enough. The soul of man, though it is in some sense derived from the world-soul, is not merely a ray of the universal energy, life, or mind, as it appears in the systems of the Ionian philosophers. It is a self-contained individual being, the ground of personality; as such it exists in the realm of pure Being before incarnation; from that realm it brings the knowledge of the Ideas manifested in reminiscence; and as such it endures through all the vicissitudes of its successive re-incarnations. Apart from its temporary association with this or that bodily organism, its activity is purely the exercise of reason and the willing of that which the reason comprehends. But, when drawn from its pure spiritual existence into the realm of matter and associated with a bodily organism, the soul exercises, in conjunction with the body, certain lower functions, namely, the higher emotions and the bodily appetites. These three modes of its activity are attributed to different parts of the soul; and in one dialogue, the *Timaeus*, they are even assigned to three distinct souls—the rational soul seated in the head, the spirited soul in the chest, and the appetitive soul in the abdomen. But it seems clear that this statement was not meant to be taken literally. Although Plato sometimes speaks of the two lower functions as belonging to a mortal soul, and leaves it an open question how far these lower functions belong to the soul when it is freed from the body; the "three parts of the soul" should, perhaps, be regarded, not as the activities of distinct souls or even distinct faculties, but rather as three levels of mental function; the highest only being exercised apart from the body.

[1] Especially Prof. J. A. Stewart in his "Plato's Doctrine of Ideas," 1909, and Prof. Natorp, ' Plato's Ideenlehre " (1903)

Reason controls the lower functions, but not always with complete success; and when the lower faculties, in their contaminating intimacy with the body, get out of control, the soul suffers a debasement, which must be expiated by future incarnation in lower bodily forms, even animal forms. From this recurring cycle of incarnations the soul can free itself only by overcoming completely the evil incitations that come to it from the body; and only when this is accomplished, does it return to its true home, the realm of eternal untroubled Being.

There can be little doubt that Plato's doctrine of the soul and of its transmigrations was largely drawn from the teachings of the Orphic theologians. His teaching and prestige raised the religious belief in the immortality of the soul (which was widely but not generally entertained at the time he began his work) to the level of a philosophic theory and secured it a wider acceptance. In fact, Plato's doctrine may be regarded as the culminating refinement of the stream of Greek Animism, of which the Dionysiac and Orphic cults were the popular aspect. Plato purified the conception of the soul of the last remnants of the dualistic materialism of primitive Animism, which still lingered in the Orphic doctrine, and, insisting upon the fundamental difference of nature between soul and body, clearly formulated for the first time the theory of psycho-physical dualism with reciprocal action between soul and body.

In spite of the great name of Plato, his psycho-physical dualism did not find many supporters among the thinkers of the immediately succeeding period. It seemed for a time almost completely submerged; the dominant philosophical trend returned to the line of physical speculation initiated by the Ionian School: the immortality of the soul was but little discussed, and Animism was at a low ebb in the philosophic world. In short, the period was, like the present time, one in which "souls were out of fashion." At the opening of this period stands the great figure of Aristotle.

Aristotle approached psychology from the point of view of biology, and by him soul ($\psi v \chi \acute{\eta}$) was ascribed to all material things that manifest powers of spontaneous movement and growth, that is to say, to all living organisms; in fact, he distinguished them from the inorganic world ($\tau \grave{\alpha}\ \acute{\alpha}\psi v \chi \alpha$) by the expression the animate or the besouled ($\tau \grave{\alpha}\ \acute{\epsilon}\mu\psi v \chi \alpha$). The word ψυχή, as used by him, would therefore be more correctly translated by our English term life, or vital principle, rather than by soul. The psyche is, in short, the vital principle, the possession of which distinguishes the living organism from inorganic things, and by that word all the peculiarities of living things, including the mental processes, are denoted; or perhaps Aristotle's conception would be more correctly expressed in modern language by saying that the soul is the sum of the vital functions. Among the vital activities, or psychic powers, of organisms, Aristotle distinguishes five principal kinds, namely: (1) the vegetative processes of nutrition, growth, and reproduction; (2) appetite, impulse, or desire, or, as we should now say, conation; (3) sensation; (4) power of spontaneous movement in space; (5) rational thought. Of these the plants enjoy only the first. The animals enjoy also the second, third, and fourth, which naturally go together and presuppose the first. Man alone enjoys all these powers; reason is his alone.

These activities are not the functions of distinct souls, or of distinct parts of the soul; for the soul is unitary. Every living thing is in a sense a combination of soul and body; yet soul and body are not distinct things in the sense that they can or do exist apart from each other. They can only be separated in thought. (This at least seems to be Aristotle's most explicit teaching, but his utterances on this point are not consistent.) The soul is not to be regarded as material, yet it is inseparable from matter. The body is the "material cause" of the organism; the soul is its "efficient cause," for it produces its movements; it is also its "formal cause," for it determines the form of the individual organism; and it is its "final cause," for it is the end for the sake of which the body exists.

The dictum which has been generally held to express most concisely Aristotle's notion of the psycho-physical relation is that the soul is the form of the body. This expression conveys no definite meaning to the modern mind, unless it is familiar with Aristotelian thought. The reader may find himself helped to grasp Aristotle's notion by a collection of the most significant passages. Among these are the following:—
"The soul is the principle by which, in an ultimate sense, we live and feel and think; it is a sort of idea and form, not matter and substrate."[1] "Soul is the primary actuality of a natural body en-

[1] "De Anima," Bk. II. chap. ii.

dowed with the capacity of life. . . . It is, therefore, unnecessary to ask whether body and soul are one, as one would not ask whether the wax and the figure impressed on it are one, or, in general, whether the matter of a particular thing and the thing composed of it are one."[1] After likening the relation between soul and body to that between vision and the eye, he adds: "It is, therefore, clear that the soul cannot be separated from the body." Yet in the following paragraph he goes on: "Yet it is uncertain whether the soul may not be the actuality of the body, as the sailor is of the ship."[2] This uncertainty as regards the separability of the soul applies only to its reasoning part; and it arises from the fact that, whereas the other psychical functions are the actualities or realizations of certain bodily organs, as vision is the realization or notional essence of the eye, reason is not the realization of any bodily organ. And so his opinion fluctuates: "In regard to reason and the speculative faculty there is no certain evidence, but it seems to be a generically distinct kind of soul, and it alone is capable of separation from the body, as that which is eternal from that which is perishable. But the other parts of the soul are, in view of the foregoing considerations, evidently inseparable."[3] Again, he wrote: "A difficulty presents itself in regard to the affections of the soul, namely, whether all its affections are common to the soul and to the body which contains it, or whether there is something that belongs to the soul alone. It is necessary, though hard, to solve this difficulty. In most cases the soul apparently acts, or is acted on, only in conjunction with the body; for example, in the feelings of anger, courage, desire and, in general, in sense-perception. Thought, if anything, would seem to be peculiar to the soul. Yet, if thought is a sort of representation in terms of a sense-image, or is impossible without it (which he affirms in another place [4]), then even thought could not exist independently of the body. If, then, there were any function or affections of the soul that were peculiar to it, it would be possible for the soul to exist separate and apart from the body. If, however, there is nothing which belongs to it exclusively, it cannot exist apart."[5]

---

[1] "De Anima," Bk. II. chap. i.   [2] *Ibid.*
[3] *Op. cit.*, Bk. II. chap. ii.
[4] "The soul, therefore, never thinks without the use of images" ("De Anima," Bk. III. chap. vii.).
[5] "De Anima," Bk. I. chap. i.

In this passage it is clearly laid down that the question of the separability of the soul, and therefore of the possibility of its continued existence after the death of the body, is one to be decided by empirical research into the extent and nature of the participation of bodily processes in mental life.

Aristotle's uncertainty as to the separability of any part or function of the soul applies only to that which he distinguishes as the creative reason (νοῦς ποιητικός) from the passive reason. To the latter belong the powers of imagination or sensory representation. Reason is passive in so far as it receives its content through sense-perception; but thought is more than the coexistence and succession of sensations, perceptions, and images of imagination and memory. These are but the matter of thought; that which gives them form is the active or creative reason. This highest function of the soul it is which converts the perceptually acquired contact of the mind to a system of logically ordered thought, and thus in a sense creates reality by giving it a rational form. This is the function which seems to Aristotle to have no bodily organ, to be the realization of no part of the body; and it is this to which he refers when he says that "In its separated state alone reason is its true self, immortal and eternal";[1] that potential knowledge pre-exists in the individual; that reason is of such a nature that on the one hand it becomes all things, and on the other hand creates all things; and that "it is separate, not passive, unmixed and in its essential nature an energizing force."[2]

But it seems clear that the immortality tentatively ascribed by Aristotle to the creative reason involves no personal immortality, no survival of the individual soul; but rather holds good only of the universal reason. And, since Aristotle explicitly affirms that "the passive reason is perishable and without it there can be no thought,"[2] it follows that the immortal reason is potential only, that it actually operates only in conjunction with the body, which through the senses supplies it with the matter of thought.

Aristotle's few, hesitating, and ambiguous remarks on the separability and immortality of the creative reason have given rise to an immense amount of controversy among the reverent interpreters and commentators. By some modern interpreters this part of his doctrine is regarded as an element foreign to and

[1] "De Anima," Bk. III. chap. v.   [2] *Ibid.*

incompatible with the main body of it. These look upon it as derived through Plato from the Orphic theologians, and as evidence merely that Aristotle did not completely succeed in shaking off the influence of his great teacher.

But this explanation of Aristotle's attitude on this question is hardly required. Aristotle showed himself generally inclined to take up a very critical attitude towards Plato's teaching, and ready to accentuate the differences between his own views and those of his great master.

His attitude on this question was thoroughly scientific, and just such as was demanded by an impartial consideration of the facts. His interpreters have generally attempted to show either that he taught the immortality of the soul or of the active reason, or that he denied it. We shall be wiser if we recognize the plain implication of his words, namely, that he held it impossible to return a decisive answer to this great question without further empirical knowledge of the bodily processes involved in mental activities; and we shall see in later chapters that, in spite of many centuries of heated controversy, the question still remains just where Aristotle left it, with this difference only—that we are beginning to acquire that understanding of the nature and extent of the bodily processes involved in mental activity, the lack of which necessitated suspension of judgment in the truly scientific mind of Aristotle.

Whatever degree of truth there may be in the view that Aristotle's indecision in the face of this question was due to Plato's influence, it is clear that his doctrine of the creative reason has none of the practical and ethical significance of Plato's doctrine of immortality.

As regards the relation of the soul to the parts of the body, Aristotle called attention to a number of facts which seemed to him to indicate that such psychical powers as the plants and lower animals enjoy are exercised equally in or by all parts of the body. But he held that in the higher animals the psychical functions are concentrated in, or more especially exercised by, certain parts of the body; and, rejecting the brain as the principal seat of the soul, and assigning to it merely the function of cooling the blood, he taught that the heart is the principal centre of vitality or soul life. The heart is the *sensorium commune*, or seat of the *common sense*, by which the common sensibles (i.e. those properties of things later distinguished by Locke as the primary qualities), are perceived. "The dominating organ of sensation in all sanguineous animals is found in the heart, for the 'common sense' that serves all the special senses must be situated there. There are two senses, taste and touch, whose channels lead manifestly to the heart, and what is true of these must be true of the other senses. Movement in the other sense-organs may be transmitted to the heart, but with the upper parts of the body these two senses do not communicate in any way. Apart from these considerations, if the principle of life of all animals is seated in the heart, the sensory principle must evidently be there also."[1]

These and other passages make it clear that Aristotle knew nothing of the functions of the nerves and nervous system.

It is of interest to note that Aristotle foreshadowed our modern notions of the dependence of all life on combustion or oxydation, asserting the dependence of the psychical functions (i.e. of life) on fire or heat. "Since every living thing has a soul, and the soul, as we have said, cannot subsist without natural heat, we find that in plants adequate provision has been made for the preservation of natural heat through nutriment and the surrounding air."[2] "It was said above that life and the possession of soul are accompanied by a certain degree of heat. For even the process of concoction, by which food is made ready for animal life, is not accomplished without soul and heat ; and all this is effected by fire. . . . And other functions of the soul cannot be performed independently of the nutritive principle, and this in turn cannot subsist without natural heat."[3] "Birth is the original suffusion of the nutritive soul with heat, and life is the maintenance of this heat. Youth is the period of the growth of the organ of cooling, old age that of the wasting of this organ, and the prime of life is the middle period between the two. Death and violent destruction mean respectively the exhaustion and extinction of the vital heat."[4] It is curious that while thus correctly, though vaguely, conceiving the fundamental importance of combustion for the maintenance of life, Aristotle attributed old age and death, not to failure of the processes of combustion, but rather to exhaustion, due to inadequacy of the cooling arrangements by which (according to his view) the processes of combustion are normally kept in check.

The foregoing brief statement of Aristotle's teaching in regard to the soul suffices to show that it has more affinity with the

[1] "De Juvent.," chap. iii.
[2] "De Juvent.," chap. vi.
[3] "De Respirat.," chap. vii.
[4] "De Respirat.," chap. xviii.

Hylozoism of the Ionian philosophers and the Materialism of Democritus and his successors than with the materialistic Animism of popular thought or the spiritualistic Animism of Plato.

The notion of a radical difference of nature between soul and body, between spirit and matter, which Plato established in the culture-tradition of Europe, has never passed wholly away; but the great age of Socrates, Plato, and Aristotle, was followed by one of which the principal features were Scepticism and a materialistic reaction against the spiritualistic dualism of Plato. Epicurus, adopting the Atomism of Democritus, taught that "the soul is a fine substance distributed through the whole mass of the body, and most resembles the air with an infusion of warmth"[1]; that it is an organ of the body by means of which the body shares in sensation, and that it is dissolved with the body. At death the soul-atoms are dispersed in the air. He distinguished two parts, or modes of manifestation, of the soul, namely, the reasonless part or vital force which permeates all parts of the body, and the reasonable part which resides in the breast and is the organ of understanding and volition: a distinction which reappears in the teaching of Lucretius. In his ethical and psychological hedonism, Epicurus provided a further supplement to the materialism of Democritus, a supplement which in later ages also has usually gone hand in hand with mental atomism or sensationalism and with metaphysical materialism.

The teachings of the early Stoics, although so opposed to Epicurus in respect to ethical doctrines, resembled his in following the materialism of Democritus; but, whereas the matter of Democritus had only the attributes of extension, hardness, mass, and capacity of movement, the matter of the Stoics was endowed with many forces. By them the life-principle was generally designated the *pneuma*, and this was regarded as a material principle composed of air and fire, which pervades the whole body, presides over its growth and movements, and is also the principle of intellectual life. Some of the Stoics held that death is the end of life; others suspended judgment on this problem; others again, adopting a materialistic Pantheism taught, not without some inconsistency, that the soul of the wise man maintains itself after death according to the degree of his ethical development; but that it eventually loses its individu-

[1] A. Lange, "Hist. of Materialism," vol. i. p. 106.

ality and, being consumed in fire, is reabsorbed in the divine Being. "The human soul is a part of the Deity, or an emanation from the same; the soul and its source act and react upon each other. The soul is the warm breath within us. Although it outlives the body, it is yet perishable, and can only endure, at the longest, till the termination of the world period in which it exists."[1]

Scepticism and Stoicism remained the dominant modes of thought from the time of Aristotle till the opening of the Christian era; when the contact of the two lines of literary tradition from which that of modern Europe descends, namely, the Hebrew and the Greek, gave birth to two philosophies, the Neoplatonic and the Christian, each of which developed its distinctive theory of the soul. These developments will be traced in the following chapter.

[1] Ueberweg's "History of Philosophy."

CHAPTER II

ANIMISM IN THE MIDDLE AGES

"THE greatest merit of the Middle Ages," writes Professor Höffding,[1] "lies in its absorption in the inner world of the life of the soul. Classical antiquity had paused at the harmonious relation between the inner and the outer, and its interest in the inner life was limited to its relation to outer life in Nature and the State. To the faith of the Middle Ages the eternal fate of the personality was determined by the events of the inner life. . . . No wonder that a fine and deep sense of the inner life developed. The self-absorption of the mystic was as important for the development of the psychological sense as the distinctions and argumentations of the schoolmen for that of the logical sense. It dawned upon men that the spiritual world is just as much a reality as the material world, and that in the former is Man's true home. The way was prepared for a more thorough investigation of the great problem of spirit and matter than was possible to antiquity."

We have seen that the Stoics gave currency to a new designation of the animating principle, namely, *pneuma*.[2] With the introduction of the *pneuma* began[3] that trichotomy of human personality into body, soul, and spirit which has figured prominently in the speculations of theologians; it continues to pervade the popular thought of Christendom to the present day, though the relation between *psyche* and *pneuma*, soul and spirit, has fluctuated widely and has never been clearly defined.

The *pneuma*, which was conceived by the Stoics as a material vital principle, continued to play an important part in the physiological speculations of physicians and natural philosophers; in the hands of Christian theologians, on the other hand, it became

---

[1] "History of Modern Philosophy," Eng. trans., vol. i. p. 5.

[2] It would perhaps be more correct to say that *pneuma* stood for a theory of the vital processes, the sum of which was denoted by the word $\psi v \chi \eta$.

[3] But see p. 7 for the view of Dr Charles that a similar trichotomy pervades the later eschatology of the Old Testament.

transformed into a purely spiritual immaterial soul. In this way, through the inevitable specialization of learning, the conception of the psyche or soul, which through all the Greek philosophy had covered both the animating principle of all living things and the intellectual or mental principle of man, became differentiated into two conceptions, which long continued to figure in the European culture-tradition more or less independently of one another, namely, on the one hand the vital force of the physiologists, and on the other hand the spirit or immaterial soul of man.

The latter conception was not taken over by the Fathers of the Church directly from Plato; it descended to them indirectly by way of the Neoplatonists, in whose hands it was developed under the influence of Eastern mysticism and Hebrew theology.

We have seen that among the Greek philosophers the dominant conception of the soul was that of a material substance, very thin and mobile, and having the power of spontaneous movement. The early Fathers, who shaped the doctrines of the Christian Church up to the fifth century, continued to hold this view of the soul. They were not materialists in the modern sense of the word, as applied to those who deny the existence of soul or spirit. But they were dualistic materialists; for, while they regarded man as made up of soul and body, they held both soul and body to be material. It was even held to be heretical to deny the material nature of the soul; for only material substance, it was thought, could be susceptible of physical pains and pleasures; therefore a material soul was required by the doctrine of retribution after death. A passage from Tertullian, one of the greatest of the early Fathers,[1] may serve to illustrate this doctrine. He wrote, "All that is real is body. The corporeality of God does not detract from His sublimity, nor that of the soul from its immortality. Everything that is, is body after its kind. What is not body is nothing. Who shall deny that God is body, though He is a spirit? A spirit is a body of its own kind, in its own form. The soul has the human form, the same as its body, only it is delicate, clear, and ethereal. Unless it were corporeal, how could it be affected by the body?" And St Jerome argued, "If the dead be not raised with flesh and bones, how can the damned after judgment gnash their teeth in hell?" These passages show how the teaching of the Fathers, according to which both

[1] He wrote about the end of the second century of our era.

God and the soul are corporeal, involved a return very nearly to the primitive theory of the ghost-soul, the vapour-like duplicate of the body. It was the same undifferentiated materialistic dualism.

The spiritualization of the soul seems to have been achieved by way of the refinement of the conception of God. This refining process consisted in successively denying Him all the distinctive attributes of matter, until the conception of an immaterial spirit was reached. And then the conception of the human soul was assimilated to this more refined conception of God. Thus man, having created God in his own likeness in the course of his first speculative efforts, reversed the order of procedure at a later stage and shaped his idea of himself on the model of his more refined idea of God.

It was probably through the influence of the Neoplatonists that this refinement was effected. Neoplatonism represents the culmination of a reaction against the quasi-materialism of the Stoics and a revival of the influence of Plato.

In Alexandria the men and the thoughts of many races and peoples came into contact, and Philo the Jew, a forerunner of the Neoplatonic school, attempted to combine Hebrew theology with Greek philosophy. He identified the *pneuma* of the Stoics with the breath of the Hebrew God and with the reason of both Plato and Aristotle. The Hebrews, like so many other peoples, had conceived the soul as air, wind, breath. But this air was breathed into man by God;[1] and therefore, as the conception of God was dematerialized, so also the *pneuma* emanating from him to become the soul of man became an immaterial substance. But in Philo's doctrine the process of dematerialization is not completed; the animal soul of man is generated with and destroyed with the body, and the *pneuma*, which is the rational soul breathed into him by God, is the last sublimation of the physical principle of the Stoics.[2]

[1] See p. 7.
[2] St Paul's doctrine of human personality, departing in this respect from the teachings of the other parts of the New Testament, in which soul and spirit are not distinguished, involved a similar trichotomy, body, soul, and spirit. According to Prof. Charles, the Apostle adopted the later doctrine of the Old Testament which regarded the soul "as the supreme function of the body quickened by the spirit. So conceived it naturally perishes on the withdrawal of the latter. It has, therefore, no existence in the next life. And such, in fact, appears to be the view of the Apostle. The soul, he holds, is the vital principle of the flesh ($\sigma\acute{\alpha}\rho\xi$). Hence the epithets 'fleshly' ($\sigma\alpha\rho\kappa\iota\kappa\acute{o}\varsigma$) and 'soulish' ($\psi\upsilon\chi\iota\kappa\acute{o}\varsigma$) over

Plotinus, the most prominent figure among the Neoplatonists, insisted that life and thought are not to be explained by means of any physical principle, such as the *pneuma* of the Stoics, no matter how thin or refined it may be; he seems to have been the first to describe the soul as an immaterial substance. In his doctrine, abstraction and the negation of attributes to God are carried so far that God becomes the One. This One sends forth *Nous*, the universal mind, of which in turn the human soul is an emanation. "The soul is the image and product of the *Nous*, just as the *Nous* is of the One. As being only the image of the *Nous*, the soul is necessarily of inferior rank and character, though none the less really divine and endowed with generative force. . . . The soul is an immaterial substance, not a body, nor the harmony, nor the entelechy of the body and inseparable from the latter, since not only the *Nous*, but also memory, and even the faculty of perception, and the psychical force which moulds the body, are separable from the body. There exists a real plurality of souls; the highest of all is the soul of the world; but the rest are not mere parts of the world-soul. The soul permeates the body as fire permeates air. It is more correct to say that the body is in the soul than that the soul is in the body; there is, therefore, a portion of the soul in which there is no body, a portion to whose functions the co-operation of the body is unnecessary. But neither are the sensuous faculties lodged in the body, whether in its individual parts or in the body as a whole: they are only present with the body, the soul lending to each bodily organ the force necessary for the execution of its functions. Thus the soul is present not only in the individual parts of the body, but in the whole body, and present everywhere in its entirety, not divided among the different parts of the body; it is entirely in the whole body, and entirely in every part. . . . The soul resembles God by its unity and by its possession of a centre and

---

against 'spiritual' (πνευματικός) are taken to be synonymous." The *pneuma* or spirit comes directly from God, but, since it alone is the immortal part of man, it is not reabsorbed into the Godhead on the death of the body, as in the later Hebrew conception, and is the basis of personal immortality. But, as Prof. Charles remarks, "the Pauline doctrine of the spirit is beset with difficulties" (*op. cit.*, p. 411); that is to say, the Apostle does not carry through clearly and consistently his trichotomous doctrine, does not succeed in combining in one consistent doctrine of personal immortality the conception of the soul as a function of the body that perishes with it and that of the *pneuma* as an emanation from God.

hence arises the possibility of its communion with the One"; [1] a communion which involves apprehension of a unique kind and is achieved only during rare moments of ecstasy.

In the later part of the fourth century Gregory of Nyssa argued for the immateriality of the soul and also for its immortality. Against those who, like the early Fathers, maintained that the soul is material, he urged that the spiritual nature of God, which cannot be denied, proves the possibility of immaterial existence. "We may with the same right conclude from the phenomena of the human microcosm to the actual existence of an immaterial soul, as from the phenomena of the world as a whole to the reality of God's existence. The soul is defined by Gregory as a created being, having life, the power of thought, and, so long as it is provided with the proper organs, the power of sensuous perception. As being simple and uncompounded the soul survives the dissolution of the composite body, whose scattered elements it continues and will continue to accompany, as if watching over its property, until the resurrection, when it will clothe itself in them anew." [2]

The expression "immaterial substance" does not seem to have been used by the Fathers until the fifth century, when Augustine applied it to define the nature of the soul of man. He is known to have been greatly influenced by the Neoplatonists, especially by Plotinus, and it is probable that he derived the notion and the expression from them. Augustine seems also to have been the first to make extension the distinctive attribute of matter, and the lack of it the distinctive attribute of soul. Nevertheless, he taught that the soul is present at each moment in every part of the body; he wrote, "when there is any pain in the foot, the eye looks, the tongue speaks, the hand moves, and this would not occur unless what of the soul is in those parts felt also in the foot; nor, if not present in the foot, could it feel what has there happened." And yet the soul was not to be regarded as having extension. Augustine also laid down the dictum that whatever is not matter and yet has real existence is properly termed spirit. He thus clearly distinguished two classes of real existents, the material and the spiritual, a distinction destined to be so widely accepted for long ages. And then, having conceived the soul as an immaterial substance, Augustine seems to have felt the difficulty of the question so often raised in later ages, namely, How can

[1] Ueberweg's "History of Philosophy."   [2] Ueberweg's "History."

two things so unlike as material body and immaterial soul influence one another? And in order to mitigate this difficulty he postulated a third substance intermediate in nature between matter and spirit, matter of a very subtle kind which should serve as the medium of interaction.

Augustine of course maintained the survival of the soul after death of the body, and claimed for it immortality, subject to the will of God, by which alone it could be annihilated.

No considerable change in the Church's teaching as regards the nature of the soul was effected until about the end of the twelfth century, when the diffusion of translations of the works of Aristotle and the invasion of Southern Europe by the Mohamedan commentators set the schoolmen upon the attempt to reconcile the teaching of Aristotle with the tenets of the Christian Church.

The earlier schoolmen made of the three fundamental psychical powers distinguished by Aristotle, the vegetative, the sensitive, and the intellectual, three distinct and almost completely independent souls, *anima vegetativa*, *anima sensitiva*, *anima rationalis*; the last of these only was regarded by them as immortal. But this strange doctrine was destined soon to be swept away by the greatest of the schoolmen. Thomas Aquinas taught in the later part of the thirteenth century a philosophy and a psychology which were the culmination of the scholastic efforts, and which have remained with comparatively little change the accepted doctrines of the Roman Church. His psychological writings and those of his immediate predecessor, Albertus Magnus, were largely provoked by the rapid spread of Arabian heresies in the schools of Europe, and they were mainly directed towards the refutation of Averroism. Averroes, who flourished in the later part of the twelfth century, was the most influential of the Arab philosophers. His doctrines, which claimed to be the inevitable developments of Aristotle's teaching, were widely accepted both in Spain and Italy; but they were regarded by the more orthodox schoolmen as involving heretical perversions.

A central topic of discussion throughout the three hundred years of the flourishing of the Arab philosophy was the relation of the creative reason of Aristotle to the soul of man. The master himself had, as we have seen, expressed himself incapable of forming a decided opinion on the question of the relation of the creative reason to the bodily organism. Alexander of Aphrodisias, a Greek writer of the end of the second century, had given wide currency to a theological development of Aristotle's uncertain utterances. According to this doctrine, which was propounded as a protest against the Materialism of the Stoics and a return to Aristotle, the creative reason belongs to God alone. The human soul was regarded as possessing only the passive reason, a capacity or disposition for rational thought, which remains, however, a mere potentiality until realized or brought into actuality by the "assistance" of the Divine Reason.[1] The doctrine of "Divine Assistance" played some part in the development of Neo-platonism, and, partly through that system and in part directly, brought into prominence in the Arabian philosophy the question of the possibility of the mode of "union" or "conjunction" of the human soul with the one creative reason. The latter came to be regarded in the Arab schools as a universal superior principle that mediates between God and man. After three centuries of controversy over this problem, Averroes went back to the doctrine of Alexander, and improved upon it by denying to the human soul the passive reason or intellect as well as the active reason; for, he argued, this mere potentiality of reason is nothing. Thus it might seem that in this doctrine the soul of man was stripped of all that in Aristotle's view distinguishes it from that of animals; but memory and the power of sensory representation and a quasi-intelligence, which went by the name *vis cogitativa*, in fact all but the capacity to form a pure abstract notion, were allowed it. Reason or intelligence was then a metaphysical entity, whose relation to individual human souls was purely external and accidental and temporary. The doctrine involved the denial to the human soul of immortality and of any existence apart from the body; and this implication was explicitly taught by Averroes, though it was not accepted by all who professed themselves his disciples.

It was to the refutation of this doctrine that Aquinas addressed himself in one of his principal treatises,[2] insisting that we cannot be content to explain the thought of man by the aid of a principle which is neither a part of the constitution of man, nor one in which man participates. He returned to the psychological method, and, instead of making an absolute distinction between thought and sense-presentation, he

---

[1] "Pietro Pomponazzi," by A. H. Douglas, Cambridge, 1910, p. 26.
[2] "De unitate intellectus contra Averroistas."

traced the play of intelligence through the lower mental functions, exhibiting their continuity with the higher modes of intellection. Like his predecessors in the schools, Aquinas claimed to have returned to the true Aristotelian doctrine, and he taught that the soul is the form of the body. But he denied the separability or separateness of the active reason and insisted that the soul is a unitary being; consistent adherence to Aristotle's principles would then have led him to the denial of immortality. This, of course, was impossible to him; therefore, instead of binding fast the reason in the body together with the nutritive and sensitive faculties, he rather set free all alike from the body and declared the whole unitary soul to be immortal: the soul is the form of the body, but it is the form in a new sense, for it is a "separable form."

In this new doctrine of the soul as a separable form, Aquinas attempted to combine the teaching of Aristotle with the Neoplatonic notion of a spiritual substance. The leading features of his psychology, and the nature of the arguments on which he relied for the proof of human immortality, have been concisely stated by a Roman Catholic writer in the following passage: "The keynote to Thomistic metaphysical psychology is the essential distinction between a lower or sensuous, and a higher or rational, grade of consciousness. The essential irreducibility of attention, abstraction, comparison, reasoning, self-consciousness, and free will to organic processes, such as those of the external senses, the imagination and the sensuous memory, is the ground of spirituality and immortality. The latter phenomena are accounted for by admitting the co-operation of the soul or vital principle with the organic co-factor; the former demand intrinsic independence of the organism for their display, and hence point to an inorganic principle as their exclusive subject. Thought is not a passive transformation of sensations; an inner attentive energy of the mind (*intellectus agens*) disengages at first the essentials of the sensuous presentation (*abstrahit essentiam*), and then the mind itself (*intellectus passivus*), out of this prepared datum, proceeds to generate the pure forms of thought (*exprimere intelligendo*). This was an application of the Aristotelic theory of the 'active and passive intellect' to the problem of the bridge between sensation and conception. The intellect is acknowledged to be objectively dependent on sense for the acquisition of the materials of its knowledge; it is subjectively independent of the organism, however, in the display of its irreducible activities of thought and volition. This intrinsic independence of the organism which the soul shows (even while united with the body and conditioned by the health or disease of the imagination and memory) by the very fact of its being the exclusive subject of its own higher functions, is the proof of spirituality and the pledge of immortality. This view of St Thomas does not imply an '*anima separata*' but an '*anima separabilis.*' There is only one specific substance in man—the compound self or ego. The soul was not a mere thinking machine, but the life-giving principle of the body as well, discharging the several functions of thought, feeling, and volition, either by itself or conjointly with the organism."[1] There was here a distinct advance towards the attitude adopted by those moderns who defend the conception of the soul.

Although Aquinas attributed immortality to the whole of the human soul, including the vegetative and sensitive powers, he maintained that the souls of animals are inseparable from their bodies and that they perish with them. Like Augustine and other Fathers, he denied the Platonic doctrine of the pre-existence of the soul, maintaining that each soul is created at the moment the body is ready for its operation.

During the long period between the great age of Greek philosophy and the Renascence of European learning, the conception of the soul was thus refined and developed under the influence of theological speculation, until it became set over against matter as a purely spiritual principle of a radically different nature, an immortal being temporarily associated with the body and intervening in its material processes with intelligent purposive activity. But during the same period there were not wanting speculations on the lines of the Pre-Socratic materialistic philosophers of Greece, made under the influence of natural science, rather than of theology.

In the last century B.C. the Roman poet, Lucretius, gave a complete exposition of Epicurean Materialism in the famous poem "De Rerum Natura"; and at the same time developed the theory in certain respects. His fundamental argument against the separability of the soul was one which has been reproduced and relied upon by materialists of all later ages; "the soul is born

[1] Article, "St Thomas," in Baldwin's "Dictionary of Philosophy and Psychology."

with the body, it grows and decays with the body, therefore it perishes with the body." He embodied the notion, first suggested by Empedocles, "that all the adaptation to be found in the universe, and especially in organic life, is merely a special case of the infinite possibilities of mechanical events";[1] a suggestion of great importance for the materialistic scheme, since it remained as the only materialistic explanation of the apparently teleological facts of nature, until in the nineteenth century Darwinism supplied a less inadequate one.

Lucretius found himself compelled by the observation of animal behaviour to make at least one assumption not strictly compatible with the pure materialistic atomism of Democritus and Epicurus; namely, he assumed that the atoms move not always in straight lines, but have the power of deviating spontaneously from the straight path. He recognized two forms of soul, or soul and spirit (*anima* and *animus*); nevertheless "both are corporeal and are composed of the smallest, roundest and most mobile atoms."[2] Lucretius, like Epicurus, seems to have felt the difficulty of boldly asserting that the motion of atoms is sensation, and sought to mitigate it by dwelling on the exceeding fineness of the soul-atoms.

Galen, the celebrated Greek philosopher and anatomist who practised surgery in Rome in the later part of the second century of our era, studied the structure and functions of the body by means of dissection. He established the connexion of the nerves with the central nervous system, and showed that the brain is somehow intimately concerned in our mental life. He taught that the brain is the seat of the soul and the medium through which the sensations are produced.[3]

Galen's teaching did much to give currency to the doctrine of "animal spirits," which figured largely in all later physiological writings until very recent times. Spirits (*Spiritus*) of many kinds played a great part in the cosmology and physiology of the Neoplatonic Scholastic philosophy; and early in the Middle Ages, Galen's doctrine of the animal spirits was fused with the Aristotelian psychology; thus arose that conception of *spiritus*

[1] A. Lange, " History of Materialism," vol. i. p. 138.
[2] Lange, *op. cit.*, p. 146.
[3] The honour of having first demonstrated the intimate connection of the brain with our mental life is sometimes attributed to Alcmæon of Crotona (500 B.C.). And it is said that Theophilus of Alexandria (300 B.C.) distinguished the sensory from the motor nerves.

animalis distilled in the brain from the *spiritus vitalis* of the blood, which at a later period was taken up by Descartes into his system. This conception of "spiritus," which came into the culture tradition of the Middle Ages from so many different sources, owed its deep hold to the fact that it seemed to bridge the gulf between the sensible and the supersensible, a need which was felt as well by the Neoplatonists as by the Christian theologians, by Lucretius as well as by Augustine and the followers of Descartes; for *spiritus* was the subtlest kind of matter.[1]

It is interesting to note that in the thirteenth century the philosophers whose speculations were of a naturalistic tendency, especially those of the University of Paris, adopted the ingenious subterfuge of distinguishing two forms of truth, the theological and the philosophical, in order to free scientific speculation from the restrictive influence of the Church; a practice which is paralleled at the present day by the widely prevalent fashion of distinguishing between scientific and philosophic truth. To confound this teaching by demonstrating the harmony of all truth had been one of the principal aims of Aquinas; but in spite of the great authority of his name and doctrine the distinction became widely accepted; and it continued to be so well recognized that it was urged by Giordano Bruno in his defence before the Inquisition in 1592. It was a symptom of the uneasiness of the spirit of inquiry under the bonds imposed upon it by the Church. By the loosening of those bonds the Renascence gave new life to the problem of the soul, and in the sixteenth century it was discussed with a new freedom and a renewed vigour.

[1] In the sixteenth century the conception of *spiritus* was brought back by Paracelsus very nearly to its original form, the ghost-soul; for he conceived *spiritus* anthropomorphically, peopled all things, great and small, with innumerable demons, and attributed to these all evidences of life and activity.

CHAPTER III

ANIMISM AT THE TIME OF THE RENASCENCE OF LEARNING

THE philosophy of the Renascence is rightly held, says Professor Höffding, to have been introduced by the treatise of Pietro Pomponazzi on the immortality of the soul ("De Immortalitate Animi," 1516).

Pomponazzi was a voluminous writer and an influential teacher in the schools of northern Italy; he has been called, with some reason, the last of the schoolmen and the first modern psychologist. His handling of the problem of the soul is remarkable for his indifference to authority and for his agnostic attitude.[1] The century that separated him from Aquinas had been filled with the controversy between Thomists and Averroists, in which the great question at issue was the relation of the soul to reason or intellect. Both parties claimed to adhere to the teaching of Aristotle, though their interpretations of that teaching were widely different. Pomponazzi approached this problem in an independent spirit and, setting aside the rival systems of interpretation, went back to Aristotle himself.

Accepting Aristotle's fundamental proposition that the soul is the form of the body, he rejected the Mono-psychism of Averroes (the doctrine that reason is one divine light which shines in upon the souls of men), not only because it seemed to him inconsistent with that proposition, but also on the grounds that embodiment is of the very nature of intelligence as known in man, and that the assumption of a universal reason leaves unsolved the problem of the reasoning power of individual men.

He rejected just as positively the Thomist conception of the soul as a self-subsistent and separable form or a spiritual substance capable of existing after the death of the body; insisting always

---

[1] A full account of Pomponazzi and his teaching, based partly on material only recently brought to light, has been given by Mr A. H. Douglas ("The Philosophy and Psychology of Pietro Pomponazzi," Cambridge, 1910). My brief account is extracted from this work.

on the fact that we have direct knowledge of human intelligence and activity only as it is manifested in bodily life. He thus rejected both the "collective immortality" of the Averroists and the individual immortality of the orthodox scholastics, and explicitly taught the mortality of the human soul; this, the most distinctive feature of his teaching, naturally produced a great stirring in the schools. Yet, in spite of his denial of immortality and his assertion of the dependence of all human thought on bodily organs, Pomponazzi was not a materialist. Nor was he, of course, an idealist in the sense most usually attached to that ambiguous word; for the notion that the material world may be purely a figment of our minds had not entered into the current of European speculation; philosophers still accepted unquestioningly the reality and the spatial character of physical things. He believed, like most of his contemporaries, in the existence of higher intelligences whose reason operated in pure universals, abstract and general ideas that were not achieved by way of the contemplation of particular or concrete objects. These pure intelligences constituted the highest part of a hierarchy of beings. "There were according to this scheme, three orders of beings—the immaterial and imperishable, including the Deity, and (in their essential nature and true being) the spheral Intelligences; at the other extreme, material and mortal, all sublunary beings with the exception of man: intermediate between the two, and sharing the attributes of both, the composite nature of man."[1] "Belonging to the three orders of being, there were three sorts of "souls." For the superior Intelligences were also to be regarded as in a sense the informing souls of the spheres to which they belonged. Only the difference between them and the human soul was that the act of intelligence in them did not depend in any way upon the physical spheres to which they were related only as the motor is to that which is moved; knowledge in them was a direct intuition and contemplation of abstract and immaterial objects; whereas the soul of man is dependent for the exercise of intelligence upon matter *tanquam de objecto*, and the sensitive soul, or the soul of the lower animal, resides in matter *tanquam de subjecto* as well."[2]

He held fast to Aristotle's teaching, that reason in man operates only with the aid of the presentation in imagination of the data of sense; and this dependence of human reason on sense and imagery for its objects was one of his chief grounds for

[1] A. H. Douglas, *op. cit.*, p. 124.   [2] *Op. cit.*, p. 125.

denying the possibility of its separation from the body. A second ground for this denial was the unity of the soul: the intellectual soul is one with the sensitive and vegetative soul; it is merely the same soul under a different aspect; and, since in its lower aspects the soul is obviously inseparable from body, the soul as a whole must be inseparable from it and incapable of surviving its dissolution. He held then that, though man's soul, in so far as it is capable of grasping universals, participates in immateriality and is allied to the pure Intelligences, this intellectual principle is in him so imperfect and rudimentary that it cannot raise him above the sphere of the perishable.[1]

Montaigne displayed in his celebrated "Essais" a similarly agnostic attitude in face of the problem of the soul, and attacked the dogmatism of theologians and philosophers. Contemporary with him was the Spaniard, Ludovicus Vives, who is sometimes claimed as the founder of psychology as an empirical science. He insisted that, properly speaking, we are interested, not in knowing what the soul *is*, but rather how *it is active*, and that the precepts of self-knowledge concern not the nature, but the functions of the soul. "We find it here asserted, with the greatest assurance, that we have directly to deal with mental phenomena only, and that empirical psychology can altogether dispense with the purely speculative theory concerning the nature of the soul."[2] All of which has a strangely modern ring. Nevertheless Vives regarded the soul as the principle, not only of conscious life, but of life in general; he regarded the heart as the centre of its vital or vegetative activity, the brain as that of its intellectual activity. The souls of plants and of animals, he taught, are generated by

---

[1] The following passage from Pomponazzi's commentary on the "De Anima" seems to state his position concisely: "Concerning the intellectual soul I hold, in accordance with Aristotle, that it essentially depends on body, both for its existence and for its intellection, and can neither exist without body nor operate without a corporeal organ. There is no reason to suppose that we think after death, but there is reason for believing that in this world we think through a corporeal organ in respect of the object. . . . Our soul, in so far as it is a concrete intellectual soul, uses in intellection a corporeal organ, and is not altogether independent of a corporeal organ. Yet it does not altogether and in every way need a corporeal organ, since it does not need it as the ground of its existence. In its operation it does not need a body in this way, but in reference to the object of thought it does, because whatever is thought by our mind is thought by means of something corporeal" (Douglas, *op. cit.*, p. 96).

[2] Höffding, *op. cit.*, p. 36.

the power of matter; human souls only are immediately created by God.

In Bernardino Telesio, whose comprehensive work, "De Rerum Natura," was published in 1586, the tendency of the philosophy of the Renascence to appeal to Nature rather than to Aristotle or the Scriptures found a systematic and thoroughgoing exponent. His system was thoroughly hylozoistic, i.e. it was metaphysical materialism of the kind which regards matter as endowed with mental capacities; and he saw in sense-perception the empirical basis of all knowledge. Looking on all matter as animated, he taught that human consciousness is but a development of the simple feelings of inorganic matter; he argued, in fact, in the modern fashion from the human consciousness to the feeling of inorganic matter, according to the principle of continuity. "He maintains, that is to say, the impossibility of explaining the genesis of consciousness out of matter, unless we suppose matter to be originally endowed with consciousness."[1] Telesio did not deny a soul to man; but the soul was, as with the Stoics, but the subtlest form of matter. "The spirit to which Telesio constantly refers as the natural soul, is thought of as wholly corporeal, a very delicate, rarefied substance, enclosed within the nervous system, and therefore eluding our senses. Its place, the seat of the soul, is chiefly the brain, but extends also to the spinal cord, the nerves, arteries, veins, and the covering membranes of the internal organs. Similar cavities to those visible in the brain (i.e. the ventricles), the spinal cord and the optic nerves are present in all these organs, and it is there that the spirit is enclosed, so that it is accessible to any movement from without, and is able to transmit its own movement to these parts, and thence to the limbs. The extreme mobility of the spirit, and its continuity throughout all the nervous system, are the qualities which fit it to play the part of the soul. . . . Recognizing that the nervous system is in close connection with soul-life, he frankly acknowledged that the soul in men differs only in degree from the soul of animals."[2]

"Corporeal, however, though the spirit be, yet it is different from the ordinary parts of the body. It is invisible, is akin to

---

[1] Höffding, *op. cit.*, p. 97.
[2] Article on Telesio by J. Lewis M'Intyre, in "British Journal of Psychology," vol. i.

the nature of the sun and the sky; hence the heaviness of a body from which the spirit has fled, for it was the upward striving soul that lightened it through life: hence also the soul that has left the body cannot return, for it flies upward towards its own element, like fire and air."[1]

Telesio was so far under the influence of the orthodox teachings of the Church that he assumed, beside the material soul in man, a divine non-corporeal soul directly implanted by God, which unites with the material soul. He did not make clear the relations between the two souls, and it would seem that this additional and superfluous soul was added by Telesio to his scheme either as a prudent concession to the Church, or because his philosophical and his theological opinions were formed in separate "water-tight compartments" of his mind, while he was too honest to accept the current convention which admitted two kinds of truth, the theological and the philosophical. "The proof or evidence of this divine soul which Telesio offers is that men do in fact inquire into supernatural matters, which have no reference to their bodily needs, that they find real happiness only in the knowledge and pursuit of the divine; that for these they neglect even those bodily needs which the brutes pursue without deviation. . . . The divine soul is that in man which understands, but it does so only through the natural spirit, and it can understand only these things, which the spirit offers to it for understanding."[2]

The greatest of the philosophers of the Renascence period, Giordano Bruno, made a remarkable attempt to unite an idealistic conception of the universe with the principles of physical Atomism. He is sometimes claimed as a link between ancient and modern Materialism, but only by those who regard one side only of his teachings. He distinguished spiritual and material substances, although he regarded them as ultimately of one single essence, an original and universal substance. Everything that exists is animated, and in everything the world-soul operates as the inner principle of a motion which is both mechanical and purposive. Nevertheless, the soul of the individual is a distinct being; and Bruno favours the belief in transmigration of souls or metempsychosis. The relation of the individual soul to the world-soul remains as obscure as in all other Pantheistic systems.

Physiology may be said to have been founded during the

[1] *Ibid.* [2] *Ibid.*

later part of the Renascence period. It began at once to exert upon the conception of the soul an influence of the kind which in succeeding centuries, and especially in the nineteenth century, has been a principal factor in leading to the rejection of Animism by the greater part of the learned world. In the year 1543 Andreas Vesalius published his great work, "Fabrica Humani Corporis," which was as important for physiology as for anatomy. He elaborated the doctrine of animal spirits which had fluttered down uncertainly from the ancients. He distinguished an inferior form of spirits, the vital spirits which are concerned in the bodily functions generally. From the vital spirits brought to the brain by the blood, and from the air, which makes its way into the brain directly by the pores of the skull, the brain elaborates the animal spirits in its ventricles. The animal spirits permeate all parts of the nervous system, just as the vital spirit is distributed through the arteries. Vesalius recognized also a third variety, the natural spirit. These three seem to have been regarded by him as three stages of elaboration of the spirit from the blood, the natural spirit being made by the liver, the vital spirit by the heart, and the animal spirit by the brain; in the third stage it attains so high a degree of refinement that it is to be described as "a quality rather than an actual thing." He wrote of three corresponding souls—the natural, vital, and the chief soul; but it seems clear that by each of these souls he meant to imply nothing more than the sum total of the spirit of the corresponding kind. Vesalius insisted upon the essential similarity of the brains of men and animals; he seems to have held a thoroughly materialistic view of the mind, though he cautiously abstained from maintaining doctrines that might have brought him into conflict with the Church.

Van Helmont, the leading physiologist of the opening years of the seventeenth century, who thus in point of time belongs to the modern period, may be mentioned here; for his teachings in respect to the soul belong rather to the mediæval than the modern period. Van Helmont took up Vesalius' doctrine of the elaboration of the animal spirits by successive stages, but distinguished six such stages. In addition to the animal spirits, he recognized, unlike Vesalius, a sensitive and motor soul (*anima sensitiva motivaque*). "This sensitive soul belongs to man alone; for, speaking truly and thinking correctly, we must say that there is no soul residing in plants and in brute beasts. These possess only a certain vital power, which we may perhaps regard as the forerunner of a soul. The sensitive soul as it exists in man takes to itself the reins of that forerunning governing vital power." The sensitive soul is the prime agent of all the acts of the body; and though it carries out the sensations and movements of the body by means of the brain and nerves, its actual seat is the orifice of the stomach. This sensitive soul is mortal, and co-exists in man with the immortal mind (*mens immortalis*). " The sensitive soul is, as it were, the husk or shell of the mind, and the latter works through it." Before the fall of Adam man possessed only the immortal mind, which discharged the functions of life. " At the fall, God introduced into man the sensitive soul, and with it death, the immortal mind retiring within the sensitive soul and becoming, as it were, its kernel."[1] Van Helmont's teaching as regards the soul, a strange chaotic mixture of notions derived from many sources, thus forms a link between the doctrines of Vesalius and of Descartes.

[1] I have extracted these brief accounts of the teaching of Vesalius and Van Helmont respecting the soul from Sir Michael Foster's " History of Physiology."

CHAPTER IV

ANIMISM IN THE SEVENTEENTH CENTURY

THE historians of European thought are agreed in regarding the beginning of the seventeenth century as the date that separates the distinctively modern from the mediæval period. Of the distinctive features of the modern period two are of predominant importance: first, the rapid and complete emancipation of scientific and philosophical thought from the fetters of the Church, and a complete reversal of their position of subordination to theology; secondly, the increasing definiteness of the strictly mechanical conception of nature, the continued and astonishing triumphs of this conception in its application to the explanation of one field of phenomena after another, and the consequently increasing confidence with which mechanical explanations were held to be applicable to all events without exception.

In classical antiquity, Democritus, Epicurus, and Lucretius had projected a mechanical scheme of the world, reducing all things to atoms in motion. But their doctrines remained fanciful speculations merely, like any others; they had no demonstrative force; the acceptance or rejection of them was as purely a matter of individual taste, as the preference of sherry to port, or of Wordsworth to Browning. But in the opening years of the seventeenth century, Kepler and Galileo laid the sure foundations of the splendid structure of nineteenth century Materialism, by initiating the exact quantitative study of motion; and the work they began has been carried on by a long line of brilliant thinkers and investigators—Gassendi, Hobbes, Newton, Boyle, Kant, Laplace, Holbach, Mayer, Joule, Helmholz, Kelvin —with such striking success that, in our own day, the truth of the purely mechanical conception of nature has become a confidently held dogma of the scientific world, accepted not only by physicists and chemists, but also by the greater number of the biologists, psychologists, and philosophers, as a fundamental principle to which all their assumptions and conclusions must conform. Accordingly, the labours of philosophers have been increasingly concerned with attempts to reconcile a belief in spiritual modes of action and existence with the mechanical scheme of the world, and with attempts to show that the belief in purposive or teleological determination is not merely a mythical survival from the dark ages.

In this great process of the development of modern thought, which may without exaggeration be described as the reaction of the human mind on the affirmation by the natural sciences of the universal sway of mechanical laws, a central place has been occupied throughout by the problem of the relation of the mental to the physical, of mind to body.

In all earlier ages men believed implicitly in the real efficiency of their wills; they knew themselves able to imagine alternative courses of events in the physical world; they believed they could freely choose to influence this course of events, and that, purposing or desiring to see one course realized rather than another, they could by their efforts contribute to the realization of their purpose. This was the essence of the conception of animation, and, in attributing animation to beings other than themselves, men attributed to them a similar capacity for teleological determination of phenomenal events. Very early in the modern period, the work of Kepler, Galileo, Gassendi, and their successors, resulted, for the majority of men of science, in the banishment of animation (in this full and original sense) from the whole realm of inorganic nature.

In the course of Kepler's own intellectual development this decisive step was made: beginning with an animistic conception of nature, according to which all things, especially the planets, are moved by souls; he ended by extruding souls entirely from his scheme and supplanting them by the conception of forces. And Galileo made the decisive step by affirming that "it is only possible to understand the qualitative changes in nature when these can be traced back to quantitative changes, which means here to motions in space."[1] But, with few exceptions, men continued to believe in the animation of organic beings; though the Cartesians, it is true, gave up the whole organic realm, with the exception of man alone, to the sway of purely mechanical laws (an intrinsically unstable compromise which owed its career only to the influence of theology).

[1] Höffding, *op. cit.*, p. 181.

Thus the soul, especially the human soul, became the centre of interest of all the great controversies of the eighteenth century. The materialists sought to show that all the phenomena of organic life (including human actions) are mechanically explicable, and to exhibit human consciousness as entirely dependent upon matter. The defence of the conception of animation was conducted along two different lines; on the one hand, the vitalists maintained the inadequacy of mechanical principles to explain the physiological processes of organic bodies; on the other hand, philosophers continued to demand a soul as the substrate of consciousness and the agent of the intellectual activities of man. Then in the nineteenth century the rapid progress of mechanical explanations in physiology and the appearance of the Darwinian principles seemed to deal a final blow at physiological Animism with its vital force; about the same time the discovery that the whole brain is a vast and complex system of reflex nervous paths, in which prevails unbroken continuity of physical process from sense-organ to muscle, seemed to be equally fatal to psychological Animism; while the establishment of the law of conservation of energy seemed to clinch the matter in both cases, to establish finally the universal sway of the law of mechanical causation throughout both organic and inorganic nature, and to secure the final triumph of Materialism over Animism.

These results of the splendid progress of the empirical sciences have been accepted by most of the philosophers. And this acceptance was not difficult for them; for they had learned to believe that a thoroughgoing Materialism is not the only alternative to Animism, but that it is possible to reject Animism without accepting those features of thoroughgoing Materialism which render it intellectually disreputable. Two such alternatives have gained wide acceptance among them. On the one hand, a way was found which seemed to make possible the combination of mechanical Materialism, of even the most extreme form, with Animism, and even with a return to the doctrine of universal animation, namely, by sacrificing the most essential element of Animism (the power of teleological determination) and retaining only as the connotation of animation the capacity for feeling or consciousness. This is the alternative of which Fechner was the principal exponent. On the other hand, philosophers had learnt from Hume, Berkeley, and Kant how, while giving up Animism, to withdraw themselves to a position from which they could look down upon both

ANIMISM IN THE SEVENTEENTH CENTURY

Materialism and Animism with indifference, namely, the subjectivist position from which matter and soul are regarded as equally unreal, as equally existing only as ideas in one's own consciousness.[1]

Such, in briefest outline, is the history of the conception of the soul in the modern period. This history we have now to follow in a little more detail, in order to arrive at a clear understanding of the present state of opinion and controversy regarding the soul. I shall first describe the teachings regarding the psychophysical problem of the principal thinkers who have dealt with it in the modern period; and afterwards I shall trace those developments of the natural sciences by which Animism has been, in the opinion of the great majority of scientists and philosophers, driven finally from the field.

Although Descartes set himself to lay anew the foundations of philosophy, a large number of the notions and distinctions thrown into the European culture-stream by his predecessors were incorporated in his system. His principal achievement was to clarify many of the distinctions and notions current in his time, and to set them in definite relations to one another in a single large scheme of things.

Descartes distinguished sharply between matter and spirit, defining the former as extended substance, the latter as inextended thinking substance. He held that the whole material world and all its processes are to be explained mechanically by means of the conceptions of extension, divisibility, and mobility. He was the first of the moderns to attempt to give a mechanical theory of the evolution of the world, teaching that purely mechanical explanation in terms of matter and motion must apply not only to the planetary movements and to all the realm of inorganic matter, but also to the processes of organic bodies; physiology was to be made wholly a branch of mechanical science. His confidence in this bold assertion was greatly strengthened by Harvey's explanation of the circulation of the blood, according to the mechanical principles; for this seemed to show that the general laws of motion are valid within, as well as without, the body. He wrote: "All the functions of the body follow naturally from the sole disposition of its organs, just in the same way that the movements of a clock

---

[1] I am aware that many readers will regard this as an unfair description of the attitudes of anti-animistic philosophers; but I shall attempt to justify it in later chapters.

or other self-acting machine or automaton follow from the arrangement of its weights and wheels. So that there is no reason on account of its functions to conceive that there exists in the body any soul whether vegetative or sensitive, or any principle of movement other than the blood and its animal spirits agitated by the heat of the fire which burns continually in the heart, and which does not differ in nature from any of the other fires which are met with in inanimate bodies." He devised a hypothetical scheme for the explanation of all the bodily movements of animals in a purely mechanical fashion; and, though this was little more than a brilliant guess, it came strangely near the modern conception of reflex automatism. Not content with this, he attempted to show in more or less detail how the whole human body may be adequately conceived as a machine working on purely mechanical principles. Descartes thus definitely gave up the vegetative functions of the soul, and taught that animals are inanimate machines having no capacity for thought.[1] But man enjoys consciousness, or the power of thought; and this fact, which cannot be explained from the motions of matter, necessitates the assumption that in him the thinking substance is somehow conjoined with matter, that an immaterial soul co-operates with the material body, intervenes in its otherwise purely mechanical operations, and is in turn affected by these. The assumption of the soul in man is also necessitated, he held, by the fact that the bodily movements of men, unlike those of the animals, reveal by their complexity and their nice adjustment to an infinity of varied situations that they are guided by reason.

A third line of reasoning by which he justified the conception of the soul runs as follows: "Because I know with certitude that I exist, and because, in the meantime, I do not observe that aught necessarily belongs to my nature or essence beyond my being a thinking thing, I rightly conclude that my essence consists only in my being a thinking being. And although I may, or rather, as I will shortly say, although I certainly do possess a body with which I am very closely conjoined: nevertheless, because, on the one hand, I have a clear and distinct idea of myself, in as far as I am only a thinking and unextended thing, and as, on the other

---

[1] Descartes' doctrine seems to imply the denial of all psychical life or consciousness to animals; and it has generally been interpreted in this way. But Descartes, inconsistently enough, attributed mere sensation and feeling to the animals.

hand, I possess a distinct idea of body, in as far as it is only an extended and unthinking thing, it is certain that I myself am entirely and truly distinct from my body, and may exist without it."[1] Again, he wrote that we "perceive clearly that neither extension nor figure nor local motion ... pertains to our nature, and nothing save thought alone; it then becomes plain that I am not the assemblage of members called the human body; I am not a thin and penetrating air diffused through all these members, or wind, or flame, or vapour, or breath; for the notion we have of our mind precedes that of any corporeal thing, and is more certain, seeing that we still doubt whether there is any body in existence, while we already perceive that we think." He argued also that the reasoning soul "can by no means be educed from the power of matter, but must be expressly created; it is of a nature wholly independent of the body, and consequently is not liable to die with the latter; and, finally, because no other causes are observed capable of destroying it, we are naturally led to judge that it is immortal."

Descartes adopted the conception of animal spirits current among the physiologists of his time; but he divested it of all animistic meaning; for him the animal spirits were purely material. These animal spirits consist of the finest particles contained in the blood, which are filtered from the arteries through minute pores into the central cavity or ventricle of the brain. From this ventricle they pass into the nerves, and, by flowing down the motor nerves and from them into the muscles, they cause the latter to become distended laterally, and therefore to shorten and so bring about the movements of the parts of the body. According to Descartes' scheme of the nervous system, the motor nerves open from the ventricle of the brain by valved mouths; the sensory nerves also have their central terminations in the ventricle, each being connected with the valve of one of the motor nerves; when, then, any impression is made on a sense-organ, the sensory nerve affected plays the part of a bell-wire, it pulls open the valve to which it is attached and so allows the animal spirits to flow down the corresponding motor nerve and to bring about the appropriate reflex movement. Descartes, having devised this mechanical scheme of reflex action, and holding that all other bodily processes also are purely mechanical, did not find it necessary to assume, as was done by Augustine and others of

[1] Meditation VI., Veitch's translation.

his predecessors, that the soul is present in every part of the body; accordingly he assigned it a seat in the pineal gland, or rather he assumed that it acts on, and is acted on by, the body only through the medium of this part of the brain; being led to this view by the fact of the central position of the pineal gland in close proximity to the ventricle. (This was an unfortunate shot in the dark; for modern research has shown that no part of the brain is less concerned in our mental processes than the pineal gland, which seems to be a vestigial remnant of a median eye carried on the top of the cranium by a remote ancestor of the human species.) The soul, he taught, is able, by inclining the pineal gland this way or that, to direct the motion of the animal spirits of the brain towards this or that motor nerve, and to secure in this way the execution of the actions that it wills—a rude foreshadowing of the conception of guidance without work done, which in more recent times has been adduced as the probable mode of action of the soul on the bodily processes.

It is noteworthy that Descartes distinguished two kinds of memory:—" one of material things which depends on after-effects or traces of preceding excitations of the brain, and the other of mental things, depending on permanent traces in consciousness itself. Thought proper (*intellectio*) and imagination (*imaginatio*) may be distinguished from one another by this, that in thought proper the soul alone is active, while in imagination it makes use of sensuous images. Imagination, like perception and the material remembrance of the soul, only belongs to the soul in as far as it is united with the body; but the soul in its pureness, *anima pura*, can be thought without either imagination or perception. The difference between instinct and will similarly rests on the fact that while the former arises in the body, the will belongs to the soul itself. . . . The emotions are due to the influence of the body upon the soul; but the inner feelings arise in the soul as a consequence of its own thoughts and judgments." Thus Professor Höffding summarizes the main points of Descartes' consistently dualistic psychology.[1]

The teachings of Descartes exerted a far-reaching influence on subsequent science and philosophy, of which, as regards the conception of the soul, we may distinguish four principal and diverse lines. First, his description of the soul as an immaterial

[1] *Op. cit.*, p. 238.

inextended being, interacting with the body through the medium of the brain and nervous system only, gave the animistic theory a more definite and more defensible form than it had previously received. Secondly, by attributing to the soul the function of thought or of conscious activities only and denying to it the vegetative functions commonly attributed to it by his predecessors, he completed the separation of the conceptions of vitalizing principle and thinking principle which some of his predecessors had proposed; and it is largely owing to his influence that this separation has continued to the present day, the former surviving as the vital force of the vitalistic physiologists, the latter as the thinking feeling willing soul, the ground of all individual consciousness. Thirdly, by his bold assertion of the purely mechanical nature of all animal behaviour and by his ingenious speculations in support of this assertion, he hastened the advent of the time when all the behaviour of men also should be asserted with equal confidence to be the product of purely mechanical factors. Fourthly, by distinguishing so sharply between the natures of soul and body respectively, he brought into clearer view the difficulty of understanding the mode of interaction of soul and body, and thus provoked attempts to find other formulations of the psycho-physical relation.

Descartes' own disciples were not slow to raise this difficulty: How can there be reciprocal action between two such wholly unlike things as body and soul? And some of them, notably Geulincx and Malebranche, said: It is not possible; there can be no such interaction; the correspondence that clearly obtains between our thought and our bodily processes is maintained by the continual interposition of God, a change in one being the occasion for God to produce a corresponding change in the other. This doctrine of "Occasional Causes," or "Occasionalism," devised by Geulincx to meet the difficulty of conceiving psycho-physical interaction, was extended by Malebranche to the explanation of all transient action.

A different answer to this problem of the correspondence of bodily and mental changes—one that has had a greater influence upon subsequent thought—was given by Leibnitz in his doctrine of pre-established harmony. This can only be understood in connexion with his metaphysical doctrine of monads. Leibnitz rejected Descartes' distinction of thinking and extended substances; he regarded extension as merely phenomenal, and sought to describe in other terms the reality which appears to us as extended matter. He conceived all things after the pattern of that of which he had the most immediate awareness, namely, the unity of his own self as a thinking conscious being. He taught that the universe created by God consists of an infinite number of real beings, each different from every other, each containing from the first the potentiality of its whole subsequent history, each indivisible and incapable of being destroyed save by an act of God. These enduring beings or substances are the monads, the elements of which all things are composed. The soul of each man and of each animal is such a monad; but the soul of man is a monad of a higher order than all others and is properly called a mind, because its consciousness is richer and its psychical activities are of a higher order; it knows more of the world, or as Leibnitz says, it expresses or reflects the world more fully and knows also God. We learn from our experience of sleep, dreams, states of fainting, dizziness, confusion, and coma, that the human soul passes through states of consciousness of many degrees of clearness and fulness; and, as we may suppose the soul of any one of the higher animals to be incapable of a clearer and fuller consciousness than that of our duller half-waking states, so the soul of an animalcule must be supposed to be a monad enjoying a consciousness which is to that of the higher animal, as this is to the fully waking consciousness of man. But there is no lower limit to this descending scale of psychical life; and what we commonly call a mass of inert matter, is the phenomenon or appearance to us of an aggregation of monads of a still lower order than the soul of the animalcule.[1] Our bodies, then, and the bodies of animals are orderly aggre-

---

[1] In the following paragraphs of the "Monadologie" this scheme is expressed, perhaps more succinctly than in any other of Leibnitz's writings: "All simple substances or created monads may be called Entelechies because they have in themselves a certain perfection. There is in them a sufficiency which makes them the source of their internal activities, and renders them, so to speak, incorporeal automatons." "If we wish to designate as soul everything which has perceptions and desires in the general sense that I have just explained, all simple substances or created monads could be called souls. But since feeling is something more than a mere perception, I think that the general name of Monad or Entelechy should suffice for simple substances which have only perception, while we may reserve the term Soul for those whose perception is more distinct and is accompanied by memory. We experience in ourselves a state where we remember nothing and where we have no distinct perception, as in periods of fainting, or when we are overcome by a profound, dreamless sleep. In such a state the soul does not sensibly differ at all from a simple Monad. As this

gations or systems of monads belonging to many different levels in this scale of psychical being; and the soul of each man or animal is but the dominant monad of one such system. Leibnitz maintained (though why he did so is not clear to my mind) that every soul exists always in association with some body, i.e. some system of lower monads.[1] What, then, is the nature of the relation between soul and body, between that higher monad which is the soul of the man and that system of lower monads which is his body? Leibnitz rejected both Descartes' doctrine of interaction and the doctrine of occasional causes. In fact, he rejected completely the conception of causal interaction between monads. The monads do not influence one another in any way. How then does he account for the harmony of the world-order, including the correspondence between the changes of our bodies and the changes of our consciousness? The temporal correspondence of changes in all monads is due to the harmony of their natures pre-established by God at the moment of their creation. This bold and original speculation cannot be more clearly expressed than in Leibnitz's own words: "Every present state of a simple substance (i.e. of a Monad) is a natural consequence of its preceding state, in such a way that its present is big with its future."[2] And again: "The union of the soul with the body, and even the action of one substance upon another, consists only in the perfect mutual accord, expressly established by the ordinance of the first creation, by virtue of which each substance following its own laws falls in with what the other requires, and thus the activities of the one follow or accompany the activities or changes of the other."[3] In seeking to make clear to others this conception, as applied to the relation of soul to body, he wrote, "Suppose two clocks, or two watches, which perfectly keep time together. Now that may happen in three ways. The first way consists in the mutual influence of each clock upon the other; the second, in the care of a man who

---

state, however, is not permanent and the soul can recover from it, the soul is something more."

Again, "But the knowledge of eternal and necessary truths is that which distinguishes us from mere animals and gives us reason and the sciences, thus raising us to a knowledge of ourselves and of God. This is what is called in us the Rational Soul or the Mind" ("Monadology," paragraphs 18, 19, 20 and 29, Montgomery's translation).

[1] "Neither are there souls wholly separate from bodies, or bodiless spirits. God alone is without body" ("Monadologie," paragraph 72).

[2] "Monadologie," paragraph 22.

[3] Letter to Arnauld of March 23rd, 1690.

looks after them; the third, in their own accuracy. Now, put the soul and the body in the place of the two clocks. Their agreement or sympathy will also arise in one of these three ways. The way of influence is that of common philosophy, but as we cannot conceive material particles, or immaterial species, or qualities which can pass from one of these substances into the other, we are obliged to give up this opinion. The way of assistance is that of the system of occasional causes; but I hold that this is to introduce *Deus ex machina* in a natural and ordinary matter; in which it is reasonable that God should intervene only in the way in which He supports all the other things of nature. Thus there remains only my hypothesis, that is to say, the way of the harmony pre-established by a contrivance of the Divine foresight, which has from the beginning formed each of these substances in so perfect, so regular, and accurate a manner that by merely following its own laws each substance is in harmony with the other, just as if there were a mutual influence between them."

Thus Leibnitz solved to his own satisfaction the problem of the relation between soul and body. His scheme raises many difficulties that he did not adequately deal with. Many of these were pointed out by his correspondent, Arnauld, especially the problems raised by the association of each soul with a succession of bodies in the course of its career from the beginning to the end of the world. This difficulty, like most others, especially every problem of causation, Leibnitz solved by the easy method of invoking the designing skill of God at the creation of the world. In thus abolishing all causation and transient action from his scheme of the created world, and reducing the relation between changes to mere temporal concomitance, Leibnitz really abolished science; for the work of science is to discover the causal relations between events.

The objection may be stated more fully in the following way. To answer, in face of any particular problem, this event takes place because God ordained it so, is no explanation; or we may say that, like the explanation of all events offered by the extreme Occasionalists, namely, the direct interposition of God, the proposed explanation is of no value because it explains too much. Admitting, as Leibnitz does, the existence of souls and bodies as distinct beings, the question all the world asks is: Why do certain changes in each particular soul correspond in a regular manner with certain changes in one particular body? And Leibnitz puts us off with the answer—Because God has ordained it so.

Moreover, Leibnitz's scheme of monads does not enable him to get rid of dualism. He maintains with Descartes and Spinoza the strictly mechanical ordering of nature, yet he maintains also the teleological character of psychical activity: "Souls act in accordance with the laws of final causes, through their desires, purposes and means. Bodies act in accordance with the laws of efficient causes or of motion. The two realms, that of efficient causes and that of final causes, are in harmony, each with the other."[1] This parallelism of the mechanical and of the teleological we shall have to notice again as a principal difficulty of all systems akin to that of Leibnitz. It is true that in the "Théodicée" he gives the primacy to teleological determination, but only at the cost of inconsistency with his earlier doctrine.

Further, Leibnitz finds himself driven to represent human souls as differing in several very important respects from other monads; thus he writes: "With regard to spirits, that is to say, substances which think and which are able to recognize God and to discover eternal truths, I hold that God governs them according to laws different from those with which He governs the rest of substances," namely, "according to the spiritual laws of justice, of which the others are incapable."[2] Again, "Such a creation is true, I admit, only in the case of reasoning souls, and hold that all forms which do not think, were created at the same time that the world was"[3]; and yet again, "Intellects or souls which are capable of reflection and of knowing the eternal truths and God (i.e. human souls), have many privileges that exempt them from the transformation of bodies."[4]

It was no doubt owing to these unsatisfactory features of the doctrine of pre-established harmony that it never became generally accepted as the solution of the psycho-physical problem.

Descartes' sharpening of the psycho-physical problem provoked Spinoza to suggest a solution which has had, perhaps, a greater influence on subsequent thought than that of Leibnitz. Although in point of time this suggestion preceded Leibnitz's, I have dealt with it after the latter, because Leibnitz does not

---
[1] "Monadologie," paragraph 79.
[2] Letter to Arnauld, October 6th, 1687.   [3] *Ibid.*
[4] Letter to Arnauld, March 23rd, 1690.

mention it among the possible solutions, and because it seems to come after his scheme in the natural order of evolution of philosophical speculation.

Spinoza taught that soul and body are not two distinct substances or things, and that we must regard thought and extension as but two of the many attributes or aspects of the one real substance, which is God. Reverting to Leibnitz's illustration of the two clocks that keep time, we may say that Spinoza's suggestion would constitute a fourth way of explaining their concomitance, and would consist in saying that the two clocks are but two reflections at different angles of one real clock. Or we may alter the illustration a little, and may liken the relation of mental to bodily events in any individual to the relation between the visual and the auditory presentations of one clock; the auditory and the visual appearances exhibit regular and orderly temporal relations, but there is no direct causal relation between them: the seen movements of the hands and the sounds heard are two of many modes in which the clock might be apprehended. In Spinoza's own words: "The mind and the body are one and the same thing, conceived at one time under the attribute of thought, and at another under that of extension. For this reason the order and concatenation of things is one, whether nature be conceived under this or that attribute, and consequently the order of the actions and passions of our body is coincident in nature with the order of the actions and passions of the mind."

Spinoza thus sought to abolish at one stroke the distinction between body and soul as material and immaterial substances, which the labours of philosophers through two thousand years had gradually evolved. It was a bold attempt to avoid the difficulties of both Animism and Materialism.

Like the doctrines of occasional causes and of pre-established harmony, the hypothesis was framed to meet, or rather to avoid, the difficulty of conceiving causal interaction between mind and matter; but, unlike the authors of those doctrines, Spinoza did not reject the causal relation as illusory, a figment of our minds only; rather he held that the causal relation obtains between the real events that we apprehend under the two modes of material and mental events, and that this real causal relation is likewise apprehended by us under the two modes of material or mechanical and of mental causation. Hence each series appears for us as a closed causal series, the two series having no causal interaction; "so long as things are regarded as mental phenomena we must explain the order of nature or the causal connexion by the attribute of thought alone; and so long as we regard them as material phenomena, we must explain the whole order of nature by the attribute of extension alone."[1]

"If," says Professor Höffding, "we ask for the real reason why the mental side of existence cannot be explained by the material, nor the material by the mental, we shall find the answer in Spinoza's ideal of explanation through causes, according to which cause and effect must resemble one another. In a letter Spinoza says clearly: 'If two things have nothing in common with one another, the one cannot be the cause of the other: for, since there would be nothing in the effect that was also in the cause, everything that was in the effect would have arisen out of nothing.' If we keep this fundamental principle consistently before us we shall have the key to Spinoza's whole system."[2]

The middle years of the seventeenth century produced yet another reaction against Descartes' spiritualistic Dualism in the Materialism of Thomas Hobbes, a Materialism as consistent and thorough-going as Materialism can be. For Hobbes, who was acquainted with the works and the persons of Galileo and Gassendi, everything that exists is corporeal, body and substance are one and the same; the essential attributes of body are extension and motion; all change is motion. Sensation is nothing else but motion; pleasure is really nothing but motion about the heart; "*mens nihil aliud erit præterquam motus in partibus quibusdam corporis organici.*"

Thus the thinkers of the seventeenth century brought to a sharper issue than ever before the problem of the soul and of its relation to the body, and formulated definitely and clearly four distinct solutions of the problem; namely, the animistic Dualism of Descartes, the parallelistic Animism of Leibnitz, the identity-hypothesis of Spinoza, the Materialism of Hobbes, each of which has continued to find respectable supporters up to the present day. These four rival doctrines, each associated with the name of one of the four most celebrated philosophers of the seventeenth century, were handed on to the eighteenth century. No wonder, then, that the problem of the soul was eagerly discussed, and that, as Lange says, the human soul was the point around which

[1] Höffding, *op. cit.* 310.   [2] *Op. cit.*, p. 310.

all controversies turned in the eighteenth century.[1] Descartes had taught that man is compounded of soul and body acting and reacting upon one another; Leibnitz that, though he is compounded of soul and body, these do not influence one another; Spinoza that mind and body are equally real or unreal, because but two aspects of one reality; Hobbes that man consists of body alone, the soul being a mere figment of his imagination.

Two possibilities only remained, namely, first, that the soul alone is real, the body being fictitious or appearance only; secondly, that both body and soul are fictitious. And the ingenuity of the eighteenth century proved equal to the task of propounding and maintaining these doctrines also; before the century passed away, these two were added to the list of rival doctrines by philosophers, namely, Bishop Berkeley and David Hume, whose penetration and high reputation secured for their views a respectful hearing and a career whose end no man can yet foresee.

[1] *Op. cit.*, vol. i. p. 244.

CHAPTER V

ANIMISM IN THE EIGHTEENTH CENTURY

IN the metaphysic of the Schoolmen the notion of "substance" occupied a position of fundamental importance. In their mouths, the word implied something permanently self-identical and unchanging beneath the flux of appearances, an unalterable substratum or core of real being which supports the accidents, qualities, or attributes in which substance manifests itself; and, as we have seen, the soul was generally defined as an immaterial substance. The philosophers of the seventeenth century had continued to use the word substance in a similar way, though the meanings they attached to the word were not strictly identical. Descartes had assumed substances of two kinds, the thinking and the extended substances; for Spinoza, all substance was one only; for Leibnitz, a substance is an ultimate logical subject, and the infinitely numerous monads were such substances. The philosophical controversies of the eighteenth century revolved around this notion of substance. Conservative thought held fast to substance as to a sheet-anchor; progressive thought turned to rend it to tatters, and left it at the end of the century covered with contempt, merely a discredited shadowy remnant of its former self. And the fate of the notion of the soul was closely bound up with that of substance; it suffered discredit in an almost equal degree.

In the attack upon "substance," John Locke was the forerunner of both Hume and Berkeley; and, with that temperate sagacity which characterizes all his writings, he anticipated the reasonings of both his brilliant successors upon the psycho-physical problem, without, however, accepting the extreme conclusions of either. He wrote, "When we talk or think of any particular sort of corporeal substances, as horse, stone, etc., though the idea we have of either of them be but the complication or collection of those several simple ideas of sensible qualities which we used to find united in the thing called "horse" or "stone," yet because we cannot conceive how they should subsist alone, nor one in another, we suppose them existing in, and supported by, some common subject; which support we denote by the name "substance," though it be certain we have no clear or distinct idea of that thing we suppose a support. The same happens concerning the operations of the mind; namely, thinking, reasoning, fearing, etc., which we concluding not to subsist of themselves, nor apprehending how they can belong to body, or be produced by it, we are apt to think these the actions of some other substance which we call "spirit," whereby yet it is evident, that having no other idea or notion of matter, but something wherein those many sensible qualities which affect our senses do subsist; by supposing a substance wherein thinking, knowing, doubting, and a power of moving, etc., do subsist; we have as clear a notion of the substance of spirit as we have of body; the one being supposed to be (without knowing what it is) the *substratum* to those simple ideas we have from without; and the other supposed (with a like ignorance of what it is) to be the substratum to those operations which we experiment in ourselves within. It is plain, then, that the idea of corporeal substance in matter is as remote from our conceptions and apprehensions as that of spiritual substance, or spirit; and therefore, from our not having any notion of the substance of spirit, we can no more conclude its non-existence than we can, for the same reason, deny the existence of body; it being as rational to affirm there is no body, because we have no clear and distinct idea of the substance of matter, as to say there is no spirit, because we have no clear and distinct idea of the substance of a spirit."[1] That is to say, Locke saw that our conceptions of matter and of soul are alike hypotheses which we make for the better interpretation of our experience and the guidance of our actions, and that what knowledge we have of them is not direct, but is hypothetical and inferential only, is inferred from the facts of immediate experience.

Locke strongly insisted that the conceptions of an immaterial soul and of its action upon the body involved no more obscurity than those of material substance and of the action of one body upon another. "If any one say, he knows not what it is thinks in him, he means, he knows not what the substance is of that thinking thing; no more, say I, knows he what the sub-

[1] "An Essay on the Human Understanding," Bk. II. chap. xxiii.

stance is of that solid thing. Farther, if he says, he knows not how he thinks, I answer, Neither knows he how he is extended; how the solid parts of body are united or cohere together to make extension."[1] And in the following passage he anticipated Lotze's reply to those who raise the difficulty of the Occasionalists. "Another idea we have of body, is the power of communication of motion by impulse; and of our souls, the power of exciting motion by thought. These ideas, the one of body, the other of our minds, every day's experience clearly furnishes us with; but if here again we inquire how this is done, we are equally in the dark. For in the communication of motion by impulse, wherein as much motion is lost to one body as is got to the other, which is the ordinariest case, we can have no other conception but of the passing of motion out of one body into another; which, I think, is as obscure and inconceivable, as how our minds move or stop our bodies by thought; which we every moment find they do."[2] Hence, he contended, "we have as many and as clear ideas belonging to spirit as we have belonging to body, the substance of each being equally unknown to us; and the idea of thinking in spirit, as clear as of extension in body; and the communication of motion by thought, which we attribute to spirit, is as evident as that impulse which we ascribe to body. Constant experience makes us sensible of both of these, though our narrow understandings can comprehend neither."[3]

Locke, then, held a distinctly dualistic view of human personality, though he held it, not dogmatically, but only as the most reasonable and probable view; for the temper of his mind was scientific rather than metaphysical. He was prepared to admit that God may have endowed material substance with the power of thought; for, said he, "It is not much more remote from our comprehension to conceive this than to conceive that God should superadd to matter another substance with a faculty of thinking; since we know not in what thinking consists nor to what sort of substances the first eternal thinking Being has been pleased to give that power."

This passage shows that Locke was familiar with, and regarded as not altogether untenable, that kind of mechanical materialism, professed by his great countrymen, Newton, Boyle, and Priestly, which reconciled itself with religion by postulating God as the designer and creator of the great machine; and his adherence to

[1] Essay, Bk. II. chap. xxiii.   [2] *Loc. cit.*   [3] *Loc. cit.*

the dualistic view seems to have been determined by the fact that it was more in harmony with the religious teachings which claimed to be founded upon divine revelation.

The more fervid temperament and stronger theological bias of Bishop Berkeley would not allow him to rest content with Locke's calm, balanced, and strictly scientific attitude towards the problem of spirit and matter, or to follow him in accepting the dualistic answer to the problem as the most probable of the rival possibilities. He was a metaphysician by nature and sought for absolute truth. Since, then, it had been made clear by Locke that matter is but an obscure and hypothetical conception based only on inference from the facts of sensation; and since Berkeley was convinced of the absolute reality of Spirit, on grounds which he never thought of questioning; he hastened to deny the reality of matter, in order to stem the dangerous flood of Materialism, which seemed to him to threaten all true religion. Locke had ascribed our sensations to the influence of material things, operating indirectly upon our souls through the medium of the sense organs. Berkeley insisted that, if we believe in the omnipotence of God, the assumption of material things as the causes of our sensations is an unnecessary hypothesis; for we must believe that God can evoke our sensations by the direct action of his Spirit upon ours.

Berkeley sets out by agreeing with Locke that all the objects of human knowledge are "ideas"—"either ideas actually imprinted on the senses; or else such as are perceived by attending to the passions and operations of the mind; or lastly, ideas formed by help of memory and imagination."[1] "But," he goes on, "besides all that endless variety of ideas or objects of knowledge, there is likewise something which knows or perceives them; and exercises divers operations, as willing, imagining, remembering, about them. This perceiving, active being is what I call Mind, Spirit, Soul, or Myself. By which words I do not denote any one of my ideas, but a thing entirely distinct from them, wherein they exist, or, which is the same thing, whereby they are perceived—for the existence of an idea consists in being perceived."[2]

As regards the alleged independent existence of material things, he writes—"It is indeed an opinion strangely prevailing

[1] "Of the Principles of Human Knowledge," § 1. [2] *Op. cit.*, § 2.

amongst men, that houses, mountains, rivers, and in a word all sensible objects, have an existence, natural or real, distinct from their being perceived by the understanding. But, with how great an assurance and acquiescence soever this principle may be entertained in the world, yet whoever shall find in his heart to call it in question may, if I mistake not, perceive it to involve a manifest contradiction. For, what are the forementioned objects but the things we perceive by sense? and what do we perceive besides our own ideas or sensations? and is it not plainly repugnant that any one of *these*, or any combination of them, should exist unperceived?"[1]

And again he writes: "Some truths there are so near and obvious to the mind that a man need only open his eyes to see them. Such I take this important one to be, viz., that all the choir of heaven and furniture of the earth, in a word, all those bodies which compose the mighty frame of the world, have not any subsistence without a mind—that their *being* is *to be perceived or known*; that, consequently, so long as they are not actually perceived by me, or do not exist in my mind or that of any other created spirit, they must either have no existence at all, or else subsist in the mind of some Eternal Spirit—it being perfectly unintelligible, and involving all the absurdity of abstraction, to attribute to any single part of them an existence independent of a spirit. To be convinced of which the reader need only reflect, and try to separate in his own thoughts the *being* of a sensible thing from its *being perceived*. From what has been said it is evident there is not any other Substance than *Spirit*, or *that which perceives*."[2]

As regards the existence of spirit, after denying all power or agency to ideas, he writes: "We perceive a continual succession of ideas; some are anew excited, others are changed or totally disappear. There is, therefore, some Cause of these ideas, whereon they depend, and which produces and changes them. That this cause cannot be any quality, or idea, or combination of ideas is clear from the preceding section. It must, therefore, be a substance; but it has been shown that there is no corporeal or material substance: it remains, therefore, that the cause of ideas is an incorporeal active substance or Spirit." "A Spirit is one simple, undivided, active being—as it *perceives* ideas it is called the *Understanding*, and as it *produces* or otherwise

---

[1] *Op. cit.*, § 4. [2] *Op. cit.*, §§ 6 and 7.

operates about them it is called the *Will*. ... Such is the nature of Spirit, or that which acts, that it cannot be of itself perceived, but only by the effects which it produceth."[1] Then, after remarking that "I find I can excite ideas in my mind at pleasure, and vary and shift the scene as often as I think fit," he goes on, "But, whatever power I may have over my own thoughts, I find the ideas actually perceived by Sense have not a like dependence on my will. When in broad daylight I open my eyes, it is not in my power to choose whether I shall see or no, or to determine what particular objects shall present themselves to my view; and so likewise as to the hearing and other senses, the ideas imprinted on them are not creatures of my will. There is, therefore, some *other* Will or Spirit that produces them."[2]

Berkeley, then, regardless of the statement with which his enquiry opens, namely, the statement that all the objects of human knowledge are "ideas," goes on to tell us that "from the Principles we have laid down, it follows Human Knowledge may naturally be reduced to two heads—that of *ideas* and that of Spirits."[3] "*Thing* or *Being* is the most general name of all: it comprehends under it two kinds entirely distinct and heterogeneous, and which have nothing common but the name, viz., *Spirits* and *Ideas*. The former are active, indivisible, incorruptible substances: the latter are inert, fleeting, or dependent beings, which subsist not by themselves, but are supported by or exist in minds or spiritual substances."[4]

Other passages that throw light on Berkeley's conception of the soul are the following: "It is a plain consequence that the *soul always thinks*; and in truth, whoever shall go about to divide in his thoughts, or abstract the *existence* of a spirit from its *cogitation*, will, I believe, find it no easy task."[5] "By the word *spirit* we mean only that which thinks, wills, and perceives; this, and this alone, constitutes the signification of that term."[6]

"The knowledge I have of other spirits is not immediate, as is the knowledge of my ideas; but depending on the intervention of ideas, by me referred to agents or spirits distinct from myself, as effects or concomitant signs."[7]

---

[1] *Op. cit.*, §§ 26 and 27. [2] *Op. cit.*, § 29. [3] *Op. cit.*, § 86.
[4] *Op. cit.*, § 89. [5] *Op. cit.*, § 98.
[6] *Op. cit.*, § 138. [7] *Op. cit.*, § 145.

"Nothing can be plainer than that the motions, changes, decays, and dissolutions which we hourly see befall natural bodies (and which is what we mean by the *course of nature*) cannot possibly affect an active, simple, uncompounded substance; such a being, therefore, is indissoluble by the force of nature; that is to say—the soul of man is *naturally* immortal." [1]

Locke, then, had shown clearly enough that our conceptions of matter and spirit, of body and soul, are obscure and uncertain, and that they are arrived at only indirectly by reflection upon the facts of immediate experience: but he accepted them as being useful and reasonably probable: Berkeley, carried away by his desire to confound the materialists, rejected altogether the "unknown somewhat" that we call matter, while retaining the equally unknown somewhat that we call spirit; thus he let loose the modern flood of subjectivism and scepticism, and led to the adoption of the critical attitude in philosophy. For Hume, approaching the same problems without Berkeley's theological bias, but in a similar metaphysical spirit, forcibly argued, as Locke had done, that our conception of spirit is in no better case than that of matter, and that, if, with Berkeley, we reject the conception of matter, we must also reject the conception of spirit.

The essential novelty of Hume's reasoning was his rejection of the validity of the notion of causation. Both Locke and Berkeley had accepted and used the principle of causation without serious question; noting that our sensations rise to consciousness independently of our volition, they regarded them as the effects of some causes lying outside or beyond the mind, and confidently inferred the reality of the causes from these effects revealed in our immediate experience—Locke conceiving them as the actions of matter on mind, Berkeley as the direct actions of God. But Hume asked: What is our warrant for thus accepting the principle of causation, and for inferring the existence of causes, whether material or spiritual, of our sensations? And to this question he could find no good answer. "It is only *causation*," says Hume, "which produces such a connection as to give us assurance from the existence or action of one object, that it was followed or preceded by any other existence or action." [2] "It appears that of those three relations which depend not upon the mere ideas (namely identity, the situation in time and place, and

[1] *Op. cit.*, § 41.   [2] "A Treatise of Human Nature," Part III. § 2.

causation) the only one that can be traced beyond our senses, and informs us of existences and objects, which we do not see or feel, is causation."[1] He then goes on to say that our idea of the relation of causation obtaining between events is derived from the observation of their contiguity in space and their immediate succession in time. But, says he, "Shall we then rest contented with these two relations of contiguity and succession, as affording a complete idea of causation? By no means, an object may be contiguous and prior to another, without being considered as its cause. There is a *necessary connection* to be taken into consideration."[2] Hume then investigates through the course of several chapters "the nature of that *necessary connection* which enters into our idea of cause and effect." And the outcome of his research is summarized as follows:—

"The idea of necessity arises from some impression. There is no impression conveyed by our senses, which can give rise to that idea. It must, therefore, be derived from some internal impression or impression of reflection. There is no internal impression, which has any relation to the present business, but that propensity which custom produces, to pass from an object to an idea of its usual attendant. This, therefore, is the essence of necessity. Upon the whole, necessity is something that exists in mind, not in objects, nor is it possible for us ever to form the most distant idea of it, considered as a quality in bodies. Either we have no idea of necessity or necessity is nothing but that determination of the mind to pass from causes to effects, and from effects to causes, according to their experienced union."[3] For, "When any object is presented to us, it immediately conveys to the mind a lively idea of that object which is usually found to attend it; and this determination of the mind forms the necessary connection of these objects. But when we change the point of view from the objects to the perceptions, in that case the impression is to be considered as the cause, and the lively idea as the effect; and their necessary connection is that new determination, which we feel to pass from the idea of the one to that of the other."[4] Hence he concludes "A *cause* is an object precedent and contiguous to another, and so united with it that the idea of the one determines the mind to form the idea of the other, and the impression of the one to form a more lively idea of the other."[5]

[1] *Loc. cit.* [2] *Loc. cit.* [3] *Op. cit.*, chap. xiv. [4] *Loc. cit.* [5] *Loc. cit.*

Hume, having thus proved to his own complete satisfaction that the conception of causal relation is purely subjective, that it stands for no real action or influence exerted by one thing on another, has (for those who accept his reasoning) undermined both the reasoning by which Locke justified our conception of matter as the cause of our sensations, and that by which Berkeley sought to prove our sensations to be directly caused by the will of God.

Hume had already dismissed to the class of baseless fictions the conception of a thing, or substance, or enduring being, with the dictum that "the idea of a substance is nothing but a collection of simple ideas that are united by the imagination and have a particular name assigned them," and that "we have no idea of substance, distinct from that of a collection of particular qualities, nor have we any other meaning when we either talk or reason concerning it."[1] But his reasoning about causation (if it be sound) invalidates even more effectively the conception of thing or substance; for a thing is essentially that which exerts power or action upon another.

Hume undertook to refute also the special arguments by which Berkeley had sought to establish the reality of God and of the human soul as real beings, things, or substances.

Berkeley had made merry over those philosophers who spoke of the substance of matter as the support or *substratum* of its accidents or sensible qualities. "If we inquire into what the most accurate philosophers declare themselves to mean by *material substance*, we shall find them acknowledge they have no other meaning annexed to those sounds but the idea of *being in general*, together with the relative notion of its *supporting accidents*. The general idea of Being appeareth to me the most abstract and incomprehensible of all other; and as for its supporting accidents, this, as we have just now observed, cannot be understood in the common sense of those words; it must, therefore, be taken in some other sense, but what that is they do not explain. So that when I consider the two parts or branches which make the signification of the words *material substance*, I am convinced there is no distinct meaning annexed to them."[2] Yet, when in the course of the same essay Berkeley came to treat of souls, he naïvely described them as spiritual substances by which ideas are

[1] *Op. cit.*, Part I. § 7. [2] "Principles of Human Knowledge," § 16.

supported and in which ideas exist as "inert, fleeting, or dependent beings"; without in any way rendering more clear the meaning to be attached to the sounds "substance" and "supporting."

Hume, regarding the problem in complete freedom from Berkeley's theological bias, metes out to spiritual substance the same treatment that Berkeley gave to material substance. Referring to "the curious reasoners concerning the material or immaterial substances in which they suppose our perceptions to inhere," he says: "In order to put a stop to these endless cavils on both sides, I know no better method than to ask these philosophers in a few words, what they mean by substance and inhesion? This question we have found impossible to be answered with regard to matter and body; but besides that in the case of the mind it labours under all the same difficulties, it is burdened with some additional ones, which are peculiar to that subject." And after displaying these, he concludes: "Thus neither by considering the first origin of ideas, nor by means of a definition, are we able to arrive at any satisfactory notion of substance, which seems to me a sufficient reason for abandoning utterly that dispute concerning the materiality and immateriality of the soul, and makes me absolutely condemn even the question itself. We have no perfect idea of anything but of a perception. A substance is entirely different from a perception. We have therefore no idea of a substance. Inhesion in something is supposed to be requisite to support the existence of our perception. Nothing appears requisite to support the existence of a perception. We have therefore no idea of inhesion. What possibility then of answering that question, *Whether perceptions inhere in a material or immaterial substance*, when we do not so much as understand the meaning of the question?"[1]

Berkeley, having opened his essay with the emphatic assertion that all the objects of human knowledge are ideas and ideas only; having shown that (in accordance with his general principles of knowledge) "it is evident there can be no idea of a spirit"; and having said "that this substance (spirit) which supports or perceives ideas should itself be an idea or like an idea is evidently absurd"; may justly be held to have anticipated Hume's denial of spirit; or at least to have shown that, according to his own principles, we can have no knowledge of

[1] "Treatise of Human Nature," Book I. Part III. § 5.

spirit. But, regardless of logic, he went on to say somewhat lamely that "In a large sense indeed, we may be said to have an idea or rather a notion of spirit."[1] And in another work he attempted to defend this "notion," this "sort of an idea," so manifestly inconsistent with his own statements and principles, by saying: "*I know or am conscious* of my own being, and that *I myself* am not my ideas. But *I am not in like manner conscious* of the existence or essence of Matter. On the contrary, I know that nothing inconsistent can exist, and that the existence of this abstract matter implies inconsistency. There is, therefore, no parity of case between Spirit and Matter."[2]

Berkeley's defence of soul or spirit against his own fundamental principles being so halting and wanting in logic, it was no great step for Hume to refute it and so to bring back the discussion to the position in which it had been left by Locke. But in doing so he gave the agnostic conclusion as to the existence of both spiritual and material substances, a more positively sceptical or negative flavour; and indeed he showed an inclination towards the materialistic view, rather than towards Berkeley's pure spiritualism or Locke's attitude of impartial agnosticism towards both spirit and matter. In reference to such affirmations of our immediate awareness of the self as Berkeley had made, he wrote: "Unluckily all these positive assertions are contrary to that very experience which is pleaded for them; nor have we any idea of self, after the manner it is here explained. For, from what impression could this idea be derived? This question it is impossible to answer without a manifest contradiction and absurdity; and yet it is a question which must necessarily be answered if we would have the idea of self pass for clear and intelligible. It must be some one impression that gives rise to every real idea. But self or person is not any one impression, but that to which our several impressions and ideas are supposed to have a reference. If any impression gives rise to the idea of self, that impression must continue invariably the same, through the whole course of our lives; since self is supposed to exist after that manner. But there is no impression constant and invariable. Pain and pleasure, grief and joy, passions and sensations succeed each other, and never all exist at the same time. It cannot, therefore, be from any of these impressions, or

[1] *Op. cit.*, § 140.
[2] Third Dialogue between Hylas and Philonous.

from any other, that the idea of self is derived; and consequently there is no such idea."

"But further, what must become of all our particular perceptions upon this hypothesis? All these are different, and distinguishable, and separable from each other, and may be separately considered, and may exist separately, and have no need of anything to support their existence. After what manner, therefore, do they belong to self, and how are they connected with it? For my part, when I enter most intimately into what I call *myself*, I always stumble on some particular perception or other, of heat or cold, light or shade, love or hatred, pain or pleasure. I never can catch *myself* at any time without a perception; and never can observe anything but the perception. When my perceptions are removed for any time, as by sound sleep, so long am I insensible of *myself*, and may truly be said not to exist. And were all my perceptions removed by death, and could I neither think, nor feel, nor see, nor love, nor hate, after the dissolution of my body, I should be entirely annihilated, nor do I conceive what is further requisite to make me a perfect nonentity. If anyone upon serious and unprejudiced reflection, thinks he has a different notion of *himself*, I must confess I can reason no longer with him. All I can allow him is, that he may be in the right as well as I, and that we are essentially different in this particular. He may, perhaps, perceive something simple and continued, which he calls *himself*, though I am certain there is no such principle in me."

"But setting aside some metaphysicians of this kind, I may venture to affirm of the rest of mankind, that they are nothing but a bundle or collection of different perceptions, which succeed each other with an inconceivable rapidity, and are in a perpetual flux and movement. Our eyes cannot turn in their sockets without varying our perceptions. Our thought is still more variable than our sight; and all our other senses and faculties contribute to this change; nor is there any single power of the soul which remains unalterably the same perhaps for one moment. The mind is a kind of theatre, where several perceptions successively make their appearance; pass, repass, glide away, and mingle in an infinite variety of postures and situations. There is properly no *simplicity* in it at one time, nor *identity* in different, whatever natural propension we may have to imagine that simplicity and identity. The comparison of the theatre must not mislead us.

They are the successive perceptions only, that constitute the mind, nor have we the most distant notion of the place where these scenes are represented, or of the materials of which it is composed." [1]

And, summing up on this question, Hume wrote: "To pronounce, then, the final decision upon the whole, the question concerning the substance of the soul is absolutely unintelligible; all our perceptions are not susceptible of a local union, either with what is extended or unextended; there being some of them of the one kind, and some of the other. And as the constant conjunction of objects constitutes the very essence of cause and effect, matter and motion may often be regarded as the causes of thought, as far as we have any notion of that relation." [2]

While Locke, Berkeley, and Hume in this country were preparing the way for the critical attitude that has been the presupposition of all subsequent philosophizing, continental thought was pursuing a different course. In spite of the attempt of Spinoza to find a new solution of the psycho-physical problem, the bulk of cultivated opinion remained divided between the two doctrines that had come down from antiquity; men were, in general, either dogmatic spiritualists or dogmatic materialists.

In the earlier part of the eighteenth century the academic philosophers were, in the main, divided into two parties, the followers of Descartes and of Leibnitz respectively. The former, accepting the extreme Dualism of Descartes' metaphysic, had developed it in two divergent directions; on the one hand, those of strongly religious tendency developed it in the direction of mysticism, and succeeded in rendering it congenial to the Church in a degree which rendered it for a time the successor of Scholasticism; on the other hand, others laid more stress on the strictly mechanical view of nature, and on the sceptical attitude which Descartes had assumed at the outset of his investigations. By these divergent stresses Cartesianism was dismembered; and throughout the greater part of the eighteenth century it was overshadowed by the Leibnitzian philosophy. In the early part of the century this was made by Christian Wolff the basis of his rationalistic dogmatic system, which dominated most of the continental academies of learning till towards the end of the

[1] *Op. cit.*, Bk. I. Part IV. § 6, " Of Personal Identity."
[2] *Op. cit.*, Bk. I. Part IV. § 5, " Of the Immateriality of the Soul."

eighteenth century. In this system the immortality of the soul as a spiritual substance was established by some such reasoning as follows: The unity of self-consciousness implies the simplicity of the soul substance. Since the soul is simple or unitary it cannot be a compound or capable of division; hence it cannot be extended, for all extended substance is divisible; therefore it is a spiritual substance without extension; and, since it cannot be divided, it is incapable of being destroyed, and is therefore immortal.

On the other hand, the materialists, fascinated by the simplicity of the kinetic view of nature, and fortified by increase of biological knowledge (which showed that the animal body is the seat of many chemical and physical processes and that many of its processes may be mechanically interpreted), accepted with enthusiasm Descartes' dictum that all the processes of the animal body are mechanically explicable, and extended it without exception to the human body; thus leaving no place for the intervention of the soul. This materialistic tendency was a part of the movement of the cultivated classes in France (known as the Enlightenment), which was stimulated by the introduction of British thought by Voltaire and Montesquieu. The sensationalism of Locke and Hume, eagerly taken up and carried to an extreme length by Voltaire and by Condillac in his " Traité des Sensations " (1754), lent itself well to the materialistic interpretation of nature and of man. Condillac adhered to Animism in spite of his reduction of all thought to sensation. But Voltaire fastened eagerly upon Locke's assertion that God may have endowed matter with the power of thought; and the Enlightenment culminated in the dogmatic and atheistic materialism of Baron D'Holbach's " Système de la Nature " (1770), which found a large following in the polite world.

These acutely opposed dogmatisms were the dominant influences in the intellectual circles of continental Europe when, in 1781, Kant launched upon the world his " Critique of Pure Reason." It fell like a bombshell among the disputants, shattered for ever the dogmatic metaphysics of both parties, and became the starting-point of a powerful new movement.

Kant's attempt was, by combining the scepticism he had learnt from Hume with the idealism of Berkeley, to achieve a position which might claim to reconcile and to combine in a higher synthesis all that was most vital in the opposed dogmatisms. The great and rapid success of his doctrine was due to this fact. The arguments of the materialists had seemed incapable of refutation; yet men would not consent to resign at their bidding the belief in God, freedom, and immortality, whose stronghold was the Wolffian metaphysic. And, when Kant came forward, offering to show them how they might consistently accept the principal tenets of both parties—might reconcile the seemingly opposed teachings of science and of religion—they eagerly welcomed him.

Kant held the balance true between Hume and Berkeley, by maintaining the validity of Berkeley's inference from our sense-perceptions to some agent or agencies that evoke our sensations; while, with Hume, he denied that we can infer the nature of those agencies. As to the real nature of these agents, the famous things-in-themselves, he held that we know and can know nothing; that we are not warranted in believing them to be either matter or thinking beings; but that it is unnecessary to assume them to be of more than one kind.

By his doctrine of the subjectivity of Space and Time and of the purely phenomenal character of all the sensible world, he robbed Materialism of its offensive power, while maintaining the validity of mechanical explanation of all phenomenal processes; and, by his doctrine of the practical reason, he claimed to establish on the sure foundation of the moral nature of man the belief in God, freedom, and immortality. Man's body belongs, according to Kant, like all other bodies, wholly to the phenomenal world, and has only empirical reality; this *mundus sensibilis* is known through the understanding, or theoretical reason; but the soul belongs to the *mundus intelligibilis*, or ideal world, which is known through the practical reason.

Kant taught that the soul has three great faculties—(1) sentiency, which man has in common with the animals; (2) understanding or theoretical reason; and (3) pure reason, which in a very partial and imperfect manner man has in common with God, who is pure reason; the two latter constitute the true Ego. Paulsen summarizes as follows Kant's metaphysical doctrine of the soul [1]:—"The logical nature, understanding and reason, is really the Ego in itself, while on the other hand, time and space belong merely to sentiency, to the sense repre-

[1] "Immanuel Kant, his Life and Doctrine," p. 185.

sentation of the Ego which as phenomenal can pass away at death. But there remains the Ego as a pure, thinking essence, free from space and time, a spaceless and timeless, pure, thinking spirit. This is a thought which, although not realizable in perception, remains nevertheless a true and necessary idea."

Though Kant claimed that his Critique showed how the problem of the relation of soul to body is to be overcome (namely by reducing the body to the level of merely empirical or phenomenal reality, while assigning the soul to a sphere of higher reality); he did not attempt to show in detail how this solution is to be worked out. But he threw out a suggestion, which has been elaborated by later thinkers. His epistemological system necessarily reduced the facts of the world of consciousness, all that we discover by introspection, to the level of phenomena, if only because our states of consciousness succeed one another in time; they are phenomena perceived by an "inner sense." Thus, mental processes and the bodily processes that accompany them are alike phenomena; and there is a parallelism between psychical and physical phenomena, in the sense that the same thing which arises in my consciousness, or appears to the inner sense as sensation, idea, or feeling, would manifest itself to the perception of the external sense as a physical process in my body.[1]

This is a variation of the psycho-physical doctrine of phenomenalistic parallelism which was first enunciated by Spinoza; we shall have to examine it in a later chapter. It was merely thrown out by Kant as a suggestion. That he did

---

[1] This suggestion is embodied in the following passage: "If matter were a thing by itself, it would, as a composite being be totally different from the soul, a simple being. But what we call matter is an external phenomenon only, the substratum of which cannot possibly be known by any possible predicates. I can therefore very well suppose that that substratum is simple, although in the manner in which it affects our senses it produces in us the intuition of something extended, and therefore composite, so that the substance which, with reference to our external sense, possesses extension, might very well by itself possess thoughts which can be represented consciously by its own internal sense. In such wise the same thing which in one respect is called corporeal, would in another respect be at the same time a thinking being, of which, though we cannot see its thoughts, we can yet see the signs of them phenomenally. Thus the expression that souls only (as a particular class of substances) think, would have to be dropt, and we should return to the common expression that men think, that is, that the same thing which, as an external phenomenon is extended, is internally, by itself, a subject, not composite, but simple and intelligent" ("Critique of pure Reason." Criticism of second paralogism of transcendental psychology. Max Müller's translation).

not mean to adopt it, is shown by the opening words of the paragraph following the one which contains the suggestion ("But without indulging in such hypotheses . . .") and by an explicit statement in the next section of the Critique, which runs as follows: "The transcendental object, which forms the foundation of external phenomena, and the other, which forms the foundation of our internal intuition, is therefore neither matter nor a thinking being by itself, but simply an unknown cause of the phenomena that supplied to us the empirical concept of both."[1]

In the eighteenth century the division and specialization of intellectual labour, which had resulted from the revival of learning, had gone so far that it was no longer possible for any one man to attempt to master the whole field of science and philosophy, after the manner of Descartes and other great thinkers of the preceding century. Biology had become a relatively independent science, and was pursued for its own sake by a rapidly increasing number of workers.

Throughout this century the Animism which had been handed down from Aristotle continued to be the dominant way of thought of biologists, in spite of the large influence of Descartes' mechanical physiology and the popularity of the Materialism exemplified in "La Système de la Nature." The most influential exponents of the vitalistic physiology were G. E. Stahl and C. F. Wolff. The former (1660-1734), rejecting the distinction of vegetative, sensitive, and rational souls, to which in the hands of Aristotle's followers the master's recognition of the corresponding functions had led, ascribed all vital manifestations, especially growth and movement, to the rational soul (*anima rationalis*). C. F. Wolff departed further from the Aristotelian tradition, and may be regarded as the father of the later vitalism, which, while denying that the body is a machine merely, confined its attention to the vegetative functions, and sought to account for their peculiarities by means of the conception of some non-mechanical principle. Wolff named this principle the *vis essentialis*, and later writers, more especially the critics of vitalism, have generally denoted it by the term vital force (*Lebens-kraft*). Wolff propounded in his chief treatise, "Theoria Generationis" (1759), a vitalistic doctrine of development by epigenesis, in opposition to the generally accepted

[1] *Op. cit.*, "Criticism of Fourth Paralogism of Transcendental Psychology."

doctrine of evolution, according to which the development of an organism is merely the growth in size of a minute organism contained within the germ and having all the essential parts and organs already present within it. It has been usual to employ the word Vitalism to distinguish physiological doctrines of this type from mechanistic physiology on the one hand and from Animism on the other; but it is clear that Vitalism (understood in this way) cannot be sharply distinguished from Animism, and that it is but a form of Animism characterized by neglect of the psycho-physical problem.

CHAPTER VI

ANIMISM IN THE NINETEENTH CENTURY

THE most striking and immediate result of the success of Kant's critical philosophy was the rapid rise of the romantic speculation that dominated Germany during the first third of the nineteenth century and culminated in the system of Hegel. During this period, the psycho-physical problem was almost lost sight of, submerged in the flood of idealistic enthusiasm which, accepting the world of ideas as the only real world, hardly deigned to take account of the facts and theories of empirical science. Kant had laid it down that Materialism, though it is utterly impossible as a metaphysical doctrine, is necessarily presupposed by the natural sciences; for it is, he affirmed, an indispensable presupposition of these sciences that everything that is real manifests itself in space as a body or a function of a body. But reflection on the nature of our knowledge and our cognitive faculties shows that bodies are mere appearance, that they are real only for a perceiving and thinking subject. Therefore it is impossible that the subject and its activities should be interpreted as a function of a body. The thinking Ego or subject is the presupposition of the possibility of the corporeal world, which is a product of its activity. This was the keynote of the subsequent Idealism: Kant's thing-in-itself was rejected, and the body was regarded as but the creation of the mind; from which it followed that it is absurd to suppose that the mind can be in any degree dependent upon the body. For Idealism of this type the body was reduced to the level of unreality; and it carried the psycho-physical problem with it to that level.

But, after thirty years of dominance of the Speculative Philosophy, there came a sudden and violent reaction against it; purely logical construction fell into disrepute; men of science had learnt to regard philosophy as the secret ally of reactionary theology and an enemy to true science; and, mistrusting its methods and results, they went back to the work of faithful observation and minute experiment.[1] Thus Kant's successors, by insisting unduly on one part of his doctrine, prepared the way for the renewed outburst of Materialism of the middle of the nineteenth century; and this in turn brought to the front once more the problem of the relation between soul and body, which Kant had placed in a new light, but without either solving or removing it. It was during this period of revived Materialism that further elaboration of Kant's psycho-physical suggestion was undertaken by a philosopher who was, by training and profession, a physicist rather than a psychologist or metaphysician, namely, G. T. Fechner.

The modern phase of the psycho-physical discussion may be said to begin with the publication in 1860 of Fechner's principal treatise, the "Elemente der Psycho-physik." In this and other works, Fechner elaborated a panpsychic and pantheistic worldview, basing it upon a psycho-physical theory which dispenses with the soul and regards all processes of the universe as both physical and psychical. This theory claims, like Kant's doctrine, to enable us to reap the advantages of both Materialism and Spiritualism, to be materialists in science and idealists in philosophy; and it avoids that feature of Kant's doctrine which has been felt by so many of its critics to be wholly unacceptable, namely, the unknowable thing-in-itself. It has become, perhaps, the most widely accepted of the various allied doctrines that are commonly classed together as theories of psycho-physical parallelism. These will be stated in Chapter XI.; here it need only be said that their common claim to escape the reproach of Materialism, while accepting whole-heartedly the strictly mechanistic view of the world, has recommended them throughout the second half of the century to a constantly increasing number of philosophers and men of science.

Animism continued to find during the nineteenth century a certain number of respectable supporters besides the philosophers of the Roman Church; the latter have continued to teach a rational psychology which descends directly from Thomas Aquinas, and which implies a dualistic metaphysic of the kind formulated by Descartes.

---

[1] So violent was this reaction against the *Natur-philosophie* that in the opinion of Dr Th. Merz ("History of European Thought") it was responsible for the comparative neglect of the first expositions of the principle of the conservation of energy by Mayer and Von Helmholtz respectively.

Until nearly the middle of the century, Vitalism continued to flourish and found many defenders among the leading representatives of the several biological sciences. While most of the vitalists of this period were content to postulate a "vital force," others, like Blumenbach and Treviranus, attempted to give a more positive content to that vague notion; while a few, like Johannes Müller and R. Wagner, held fast to the conception of the soul.[1] Even in the third quarter of the century the latter notion was still maintained by a few physiologists of eminence, such as Pflüger and Goltz; but the efforts of these defenders were generally regarded at this time as merely prolonging the death throes of an exploded superstition.

Of those few German philosophers who opposed the romantic school during its period of dominance and yet managed to obtain a hearing and exert a permanent influence, the most important was J. F. Herbart. His philosophy claimed to be a development of the Kantian teachings, but it was more definitely realistic; like Kant, he taught that our ideas point beyond themselves, that we are able to infer the existence of a world of real being behind the veil of phenomena; but, not content with the mere affirmation of the existence of that world, he held that it consists of a plurality of real beings, or "Reals," each of which eternally persists, unchanging and unchanged. The soul of each man is such a "Real," and the play of ideas is the expression of the efforts of this "Real" to preserve its identity unchanged, in spite of the influences of other "Reals" upon it. But, though he professed to found his psychology on this metaphysical conception of an animating soul, Herbart's account of the course of mental life represents it as the strife and interplay of ideas or presentations, whose relation to the soul is never definitely conceived or cleared from inconsistencies. And, since the psychology of Herbart, the part of his teaching of the most enduring influence, really operated with the presentations, treated these as the foundations of all psychical life, regarded psychical laws as laws of their operations, and found no place for the soul, many of the numerous psychologists who have accepted his psychological principles have found themselves able to do so, while neglecting or rejecting his metaphysical notion of the soul as a member of the world of "Reals." Thus, although Herbart's own teaching was animistic, it has contributed, only less powerfully than the association-psychology, to the

[1] See "Vitalismus, als Geschichte u. Lehre," by Hans Driesch, Leipzig, 1902.

predominance of the "psychology without a soul" which characterizes the later part of the nineteenth century.

Another independent and original psychologist of this period, F. E. Beneke, continued to hold the conception of the soul as the ground of mental life; but he too contributed to bring about the predominance of the "psychology without a soul," by affirming the validity of purely physiological and anatomical explanations of mental disorders, and by his sympathetic presentment of Spinoza's doctrine of the relation of mind to matter.

In the middle of the century, Animism found its most brilliant and thoroughgoing modern defender in R. H. Lotze. Trained in the medical sciences, and a master of the physiology of his time, one of his first efforts was an attack on Vitalism. He exhibited the futility of the formless notion of the vital force, and, conceiving the mechanical principles in a very broad spirit, he attempted to show the adequacy of those principles to the explanation of all the facts of biology. But in his chief works [1] he defended in the most thorough and searching manner the notion of psycho-physical interaction and the conception of the soul as a being distinct from the body. His metaphysic was a realistic but spiritualistic monism; for he regarded the physical world as the appearance to us of a system of psychic existents of like nature with the soul of man, but of many grades of development. Nevertheless he maintained that "no general scruples must therefore hinder us from accepting for the two great distinct groups of physical and of psychical phenomena grounds of explanation equally distinct and independent."[2] He maintained also that "anywhere and in any form, however surbordinate (i.e. animal forms), we may see elements of mental life, intervening between the operation of the corporeal organs, and filling gaps between the single links of the chain of vital processes."[3]

It is, I think, impossible to reconcile the views expressed in these and many similar passages with Lotze's thoroughgoing rejection of Vitalism and his defense of the mechanical view of nature; for, although his conception of *mechanism* was so wide that he felt justified in speaking of the mechanical course of all mental processes, he excepted those in which he recognized the operation of explicit volition, and defended the notion of free-will, looking upon the free act as a new beginning in the universe; and Lotze attributed

---

[1] "Medizinische Psychologie," "Microcosmus," and "Metaphysik."
[2] "Mikrokosmus," I. p. 149 (Eng. trans.).   [3] *Op. cit.*, p. 135.

all mental retention to the soul alone, which was thus conceived, not as an unchanging "real" or a mere atom of soul-substance, but as the bearer of all that essentially constitutes personality. But his early opposition to the current Vitalism prevented him attributing to the soul any other than purely mental and fully conscious functions; and, not having grasped the full implications of the Darwinian principles, he made no attempt to reconcile his animistic doctrine with evolutionary biology. The argument to which he repeatedly turned for proof of the distinctness of the soul from the body was drawn from the unity of consciousness. But more must be said of this reasoning in a later chapter.

In spite of the high position accorded to Lotze, later German thought has in the main turned scornfully away from Animism; and, though the psycho-physical problem has been discussed in a multitude of books and articles, most of these discussions have aimed at rendering clearer and more intelligible the notion of psycho-physical Parallelism, very few, however, attempting to show that the principle of Parallelism can be carried through in detail. On the other hand, Animism has continued to find some notable defenders in academic circles; among them being Prof. C. Stumpf,[1] a friend and pupil of Lotze; Prof. O. Külpe, who briefly defends the dualistic metaphysic in his "Einleitung in die Philosophie"[2]; and the late Prof. L. Busse, whose book,[3] published in 1903, is at once the most thorough examination of the psycho-physical question and a critical defence of Animism on the basis of a spiritualistic metaphysic. The close of the century has witnessed a revival of Vitalism among German biologists; the common note of these Neo-Vitalists being the insistence that Darwinism fails to explain away the evidences of teleological determination presented by living organisms.

In the early years of the century, French thought on psychological problems was dominated by the teaching of Condillac and by that of the physiologist, Cabanis, who, though not strictly a materialist, gave precedence to physiological explanations of mental processes: a tendency exemplified by his famous dictum, the brain excretes thought as the liver excretes bile.

[1] "Leib u. Seele." The inaugural address to the International Congress of Psychologists at Munich, 1896.

[2] First Edition, Leipzic, 1895.

[3] "Geist u. Körper, Seele u. Leib" Leipzic, 1903. Other recent German psychologists who have accepted psycho-physical dualism are Rehmke, Volkmann, Jerusalem, Pfänder.

Maine de Biran, whose psychological writings were perhaps the most important of this period, was much influenced by Condillac and Cabanis, but held fast to the conception of the soul as a being distinct from the body and having a destiny not limited by the life of the body. He found the surest evidence for this view in our consciousness of putting forth power or energy to effect changes in the world, and in man's capacity for æsthetic, religious, and mystical experience.

But the influence of Comte and the positivist way of thought predominated in France throughout the century; until at its close a new star of great brilliance appeared in the person of Prof. H. Bergson. His thought, as so far expressed, is very difficult to characterize on its positive or constructive side; but he attacks the mechanistic view of nature by impugning the intellectual apparatus by means of which it has been built up. In his treatise on matter and memory [1] he distinguishes sharply between the habits rooted in the structure of the brain and true memory, a purely psychical mode of retention, and he regards traces of these two kinds, the material and the immaterial, as co-operating in the determination of the course of thought and action. And in his "Évolution Créatrice" he propounds a distinctly vitalistic doctrine of biological evolution. He must therefore be ranked among the defenders of Animism.

In Great Britain the scepticism of Hume had provoked by a natural reaction the common-sense philosophy of Reid and his followers, who accepted in the main the popular notion of the soul. Sir William Hamilton, whose influence in Scotland has been very great, attempted to combine the common sense of Reid with the critical phenomenalism of Kant. Consciousness, he maintained, is phenomenal only; but it points to a reality behind it, of which it is the property: and this real being, the soul, cannot be identified with the reality that underlies material phenomena. But the dominant influence throughout the middle years of the century was that of the association-psychology of Locke, Hume, and Hartley, as elaborated by the two Mills, Bain, Spencer, and Shadworth-Hodgson. This tends naturally to be a "psychology without a soul," for which the fundamental realities are sensations that cluster and combine together according to the laws of association and of "mental chemistry." The Mills hardly attempted to deal with the psycho-physical problem,

[1] "Matiére et Memoire," Paris.

though John Mill was troubled with some misgivings as to the associational doctrine that a series of states of consciousness can be aware of itself; but Spencer, Bain, and Shadworth-Hodgson definitely adopted the doctrine of psycho-physical Parallelism, the statement of which, in Spencer's "Principles of Psychology" (1855), is perhaps the earliest of the modern formulations.

The British revival of the absolute Idealism of Hegel, which has been the dominant influence of the later part of the century, has tended to divert attention from the psycho-physical problem; though a few of its prominent exponents have incidentally defended the animistic conception.[1] Prof. James Ward has maintained that psychology cannot dispense with the notion of an Ego or Subject, and has argued forcibly against psycho-physical Parallelism in his "Naturalism and Agnosticism."[2] Dr F. C. S. Schiller has maintained a Berkeleyan Idealism,[3] and the late F. W. H. Myers propounded a psycho-physical doctrine of a thoroughly animistic type.[4]

In America Prof. G. T. Ladd has ably expounded and defended the ideas of Lotze; and the late Prof. William James, in his celebrated "Principles of Psychology," has defended the notion of psycho-physical interaction, and in later works has propounded a peculiar form of Animism, of which something will be said in a later chapter.

In spite of these defenders, Animism was at a very low ebb in the last quarter of the century; its few exponents were generally regarded as survivors from an earlier age, actuated by some theological bias to offer a futile opposition to the conquering march of science.

Thoughout the nineteenth century, then, Animism has rapidly declined. Its claim to figure as the great opponent of Materialism has been successfully disputed by the parallelistic or monistic theories, which seek to combine the scientific advantages of Materialism with the philosophic respectability of Idealism. Of the three influences that have contributed to bring about this decline, namely, the critical philosophy of Kant, the absolute Idealism of the romantic school, and the astonishing and splendid development of the natural sciences, based in the main upon the

[1] Especially Mr F. H. Bradley and Prof. A. E. Taylor. (See "The Problem of Mind and Body in recent Psychology." *Mind*, N.S. No. 52.)
[2] Gifford Lectures, 1899. [3] "Riddles of the Sphinx," London 1891.
[4] "Human Personality and its Survival of the Death of the Body," London, 1903.

strictly mechanistic view of nature, the last has been the most far-reaching and decisive. From it the claim of mechanistic principles of explanation to universal and exclusive sway in the physical world has gained much greater strength than it derived from Kant's epistemology or from the natural science of his time; and it is the strength of this claim that has well nigh banished Animism from the culture-tradition of the present age. We must therefore trace the growth of the strength of this claim and notice in some detail the bearing of modern scientific discoveries upon the psycho-physical problem.

CHAPTER VII

MODERN DEVELOPMENTS OF PHYSICAL SCIENCE ADVERSE TO ANIMISM

THE epistemological reflections of Locke, Berkeley, and Hume, culminating in the critical philosophy of Kant, not only completed the list of possible answers to the psycho-physical problem, but also introduced the modern scientific or critical attitude towards it. In spite of the presence of strong elements of old-fashioned dogmatism in the teaching of Kant, and to a less extent in that of Berkeley; the enduring result of the discussions of these four thinkers was to make it clear that we can have no absolute and no immediate knowledge of either soul or body, and that the two conceptions can only be justified (or rejected) by showing that they are (or are not) necessary features of the system of conceptions which the human mind is slowly working out, for the purpose of rendering an intelligible and consistent explanation of the chaotic flux of individual experience. Though it was necessary to accept this demonstration, it was not necessary, it was not possible, to accept the sceptical attitude towards all knowledge which Hume half-seriously advocated as the only respectable one. To have done so would have been profoundly irrational and in the last degree cowardly. If man is to live, he must act; and, if he must act, he must govern his actions in accordance with conceptions of his own nature and of the world in which he is set, conceptions of whose validity he can have no absolute guarantee, and which he must choose, develop, reshape, or reject, according as he finds them more or less efficient guides to successful action. And of all conceptions, the conceptions of the nature of, and of the relations between, mind and body are those which in the long run affect most profoundly, and are of the first importance for, this guidance of conduct; for they must always exert a determining influence upon man's view of his place in the world, upon his prospects, his hopes, and his deepest purposes, and hence upon his conduct.

Although, then, Hume's scepticism has continued to secure the adhesion of certain temperaments, and is represented at the present day by a few vigorous thinkers,[1] it has not gained any wide acceptance among peoples in whom the tide of life runs strongly. Its acceptance implies the Eastern doctrine that all is illusion; it involves a thoroughgoing Solipsism, the doctrine that I, or my thoughts, alone exist; for the consistent follower of Hume must admit that his principles involve the rejection, not only of the material world, but of all thought or mental life other than his own. And among all the wide divergences of thought in our Western world, one principle has continued to secure a predominance never yet seriously shaken, namely, the principle, accepted whether explicitly or implicitly, whether as a reasoned conclusion or as a venture of faith, that each man lives, not by and for himself alone, but as a member of a community of beings of like nature with himself; that our life is not a mere dream; that our knowledge is not mere fantasy, but, however imperfect and inadequate, is yet real knowledge of a real world, and is capable of indefinitely great extension and improvement.

Hume's absolute condemnation of all discussion of the materiality or immateriality of the soul was, then, of no effect in stemming the tide of discussion. The upshot of his work and that of his British predecessors was in the main to produce a change in the mode of approach to the problem. It was made clear that no solution of it can be achieved by reasoning *a priori* or from general principles alone; but that rather we must work towards its solution by the aid of the methods of empirical science, by increasing the stock of well established facts and well grounded hypotheses.

Accordingly, we find since the time of Hume an increasing tendency for the psycho-physical problem to be regarded as belonging to the province of science, rather than that of metaphysic. We have seen that Kant himself touches on the psycho-physical problem but lightly, and that what he wrote of the soul exhibits a curious mixture of dogmatic metaphysics with the critical procedure. Nevertheless, he too contributed to bring about the relegation of the problem from metaphysics to empirical science—on the one hand, by furthering that form of

---

[1] Notably by Prof. E. Mach of Vienna and by Prof. Karl Pearson, who agree with Hume in asserting that the known and knowable world consists of sensations only.

idealistic metaphysic which regards the body as negligible, because unreal; on the other hand, by making clear the impossibility of establishing the existence and nature of the soul by theoretical reasoning from general principles in the style of the Wolffian metaphysic. Accordingly, few of the metaphysicians since Kant have put the problem of the relation between soul and body in the foreground of their discussions, after the fashion of earlier ages; they have, in fact, for the most part, left it on one side, or treated of it incidentally only and with uncertain tones, showing a disposition to accept the opinions dominant in the scientific world, and, if they have continued to speak of the soul of man, they have done so in a fashion which commits them to no definite answer to the psycho-physical problem.

The history of the psycho-physical problem since the middle of the eighteenth century is, then, in the main the history of the way in which the progress of the physical, the biological, and the psychological sciences has rendered ever more confident, and secured wider acceptance for, the belief in the universality of the laws of mechanism revealed by the study of the realm of physical phenomena; a belief which necessarily involves the rejection of Animism. And this rejection of Animism has been rendered easier by the wide prevalence of the notion that Kant's phenomenalistic epistemology somehow renders it possible to hold to God, freedom, and immortality, in spite of it.

In the following pages I propose to describe concisely the way in which the modern development of each of these branches of empirical science has contributed to bring about this result. The three lines of development of scientific knowledge and thought have acted and reacted upon one another in a way that has in the main favoured this result; but they may be briefly outlined in succession.

We have seen that, in the seventeenth century, Kepler, Galileo, Gassendi, and Hobbes had rehabilitated the atomic Materialism of the ancients. In the eighteenth century the genius of Newton, especially by the formulation of the fundamental laws of motion and of the law of gravitation, gave an immense impetus to this way of thought. Newton himself and his leading disciples and successors, Priestley and Boyle, regarded the laws of mechanism as universally valid, and saved themselves from the charge of atheistic Materialism only by acknowledging matter and its laws to be the creations of the one Supreme Being. Laplace went further and, intoxicated by the intellectual splendour of the nebular hypothesis and by the wonderful powers of the mathematical instruments of which he was a master, denied in his famous reply to the great Napoleon the necessity of the hypothesis of a Creator ; and he it was who formulated clearly and explicitly the supreme faith of mechanical Materialism by asserting that, if the state of the material universe at any one moment of time could be completely described, it would be possible in principle to arrive by calculation at the complete description of it at any other moment of its history.

Laplace's confidence in the universality of the mechanical laws was founded in the belief that all physical processes are essentially the movements of particles of matter; it was the apotheosis of atomic Materialism, developed by modern science into a scheme of universal kinetic mechanism. This scheme of kinetic mechanism has been of very great value as a working hypothesis for the guidance of physical research. It has proved so useful, is so attractive in its simplicity, is so well adapted to the powers of concrete representation or pictorial imagination which most men exercise with greater confidence and ease than any other of our intellectual faculties ; that it has obtained a very strong hold upon the scientific world. Throughout the nineteenth century it continued to win fresh triumphs in various fields of physical research, notably in acoustics, optics, and the theory of gases, repeatedly proving itself the most fruitful of all physical hypotheses. It may be said to have reached its culmination in Lord Kelvin's theory of the vortex-atom, the most successful attempt yet made to describe the nature of matter and its relation to the ether; and it has successfully withstood every attempt to supersede it, so that at the end of the century Dr Merz, judicially weighing its claims, affirms: "there is no doubt that the century ends with a very emphatic assertion of the rights and the legitimacy of the atomic- and mechanical views of nature."[1]

No wonder, then, that in the minds of very many men this scheme of kinetic mechanism has stood for a true and, in principle, an exhaustive description of the nature of the physical universe, and that it has played a very considerable part, especially in

[1] " History of European Thought in the Nineteenth Century," vol. ii. p. 198.

the minds of biologists, in determining the rejection of every form of Animism. It was argued that every physical event consists in the motion of particles, or the communication of motion from particle to particle; such communication of motion by impact being held to be the only effective cause of acceleration or change of motion. All psychical influence upon the physical world was thus ruled out by the very definition of the physical world; for in a world where all change is motion, and where all causation is of the nature of communication of motion by impact, there is no room for psychical influences.

This conception has contributed to bring about the rejection of Animism in a second way also; namely, it has served to strengthen the old argument of the occasionalists, that interaction between things so diverse as soul and body is inconceivable; for, when all physical process is definitely conceived as motion or acceleration of particles, the difficulty of conceiving how mind can in any way modify this motion becomes correspondingly definite. The difficulty has been forcibly put by a contemporary writer who bids us try to imagine the thought of a beef-steak binding two molecules together[1]; while another brilliant author has illustrated the manifest absurdity of any belief in psychical influence upon the physical world, by likening it to the belief that the wagons of a railway train might be held together by the friendly feeling of the engine-driver for the guard.[2]

But the nineteenth century has achieved a physical generalization which has played an even greater part than the kinetic view of nature in expelling Animism from scientific thought. I mean of course the great generalization known as the law of conservation of energy.

In spite of the seductiveness of the kinetic view of the physical world, in spite of the wealth of biological arguments skilfully arrayed in the " Système de la Nature," in spite of Kant's epistemological dictum, Animism continued to rear its head from time to time in the scientific world, like a snake scotched, but not quite killed. But the law of the conservation of energy has, in the opinion of many philosophers and men of science, given it its death-blow; and in contemporary demonstrations of the impossibility of Animism, the argument from this law is generally given the place of honour, as the most weighty of all.

[1] Dr C. Mercier in " The Nervous System and the Mind."
[2] W. K. Clifford, " Lectures and Essays."

The law of the conservation of energy was enunciated almost at the same time by R. Mayer and Von Helmholtz in Germany and by Joule in England (in the year 1847); Mayer being led to it by reflection on biological facts, Helmholtz by physical and mathematical considerations, Joule by experiments which proved the exact equivalence of the energy converted into heat during the performance of mechanical work. The law has received many different formulations; but since its first enunciation, it has been empirically verified by many experiments; and the more refined the methods of experimental observation that have been applied, the more exact have been the demonstrations that the quantity of energy remains unchanged in every transformation of energy; further, no exception to the law has been experimentally demonstrated.

It is claimed, therefore, that these experimental observations justify us in generalizing the statement of the facts of observation, so that it runs—The transformation of energy involved in every physical process results in no change in the quantity of energy; the quantity of physical energy is exactly conserved in every case. From this statement it follows that the total sum of physical processes of the universe result in no change of the quantity of its physical energy. From this the further deduction is made that the sum total of the energy of the physical universe is a constant quantity, remaining without the least increase or diminution throughout all time.

It has been widely held that this conclusion is confirmed by a metaphysical view which has found favour with many scientific authorities, the view namely that energy is a real thing or substance, constituting, alone or in conjunction with matter, the substance of the physical universe.[1]

Now, the law of the conservation of energy, if accepted in this form, is held to be incompatible with the belief that psychical influences can modify in any way or degree the course of physical processes; for any such influence, it is said, must either diminish or increase the quantity of physical energy of the universe and so violate the law of the conservation of energy. But the nervous changes which are the concomitants of our

---

[1] *e.g.* the late Prof. P. G. Tait, who wrote: "The only other known thing in the physical universe, which is conserved in the same sense as matter is conserved, is energy. Hence we naturally consider energy as the other objective reality in the physical universe" (Article: *Mechanics* in "Encyclopædia Britannica," Ninth Edition).

psychical activities are physical processes. Therefore, it is argued, they must run their course without being in the slightest degree affected by psychical influences.

But the argument is generally stated more briefly and more dogmatically and in a way which combines the two great arguments against Animism drawn from physical science, namely, that from the kinetic view of nature and that from the law of the conservation of energy; I quote the following passage from a lecture by the late Dr J. G. Romanes as a fair sample of such statements. Spiritualism (or Animism), said Romanes, is unsatisfactory because it is opposed to the whole trend and momentum of modern science. "For if mind is supposed, on no matter how small a scale, to be a cause of motion, the fundamental axiom of science is impugned. This fundamental axiom is that energy can neither be created nor destroyed—that just as motion can produce nothing but motion, so, conversely, motion can be produced by nothing but motion. Regarded, therefore, from the standpoint of physical science, the theory of Spiritualism is in precisely the same case as the theory of Materialism: that is to say, if the supposed causation takes place, it can only be supposed to do so by way of miracle."[1]

If the animist retorts to this argument that the law of conservation of energy is founded upon measurement of the quantities of energy undergoing transformation in the course of inorganic physical processes, and that it is illegitimate to apply the generalization to organic processes, because these form a peculiar realm in which the operation of laws of the inorganic world may be interfered with or suspended by other modes of influence; then he is met with the results of recent exact quantitative investigation of the energy transformations of the human body. These investigations[2] have shown that the energy value of the output of the human body in the form of work, heat, chemical products, and so forth, equals, almost exactly, the energy value of food and oxygen absorbed, that is, the value of the sum total of energy supplied to the body; the difference between the quantities measured being so small as to fall well within the margin of error of the most careful experiment.

[1] Rede Lecture, published in "Contemporary Review," 1885.
[2] Atwater, "Reports of British Association," 1904.

CHAPTER VIII

THE RISE OF THE MECHANISTIC PHYSIOLOGY AND OF THE "PSYCHOLOGY WITHOUT A SOUL"

THE development of modern biology has contributed not less powerfully than that of physical science to bring about the general rejection of Animism; though the bearing of its discoveries has been less simple and direct.

In all earlier ages the peculiarities of living beings, their powers of growth, assimilation, reproduction, self-restitution and so forth, had been almost universally attributed to their animation, that is, to the presence and operation of the soul within the body. Descartes was the first of the moderns decisively to reject this conception and to maintain that all the bodily processes of men and animals (with the single exception of the movements of the pineal gland of the human brain) are of a strictly mechanical nature, needing no psychical guidance or control.

While Descartes' famous dictum "*Cogito ergo sum*" became the starting-point of modern Idealism, his view of the purely mechanical nature of all bodily processes initiated the wave of confident Materialism that rose to a great height in the eighteenth century, especially in France. The most popular exponents of this doctrine were De la Mettrie[1] and Baron D'Holbach.[2] The former, "a wit, philosopher and friend of Frederick the Great, traced his own materialism to Descartes, and maintained that the wily philosopher, purely for the sake of the parsons, had patched on to his theory a soul, which was in reality quite superfluous."[3] He argued in a lively manner for a materialistic view of human nature, relying chiefly upon illustrations of the intimate dependence of our moods, feelings, and mental processes generally upon physical influences such as food and drink. Like Diderot and Holbach he was a hylozoist, that is to say, he attributed psychical life to all material things; and, though he admitted that

[1] "Histoire naturelle de l'Ame," 1745, and "L'homme Machine," 1748.
[2] "Système de la Nature," 1770.
[3] A. Lange, "History of Materialism," vol. i. p. 244.

we cannot know what matter is in itself, he made all psychical life a property of matter, maintaining that sensation and thought are modifications of matter and entirely dependent upon it. "Man," he wrote, "is framed of materials not exceeding in value those of other animals; nature has made use of one and the same paste—she has only diversified the ferment in working it up. . . . We may call the body an enlightened machine. It is a clock, and the fresh chyle from the food is the spring."

D'Holbach's treatise, written under the influence of Diderot in a more sober and dignified style, made use of similar arguments. It represents the culmination of the Materialism of the eighteenth century, and, unlike the Materialism of Newton, Priestley, and Boyle, was avowedly atheistic. It would seem to have been the conjunction of Materialism and Atheism affected by these two writers that secured for their works so wide an influence; for they aroused a violent opposition.

But these writers were merely the popular exponents of the dominant tendencies of physiological science in the eighteenth century. G. E. Stahl has been mentioned in Chapter V. as one of the leading physiologists of the earlier part of the century who continued the older animistic tradition. He "put forward and brilliantly maintained the view that all the chemical events of the living body, even though they might superficially resemble, were at the bottom wholly different from, the chemical changes taking place in the laboratory, since in the living body all chemical changes were directly governed by the sensitive soul, *anima sensitiva*, which pervaded all parts and presided over all events."[1]

"Stahl's fundamental position is that between living things, so long as they are alive, however simple, and non-living things, however composite, however complex in their phenomena, there is a great gulf fixed. The former, so long as they are alive, are actuated by an immaterial agent, the sensitive soul, the latter are not. . . . Further, the living body is fitted for special ends and purposes; the living body does not exist for itself; it is constituted to be the true and continued minister of the soul. The body is made for the soul, the soul is not made for, and is not the product of, the body."[2] Stahl himself wrote "We may therefore rightly and truly conclude that all the actions of the body, both those which concern its structure and those which relate to the

[1] Sir M. Foster, *op. cit.*, p. 168.   [2] Sir M. Foster, *op. cit.*, p. 169.

preservation of its composition, are carried out by the soul itself for its own uses and ends, and are directed and brought to completion, knowingly and properly, in the proportions and relations which fit those ends and uses." And again he wrote "Vital activities are directly administered and exercised by the soul itself, and are truly organic acts carried out in corporeal instruments of a superior acting cause, in order to bring about certain effects, which are not only in general certain, and in particular necessary, but also in each and every particular adapted, in a special and yet most complete manner, to the needs of the moment and to the various irregularities introduced by accidental external causes. Vital activities, vital movements, cannot, as some recent crude speculations suppose, have any real likeness to such movements as, in an ordinary way, depend on the material condition of a body and take place without any direct use or end or aim."

Thus Stahl from the side of physiology, as Descartes from the side of psychology, defined more clearly than any of their predecessors the issue between Animism and Materialism. By conceiving the soul as an immaterial teleological factor controlling the physical processes of the living body, he set upon its modern lines the controversy as to the reality of a teleological determination of the processes of living beings. The subsequent history of modern physiology is the history of the constantly increasing ascendancy of the purely mechanical view of the processes of the animal body over the vitalistic and teleological modes of explanation.

The first great step towards this ascendancy had been made when, in the year 1628, William Harvey announced and demonstrated his discovery of the circulation of the blood, explaining it by purely physical and mechanical reasoning. A little later in the seventeenth century, the new mode of purely mechanical and chemical explanation of physiological processes was greatly promoted by Franciscus Sylvius of Leyden and his pupils. Van Helmont had studied the chemical processes of the body, but had mingled with his chemistry strange mystical doctrines and obscure conceptions of animal spirits and *Archei*, which he had derived from Paracelsus. "The spiritualistic fancies of Van Helmont, and still more the earlier ones of Paracelsus, had had the tendency to make men think that chemical inquiry, in contrast with physical inquiry, was in some way necessarily bound up with speculations about invisible agencies of a spiritual kind; and this doubtless was more or less a bar to men of sober and exact thought entering upon that line of inquiry. To Sylvius at least is due the credit of showing that there was no such necessary connexion between chemistry and spiritualism; that on the contrary the newer chemistry in its attempts to solve vital problems trod the path of the most valued Materialism." [1]

While Sylvius and his pupils set chemical physiology, especially the chemistry of digestion, upon the path of its modern development; the influence of the more exact mechanical conceptions introduced by Galileo, the first great victory of which when applied to physiology was Harvey's discovery of the circulation of the blood, continued to bear fruit. In Italy, Borelli, a mathematician trained in the school of Galileo, first gave a clear account of the mechanics of respiration; and in England a small band of Harvey's followers, Hooke, Lower, Mayow, applied the new understanding of the nature of combustion to explain the chemistry of respiration, the relations of the respiratory and circulatory systems, and the part played by the blood in conducting air to the tissues to sustain their processes of combustion.

These various mechanical and chemical modes of explanation of bodily processes were brought together in the teaching of Boerhaave of Leyden, perhaps the most influential physiologist of the earlier part of the eighteenth century. And the tradition was given an assured predominance over the animistic doctrines of Stahl and his successors by the great influence of Albrecht Haller, generally called the father of modern physiology, whose "Elementa Physiologiae" was completed in the year 1765.

Thus, when De la Mettrie and D'Holbach wrote their popular treatises with the avowed purpose of propagating the materialistic view of the nature of man, their doctrines could find solid support in the teachings of the most influential physiologists of their time: they may in fact be regarded as expressing the influence of those teachings upon minds of a positive and materialistic tendency.

The rapid progress of the physical sciences in the early decades of the nineteenth century seemed to bring much nearer to realisation the possibility of complete physical and chemical explanations of the processes of living bodies; and at the same time much of their technical apparatus of research was found

[1] Sir M. Foster, *op. cit.*, p. 153.

to be applicable in physiological investigations. There was a renewal of physiological research and progress, in which Johannes Müller was the leading spirit; and a confident expectation of the rapid reduction of all vital processes to terms of physics and chemistry began to be widely entertained. Although Müller himself must be reckoned among the vitalists, the great school of physiology founded by him made splendid progress along these physico-chemical lines; and the continued success of this way of physiological thought and research secured for it an undisputed predominance over the vitalistic physiology and seemed to justify to the full the hopes of its adherents. This triumphant progress of the mechanistic school of physiology soon gave rise to a fresh outburst of dogmatic Materialism. This time Germany was the centre of the storm, and its moving spirits were Moleschott,[1] Karl Vogt, and Ludwig Büchner.[2] These writers, especially the last, exercised a great influence on popular thought. Their favourite dictum was— "No matter without force, no force without matter." The language and thought of all three was open to the charge of confusion, inconsistency, and philosophical crudity, to a degree that prevented them exerting any serious influence in academic circles. Nevertheless these materialists, and indeed the French materialists of the eighteenth century also, had made some refinement upon the crudity of Hobbes and others of their forerunners. Their Materialism consisted chiefly in the repudiation of the notion of immaterial or spiritual substances, agents, forces, or modes of being, rather than in any assertion so crude as that thought is nothing but matter or motion of matter. They were concerned to show that matter consists not merely of inert solid particles, capable only of moving under the influence of external forces; but that it is rather endowed with intrinsic powers of activity, of which thought and feeling are special developments. For, as Lotze has pointed out, few modern materialists have maintained doctrines so crude as those commonly attributed to them by their opponents.

In our own day Materialism has undergone a further refinement which makes it less easy to attack or refute and which has in fact rendered it extremely difficult, if not impossible, to draw any line between the more subtle forms of Materialism and doctrines that are classified under the head of Idealism.

[1] "Der Kreislauf des Lebens," 1852.   [2] "Kraft und Stoff," 1856.

THE RISE OF THE MECHANISTIC PHYSIOLOGY

Before noting the position of present day Materialism, let us follow in more detail those lines of development of biological science which have done most to bring about a wide acceptance of it and of the other psycho-physical doctrines that agree with it in rejecting all forms of Animism.

The Search for the Seat of the Soul

We have seen that the ancients entertained various notions as to the seat of the soul, assigning the several vital and psychical functions that they distinguished to this or that bodily organ, or regarding the soul as equally present and active in all parts of the body. In the second century of our era, Galen, the great Roman physician and anatomist, made a considerable advance upon Aristotle's physiology; he showed by his dissections that the brain is connected with the muscles and with the sense-organs by the nerves, and taught that it is somehow concerned in mental process. After Galen no progress in anatomy and physiology was made for more than a thousand years; in fact, the authority of Galen remained supreme until in the middle of the sixteenth century the labours of Vesalius set these sciences once more on the path of progress. We have seen that Vesalius, while he took a materialistic view of the nature of soul, distinguished three souls, the vital, natural, and chief souls, each of which was but the sum of the spirits of corresponding function, and that he assigned to the brain the chief soul, the sum of the animal spirits, whose functions were distinctly mental. He taught that the animal spirit is made in the brain and that the brain influences the muscles and other organs by sending out the animal spirit along the nerves. " He was clear that the soul was engendered in and by the brain, but beyond that he knew next to nothing. Vivisection taught him that when the brain is removed sensation and movement are lost; but it taught him little more than this."[1] He observed also "that the mass of the brain attains its highest dimensions in man, which we know to be the most perfect animal, and that his brain is found to be bigger than that of three oxen; and then in proportion to the size of the body, first the ape, and next the dog exhibit a large brain, suggesting that animals excel in the size of their brains in pro-

[1] Sir M. Foster, *op. cit.*, Lect. x.

portion as they seem the more openly and clearly to be endowed with the faculties of the chief soul (i.e. mental powers)."

A hundred years later the brain was still not fully established as the seat of the soul, for Van Helmont assigned that honour to the orifice of the stomach.

Willis, Sedleian professor in the University of Oxford, a contemporary of Descartes and one of the founders of the "Royal Society," was fully aware of the importance of the brain for mental processes, the higher modes of which, in the case of man, he attributed to a rational incorporeal soul; nevertheless he distinguished a corporeal soul consisting of two parts, one of flame residing in the blood, the other of light diffused throughout the nervous system and in a less degree through other tissues.

Although Descartes was but an amateur in physiology, his assignment of the rational soul to the brain and his speculative description of the functions of the brain, mark a distinct epoch in the search for the seat of the soul. For, from his time onwards, the brain was securely established as the seat of the mental functions and as the medium through which the soul effects its commerce with the other parts of the body; and, though Stahl regarded the soul as operating directly in all parts of the body, the search for the seat of the soul followed the lines laid down by Descartes, i.e. it continued to be the search for that part of the brain in which the nerves come most closely together.

Stensen and Borelli showed themselves to be clearly aware that the brain is the seat of sensation and originator of bodily movements. But no progress was made with this problem until the middle of the eighteenth century, when Haller applied to it his penetrating intellect. He rejected Stahl's view, that the soul acts directly in all parts of the body; but he argued "no narrower seat can be allotted to the soul than the conjoint origin of all the nerves; nor can any structure be proposed as its seat, except that to which we can trace all the nerves. For it will be easily understood that the *sensorium commune* ought to lack no feeling of any part of the whole animated body nor any nerve which can convey from any part of the body the impression of external objects. And the same may be said of the nerves of movement. Wherefore, even quite apart from the experimental results described above, we cannot admit as the exclusive seat of the soul, either the *corpus callosum* or the *septum lucidum* or the tiny pineal gland, or the *corpora striata* or any particular region of the brain."

And he concluded that "both sensation and movement have their source in the medulla of the brain. This, therefore, is the seat of the soul." By medulla he denoted the whole of the central mass of both cerebrum and cerebellum. Haller nevertheless inclined to the view that different parts of the brain are specially concerned in different mental functions; though in summing up he wrote: "Our present knowledge does not permit us to speak with any show of truth about the more complicated functions of the mind, or to assign in the brain to imagination its seat, to common sensation its seat, to memory its seat."

In spite of this vague foreshadowing by Haller of the modern doctrine of cerebral localization of mental functions, the search for the seat of the soul continued to be prosecuted under the influence of the reasoning that led Descartes to choose the pineal gland. It was held that the soul must be present at some one spot in the brain, where it could receive or be affected by all the agitations brought from the sense-organs by the converging sensory nerves, and where it could control the outflow of nervous impulses along the motor nerves; for the soul was conceived as playing upon the central ends of groups of motor nerves and originating in them impulses appropriate to the production of the movements it willed, much as a musician plays upon the keys of a piano, striking them in combinations appropriate to the production of harmonious chords. According to this way of thinking, it was necessary that the seat of the soul should be a central and single organ in the brain, and, since almost all parts of the brain exist in bilateral symmetrical duplication, the choice was strictly limited and fell in turn upon each of the single median structures, e.g. the *septum lucidum*, the *corpus callosum*, the central ventricle; all of which, however, were in turn shown to have no immediate connexion with consciousness.

No less a man than R. H. Lotze was the last psychologist of note seriously to accept this reasoning; and though his knowledge of anatomy and physiology of the brain forbade him to designate any one part as the seat of the soul, and though he afterwards relinquished this view, nevertheless, in his "Medizinische Psychologie" (published in 1851), he postulated such a central seat of the soul.

Early in the nineteenth century, the great anatomist Gall laid the foundations of our modern doctrine of the localization of cerebral functions, by means of his comparative studies of the brains of men and animals. From the time of Gall the study of cerebral functions has been carried on by an ever increasing army of keen workers. Forty years ago it was still possible for one party of experimental observers to maintain that there obtains no specialization of function of the parts of the great brain, that each part is of similar undifferentiated function with all the rest of its substance. But Broca's discovery of the motor speech-centre, a small part of the cortex of the left frontal lobe of the cerebrum, rapidly gained general acceptance. Since the establishment of this instance of the dependence of a special mental function on the integrity of a particular part of the brain, an immense amount of labour has been devoted to the problem, and has proved that the cerebral cortex, the thin surface layer of grey matter, is the part of the brain most immediately concerned in mental process[1]; it has been shown also that a large part of the cerebral cortex can be mapped out into areas, the integrity of each of which is essential to the enjoyment of certain modes of consciousness. The evidence is especially clear in the case of the sensations and perceptions of the higher senses. Let us glance at the nature of the evidence which has convinced all physiologists that all the visual perception and sensation and imagery of any normal human being are invariably accompanied by certain physico-chemical processes in the cortical grey matter of the occipital pole of his brain; and that visual sensation is normally experienced, only when these processes are excited by the arrival of nervous impulses travelling from the retina directly to this part of the cortex.

First, it has been shown that, in man and the higher animals, the retina is connected with this part of the brain cortex by a system of nerve fibres more direct and more numerous than those that connect it with any other part. Secondly, it has been shown that in animals this part of the cortex remains in a state of very incomplete development, if the animal is in any way deprived of the use of its eyes from birth onwards; while it is known that, if a human being is blind from birth, or loses his eyesight within the first two years of life, he remains devoid of all visual imagery, all power of visual representation or imagination.

Thirdly, it has been shown by the clinical and *post mortem*

[1] There is some ground for believing that some of the masses of grey matter at the base of the brain have equally intimate relation with conscious life.

study of a very large number of cases that, if, in an adult human being, the tract of nerve fibres which connects the retina of one eye with this part of the cortex is broken across in any part of its course, that eye becomes blind; and that, if both tracts are thus broken across, total and permanent blindness is the result, even though the lesion be confined to the upper part of the tract, and the connections of the retinæ with the lower parts of the brain remain uninjured. In such cases the powers of visual imagination may remain unimpaired.

Fourthly, it has been shown that destruction of, or serious injury to, this part of the cortex always impairs more or less seriously the powers of vision. If the whole of the occipital cortex of one hemisphere of the brain (say the left) is destroyed (as by the rupture of a blood vessel in that region), the patient suffers permanently the defect of vision known as hemianopsia, *i.e.* the optical impressions made on the left halves of both retinæ no longer excite visual sensation; for the left halves of both retinæ are connected directly only with the left occipital cortex.[1] In rare cases in which the occipital cortex of both cerebral hemispheres is gravely injured, visual sensation, perception, and imagination are almost completely destroyed; and, though no case of complete destruction of the occipital cortex of both hemispheres has been carefully studied, the evidence at present available is held by almost all physiologists to warrant the belief that in such a case the patient would be completely deprived of all power of visual sensation, perception, and imagination; and it seems highly probable that the deprivation would be permanent and would be so complete that he would not even be aware of the nature of the gap in his mental life.

Similar observations have yielded almost equally strong evidence that the sensations, perceptions, and representations of each of the other senses are similarly dependent on the integrity of other circumscribed areas of the cerebral cortex; that they are invariably accompanied by nervous processes in those parts of the brain, and that they are no longer experienced when the nervous structures of those parts are destroyed. We have evidence that is, if possible, even more conclusive, showing that

---

[1] This statement is perhaps not strictly true. Some authorities believe that a small central region of each retina is connected directly with the occipital cortex of both hemispheres; for in many cases of hemianopsia this small central part of both retinæ continues to function normally.

the production and control of all skilled voluntary movement is dependent on the integrity of the extensive region of the cortex known as the Rolandic or sensori-motor area; and that the skilled movements of the various parts of the body, the fingers, thumb, wrist, tongue, lips, etc., are dependent on the integrity of different specialized parts of this area. For not only is the power of production of such movements lost, when these parts of the cortex are destroyed; but it has been abundantly shown that artificial direct stimulation of these parts excites movements of the corresponding parts of the body. And in this case also, the anatomical connexions of these parts with the corresponding muscles has been worked out in considerable detail.

Again, we have now good evidence that outside these sensory and motor areas of the cortex, which together make up less than half its total extent, are parts whose integrity seems essential to such mental processes as the synthetic elaboration of the sensations involved in intelligent perception; for example, it is established that the intelligent appreciation of the significance of written words depends on the integrity of a small part of the cortex that lies a little in front of the "visual area," or area directly concerned in visual sensation. And it seems to be proved that injury to such parts may leave the patient capable of enjoying the normal range of sensations, while depriving him of the power of interpreting certain of them; so that, *e.g.*, he may remain capable of distinguishing objects in his visual field, though he is incapable of recognizing them, of naming them, or of reacting upon them in any intelligent fashion.

It is unnecessary to pursue the evidence in greater detail. Observation and experiment of the kind we have been considering seem to have established beyond serious question the doctrine of the localization of cerebral functions; that is to say that, although the functions of many parts of the brain remain obscure, we are compelled to believe that the exercise of various kinds of mental activity and the enjoyment of various modes of consciousness, including all that is properly called sensation and imagery, are invariably bound up with, and are directly dependent upon, the occurrence of nervous processes in various parts of the brain, parts consisting of nervous elements of highly specialized functions, which are distributed widely throughout the cortex of the cerebral hemispheres, and possibly in other parts of the brain also.

THE RISE OF THE MECHANISTIC PHYSIOLOGY

Thus the search for a punctual seat of the soul, for some one spot at which the sensory nerves might be supposed to converge to act upon the soul, and at which in turn the soul might be supposed to play upon the central ends of the motor nerves, has been shown to be a hopeless one: it is proved that there is no such seat of the soul.

The Doctrine of the Reflex Type of all Nervous Process

Closely connected with this search for the seat of the soul, and closely allied to the failure of this search in its bearing upon our problem, has been the development of the doctrine of reflex action.

Descartes' bold speculations anticipated the modern doctrine of reflex action; and the writings of Willis and of other physiologists of the seventeenth century also contain some vague foreshadowings of it. But it was not until the middle of the nineteenth century that the nature of reflex action was clearly understood. Descartes distinguished between the afferent and motor modes of nervous conduction, but it is not clear that he conceived the processes as taking place in two different sets of nerves; and it was Sir Charles Bell who first clearly demonstrated, early in the nineteenth century, that all the peripheral nerves are of two kinds—the afferent nerves which, entering the spinal cord by the posterior nerve-roots, carry up impulses from the sense-organs; and the efferent nerves which, issuing from the cord by the ventral roots, carry impulses from the central nervous system to the muscles and other executive organs.

It had, of course, long been observed that, in both men and animals, certain simple movements can be evoked in a regular involuntary machine-like fashion by the application of certain forms of stimulation to the sense organs; *e.g.* the winking of the eyelid and the contraction of the pupil by the sudden flashing of a light upon the eye; the withdrawal of a hand or foot by the pricking of the skin of the part. It was known also that some of these reflex movements may be excited in man, not only without his volition, but even in spite of his utmost voluntary efforts to prevent them. This remarkable fact could not fail to excite the attention of students of the nervous system; and early in the nineteenth century it was shown that some of these movements may be equally well excited in both men and animals, when the brain is destroyed or the spinal cord severed from the brain; when, for example, the spinal cord of a man has been broken across by accident, it is in some cases possible to evoke movements of the lower limbs by tickling or pricking the skin; and in such cases the stimulus evokes in the patient neither feeling nor sensation. It was clear, then, that the integrity of the spinal cord is the sufficient condition of such reflex response. In the middle of the last century a famous controversy was waged over the question whether such reflex movements, effected through the spinal cord in the absence of the brain, imply the presence of some kind of soul-life, some kind of psychical activity, associated with the nervous processes of the cord. For some of these movements are so nicely adapted to effect results beneficial to the organism, that they seemed to some observers to imply intelligent and purposive direction. But physiologists, with few exceptions, soon came to hold very decidedly the opinion that all such spinal reflex actions are determined in a purely mechanical fashion. And this opinion has received very strong support from the modern studies of the minute structure of the nervous system. These studies have shown that in almost all cases the sensory fibre, which carries up impulses from some sense-organ and enters the spinal cord by a dorsal nerve-root, sends across the spinal cord a branch which (either directly or through the medium of another neurone) comes into contact with one or more of the motor neurones, whose long branches or axones pass down to the muscles as their motor nerves. These studies, in fact, have displayed the material mechanisms by means of which the incoming impulses of the sensory nerves are distributed to motor nerves, through systems of nervous connexions in the spinal cord of various degrees of complexity; and there is little reason to doubt that, in all spinal reflexes, the paths taken by the nervous impulses, and the conjunctions of efferent nerves thus thrown into action by them, are wholly determined by the material connexions of the nervous elements, and by their physico-chemical state at the moment of the arrival of the afferent impulse.

This revelation of the material mechanism conditioning the seemingly purposive reflex action, has cut away the ground from under those who would maintain that the spinal reflexes are psychically guided in any way. But the conception of reflex action as a seemingly purposive, though in reality a mechanically determined, response to the stimulus applied to the sense-organ has exercised a much more important influence upon the consideration of the psycho-physical problem. For the incessant labours of a multitude of workers has revealed the fact that not only the spinal cord, but the whole of the brain also, is built up on the reflex plan; that the whole of the brain may properly be regarded as made up of a multitude of nervous loops, interlacing and communicating with one another, it is true, in wonderfully complex fashion, yet still being essentially loops or long bye-paths; each of these diverges from the afferent limb of some spinal reflex arc to ascend to the brain, and, after traversing the brain, descends to join the efferent or motor limb of some spinal reflex arc. Just as it is possible to trace the path of the spinal reflex impulse across the cord from sensory to motor nerve, so it is possible to reconstruct in imagination the ascent of the various sensory paths to the lower brain, thence to the appropriate sensory areas of the cortex, and thence again in great converging systems to the motor area of the cortex; whence they descend by the great pyramidal tract to be distributed to the various motor mechanisms of the cord. And this reconstruction is no mere piece of fancy, but is fully warranted by a great quantity of careful observations. Hence we have to suppose that, when a man sees an object and stretches out his hand to take it, the nervous excitation follows such a long loop-path, passing up to the visual cortex, thence by long association-tracts to the motor cortex, and so down by the pyramidal tract to the spinal centres through which all movements of the arm are effected. And we have to believe that the sensations which are involved in this perceptual reaction are somehow determined by the nervous current as it traverses the cortex of the brain in the course of this long journey.

Again, there is good reason to believe, though here we are on less firm ground, that all the processes of the brain, even those that accompany the most abstruse thought, conform to the same fundamental reflex type. Everywhere, then, in the central nervous system, in the brain no less than in the spinal cord, there seems to be continuity of the physical processes of nervous conduction; nowhere do we find the sensory nerve coming suddenly to an end at any place where its physical process might be supposed to terminate in giving rise to a sensation or any other psychical effect; and nowhere does the impulse of the efferent nerve seem to be originated as a physical process without physical cause or antecedent; rather there seems always and everywhere to be continuity of material substance and of physical process, nowhere and at no time spontaneous or psychical origination of nervous process.

The study of spinal reflex action has shown us also that the energy expended in the efferent process need bear no simple and constant relation to the magnitude or intensity of the excitation by which it is induced; that rather the nervous system contains in its various parts stores of potential energy, which may be liberated in large quantities by very small excitations, so that under favourable conditions a very slight sensory stimulus may provoke a violent reflex action. We can, therefore, no longer see in the disproportion of physical effect to physical cause, in the case of intense voluntary reaction upon a stimulus, any evidence of psychical intervention in the chain of physical events.

It is obvious that the two lines of development of our knowledge of the brain and its functions reviewed in the foregoing paragraphs, necessitate the rejection of any such conception of the interaction of the soul with the body, as was commonly entertained half a century ago and was clearly set forth by Lotze in his "Medizinische Psychologie." For this conception had postulated the abutting of all sensory paths about some central part of the brain, the seat of the soul; the abrupt termination of all the sensory nervous processes at that place; and the equally abrupt inception of the excitation of motor nerves without physical cause or antecedent. And, though the argument is seldom explicitly set forth, yet there can be no doubt that these two allied developments of physiological knowledge have done much to banish the belief that the brain is the seat of psycho-physical interactions, of action and reaction between soul and body.[1] But their influence in this direction has worked in conjunction with other lines of physiological thought; and these we must consider, before we can appreciate the full force of the physiological argument.

---

[1] Prof. Th. Ziehen regards the absence of any gap in the chains of physical causation in the brain as the most important of all the grounds on which he bases his rejection of psycho-physical interaction. "Gehirn u. Seelenleben." Leipzig, 1902, p. 39.

Unconscious Cerebration

We have seen that reflex movements of a seemingly purposive character may occur without, and even in spite of, the volition of the subject, and, in fact, without the subject becoming aware of the stimulus that evokes the movement or of the movement itself. Now, in certain abnormal states, actions of much more complicated character are performed, while the subject seems to remain unconscious of them. Thus, epileptics sometimes execute, in the period succeeding to an acute attack, long trains of action that imply intelligent design and choice of means, as well as nice control and regulation of all bodily movements; and yet the subject, returning after a time to his normal state, asserts that of the whole period during which these actions were performed he retains not the slightest remembrance, that he is absolutely ignorant of all that he did and of all that happened to him during this space of time. Similar examples of the intelligent performance of complex actions of which no recollection can be evoked, are afforded by subjects in a state of trance or somnambulism, and by others suffering from lesions of the brain. Other persons, apparently normal in all respects, have wakened up from sleep to find that they have written down original verses or the solution of some problem that had remained insoluble up to the moment of falling asleep.

The feature common to all these cases is the inability of the subject to remember anything of the execution or the circumstances of actions that seemed to imply perception, feeling, reasoning, and volition. Now the recollection of any past action is our only direct evidence that that action was consciously performed, especially if, as in many of these cases, the subject is irresponsive to all questioning during the execution of the actions. It is argued, then, that we have in these cases examples of highly complex, purposive, and intelligently controlled action taking place without consciousness; it would seem to follow that in these cases the material mechanisms of the nervous system suffice for the execution of such actions, independently of all consciousness or psychical guidance; and, therefore, we seem compelled to believe that, when similar actions are executed consciously, the nervous mechanisms are the only essential conditions; that their physico-chemical processes constitute the complete causal sequences intervening between the sense-impressions and our reactions upon them; and that consciousness is a superfluous accompaniment, so far as the causal sequence is concerned.[1]

The Association-Psychology and the Law of Habit

The association-psychology, founded by Locke and Hume, and developed by a succession of British writers, reached its climax of confident explanation of all mental process in the works of Alexander Bain and Herbert Spencer, about the same time that the physiological facts and inferences described above were brought to light. From the first it had been clear that the association-psychology lends itself admirably to a physiological interpretation of mental process; and, as early as the middle of the eighteenth century, Hartley sketched a system of physiological explanation of mental process, based on the assumption that all mental processes consist in the association and associative reproduction of ideas. But the increase of knowledge of the nervous system brought by the researches of the nineteenth century, provided a much less inadequate basis for such a system of explanations than was available to Hartley. According to the association-psychology, all mental process consists in the reception of impressions by the senses and in the revival of these impressions in various conjunctions and sequences, as the simple and complex ideas of memory and of imagination, according to the laws of association and associative reproduction; and it was held that, by the careful analysis of instances of all types, the various laws of association recognized by the earlier writers may properly be reduced to a single principle, namely, that of association of ideas in virtue of their immediate succession in time.

Now, a fixed habit of action resembles very closely a reflex action; an habitual action may be effected involuntarily, without design or reflection, and with very little or no consciousness of the action or of the impressions on the senses by which it is evoked and guided. We have, therefore, good warrant for believing that nervous mechanisms, such as have been shown to be the essential conditions of reflex actions, are the sufficient conditions of habitual actions. Further, a habit is formed by the repetition of an action on the repetition of a particular sense-impression; that is to say, the repeated sequence of a particular

---

[1] The late Prof. Huxley described a case of such apparently unconscious, yet intelligent and complex, activities, and attached great weight to such cases as justifying the denial of psycho-physical interaction (Collected Essays, vol. i.).

action upon a particular sense-impression results in the formation of a mechanism consisting of a system of nervous connexions in the brain, which system is capable of bringing about the appropriate response to the sense-impression in a purely mechanical fashion. The nervous system, then, is plastic and has a tendency to take on habits; wherever the nervous current runs from one part to another, it leaves behind a more or less enduring tendency for the path it has traversed to be an open path, a path of low resistance, between the two parts. Here, then, is a basis for the physiological and mechanical explanation of the course of all mental process in terms of the association-psychology. We have only to suppose (as we have good warrant for doing) that the rise to consciousness of each idea is accompanied by the excitation of some particular group of nervous elements in the brain; and to assume that, when one sense-impression following upon another gives rise to a second idea following immediately upon another, the nervous current strikes across from the one group of nervous elements to the other. If so much be assumed, then it follows from the law of habit that the revival of the one idea[1] will tend to be followed by, or accompanied by, the revival of the other; and we have in outline a scheme for the explanation of all that clustering, cohesion, and succession of simple ideas, which, according to the principles of the association-psychology, constitute the whole of mental process. For this scheme is held to afford a mechanical explanation, not only of the facts of association and reproduction of ideas, but also of memory itself; it is said the idea is merely a cluster of simple ideas or sensational elements (as Locke first taught), which cohere, in virtue of the principle of habit, in the groupings in which they are evoked by the fortuitous conjunctions of sense-impressions.

Such is the conception of mental process which has gained a wide currency, especially among the biologists; and, since this conceptual scheme makes use of no other principles and faculties than those inherent in the nervous system, it has played no inconsiderable part in banishing the belief in psychical intervention with the course of the physical processes of the brain.[2]

[1] I here use the word *idea* in the sense given it by Hume and the Associationists, as equivalent to presentation, and as covering both percept and image.
[2] The most consistent elaboration of this mechanical system of explanation of mental process may be found in Prof. Ziehen's "Outlines of Physiological Psychology."

The four lines of development of physiological fact and theory reviewed in the foregoing pages have, then, all tended to the one conclusion, namely, that the actions of man are capable of being fully explained in terms of mechanism—that a sufficient knowledge of the structure and physico-chemical constitution of the nervous system would enable us to describe completely in terms of physical and chemical changes the causal sequence of events that issues in any action, no matter how much deliberation, choice, and effort may seem to be involved in its preparation and determination.

Long ago, Spinoza, in proposing to regard mind and body as but two aspects of one reality, found himself compelled to make this assumption. He wrote: "Certainly no man hath yet determined what are the powers of the body; I mean that none has yet learnt from experience what the body may perform by mere laws of nature, considering it only as a material thing, and what it cannot do without the mind's determination of it. For nobody has known as yet the frame of the body so thoroughly as to explain all its operations; not to say that in brutes much is noted which doth far surpass human cunning, and that men walking in their sleep often perform, so sleeping, that which they would never dare waking: which is proof enough that the body may, merely by the laws of its own constitution, do much that its own mind is amazed at. Again, there is none can tell how and in what manner the mind moves the body, what measure of motion it can impart to it, or with what velocity."

Spinoza, in making this great assumption so contrary to all the accepted ways of thought of his time, could appeal only to men's profound *ignorance* of the body and its processes; whereas those who make the same assumption in the present age appeal with confidence and good show of reason to our *knowledge* of the body and its processes, claiming that the knowledge which we now have amply justifies the assumption and allows us to understand in a general way the mechanics of human conduct.

In strict logic, the physiological knowledge we have been considering does not do more than this; it does not provide any positive argument against psycho-physical interaction, although in the minds of many it has seemed to justify and necessitate this negative conclusion.

But we have now to consider certain other physiological and

biological arguments which are held to prove the dependence of all mental process on the brain.

The dependence of Thought on Brain-function.

The materialists of the eighteenth century based their arguments very largely on facts of the kind we have to consider in this section. But modern research has rendered much more exact and extensive our knowledge of these facts.

First and foremost, we have to put all the facts which, in the course of our description of the search for the seat of the soul, were referred to as proving the localization of cerebral functions; especially the facts of brain-lesion, which show that the sensations and imagery of each of the senses are dependent upon the integrity of special parts of the cerebral cortex and that other special mental functions are abolished by injuries of other parts. But there are many other evidences of the intimate dependence of mental processes upon the brain-functions, of which the principal are indicated in the following paragraphs.

There obtains throughout the animal scale, and also within the course of development of each human being, a close correspondence between the degree of development of the brain and the degree of development of intelligence or mental capacity in general. Passing over the facts of the comparative size of the brain in the various animal species, let us consider for a moment the parallelism of mental and cerebral development in the human being. The lack of all but a vague sentiency and appetition in the new-born infant corresponds to a very undeveloped state of its brain: not only is its mass very much less than that of the adult brain; but also, microscopic study has shown that, for some time after birth, the majority of the nervous elements of the cerebrum are in a condition in which they cannot take part in any concerted nervous activities. Gradually, throughout all the years of childhood and adolescence, more and more of these elements become perfected and organized within the general system or hierarchy of minor systems; first, as the sensory powers develop, the neurones of the sensory areas become organized, later those of the intervening "association-areas," which subserve the higher mental functions; and this process of the organization of fresh neural elements continues far on into adult life, multitudes of new branches and twigs growing out from millions of nerve cells to establish a plexus or network of constantly increasing complexity in correspondence with the development of knowledge and intellectual power. Then, as middle age begins to pass over into old age, this multiplication of twigs and branches and this formation of new connexions between the neural elements come to an end; and at the same time the mind becomes less and less capable of making new acquisitions of knowledge, of skill, of capacity of any kind; until in advanced age the powers of acquisition and retention are reduced to a minimum: the old man lives again in the scenes of his youth, and remembers hardly, if at all, the events of yesterday.

Again, we know how, when the surface of the brain becomes chronically inflamed, the mental powers of the patient exhibit a progressive deterioration running parallel with the deterioration of the grey matter of the cortex; so that a man of splendid intellect and fine character may be gradually reduced to a state in which he stands, both intellectually and morally, below the level of the higher animals; a state of complete mental degradation, from which he is released only by death. Surely the most terrible object the mind of man can contemplate! And modern medical science is showing more and more clearly that many mental disorders are primarily due to disorders of the body which, by poisoning the blood, secondarily produce a chronic poisoning of the brain, and thereby a degradation of intellect and character.

We have to take account also of the many modes in which mental process may be profoundly affected or arrested by physical agents acting on the body. A very small quantity of laughing gas, chloroform, or ether, in the blood quickly deranges all our mental processes, and a slightly larger dose seems to arrest all mental activity and completely to abolish consciousness. In the case of alcohol, the steps by which the activity of the mind is arrested and consciousness abolished may be followed, the change being greater in proportion to the dose of the drug introduced into the blood, and, through it, into the brain-substance: the highest, most delicate functions seem to be first abolished, and then in turn the functions successively lower in the scale of complexity and delicacy; until, when the dose is large enough, all the parts of the brain are paralysed, and consciousness seems as completely abolished as in chloroform narcosis. Various other drugs, such as Indian hemp and mescal, produce specific alterations of our mental processes, without arresting them.

A copious stream of blood, rich in oxygen, is constantly supplied to the brain during waking life; the more active the mind at any moment, the more copious is the supply of blood pumped up to the brain, the more rapidly is oxygen taken up from the blood, and the more rapidly is the substance of the nervous tissues oxidised and consumed and cast out into the bloodstream, in the form of carbonic acid and other waste products of combustion. On the other hand, any checking of the stream of blood flowing through the vessels of the brain, or any diminution of the quantity of oxygen contained in it, produces at once some disturbance of mental process; and a sudden stoppage of the supply of oxygen to the brain arrests almost instantaneously all mental process and abolishes consciousness—as we see in the case of the ordinary fainting caused by insufficiency of the heart's action.

A mechanical shock or jar of the brain will also instantaneously arrest all mental activity and abolish consciousness, if only it is sufficiently severe.

Not least important among the facts of this order are those which indicate the dependence of memory upon the nervous system. A blow on the head seems in some cases to abolish throughout a period of minutes or hours all memory of experiences preceding the moment of the blow. Local lesions, *i.e.* injuries of small parts of the brain, seem in some cases to destroy memories of some one class, *e.g.* visual memories; as we have noticed in discussing the localization of cerebral functions.

The effectiveness with which we can commit any matter to memory varies greatly with the bodily state at the moment, with the degree of fatigue, the state of general bodily vigour and health, with youth and age.

And, most significant of all perhaps, the minute study in recent years of the processes of mental association and reproduction has shown that they obey laws which seem to be identical with those of the formation and operation of habits. Now, there is no room for doubt that the acquisition of a habit consists in the formation of material connexions between nervous elements and in the consolidation, improvement, or wearing smooth of such paths of communication between nerve cells, or, as it is commonly put, in the formation of paths of low resistance in the nervous system.

All these facts, and many others of the same order, show

that the continuance of our mental processes and of consciousness, in the only form of which we have any positive knowledge, is intimately dependent upon the metabolism of the brain and upon the maintenance of certain very complex chemical conditions, conditions which cannot vary beyond very narrow limits without producing disorder or arrest of the brain's metabolism and, with it, of the stream of mental life.

The Law of Psycho-neural Correlation or Concomitance.

The physiological facts of the kind we have been considering are generally held, and with good reason, to justify the empirical generalization known as the law of psycho-neural concomitance, which runs as follows:—All mental process is accompanied by neural process in the brain, each thought or idea having its specific neural correlate, or, in the language of Huxley—every *psychosis* is definitely correlated with a *neurosis*.

The Composite Nature of the Mind.

In former years, the proposition that the mind of each man is a unity was very generally accepted as a fundamental and unquestionable truth. But modern research has shaken very seriously even this inner stronghold of the castle of Animism.

Biology has made clear that the human body is a vast and harmoniously coöperating aggregation of cells, each of which is in a sense a vital unit, which seems to have a life of its own, relatively independent of that of the rest of the body. Embryology has shown that this aggregation of cells is formed by the repeated division of a single parent-cell, the germ-cell, and the cohesion of the many cells thus formed. Now, the principle of continuity and the analogy presented by the unicellular animals, each of which divides repeatedly into two or more cells that lead independent lives, seem to compel us to suppose that the germ-cell has not only life but also mind, that it enjoys psychical life in however lowly a manner or degree, and that, on the division of the germ-cell, each of the cells derived from it has also its psychical capacities. This line of thought leads us inevitably to the view that the developed human being is, as it were, a vast colony of cells of more or less highly-specialized functions; that in the cells constituting the nervous system the psychical functions are most highly developed and specialized; and that the consciousness of each man is in some sense the sum, or aggregation, or resultant, of the consciousnesses of the cells of his brain. This view of the composite nature of mind and consciousness, which has now gained very wide acceptance, seems to be borne out by two classes of very striking and curious facts.

The facts of the one class are those established by the experimental division of lower animals; their significance did not escape the observation of Aristotle, but they were first studied in detail in the eighteenth century by Charles Bonnett. Many of the lower animals, notably some of the segmented worms, may be divided by the knife into two or more portions, each of which continues to live and to manifest all the indications of psychical life proper to the species. In such cases we seem compelled to believe that, in dividing the body and nervous system, the knife divides also the psychical life of the creature; if indeed the psychical life of the parts of the intact creature is integrated to a unitary consciousness.

The reproduction or genesis of each human being takes place by a process of fission which is essentially analogous to such simple transection of an animal; for the inception of the new individual is a budding off of the germ-cell from the mass of cells constituting the body of the parent, a cell which seems to carry with it the rudiment, or at least the potentiality, of the psychical life of the developed man.

Consideration of these facts has led many competent thinkers [1] to assert that the consciousness of any man is composite, is a great stream formed by the flowing together of the many little streams of consciousness, the consciousnesses of the vital units of which his body or brain is composed; [2] and they have not hesitated to assert that, if a man's brain could be mechanically divided into two parts (as by the transection of the *corpus callosum*) without arresting the life of the parts, the nervous activities of each part would be accompanied by its own stream of consciousness; that, in fact, the condition or ground of the unity of personal consciousness is the material and functional connection between the cells of which the brain is composed.

Secondly, since Fechner boldly propounded this view fifty

[1] Notably G. T. Fechner in the "Psycho-physik," and Von Hartmann in "The Philosophy of the Unconscions."
[2] This view is strictly in harmony with the widely accepted speculation of philosophers that an absolute mind or consciousness comprehends or includes the consciousness of all lesser minds.

years ago, it has received very strong support from modern studies in mental pathology. Students of hysteria, of hypnosis, of trance, and of automatic speech and writing, medical psychologists of the school of Charcot and Janet, loudly proclaim that the doctrine of the unity of the individual consciousness is an exploded dogma, and that, even in the normal individual, many obscure currents of thought and consciousness flow on independently beside or beneath the main stream; and that this multiplicity of consciousness is but accentuated and brought more clearly to view in the abnormal states that they have studied with so much success.[1] For these abnormal states, known as states of multiple personality, dual or divided consciousness, and so forth, seem to afford evidence of the existence of two or more streams of mental activity and consciousness associated with the processes of a single brain and body, the two streams of consciousness alternating with one another in time in cases of the commoner type, but seeming in rarer cases to run on contemporaneously and independently of one another.

Now there is very good reason for believing that in all cases of these kinds, the kinds that are now commonly classed under the head of *mental dissociation*, there obtains some degree of functional dissociation among the elements of the brain; in fact, the evidence of such neural dissociation is much more clear and direct than the evidence for dual or multiple consciousness.[2] It is, then, easy to see in these facts a confirmation of the view that such unity of consciousness as we normally enjoy is conditioned by the functional continuity of the elements of the brain; for in these cases we seem to find that rupture of this neural continuity is accompanied by a rupture or division of consciousness, just such as, according to the view of Fechner and Von Hartmann, would result from division of the brain by the surgeon's knife.

[1] For an authoritative statement of this kind see an article by Prof. Th. Flournoy, "Esprits et Médiums," in the *Bulletin de l'Institut général psychologique*, 1909, No. 3: "En resumé, au cours de ce dernier demi-siècle, les expériences d'hypnotisme, l'étude des alterations spontanées de la personnalité, et l'observation même de nos procès psychologiques courants, ont révélé dans l'âme humaine une complexité de nature, et des possibilités de dissociation intérieure ou de polymorphisme, dont on ne se doubtait guère à l'epoque d'Allan Kardec, et qui ont totalement ruiné l'axiome servant tacitement de pilier principal à sa théorie" (the axiom, namely, that the consciousness of the individual is unitary).

[2] The nature and production of such states of neural dissociation has been discussed by the author in a paper in *Brain*, vol. xxxi., "The State of the Brain during Hypnosis."

CHAPTER IX

THE INFLUENCE OF THE DARWINIAN THEORY

WE have now reviewed the principal ways in which the development of our knowledge of the nervous system and its functions has contributed to the rejection of Animism. But the progress of other branches of biology has contributed powerfully towards the same result, especially the establishment of the doctrine of biological evolution through the influence of the ideas of Charles Darwin.

The multitude of nice adaptations of animal structure and function to the situations and circumstances and needs of the animals had always been looked upon as evidence of the operation of a teleological factor in the determination of those structures and functions; whether this factor was regarded as operating from outside to mould the development of the animals, or was identified, as by Lamarck, with the minds of the animals, with their intelligent psychical efforts to achieve their purposes and to adapt themselves more perfectly to their environment. Then, in the middle of the nineteenth century, just when the triumphs of physical science and the rapid progress of physiology were leading men to regard all animal growth and behaviour as capable of mechanical explanation, came the Darwinian hypothesis of the evolution of species and the adaptation of species to their environment by the blind mechanical operation of natural selection. Darwin himself retained the hypothesis of Lamarck and continued to regard mind as a teleological factor in the evolutionary process. But to a great number, perhaps the majority, of biologists who came after Darwin, his hypothesis has seemed capable of explaining as mechanically engendered all instances of adaptation of structure and function; and it is maintained by those who accept the view of this Neo-Darwinian school, of which Weismann is the leader, that the last ground for the recognition of any teleological factor in the biological realm has been washed away for ever by the Darwinian principles.

The modern doctrine of biological evolution contributes in a second way also to the abolition of Animism. It compels us to believe in the continuity of the evolution of the animal kingdom from the simplest to the most highly developed animal, namely man; and it regards man's mental organization as having been continuously evolved from that of his animal ancestry, by means of the same processes of natural selection and inheritance of chance variations that have produced his bodily organization.

Now it is obvious that the acceptance of this view raises new difficulties for any animistic doctrine. If man has a soul, what is its relation to the souls of animals? If it is of an altogether different order from these, at what point in the scale of evolution did the human soul replace the animal soul? and so on and so on. The doctrine of the continuity of the evolution of man's mental powers from those of his animal ancestry forbids us to accept Descartes' easy way of escape from these difficult problems, namely, the denial of all psychical life to the animals. But in addition to the raising of these unanswerable conundrums, the doctrine of the continuity of evolution seems to make against Animism in yet another way. It is said that the principles of continuity and of economy justify us in regarding the world of living things as having been gradually evolved from inanimate or non-living matter,[1] and that the rejection of this view involves the assumption of a miraculous interference with the course of nature for the first production of living organisms. And it is held that the successes of modern chemistry in analyzing the substance of living matter and in synthesizing complex organic molecules from the chemical elements justify us in believing that living matter will one day, perhaps at no distant date, be synthesized in the laboratory. If, then, such continuity of evolution of the organic world of living things from the inorganic world is established, it justifies the belief that all organic processes, including those of the human brain, are determined according to the laws of mechanism to which all inorganic matter has been proved by exact experiment to conform; for we cannot suppose that the mere aggregation of the chemical elements in the more complex molecules of organic matter removes them in any degree from the sway of those laws. Hence there is no room

[1] Prof. Lloyd Morgan is one of those who have laid great stress upon this argument: see his "Introduction to Comparative Psychology."

for psychical guidance among the strictly mechanical processes of human brains.

The evolutionary speculations of Herbert Spencer must also be mentioned here as having played a considerable part in establishing "the psychology without a soul." For in his "Principles of Psychology" (the first edition of which preceded by a few years the "Origin of Species") Spencer applied the physiological principles of the association-psychology to explain not only the development of the individual mind, but also the evolution of the mental powers of the race; claiming to show how all the powers of the human mind have been built up by the transmission and accumulation from generation to generation of the experience of each, embodied in the form of associated groups of nervous elements. And these speculations met with very general approval and exerted a widespread influence.

Thus, just ten years after physical science had launched its heaviest bolt against Animism, in the shape of the law of conservation of energy, the Darwinian theory seemed to undermine its last prop. To the scientific world in general it seemed that Animism was forever dead; and when, in the year 1874, Prof. Tyndall gave to his presidential address before the British Association the double character of an inquest into the death of Animism and a funeral oration over its corpse, the mind of the cultured public was well prepared to bid it a regretful farewell. We have it on the authority of a leading newspaper of that date,[1] that "The Address has been received with a unanimity of commendation that has fairly bewildered those who make it a business to study the drifts and currents of public sentiment."

[1] *The New York Tribune.*

CHAPTER X

CURRENT PHILOSOPHICAL ARGUMENTS AGAINST ANIMISM

BESIDE the weighty arguments against Animism provided by the results of modern physical and biological research, other arguments of a metaphysical or epistemological character, which have long been current, have been presented again and again with great force and liveliness, and still carry great weight with many minds.

Of these, one of the most widely influential is still undoubtedly the objection raised by the Occasionalists to Descartes' teaching. It is inconceivable, it is said, and therefore impossible, that things so utterly unlike as body and soul should act upon one another; that the immaterial inextended soul or thinking substance postulated by Descartes should be capable either of acting upon, or of being acted upon by, the material extended substance of the brain. The development of physical science with its more exact notions of physical causation has strengthened the appeal of this argument; it is therefore still much relied upon, and has been stated again and again in recent years and given a variety of slightly different forms. To all those who accept the scheme of kinetic mechanism as a literal description of the constitution of the physical world, it is most effective when stated in the form that we cannot conceive how consciousness can affect the movements of molecules.[1] One of the best known and authoritative statements of it is that contained in the late Prof. Tyndall's famous Belfast address; others were cited in Chapter VII.

Some philosophers prefer to give to this argument a logical flavour. They say that all our conceptions of physical phenomena are built up on the mechanical type, all involve the notions of extension, of position and of changes of position in space; that we can only conceive of physical processes in this way; and that to regard psychical agencies as affecting physical

[1] See the passage quoted on p. 93 from Romanes' Rede Lecture.

processes is to attempt to combine two systems of ideas that have no relation to one another; that, in short, any such attempt is illegitimate, because the two systems of conceptions have been evolved for dealing with different aspects of experience.

Dr Stout has presented this argument in a way which combines these two rather different formulations of it, without implying the acceptance of the scheme of kinetic mechanism. "The main objection to this view (interaction of soul and body) is that the kind of interaction presupposed is utterly incongruous with the conception of causation on which the whole system of our knowledge both of physical and psychical process is based. It is the function of science to explain how events take place, or, in other words, to make their occurrence intelligible; but this is only possible in so far as we can discover such a connection between cause and effect as will enable us to understand how the effect follows from the cause; or, in other words, we must exhibit cause and effect as parts of one and the same continuous process. To explain is to exhibit a fact as the resultant of its factors. This is the ideal of science, and it is never completely attained. But in so far as it is unattained, our knowledge is felt to be incomplete. Now when we come to the direct connection between a nervous process and a correlated conscious process, we find a complete solution of continuity. The two processes have no common factor. Their connection lies entirely outside of our total knowledge of physical nature on the one hand, and of conscious process on the other."[1]

These may be said to be the modern attenuated forms of Kant's epistemological dictum that all processes of the phenomenal world must be conceived as the movements of bodies and be regarded as strictly subject to mechanical law.

A thoroughly metaphysical objection to the soul is the following:—We have no immediate experience of the soul; the conception is reached by inference only; therefore it is bad metaphysics to assign a higher or greater reality to the soul than to consciousness; for of the latter we have immediate knowledge. Professor Strong, who makes much of this objection in his discussion of the question,[2] supports it with closely allied arguments, which

[1] "Manual of Psychology," chap. iii.
[2] In his book, "Why the Mind has a Body," a lucid and forcible presentation of the argument for the position designated on a later page (chap. xi.) Psychical Monism.

may best be given in his own words. "But the hypothesis of a soul involves a second difficulty equally great, in regard to the nature to be ascribed to it if assumed. What could the soul itself, apart from consciousness, be like? It has been carefully distinguished from and opposed to consciousness, therefore it cannot have the latter's luminous nature. We are forced to conceive it as a dark and mysterious source from which consciousness in some unintelligible manner flows. Insensibly we are drawn to picture it by the aid of that illegitimate notion of matter existing with all its materiality apart from consciousness, —in short, as a mind-atom. But, no matter how carefully we define it as immaterial, since we contrast it in nature with consciousness, the origin of the latter out of it is as irrational, as much "the birth of a new nature," as its origin out of matter. Thus the nature of the Soul in itself is as unassignable as our knowledge of it is inexplicable." Other writers who urge this argument hide its purely metaphysical nature under the disguise of an *argumentum ad hominem*; they say that to posit a soul is but a disguised Materialism; they assert that, describe it how we may, the soul remains essentially of the same nature as our naïve conception of matter, that the two conceptions arose from, and owe their survival to, the same weakness of the human intellect. Professor Strong goes on to say — "Finally the phenomena-transcending assumption that occasions these difficulties is irreconcilable with the fact that our existence is something of which we are immediately aware. For the existence of consciousness is our existence. If the Soul should continue but consciousness cease, we should be as good as non-existent; whereas, if the Soul should be annihilated but consciousness still go on, we should exist as truly as now. Thus our existence is bound up with that of consciousness, not with that of the Soul; or, as I said before, the existence of consciousness is our existence."[1]

It only remains to point out that the almost universal rejection of Animism by the learned world of our time is due not merely to the force of the arguments provided by the physical and biological sciences, nor to the reasonings of epistemologists and metaphysicians, but to the co-operation of these influences. In earlier ages the materialistic tendencies of science and the spiritualistic affirmations of philosophy had generally arrayed the men of science and the philosophers

[1] *Op. cit.* pp. 199 and 200.

in hostile parties, the opposition between which reached its climax towards the close of the eighteenth century. Then came Kant, who taught the philosophers that they might accept the materialistic conclusions of science without giving up all that they held most dear; and the men of science, on the other hand, mollified by these great concessions to their claims, and finding their most cherished tenets no longer imperilled by the prepossessions of the philosophers, have sought to make what concessions seemed possible, and have found that an agnostic or neutral Monism is at once more defensible and more respectable than the crude Materialism of their predecessors. Hence, in the course of the nineteenth century, these parties have drawn closer together; until now they are united in a common opposition to Animism under the twin banners of Monism and Idealism, each confirmed in its opposition to Animism by the knowledge that it can claim the support of its powerful ally.

In this process of reconcilement of science and philosophy at the cost of Animism, which only in recent years has made rapid progress, a great part has been played by the exposition of a variety of solutions of the pyscho-physical problem; the essential features common to all these are the denial of all psycho-physical interaction, and the insistence that all the processes of the organic world (including all the behaviour of men and animals) are capable in principle of being fully explained in mechanical terms. They may therefore be classed together under the head of automaton theories; though the clumsy expression, anti-animistic theories, would bring out more clearly their common opposition to Animism. In the following chapter I propose to describe the varieties of the automaton theory most widely accepted at the present time.

CHAPTER XI

THE AUTOMATON THEORIES

OF the many authors who have adopted and presented an anti-animistic solution of the psycho-physical problem, each has given to his doctrine some peculiar turn and flavour.[1]

The formulations range from the crudest materialism on the one hand to the grossest subjective idealism on the other, and not a few authors oscillate uncertainly between these two extreme varieties of Monism.

These many formulations fall into four groups, although of some of them it is difficult to say to which group they properly belong. I adopt the plan of describing the type formulation of each of these four groups. The first, generally known as *Epiphenomenalism*, is the modern representative of Materialism. The others are often loosely classed together under the title, theories of *psycho-physical Parallelism*, and many writers signify in general terms their adhesion to "the theory of psycho-physical parallelism," without specifying which of its three distinct forms they approve, and, it may be suspected, without distinguishing between them in their own minds.

Epiphenomenalism

The simplest formulation of the monistic view is of course the materialistic. Perhaps no reputable writer of the present time formulates Materialism so crudely as some of the older writers. Since Hobbes asserted that sensation is nothing but motion, the statement of the materialistic creed has undergone considerable refinement. Even the dictum of Cabanis, that the brain secretes thought as the liver secretes bile, marked a considerable refinement; and a further refinement is implied by the formula that

[1] It is surprising and amusing to anyone who forages among the literature of this subject to find that so many authors have put forward one or other of these allied doctrines, claiming it in all good faith as an original discovery.

consciousness is a function of the brain. But the modern materialist refines still further upon his predecessors. He will not commit himself to the statement that the brain secretes consciousness or thought, and he hesitates to say that the processes of the brain are the cause of sensation or of consciousness of any kind; he prefers to say that the stream of consciousness accompanies the flow of brain-processes, each detail of the stream of consciousness being dependent upon some specific feature or detail of the total brain-process with which it coincides, or to which it immediately succeeds, in time. Huxley did more than anyone else to define and to give currency to this formulation, and to him it owes the name by which it is generally known; for he it was who suggested that the stream of consciousness should be called epiphenomenal, or the epiphenomenon of the brain-process.[1] Now, though some of those who have adopted this view are shy of using the word cause in this connexion, and especially of describing the relation of consciousness to brain-process as one of causal dependence, yet others are less reticent; and it cannot be denied that the doctrine of Epiphenomenalism as widely entertained by scientific men does imply this causal dependence. The doctrine may, then, be stated succinctly in the form of the following propositions:—(1) The universe is a system of forces, or of matter and energy, in which every event or process is completely determined or caused by antecedent physical process according to the laws of mechanism (the bodies and brains of all organisms, including those of men not excepted). (2) Certain complex physico-chemical processes, taking place in those very highly specialized collocations of matter which we call brains, produce or cause (in their own right, as it were) all that we call consciousness, all sensation and imagery, all feeling, emotion, thought and sense of effort, or other mode of consciousness; that is to say, every feature or element of the content of the consciousness of any organism is caused by some immediately preceding physical or chemical change occurring in the brain of that organism, and all that we call psychical process is merely the successive and momentary appearance of new elements in the stream of consciousness, each new element being called into existence by a corresponding process in the brain, and ceasing to exist when that process comes to an end.

[1] Dr Shadworth Hodgson is perhaps the most thorough and consistent exponent of this view among contemporary writers.

According to this doctrine, then, there is no true psychical activity; all psychical existence is consciousness only, and consciousness consists of a stream of fragments or elements of consciousness, appearing simultaneously or successively, merely subsisting for a moment and then disappearing, without in any way influencing one another and without reacting in any way upon the brain-processes by which they are produced; the causal sequence and all true activity and effectiveness belong to the brain-processes. The relation of consciousness is one of dependence without reciprocity of influence. The consciousness of any moment is a passive conjunction of "epiphenomenal" elements. Huxley and others have illustrated this doctrine by likening this stream of epiphenomenal elements to the shadows cast by the moving parts of a machine, or to the noise fortuitously produced by them—the creaking of the wheels. Perhaps a better simile would be the electrical disturbances that always are incidental to the strains and frictions of the working of a machine.

Epiphenomenalism may be illustrated and fixed in the mind by help of the diagram (Fig. 1),

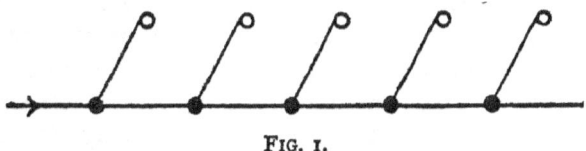

FIG. 1.

or, less inadequately but less simply, by the second diagram (Fig. 2).

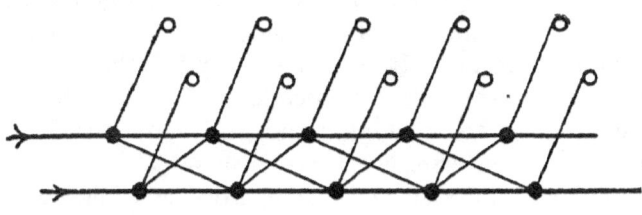

FIG. 2.

In these, as in the following diagrams, physical processes of the brain are indicated by the black discs below; the circles above stand for elements of the stream of consciousness; causal links are indicated by the lines, and the time-direction by the arrowheads. The diagram thus indicates the causal network connecting the physical processes of the brain, and the causal dependence of each element of consciousness upon some one of the brain-processes.

This doctrine is very widely held among men of science at the present time, especially perhaps among the physiologists; for the facts with which they are most familiar, those which seem to indicate the dependence of all mental process upon the material brain-processes, are those which incline the mind most strongly towards this view. Although this doctrine escapes some of the most obvious crudities of the older Materialism, it must be classed as materialistic; for it gives the primacy to matter. Material collocations and their forces are held to be the real and effective agents in the production of all change and process. The material universe is held to have existed throughout an indefinitely long time, and to have undergone an immensely prolonged evolutionary process of a purely mechanical nature, as described by Herbert Spencer; which process has resulted at a certain point of time in the production of living organisms, through the increasing complexity of the atomic structure of certain molecules. In these organisms further evolution of the same kind has resulted in a further increase of complexity of atomic structure and molecular arrangement; until, when the brains of some organisms attained a certain degree of this complexity of atomic and molecular structure, their physico-chemical processes began to be accompanied by consciousness. Consciousness, or mind, was thus called into being for the first time in the history of the universe; which consciousness continued to increase in complexity as brains grew larger and more complex and more highly integrated, and has attained its greatest richness and complexity in the case of the large and very complex brain of the human species. It is further implied that, if and when these very highly specialized collocations of matter which we call brains shall cease to exist, all mind and consciousness will disappear from the universe.

The material universe is thus regarded as rolling on through the ages according to eternally fixed mechanical principles, and as producing now and again, on one or more of the stellar bodies on which brains happen to be evolved, little flecks of consciousness, which flash out like sparks of light, flicker for a moment and disappear, coming and going without affecting in the slightest degree the secular evolution and dissolution of material systems.

There are no special arguments advanced in favour of this view, beyond all those objections to Animism which we have noticed. It is the only alternative to Animism open to the crude realist, who believes the physical world to consist of matter such as we perceive or as physical science describes.

An interesting variation of this doctrine has been proposed a few years ago by Professor W. Ostwald,[1] who claims that his suggested modification would remove it from the category of Materialism. The suggestion is bound up with his attempt to show that the conception of matter is a false and improper, because useless, hypothesis, and that we may profitably do away with it altogether and replace it by the conception of energy. Energy, according to this doctrine of "Energetics," is the only enduring reality; it is capable of assuming, or transforming itself into, many different modes or species; and of these species consciousness or psychical energy is one among the rest. All mental process is thus conceived as the interplay of psychical energy with other species of energy. It seems possible that this suggestion might be developed in a way not inconsistent with Animism;[2] but as presented by its author it would seem to be very closely allied to Epiphenomenalism. It may be illustrated by developing the simile in which we likened the consciousness that accompanies the brain-processes to the electrical disturbances that accompany the strains and frictions incidental to the working of a machine. Just as man-made machines continued through long ages to develop incidentally feeble electrical disturbances which played no effective part, so through long ages natural mechanisms developed incidentally feeble psychical energies which played no effective part. And, just as man evolved machines (namely dynamos) in which, by the special arrangement of the parts, the electrical energy generated became much greater in quantity and was given an essential and dominant role in the working of the system, so certain natural mechanisms (namely organisms), through the evolution of brains, became capable of generating psychical energy in larger quantity; which energy, with each further evolution of the brain, has played a more important part in the working of the whole organism.

[1] "Vorlesungen über Naturphilosophie," Leipzig, 1902.
[2] This development (if I rightly comprehend them) seems to be attempted by several Russian authors, especially Grot, Krainsky, and Bechterew. (See "Psyche und Leben," W. Bechterew, Wiesbaden, 1901.)

Psycho-physical Parallelism

The expression, psycho-physical parallelism, is conveniently used in a loose way to denote all the doctrines that deny psycho-physical interaction, but in this section I am concerned only with that one to which in strictness the designation should be confined.

According to this view physical and psychical processes are equally real; but there is no causal relation between psychical and physical processes; the two series of events, the psychical processes of any mind and the physical processes of the brain with which they are associated, merely accompany one another in time; their relation is one of simple concomitance only; the two series of events merely run parallel to one another in time, as two railway trains running side by side on a double track, or two rays of light projected towards the same infinitely distant point, run parallel with one another in time and space. Within each series the law of causation holds good, the successive steps being related to the preceding and succeeding steps as effects and

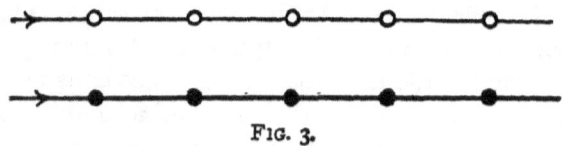

FIG. 3.

causes; but no causal links stretch across from one series to the other. The diagrams illustrate this view, the one (Fig. 3) in the

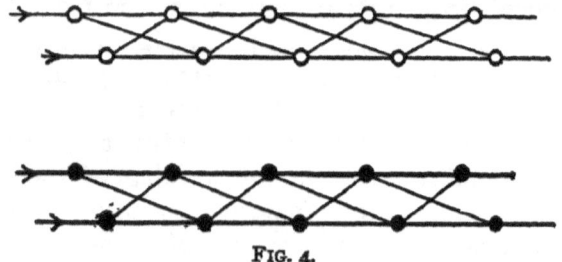

FIG. 4.

simplest possible manner, the other (Fig. 4) rather less inadequately. In the latter figure the clear circles are supposed to lie in one plane at right angles to the plane of the paper, the black circles in another.

This doctrine is held in either of two forms, restricted or universal parallelism. In the former case, brain-processes alone of all physical processes are supposed to be accompanied by psychical events corresponding to them point for point in this mysterious fashion. In the latter case it is assumed that all physical processes alike, those of the inorganic realm no less than those of brains, have their psychical concomitants. This doctrine of parallelism without interaction was, as we have seen, suggested by Leibnitz; but it may be and is held without accepting the doctrine or pre-established harmony by means of which Leibnitz sought to make it intelligible. It may be, and in fact usually is, held only as a working hypothesis or as a heuristic principle making no claim to metaphysical validity.

Those who are not content with the bare affirmation of temporal concomitance of brain-process and consciousness, and who, while denying all psycho-physical interaction, seek to make their relation intelligible, find themselves compelled to adopt the doctrine of the identity of mind and body in one or other of the two forms in which it is current. Both of these necessarily claim to embody metaphysical or ontological truth, i.e. to give us some account of the nature of real being, or at least to make certain assertions in regard to it.

Phenomenalistic Parallelism (Identity-Hypothesis A)

Under this heading we may put together the closely allied formulations of the psycho-physical relation suggested by Spinoza and by Kant respectively; for both regarded mind and body as but two aspects of one reality; Spinoza's doctrine is more properly called "the two-aspect view"; Kant's, "phenomenalistic parallelism." The diagram (Fig. 5) may serve to illustrate both

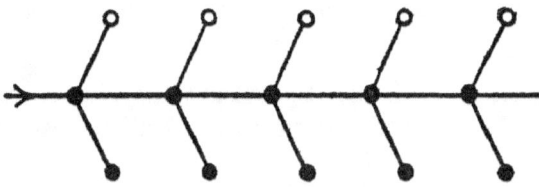

FIG. 5.

varieties. As the diagram implies, the causal links belong wholly to the unknown series of real processes which appear to us under the two aspects, the physical and the psychical, although both series of appearances will seem to be causally linked, just as one shadow may seem to draw another shadow after it. This form of the identity-hypothesis thus implies the metaphysical doctrine known as realistic Monism. It asserts that reality or real being, of which mind and body are appearances only, is not immediately given to or known by us. This underlying reality may be regarded as an unknown and unknowable X. This was the teaching of Herbert Spencer, as also of Kant, who declared that it is "weder Materie noch ein denkend Wesen."[1] But those who, on other grounds, adopt a pantheistic metaphysic will naturally follow Spinoza in affirming that this real being is God.

Psychical Monism (Identity-Hypothesis B)

The alternative formulation of the identity-hypothesis runs as follows:—Consciousness is the only reality, and the consciousness of each of us partakes of this real nature; all that each man calls matter or the physical world is but the form under which consciousness other than his own is manifested to him, so that, if I could observe the processes of your brain while you are thinking, I should be observing the phenomenal manifestation of your consciousness. According to this doctrine, then, the causal efficiency is wholly confined to the psychical series; and matter and its processes (all that we call the physical world or Nature) are but, as it were, the shadows thrown by thought. It is thus the converse of Epiphenomenalism, which regards thought as the shadow thrown by matter. It may be illustrated by the diagram (Fig. 6).

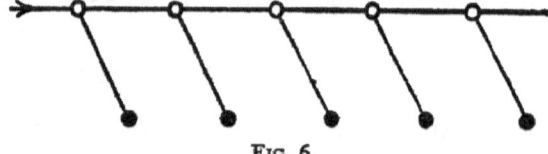

FIG. 6.

This form of the identity-hypothesis implies a metaphysical doctrine which is usually designated idealistic Monism, but is better described as realistic or objective psychical Monism. It must not be confused with subjective Idealism or Solipsism; this also is a psychical Monism, for it maintains that my thought or consciousness alone exists. But, while the latter denies the existence of the physical world and of other minds than my own (except as ideas of my own mind), the former maintains the

[1] See p. 77.

objective existence both of the things which appear to me as composing the physical world and of other minds like my own, while holding that they are all of the same nature, namely consciousness. It will be convenient to designate it simply "Psychical Monism." A diagram illustrating Solipsism on the plan of the foregoing diagrams may help to make clear the difference between these two forms of psychical Monism. It would take the form of figure 7, though the links joining the

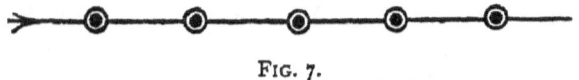

FIG. 7.

circles would not stand for causal links, since Solipsism necessarily denies validity to the principle of causation.

In order to complete the series of diagrams illustrating the various psycho-physical doctrines which reject Animism, I add

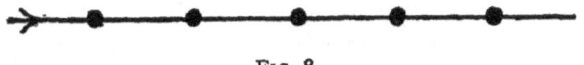

FIG. 8.

figure 8; this may stand for the crude Materialism which asserts that consciousness is matter or the movement of matter.

Of all the anti-animistic answers to the psycho-physical problem this second form of the identity-hypothesis is the one which is most widely accepted at the present time and which has been the most thoroughly elaborated. It is therefore important that it should be clearly grasped, and I restate it in the words of the late Professor Paulsen, one of its most enlightened and thoroughgoing advocates of recent years. "Alle körperliche Wirklichkeit ist durchaus und überall Hinweisung auf eine Innenwelt, die der verwandt ist, die wir in uns selber erleben. Und allerdings werden wir nun sagen: in der Innenwelt, die uns freilich nur an einem Punkt unmittelbar gegeben ist, im Selbstbewusstsein, darüber hinaus erreichen wir sie nur durch stets unsichere Interpretation und jenseits der Tierwelt nur durch schematisierende Konstruktion, und durch idealisirende Symbolik; in der Innenwelt offenbart sich die Natur des Wirklichen, wie es an und für sich ist: die Körperwelt ist im Grunde nur eine zufällige Ansicht, eine unadäquate Darstellung der Wirklichkeit in unserer Sinnlichkeit."[1] And again, "Das Dasein der Seele besteht in ihrem Leben, in der

[1] "Einleitung in die Philosophie," p. 126, twelfth edition, 1904.

Einheit aufeinander bezogener psychischer Vorgänge; nehmen wir diese weg, so bleibt kein Rückstand, Bewusstseinsvorgänge sind das an und für sich Wirkliche, sie bedürfen nicht eines anderen, eines Seelensubstantiale, das ihnen erst zur Wirklichkeit helfen oder sie in der Wirklichkeit halten und tragen müsste; so etwas gibt es überhaupt nicht."[1] "Seele ist die auf nicht weiter sagbare Weise zur Einheit verbundene Vielheit innerer Erlebnisse." This is the conception of "the actual soul" which we are told on all hands must replace that of "the substantial soul."[2]

More recently, Prof. C. A. Strong, in a book bearing the significant title "Why the Mind has a Body," has presented this form of the identity-hypothesis and the metaphysical argument for it with admirable force and clearness. He demands that metaphysic should give some clear account of the nature of the realities it recognizes; and defining a reality as "something that exists of itself and in its own right, and not merely as a modification of something else," he maintains that consciousness, the only mode of being of which we have immediate knowledge, has the best possible claim to be regarded as real being or reality.[3] Then, having demonstrated the necessity of the assumption of things-in-themselves, of which physical objects are the phenomena or appearances to us; he asks—Why should we postulate two modes of real being, namely these things-in-themselves and consciousness? Why not make the simplest possible assumption and regard them as identical? "No solution of the problem, in fact, could be simpler or more economical. We have two things, the brain-process and consciousness, and the question is as to their relation. The brain-process is a phenomenon, and every phenomenon symbolizes a reality, and consciousness is a reality. Therefore, conclude the psycho-physical materialists and monists (i.e. those who accept Epiphenomenalism or identity-hypothesis A), the brain-process symbolizes a reality of which consciousness is the manifestation or on which it is dependent. They actually go out of their way to avoid the solution! For, if the reality symbolized by the brain-process is distinct from consciousness, then the two are loosely and externally attached as we commonly conceive brain and mind to be attached, and the problem is simply transferred to another sphere and perpetuated. Whereas,

---

[1] *Op. cit.*, p. 384.
[2] "Aktualitätsbegriff der Seele," or "Die aktuelle Seele," in the language of Wundt.   [3] P. 194.

if the reality symbolized by the brain-process is consciousness itself, their connexion is explained and the problem solved. Indeed, this is the only conceivable solution of a problem which all other hypotheses necessarily perpetuate. On every other hypothesis, the duality of mind and body is either a duality of existences or a duality of disparate phenomena; in either case their connexion is a new fact, not provided for in their nature, and consequently inexplicable. On this hypothesis, the duality is that of a reality and its phenomenon; this, for believers in things-in-themselves, is a *vera relatio*, and the connexion is therefore explained by being subsumed under the relation of phenomenon and thing-in-itself."[1]

Professor Strong supports this metaphysical argument for this form of the monistic doctrine as follows: we have an ineradicable conviction that our consciousness is a real factor in the course of things, and a review of the evolution of mind in the animal world justifies this conviction of the efficiency of consciousness. Now Psychical Monism (the identity-hypothesis B) does no violence to this well-based belief; for in a world where all is consciousness and all causal action is of consciousness on consciousness, our own consciousness finds a natural sphere of influence. The other monistic doctrines on the other hand ask us to reject as a delusion our belief in the effective agency of our consciousness.

Among the clearest statements of this doctrine is that of the late Prof. W. K. Clifford in his essay entitled " On the Nature of Things-in-themselves."[2] He asserted that " consciousness is made up of elementary feelings grouped together in various ways "; that " the elementary feeling is a thing-in-itself "; that " consciousness is a complex of ejective facts,—of elementary feelings, or rather of those remoter elements which cannot even be felt, but of which the simplest feeling is built up "; and, proposing to give to these remoter elements of which the simplest feeling is built up the name mind-stuff, he asserted that " mind-stuff is the reality which we perceive as matter " and that " the universe consists entirely of mind-stuff." He wrote further that " a moving molecule of inorganic matter does not possess mind or consciousness, but it possesses *a small piece of mind-stuff.*" This should have run—the molecule, or what we conceive as a molecule, *is* a small piece of

[1] " Why the Mind has a Body," chap. xv.
[2] " Lectures and Essays," vol. ii.

mind-stuff. Lastly it must be noted that with complete consistency Clifford asserted that these eject-elements, these small pieces of mind-stuff "are connected together in their sequence and coexistence by counterparts of the physical laws of matter"; that is to say, what we call laws of matter are the laws of mind-stuff.

Clifford ascribed the first distinct enunciation of this doctrine to Prof. Wundt, but it appears in the writings of Wundt's master, G. T. Fechner. We owe to him, I believe, the first statement and the most elaborate defence of it.

The language in which Fechner sets forth his view is not always strictly consistent; it seems sometimes to imply psychophysical parallelism in the strict sense defined on page 131, sometimes the first, and sometimes the second, form of the identity-hypothesis; and it may be doubted whether he always distinguished clearly between these three formulations. But, as it was Fechner who, by the publication of his celebrated treatise "Elemente der Psycho-physik,"[1] brought the identity-hypothesis into fashion in the scientific world, I quote from that work the following passage in which he illustrates his view. "When anyone stands inside a sphere[2] its convex side is for him quite hidden by the concave surface; conversely, when he stands outside, the concave surface is hidden by the convex. Both sides belong together as inseparably as the psychical and the bodily sides of a human being, and these also may by way of simile (*vergleichsweise*) be regarded as inner and outer sides; but it is just as impossible to see both sides of a circle from a standpoint in the plane of the circle, as to see these two sides of humanity from a standpoint in the plane of human existence."[3]

Again, he wrote—"The solar system seen from the sun presents an aspect quite other than that which it presents when viewed from the earth. There it appears as the Copernican, here as the Ptolemaic world-system. And for all time it will remain impossible for one observer to see both systems at the same time, although both belong inseparably together, and, just like the concave and the convex sides of a circle, they are at bottom only two different modes of appearance of the same thing seen from different standpoints;"[4] and yet again—"What appears to you,

[1] Leipsic, 1860.
[2] The word used is *Kreis*, but a sphere seems to be implied by the first sentence.
[3] "Elemente der Psycho-physik," vol. i., Introduction.
[4] *Loc. cit.*

who yourself are spirit, when at the inner standpoint as spirit, appears from the outer standpoint as the bodily substratum of this spirit."[1]

The first and second passages may seem to imply phenomenalistic Parallelism (identity-hypothesis A); the last, on the other hand, would rather imply Psychical Monism (identity-hypothesis B); and the passage following upon the last sentence makes it clear that this was the view Fechner adopted and defended with such admirable industry and ingenuity. It runs—
"The difference of standpoint is whether one thinks with one's brain or looks into the brain of another thinker. The appearances are then quite different; but the standpoints are very different, there an inner, here an outer standpoint; and they are indescribably more different than in the foregoing example (i.e. the circle and the solar system), and just for that reason the difference of the modes of appearance is indescribably greater. For the double mode of appearance of the circle, or of the solar system, is after all only obtained from two different outer standpoints over against it; at the centre of the circle, or on the sun, the observer remains outside the line of the circle, or outside the planets. But the appearance of the spirit to itself is obtained from a truly inner standpoint of that underlying being over against itself, namely the standpoint of coincidence with itself, while the appearance of the bodily self is obtained from a standpoint truly external to it, namely, one which does not coincide with it."[2]

"Therefore no spirit perceives immediately another spirit, although one might suppose that it should most easily apprehend a being of like nature with itself; it perceives, in so far as the other does not coincide with it, only the bodily appearance of that other. Therefore no spirit can in any way become aware of another save by the aid of its corporeality; for what of the spirit appears outwardly is just its bodily mode of appearance."[3]

Fechner worked for the establishment of his view along two very different lines. On the one hand he sought an exact empirical foundation for it by means of laborious psycho-physical experiment, on the other, he appealed to the æsthetic side of human nature. We may briefly notice these two main lines of his argument. Fechner's view necessarily involves the assumption that all the objects and events composing the physical world are, like the processes of the cortex of our brains, the outward

[1] *Loc. cit.*   [2] *Loc. cit.*   [3] *Loc. cit.*

appearances of what is really consciousness or consciousnesses. For to set certain of the processes of the brain apart from all other physical processes, attributing to them alone this peculiar relation to consciousness, would be but to deepen the mystery of the psycho-physical relation. Fechner, far from shrinking from this necessary implication, revelled in it; and his two chief lines of endeavour were, on the one hand to provide some empirical evidence of the psychical nature of all that we call physical processes, and on the other to show how pleasing and inspiring the world becomes when thus regarded.

The former line he pursued in the following way. His friend, E. H. Weber, had formulated on the basis of experiment the empirical generalization know as Weber's law. This law may be briefly expounded as follows: the application of a physical stimulus to a sense-organ evokes a sensation of a certain intensity; and, if a second stimulus of greater intensity is then applied, the subject experiences a sensation of greater intensity, provided the increase of the stimulus is not too small. Now it is possible to determine with some exactitude the least increment of stimulus-intensity which will suffice to evoke a sensation just perceptibly more intense than that evoked by the weaker stimulus. Weber's experiments showed that, in the case of several of the senses, the amount by which the intensity of a stimulus must be increased in order to evoke such a just perceptibly more intense sensation is not a constant quantity, but that it varies with the intensity of the stimulus, being always a certain fraction of the total value of the stimulus; for example, in the case of vision, the intensity of the light stimulating the retina must be increased by about one per cent. of its total value, in order to evoke a just perceptibly more intense sensation.

Fechner saw in this generalization the indication of a definite mathematical relation between physical and psychical magnitudes, between the magnitude of a sensation and that of its phenomenon, the brain-process. He first strove to render the empirical basis of this generalization more exact and to explain away the apparent exceptions to it; and then he sought to deduce from it a more definite mathematical statement of the relation.

The gist of his argument was this: Just perceptible increments of sensation-intensity are equal increments; therefore we may state Weber's law more generally thus—Equal increments of sensation-intensity are determined by increments of stimulus-intensity whose value is in each case a certain fraction or percentage of the total value of the stimulus. Now let this percentage be made equal to one hundred per cent.; that is, let the intensity of the stimulus be increased by a series of steps such that the value of the stimulus at each step is double that of the stimulus of the preceding step; then from our empirical law we may deduce that the sensations evoked by this series of stimuli will differ in intensity by equal amounts. That is to say the sensation-intensities will form a series of values in arithmetical progression, while the corresponding stimulus-values will form a series in geometrical progression. This inference may be stated in the form of geometrical curves. Construct two curves, Sn and St, representing the two series of intensities, the sensation-intensities and the stimulus-intensities respectively, in the following way:—

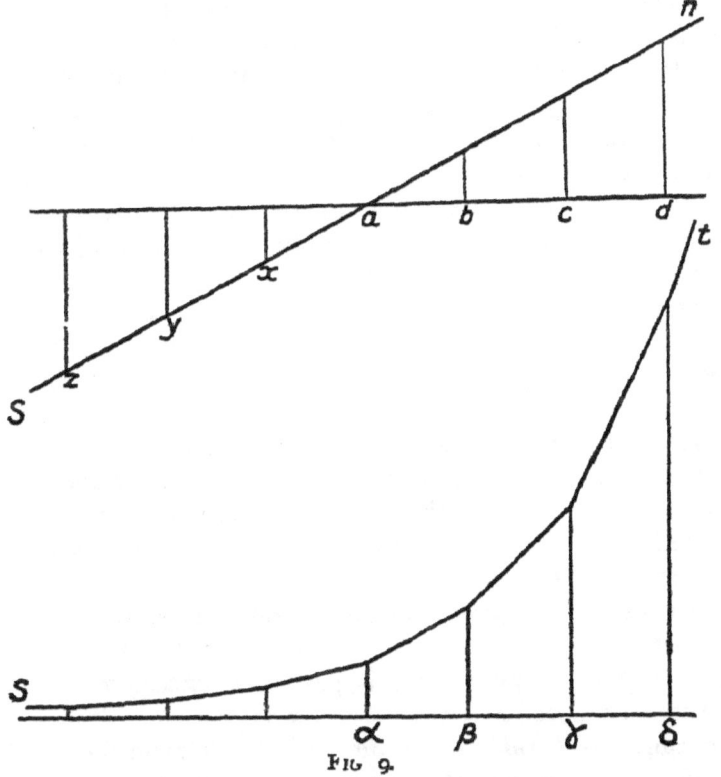

Fig 9.

The ordinates of Sn (a, b, c, d, e) represent the values of the sensation-intensities, those of St the values of the corresponding stimulus-intensities $\alpha, \beta, \gamma, \delta, \epsilon$.

Now, if we apply to any sense organ the slightest possible stimulation we find that it evokes no perceptible sensation, and that the intensity of the stimulus must be raised to a certain definite value, before it suffices to evoke a just perceptible sensation. Fechner argued that the stimuli which are too feeble to evoke perceptible sensations cannot be supposed to produce no effect at all; and that they must rather be supposed to produce imperceptible sensations, or, as he preferred to say, sensations which do not rise above the threshold of consciousness. And he saw in the definite mathematical relation of the two series of intensities, represented by the two curves, a proof of the reality of these sensations below the threshold of consciousness. For, let a be a stimulus of such intensity that it just suffices to evoke the sensation a of just perceptible intensity. Then the horizontal line passing through a represents the threshold of consciousness; whereas the ordinate expressing the intensity of stimulus a rises to a definite height above the base line representing zero of stimulus intensity. Now the two curves having definite mathematical properties may be produced in both directions, each according to its own law. When we thus produce the curves, we find that, while the curve St (representing the stimulus-intensities) approaches the base line asymptotically, Sn (representing the sensation-intensities) sinks at once below the line representing the threshold of consciousness. The part of the curve St between a and the base line, which represents a series of subliminal stimuli, implies the corresponding part of the curve Sn, *i.e.*, the part below the line which represents the threshold of consciousness. Here, said Fechner, we have proof that a series of sensations, x, y, z, which remain below the threshold of consciousness, is evoked by the series of subliminal stimuli. This was the line of argument developed at length by Fechner in the "Elemente der Psycho-physik."

The æsthetic argument or persuasion was set forth at great length in several works.[1] Professor James has recently published[2] a vivid summary of this part of Fechner's work, and I may therefore describe it in a very few words.

Fechner, as I said above, did not shrink from the corollary implied by his psycho-physical doctrine, the corollary that all the universe consists of consciousness; rather he gloried in it,

---

[1] "Die Seelenfrage," "Zendavesta," "Nana."
[2] "A Pluralistic Universe," chap. iv.

regarding it as the chief claim of his view to acceptance. He called this peculiar view of the constitution of the world, the "day-view" of Nature, and favourably contrasted this view, that all Nature enjoys or is consciousness, with the view, prevalent in the scientific world, that the inorganic part of Nature is inert and unconscious, the "night-view" as he called it. He held up his day-view as revealing a Nature infinitely more pleasing and satisfying to our contemplation than the Nature of the night-view; he drew a glowing picture of all Nature rejoicing together, delighting in the sense of its own beauty and orderliness; he even regarded each planet and star as enjoying an individual consciousness and glowing with joyful pride as it rolls on its majestic way through space. For, just as he regarded the individual consciousness of each man as in some sense a sum or aggregate of the feebler poorer consciousnesses of the vital units, the cells, of which his body is composed, and as in turn entering as a component into the wider richer consciousness of the whole human race; so he regarded the consciousness of each stellar body as being in a similar way the mighty stream of consciousness formed by the flowing together of the consciousnesses of all its constituent parts, both organic and inorganic, human and infrahuman, and as in turn entering into a still mightier stream, the universal consciousness. How much more satisfying, said Fechner, is the contemplation of the universe when so conceived, than when we look upon it as consisting of immense systems of lifeless matter, forming a stage on which men spend their brief moments of conscious life, oppressed by the dreary vastness of the spaces, times, and forces that compass them about!

We have seen that the doctrine or postulate of the continuity of evolution of the organic and inorganic worlds is used as an argument against Animism. The same postulate is used in a rather different way as the basis of a special argument in favour of the identity-hypothesis in one or other of its two forms, and by some authors, notably by Tyndall[1] and by Professor Lloyd Morgan,[2] this argument is regarded as of the greatest weight. It runs thus:—The evolution of organic life has been continuous from the lowliest unicellular form up to man; at no point is there

[1] The Belfast Address to British the Association, 1874.
[2] "Introduction to Comparative Psychology," chap. xviii.

an absolute break in the series, or any indication of the incoming of mind as a new factor in the evolutionary process. Now we have evidence that the earth has existed in isolation (so far as any material continuity is concerned) from all other parts of the material universe, since a date long preceding that at which the existence of organic matter upon it became possible; for such matter cannot exist at high temperatures and could only begin to exist when the crust was pretty well cooled down. Hence organic matter must be presumed to have been evolved from inorganic matter by a continuous and gradual process; hence what we call life and mind or soul or consciousness[1] must have been present in some very lowly forms in the inorganic matter from which organic matter was evolved, and therefore in all inorganic matter; that is to say, all matter must be regarded as in some sense and degree conscious or endowed with psychical life; and, since inorganic matter is wholly subject to the strictly mechanical laws in spite of its consciousness, so organic matter must be likewise subject to the strictly mechanical principles, and psychical life or process accompanying the physical processes of matter, must be devoid of all influence on the physical processes —a conclusion which is compatible only with one or other of the parallelistic theories, and not at all with interaction theories.

This reasoning from the continuity of the evolution of the animal kingdom from non-living matter is supplemented by the following argument, which I give in the form in which it was presented by F. A. Lange in a well-known passage of his "History of Materialism." Let a pair of mice be shut up in a room with a sack of flour and allowed to breed undisturbed. After a few months the whole of the flour has disappeared, the greater part of its substance having been converted into the bodies of a swarm of mice. Whatever consciousness or psychical capacity may be enjoyed by the mice must then, it is said, have been present in some form in the flour.

In addition to the special arguments in favour of the several automaton theories that we have now reviewed, we must notice certain considerations which may be adduced in favour of a monistic solution in general. These considerations are appeals to various motives, various sentiments and prejudices, rather than logical arguments. The motives brought into operation

[1] Infra-consciousness is the term preferred by Prof. Lloyd Morgan, (*loc. cit.*).

by these appeals have played a great part in determining the choice of the monistic theories by so many moderns.

The most important of these motives is probably the desire for a well-rounded, self-consistent, conceptual scheme of the physical world. Now the rejection root and branch of all psycho-physical interaction enables us to entertain such a conceptual scheme; while the adoption of any one of the parallelistic hypotheses enables us to hold it without incurring the reproach of philosophical crudity or absurdity which, as all with few exceptions can see, lies against crude Materialism. The adoption of any one of the monistic hypotheses, then, brings with it all the advantages of a materialistic metaphysic while avoiding its principal drawback. And that is, doubtless, the explanation of the fact that these monistic hypotheses have secured the adhesion of so large a proportion of the students of the natural sciences.

The peculiar advantage of the materialistic scheme of things, to which it chiefly owes its attractiveness, is that its acceptance brings with it a confident sense of intellectual mastery. So long as we can confidently believe that all the events to be reckoned with by science are but the motions of masses, or the transformations of measurable quantities of energy according to exact equations that can be calculated and therefore foretold, the mind feels itself at home and master of what it deals with, and there lies before it the prospect of a continued approach towards a completed power of prediction and control of the future course of events. Under these conditions, the working hypotheses of the natural sciences become confidently held doctrines from which we feel ourselves able to deduce the limits of the possible; and we seem able to rule out from our scheme of the universe all that confused crowd of obscure ideas which, under the names of magic, occultism, and mysticism, have been at war with science, ever since it began to take shape as a system of verifiable ideas inductively established on an empirical basis. Once admit, on the other hand, that psychical influences may interfere with the course of physical nature and—"you don't know where you are," you can no longer serenely affirm that "miracles" do not happen; they may happen at any moment and may falsify the most confident predictions of physical science. Thus the gates are opened to all the floods of Spiritualism and superstition of every kind, which to some gloomy scientists seem to threaten to light up once more the fires of persecution and to drag down our civilization from its hardly-won footing upon the steep path of progress.

Paulsen urges his Psychical Monism upon our acceptance in a rather different way. The function of philosophy, says he, is to mediate between science and religion, to reconcile their teachings and aspirations. Now, the physical scientists will never tolerate the intervention of non-physical agencies in their physical world; they will always assume that every event is determined strictly according to the laws of physical or mechanical causation; that such explanation of all events in the universe without exception is possible, is the fundamental axiom of science.[1] Therefore a reconciliation of science with religion can only be effected by admitting the claim of science to furnish causal explanations of all events in terms of mechanism, while reserving for religion the task of providing an idealistic *interpretation* of the mechanically caused events. "Also: *Alles muss physisch zugehen und erklärt werden*; und: *Alles muss metaphysisch betrachtet und gedeutet werden*. Das ist die Formel, *in der Physiker und Metaphysiker übereinkommen können*."[2] The establishment of the monistic solution of the psycho-physical problem thus becomes the principal task of philosophy; and we ought to welcome and accept this solution, because it allows us as men of science to be rigid materialists, to accept without scruple and without regret the most rigidly materialistic conclusions and tendencies of science, while as philosophers we remain idealists, asserting that all reality is at bottom mental.

Another argument for Parallelism or psycho-physical Monism is found in the desire for a monistic scheme of the universe. Many philosophers seem to experience this desire to conceive the

---

[1] "Darüber täusche man sich nicht: die Naturwissenschaft kann und wird sich von ihrem Wege nicht wieder abbringen lassen, eine *rein physikalische* Erklärung *aller* Naturerscheinungen zu suchen. Es mag tausend Dinge geben, die sie gegenwärtig nicht erklären kann, aber das prinzipielle Axiom, dass es auch für sie eine physische Ursache und also eine naturwissenschaftliche Erklärung gebe, wird sie nicht wieder fahren lassen. Daher wird eine Philosophie, die darauf besteht, gewisse Naturvorgange könnten nicht ohne Rest physisch erklärt werden, sondern machte die Annahme der Wirkung eines metaphysischen Prinzips oder eines supranaturalen Agens notwendig, die Naturwissenschaft zur unversöhnlichen Gegnerin haben. In Frieden kann sie mit ihr nur leben, wenn sie sich der Einmischung in die *kausale* Erklärung der Naturerscheinungen grundsätzlich enthält und die Naturwissenschaft ruhig ihren Weg bis zu Ende gehen lässt" ("Einleitung in die Philosophie," p. 180).

[2] *Op. cit.*, p. 181.

universe as at bottom consisting of only one kind of real being; and not a few claim that this desire is a demand that our intellectual nature inevitably makes, and one that carries with it a guarantee of the validity of the monistic interpretation. Closely connected with this in many minds is the conviction that a universe monistically conceived, that is, conceived as a unitary whole of which all the parts are of one nature, is indefinitely nobler than one consisting of ultimate real beings of diverse natures.

To many, again, it seems that the second form of the identity-hypothesis is preferable to all others, because it is essentially and necessarily an idealistic doctrine; that is to say, because it is one which regards all reality as of the nature of mind: and such a view of the universe seems to them æsthetically superior to, or in some indefinable way nobler than, any scheme which recognizes the real existence of anything not mental in nature. This was the line of persuasion which, as we have seen, Fechner developed at great length.

Least in worth, though not perhaps of least effect, among the influences that have brought about the very general acceptance of Parallelism, is the feeling that such a doctrine derives a certain distinction from being so entirely different from and opposed to the scholastic doctrine and all popular conceptions and common-sense views. For to many minds there is something attractive in any esoteric and difficult doctrine that rises above the reach of the common herd. And this feeling is given the form of an appeal to reason, in the following way: it is pointed out that the doctrine of Animism was originated by the first crude efforts of speculative reason, at a time when man was but a naked savage following a bestial mode of life, knowing little of the laws of nature, ignorant of their harmony and constancy; that it was a monstrous birth begot by fear out of greed; a conception not without its social uses in the earlier stages of social evolution, serving through superstitious fear to discipline man in the control of his cruder impulses; but one which no longer serves any useful purpose, and which is fit only to be set up in the ethnographical museums of primitive customs and beliefs alongside of its monstrous progeny, totemism and magic, witch-craft and polytheism, vitalism and possession, free-will, human immortality and divine retribution, heaven, hell, and the devil, and all the crowd of spectres with which man's wayward and fearful imagination has for so many ages oppressed him, cumbering his progress in true knowledge and in command over the forces of nature.

We have seen now how, in the long course of development of thought, the conception of the soul, which came into the culture tradition of Europe as a heritage from our savage ancestors, has been refined in successive ages, until it has been refined away altogether: how the soul, beginning as a material or quasi-material shadowy duplicate of the body, became divested of its bodily characters; so that it remained a mere spirituous tenuous vapour, diffused equally throughout the body or concentrated more or less in certain of its parts or organs, and somehow playing an essential and dominant role in the life of the body: how the specialization of learning along the biological and psychological lines led to the division of the soul into two souls, one concerned in the governance of the bodily functions, the other the substrate of the intellectual functions, while those organic functions in which the co-operation of mind and body is most strikingly obvious continued to hover uncertainly between the two souls or to demand a third as their substrate: how the two souls became, the one the vital principle of the physiologists, the other the immortal inextended substrate or support of the mental functions: how then the progress of physiology led to the rejection of the vital principle, and how increasing insight into the structure and functions of the nervous system seemed to render superfluous the notion of the teleological agency of the soul and to reduce consciousness to an epiphenomenon: how the development of exact quantitative notions in physical science, first under the form of the scheme of kinetic mechanism, later as dynamic mechanism obeying the law of the conservation of energy, confirmed the physiologists in their rejection of both the vital principle and the soul, by affirming that the physical world constitutes a closed system of causally related processes insusceptible of being influenced by other than physical agencies: how the philosophers discovered that the conceptions of both soul and body are mere inferences from our immediate experience and that neither can be regarded as above suspicion: and how, under the influence of physical and biological science, they have excogitated solutions of the psycho-physical problem that escape the absurdities of Materialism and Subjective Idealism, while claiming to reconcile the materialistic conclusions of modern science with our ineradicable belief in the reality and efficiency of mind, with the principles of the most exacting metaphysic, and even in some degree with the demands of religion. Who then would hesitate to accept the conclusion towards which all branches of science, all those lines of exact research whose results we have noted, seem to drive us irresistibly? Who would seek to deny the universal sway of the laws of mechanism and to subvert the vast and splendid pyramid of modern science to which the monistic interpretation of the psycho-physical problem is the very crown, the glorious consummation which heals the age-long struggle between scientific Materialism and the philosopher's conviction of the reality and primacy of mind? Who would still hanker after that vague elusive notion of the soul, first launched into the stream of thought by the troubled fancy of savage man, while yet he lived like a beast, knowing nought of the wonderful harmonies of nature and seeing in all her motions neither law nor order but only the vengeful caprice of a host of spirits, before which he grovelled muttering spells and incantations? Surely only a fool or a fanatic!

Yet hesitate we must until we shall have critically examined the arguments, drawn from epistemology, from metaphysic, and from the natural sciences, which seem to make Animism untenable, and the special and general arguments advanced in favour of the several monistic interpretations; and until we shall have inquired whether any one of the automaton theories allows us to construct an intelligible and self-consistent account of human personality. This part of our task will occupy us in the following chapters.

CHAPTER XII

EXAMINATION OF THE AUTOMATON-THEORIES AND OF THE SPECIAL ARGUMENTS IN THEIR FAVOUR

IN this chapter I propose to examine in turn the four principal monistic interpretations of the relation of mind to body, to weigh the special arguments advanced in their support, and to point out the special difficulties in the way of each of them. Beside these special difficulties there is a number of empirically-based objections of a more general kind, which may be more suitably dealt with in later chapters under the head of positive arguments in favour of Animism.

Epiphenomenalism

To some persons it seems sufficient for the refutation of Epiphenomenalism to assert the absurdity of the supposition that the existence of mind should be dependent on that of matter, or that mind and consciousness should have been generated by the mere increase in complexity of molecular organization of certain forms of inanimate matter; for, they say, it is only through and by mind that matter can be known. But this assertion does not confute the epiphenomenalist. He may reply—But suppose for a moment that my account of the case is the true one, that matter really did precede mind, did generate it in the course of the evolution of material processes of ever greater complexity; then, he might say, your attitude might still be just what it is now; mind, once evolved and once having learnt to reflect upon itself and its relation to matter, would inevitably use just your arguments; it would claim a primacy over matter, the primacy of the knower over the known, and in the pride of self-consciousness would despise its parent, matter, and would incline to assert its independence of it. In face of this reply a repeated assertion of the conviction of the primacy of mind would have little effect.

Nor will it suffice to assert that the human mind will never rest satisfied with this account of itself as a mere by-product of matter and its evolutions, but will always continue to seek some position that will do less outrage to the reality of experience.

Epiphenomenalism must be met in a different way, namely, by pointing out that just those considerations which are held to make the doctrine of psycho-physical interaction impossible tell equally strongly against it, while the motives which make for the parallelistic doctrines find no satisfaction in it; that, in fact, it combines the principal weaknesses of both the parallelist and the interaction doctrines, while it lacks the principal advantages of either. Thus, the biological argument from continuity of evolution makes against Epiphenomenalism; for the appearance of consciousness at some undefined point in the course of the evolution of the animal kingdom, as postulated by it, constitutes a distinct breach of continuity. The argument from inconceivability also makes against Epiphenomenalism more strongly than against Animism; for the notion that material processes should generate consciousness out of nothing is certainly a more difficult conception than that of the interaction of soul and body. Again, Epiphenomenalism, though it may perhaps be consistent with the law of the conservation of energy, offends against a law that has a much stronger claim to universality, namely the law of causation itself; for it assumes that a physical process, say a molecular movement in the brain, causes a sensation, but does so without the cause passing over in any degree into the effect, without the cause spending itself in any degree in the production of the effect, namely, the sensation. It thus saves the law of conservation of energy at the expense of the law of causation; and such similes as those used by Huxley to illustrate his exposition and offered by him as examples of the production by mechanism of effects that are indifferent to its workings—the shadow thrown by the wheel, the whistling of the locomotive engine and so on—all such similes are misleading and fallacious if regarded as analogies; for in every case the production of the effect, even though it be but a shadow or a reflection, leaves the machine and its processes other than they would have been if the effect had not been produced.

Again, the identity-hypothesis claims with some show of reason to reconcile the teachings of science and philosophy; but Epiphenomenalism, in assigning to mind an altogether insignificant, dependent, and ineffective position in the scheme of the universe, sets itself in direct opposition to the overwhelmingly large majority of philosophers of all times and of all races.

It is for these reasons that Epiphenomenalism has been accepted by few or none of those who have seriously tried to think out the psycho-physical problem; and it is, I hope, unnecessary to say more in order to convince any reader that, if the balance of argument seems to him to incline against Animism, he must not prefer Epiphenomenalism.

Before finally dismissing Epiphenomenalism, I must remark upon the illegitimate attempt made by some of its defenders to redeem it from the charge of Materialism. After assuring us that science has proved the absolute dependence of all mind on the material processes of animal organisms, and that the evolution of these material organisms was but a trifling incident in the life of a universe which consists only of matter and physical energy in eternal agitation; they turn round upon matter and ask—But what is this matter? You charge me with being a materialist, but I know as well as you that matter is only a figment of my imagination, that in seeing, touching, tasting, I perceive only certain states of my own consciousness, that material phenomena are but my own perceptions or ideas. Have I not, therefore, as good a right to call myself an idealist as you, or Bishop Berkeley, or any man? Now, this is Solipsism or Subjective Idealism pure and simple; it is the denial of all existence save one's own consciousness; and, in attempting to save himself in this way from the absurdity of Materialism, the epiphenomenalist does but take upon himself the additional absurdity of Solipsism, and crowns himself with the final absurdity of professing adherence to both of the two most violently opposed metaphysical dogmas. Yet absurd as this procedure is, it is not unnecessary to utter a warning against it, for no less a writer than T. H. Huxley was guilty of it, as also, to the best of my judgment, the admirable historian of Materialism, F. A. Lange. "The Idealist," he wrote, "can and must in fact in natural science everywhere, apply the same conceptions and methods as the Materialists; but what to the latter is definitive truth, is to the Idealist only the necessary result of our organization."[1] Lange, having accepted whole-heartedly the teaching of Materialism that mind is evolved from, and wholly dependent upon, matter, goes on to tell us, in the language

[1] *Op. cit.*

of a glowing enthusiasm for humanity which commands our sympathy, that the human mind creates for itself a world of ideals in which it finds its true home—that man's spirit must soar above the vulgar real into the realm of ideas which are symbols of the Unknowable Absolute. It is true that Lange seems in some passages to accept Kant's notion of the thing-in-itself; but, as Professor Höffding says, he wavers between the acceptance and the rejection of it, and on the whole his language justifies the assertion that for him matter is the only reality and the ideal is the unreal. Lange was thus an idealist only in the sense in which any materialist may be an idealist, namely, that he entertained ideals and, in splendid defiance of logical consistency, strove to make them real.

Psycho-physical Parallelism

The doctrine that psychical processes and physical processes run parallel with one another without any causal relation is not seriously maintained save in the form of universal parallelism of the physical and the psychical. To assume that of all physical processes just certain brain-processes alone are accompanied by conscious concomitants, would leave the relation too obviously mysterious; the coming into being of the sensation, at the moment of the occurrence of a brain-process of a certain quality, would be too decidedly miraculous. If we accept the principle of causation at all, we must assume that the rise of a sensation in consciousness is in some sense the effect of some cause. And, if we do not accept the principle of causation, we have no ground for believing in the existence of the brain-process, save as one's own thought of it; and it then would be absurd to speak of parallelism, for my sensations do not run parallel with, are not temporal concomitants of, my thoughts of my brain-processes.

This insuperable objection to partial Parallelism is avoided by universal Parallelism; for, according to this doctrine, every physical process has its psychical concomitant, and both series are closed causal series. Thus, when a sense-stimulus seems to evoke a sensation in my consciousness, the physical stimulus causes only the sequence of physical changes in sensory nerves and brain; and the sensation is a member of a causal sequence of events which runs parallel in time with every step of the physical sequence, stimulus, sense-organ-processes, processes of conduction throughout the sensory nerves and lower nervous centres; and the sensation itself actually coincides in time with, or is the concomitant of, that part of the physical sequence which consists in the transmission of the nervous impulse through the cortex of the brain.

Now this statement of the doctrine of Parallelism at once raises the question—Why, then, of all the steps of the psychical sequence does this one alone appear as an element of my consciousness, and why does it become conjoined with similar elements (concomitant with the cortical steps of other physical sequences) to form the coherent field of consciousness of the moment in which these several cortical processes occur? A similar difficulty stands in the way of every form of psycho-physical monism, and is an insuperable difficulty for all of them. And, therefore, I will not insist upon it here. It is sufficient for my purpose to point out that strict Parallelism is less acceptable than the identity hypotheses; because it is open to all the principal objections that can be made to these, and incurs in addition a very great reproach which does not lie against them, namely, it asserts the relation of universal concomitance and leaves it absolutely mysterious and unintelligible. In this connexion it must be remembered that the doctrine asserts, not merely the temporal concomitance of some psychical process with every physical process, but that every event of the one kind corresponds qualitatively and in a perfectly definite and constant manner with an event of specific quality or character of the other kind, in such a way, indeed, that a sufficient empirical acquaintance with the two series would enable us to establish exact empirical laws of this temporal and qualitative correspondence, and to infer the one series from the observation of the other.

This doctrine, then, involves the admission of ultimate unintelligibility; and it also obviously involves an ultimate or metaphysical dualism, which can only be got rid of by adopting the identity-hypothesis; it therefore cannot claim to compete seriously with it for our acceptance.

The alternative to Animism, then, must be the identity-hypothesis in one or other of its two forms. Before going on to the criticism of these, I would meet a possible exception that may be taken to the foregoing remarks on strict psycho-physical Parallelism. It may be said that the doctrine may be rendered intelligible and acceptable by adopting Leibnitz's conception of pre-established harmony. To this I reply that Leibnitz's conception is essentially animistic, and differs from other animistic doctrines chiefly in that Leibnitz's view of causation was peculiar. He assigned to each organism a soul, and though the soul was called a monad, and though the body and all other material things also were said by him to consist of monads, yet, as we have seen (p. 57), he assigned to the human soul a position and a nature very different from those of other monads. The essential peculiarity of his view, which marks it off from other animistic doctrines, is that it substitutes for the principle of causal interaction that of the pre-established harmony of the internal evolution of all monads, just as thoroughgoing Occasionalism substitutes for it the conception of the perpetual action of God. And, since it is the behaviour of things which we are interested to understand, it matters little or nothing, from the point of view of science, whether we call the bond between them which secures the harmony of their changes one of causal interaction or of transient influence, or one of harmony pre-established by the design of the Creator, or one consisting in the perpetual adjustment of their states by the direct act of God.

Some of those who accept psycho-physical Parallelism in the strict or narrow sense tell us that we ought to accept it as a heuristic principle or a necessary working hypothesis for psychology. Wundt and Münsterberg are the most prominent exponents of this doctrine; though I speak with diffidence about Wundt's views, because, like some others, I have wrestled long and earnestly with his exposition of Parallelism, without being able to discover that he presents a consistent and intelligible doctrine. For Wundt, Parallelism is an empirical postulate; for Münsterberg it is a postulate which we are driven to accept, not by empirical fact, but by epistemological theory.[1] Both agree that the parallelism is only true of the sensory content of consciousness, and that therefore psychology can base itself on Parallelism only on the condition of regarding the whole of our psychical life as consisting in the conjunction and succession of elements of sensation, or of sensation and feeling.[2] Both admit that to describe our mental life in this way is to falsify it; and Münsterberg goes so far as to insist that the "scientific" psychology constructed on the basis of Parallelism has no bearing whatever upon real life

---

[1] "Grundzüge der Psychologie," p. 435.

[2] Thus Münsterberg (*op. cit.*, p. 429), "Alles Psychische besteht aus Empfindungen und aus nichts als Empfindungen." Wundt adds to the elements of sensation also elements of feeling.

EXAMINATION OF THE AUTOMATON THEORIES

and its problems. It is then a little difficult to understand what it is hoped to gain by basing psychology upon this postulate. Surely, when it is found that any working hypothesis so falsifies a science as to render it incapable of having any bearing upon practical life, only a mind having some curious twist can continue to retain it.

The culminating absurdity of Wundt's position is that, after arguing at great length to show that psychology must accept psycho-physical Parallelism as a "heuristic principle" empirically based, he turns round and tells us that in considering voluntary movements of the body we must treat them as being psychically originated, because we cannot ascertain the nature of the physiological process which initiates them; and that we must make use of the conception of psycho-physical interaction, so long as we cannot complete our account of the brain-processes.[1]

Münsterberg's *reductio ad absurdum* of his adopted principle is more elaborate. After writing two books[2] to prove that his psychology, being based on "Parallelism," can have no application to real life, he has produced several very able and interesting books which are models of the application of psychology to problems of real life,[3] and promises others which shall deal with the whole field of applied psychology.

Phenomenalistic Parallelism (Identity-hypothesis A.)

Against the doctrine that the psychical process and its concomitant physical process in the brain are but two different modes of appearance or aspects of one real process, two very serious objections must be made, in addition to all those that lie against all forms of psycho-physical monism.

When we apply the phrase "two modes of appearance" or "two aspects" to explain the psycho-physical relation, we are using a phrase which has meaning for our minds only in virtue of certain of our experiences connected with physical phenomena. These experiences are of several kinds and the phrase has accordingly several corresponding meanings. In experiences of the one class we observe a series of events of a certain kind on two successive occasions, on each occasion from a different stand-

---

[1] "Physiologische Psychologie," 5th ed., vol. iii., p. 647.
[2] "Grundzüge der Psychologie," and "Psychology and Life."
[3] "The Americans," "Psychology and Crime," "Psychology and the Teacher," "Psycho-therapeutics."

point; thus, to use the illustration suggested by Fechner, it is in principle possible for one person to observe the passage of the moon round the earth, at one time from a standpoint on the earth and at another from a standpoint on the moon. That is the type of one great class of experiences in which the difference of the appearances of a thing depends upon difference of standpoint: the observation of movements in space from two different points in space.

Another kind of experience which gives meaning to the phrase "two aspects of the same thing or process," is the abstraction by thought of two features of a process successively; thus, on considering the motion of a particle, one may fix one's attention successively upon the direction or changes of direction of its motion and upon the velocity or changes of velocity of its motion; or, on observing a series of changes of colour, one may direct one's attention to the changes of colour-tone or to the changes of brightness or of saturation; on hearing a melody, one may pay attention to the rhythm or to the harmonic relations. In all cases of this class the difference of aspect is secured by a difference of the setting of the attention, and the resulting conceptions are abstractions merely. Again, one may apprehend a physical event successively through two different senses, e.g. one may see the strokes of a hammer upon a gong, or one may hear them; the one series of physical events appears then under two different aspects.

There are, I think, no other radically different classes of experience that give meaning to the phrase "two aspects of the same process."

The question is then—Does the phrase derive from any one of these classes of experience a meaning which is applicable to the psycho-physical relation? Or, in other words, is the difference of aspect apprehended in any of these experiences truly analogous to the difference between physical and psychical processes?

As regards the experiences of all these classes it is to be noted that that which appears under two different aspects appears in every case as of the same order in both aspects, and is apprehended in a similar way in both cases; in the first class both aspects are of the order of paths of motion in space; in the second class the two aspects are simultaneously given as qualitative changes of one series of sensations; in the third class the two aspects of the one process are the sensations of two different classes simultaneously excited in the same consciousness and referred to the same cause, the physical process. But the brain-process and the rise of a sensation in consciousness, which are said to be two aspects or appearances of one real process, are two events of radically different orders, and are apprehended in two radically different ways, the one by sense-perception, the other by reflective introspection.

Again, in the experiences of the first class we do not really observe the same process under two aspects, we merely observe the repetition of a process of a certain kind on two successive occasions. Further, it is characteristic of the experiences of this class, that the appearance of the process at the one standpoint can be inferred or exactly calculated from the appearance at the other standpoint, by a purely logical process. Nothing of this sort is true of the relation of the psychical to the physical; we cannot in the least degree deduce the nature of the one series from the observation of the other.

The experiences of the second and third classes fail in another way to afford a true analogy to the supposed relation of the physical to the psychical and therefore fail to give meaning to the phrase in which the relation is described. It is of the essence of the two-aspect doctrine that, as Spinoza explicitly affirmed, the causal sequence shall be completely given under both aspects, the physical and the psychical. But, when we abstract the direction of a motion from its velocity, or the change of quality of a colour-sensation from the change of its saturation or intensity; or when we apprehended simultaneously the series of auditory and visual sensations evoked by the hammer; in all these cases the causal sequence is not given or apprehended under both aspects, for in each case we are dealing with partial aspects achieved only by a process of mental abstraction and by a deliberate neglecting of the remaining aspects simultaneously presented.

A still more serious objection to this "two-aspect doctrine" remains to be stated. A thing or being or process can appear under two different aspects, can manifest itself in two different modes, only if and when both aspects are apprehended by the mind of some observer; either one observer must occupy the two standpoints successively, or two or more observers must apprehend it from the different standpoints. Now, in the case of the physical and the psychical processes which are said to be two aspects of one real process, there is no such observer occupying the inner standpoint and apprehending the inner or psychical aspect of the real event, except in the altogether exceptional case of the introspecting psychologist; in which case a part of the stream of consciousness may, perhaps, be said to be apprehended by a later coming part. The process of apprehending a physical change is itself, according to this doctrine, the inner aspect of a real process; but, when the observer (let us call him A) is apprehending a physical event, say the fall of a stone, he is not normally at the same time observing his own consciousness; he is occupying the outer, not the inner standpoint. In such a case, then, the real process, (the two aspects or phenomenal appearances of which are on the one hand A's consciousness of the falling stone, and on the other hand the corresponding process in A's brain) is apprehended neither from the inner nor the outer standpoint, although in principle it is capable of being observed from both; but now the phenomenal appearances consist in being apprehended, their *esse* is *percipi*, they are by the hypothesis merely appearances for an apprehending mind; hence, in the case we are considering and in all similar cases, i.e., (in all cases of perception in which the subject's attention is wholly given to his external object), we are led by the hypothesis to the following conclusion—neither the phenomenal process in A's brain nor his consciousness of the falling stone have any being whatever, since their *esse* is *percipi*, and they are not perceived or apprehended. Now the denial of the brain-process raises no insuperable difficulty, it is acceptable to many philosophers; but the denial of A's consciousness of the falling stone is more serious. Suppose A to be yourself, and suppose that you play a sharp rally in the course of a game of tennis, or play a difficult ball at the wicket; then your attention at the moment of expecting the ball was wholly directed to the object. A moment later you sit down to describe in detail the way you took that ball; and a philosopher then undertakes to prove to you, by the reasoning outlined above, that you were not conscious of the ball at the moment of its approach. Will he succeed in convincing you of the truth of his thesis? I think not. It is true that among a certain class of philosophers there is still current the dogma that all consciousness is self-consciousness, and that in all knowing you know that you know. But, even if this dogma were admissible in the case of human knowing, it is certainly not admissible for the infra-human intelligences; to the animals we cannot deny consciousness or at least sentiency; and the double-aspect hypothesis necessitates the assumption of an inner or psychical aspect to the events of the infra-organic realm also.

These considerations seem to me to raise an insuperable objection to this form of the identity-hypothesis; namely there is lacking, except in certain special cases, any observer occupying the inner standpoint. The difficulty is not met by saying that in knowing or perceiving one knows that one knows, or that one's knowing is an appearance to oneself. For such knowing as that is peculiar to the most highly developed minds; lower types of mind cannot be credited with reflective introspective self-consciousness, or self-consciousness of any kind, and yet they must be allowed to be conscious, their brain-processes must be allowed to have their psychical correlates: their knowing is directly known by no one, is not an appearance for any observing mind, and yet it exists or goes on.

Perhaps at this point some reader will wish to remind me of Kant's doctrine of the "inner sense," which perceives the "phenomena of consciousness" as the outer sense perceives the phenomena of the physical world. Of this "inner sense" I need only say that it was merely a faculty invented by Kant to meet the exigences of his peculiar system, that it is now generally regarded as indefensible, and that, even if we accept the notion, the difficulty of the "two-aspect doctrine," pointed out in the foregoing paragraph, is in no way diminished.

As to Spinoza's form of this hypothesis, it is now generally admitted, even by ardent admirers of Spinoza's philosophy, that it cannot be consistently worked out. Sir F. Pollock, for example, demolishes it with the following unanswerable criticism: "Spinoza's Attributes are in effect defined as objects, or rather as objective worlds. But the general form of the definition disguises the all-important fact that the world of thought, and that alone, is subjective and objective at once. The intellect which perceives an Attribute as 'constituting the essence of Substance,' itself belongs to the Attribute of Thought. Thus, if we push analysis further, we find that Thought swallows up all the other attributes; for all conceivable Attributes turn out to be objective aspects of Thought itself."[1]

[1] "Spinoza: His Life and Philosophy," p. 179.

We may then fairly say, with Professor Stumpf,—" the one substance which is supposed to manifest itself in the two attributes, the physical and the psychical, is nothing but a word which expresses the desire to escape from dualism, but which does not really bridge the gulf for our understanding."[1]

This form of the identity-hypothesis lies open also to all the metaphysical objections that are raised against the conception of substance or substantiality, and, though I do not attach great importance to them, they cannot be set aside as of no weight, since many acute minds take a different view.

The difficulties of phenomenalistic parallelism are, then, very great, indeed insuperable; accordingly we find that the second form of the identity-hypothesis, namely, Psychical Monism, is the form of Parallelism that can claim the most influential supporters at the present day; and it is this second form that we must chiefly keep in mind, on weighing against one another the rival claims of the animistic and the parallelistic interpretations of the psycho-physical relation.

Psychical Monism (Identity-hypothesis B)

According to the second form of the identity-hypothesis, consciousness or conscious-process is the thing-in-itself, the fundamental and only reality, while all physical processes are the phenomenal appearances of conscious process; this is now generally regarded as being the strongest and the most subtle of the monistic interpretations of the psycho-physical relation. But this also has its peculiar difficulties, in addition to those common to all psycho-physical Monism. We must begin our criticism of this view by insisting that its supporters shall stand faithfully by the pre-suppositions from which they have chosen to set out and which they have made the very foundation of their argument These fundamental propositions are three : (1) consciousness or conscious-process (or something of the same nature, but so very much simpler as to require a different name, such as mind-stuff or infra-consciousness) is the only reality, the only mode of existence or of real being. (2) By each one of us only one tiny fragment of reality is directly known, namely the stream of his own consciousness; although all the rest of the universe consists of other conscious processes, it can be apprehended by him only under the form of

[1] " Leib und Seele," p. 16.

material or physical phenomena. (3) The appearances to us of other real or conscious processes under the forms of physical objects and processes bear some constant and orderly relation to those real processes, so that the descriptions and explanations of the universe given by physical science are valid, though they are symbolic only ; that is to say, all the processes which constitute the universe proceed according to, or can be fully explained in terms of, the laws of mechanical causation.

This last is the pre-supposition on which it is especially necessary to insist; for it is this one which is most apt to be tacitly let slip by those who accept Parallelism in this form. But it is the acceptance without reserve of the teachings of physical science, especially of its doctrine that the laws of mechanical causation hold universal sway, which constitutes, we are told, the chief claim of the monistic view upon our acceptance ; while the rejection by Animism of the claim of the mechanical principles of explanation to universal validity is its great offence.

Now, according as the psychical monist inclines to an intellectualistic or a voluntaristic psychology, he regards knowing or willing as the essence of conscious process. In the former case, then, he claims that all that exists is "knowing," though there is no one who knows and nothing, save knowing, to be known; or, in the latter case, that all that exists is "willing," though there is no one who wills and nothing to be willed but willing. I confess that, if a philosophical gourmet should tell me—"All that exists is 'eating,' though there is no one who eats and nothing to be eaten but eating," his statement would seem to me hardly less paradoxical.

But parody is not serious criticism. The principal positive superiority over its rivals claimed for this form of Monism is its rejection of the notion of substance or thing and its replacement of it by the notion of activity or process. Substance, whether material or spiritual, is rejected as an antiquated bit of popular metaphysic ; and with it to the same limbo must go all such notions as substantial beings or things, beings that remain self-identical in spite of partial changes. If we object that we find those notions essential to our thought, that we cannot think of relations without terms, of activities without things acting and acted upon, of changes without things that change, of movements without things that move, of knowing without subjects that know and objects that are known; we are told that this is a false or psychological necessity of thought engendered merely by bad habits, a necessity to be carefully distinguished from true or logical necessities of thought.[1]

Let us first examine, from the point of view of physical science, this proposal to banish things from the universe. Science distinguishes between rest and change, between potential and active energy, between the mere persistence of a given state of a system and its change; and it regards all changes as involving transformations of energy. Even though it may resolve all things into swarms of atoms in perpetual motion and atoms into ether vortices, yet this is only to drive back the notion of substance or thing; for the ether remains as the enduring basis of all this process. And even when it is proposed to replace mechanics by energetics and matter by energy, this can only be done by conceiving energy as something capable of enduring, as something whose quantity persists unchanged in spite of qualitative transformations. What then, in the metaphysical translation of the description of the world given by physical science, is to correspond to this distinction between systems of matter or energy at rest, or doing no work, and those that are doing work or transforming energy?[2]

But the impossibility of banishing altogether the notion of substance is even clearer in the case of psychological than of physical science. My consciousness is a stream of consciousness which has a certain unique unity; it is a multiplicity of distinguishable parts or features which, although they are perpetually changing, yet hang together as a continuous whole within which the changes go on. This then is the nature of consciousness as we know it. Now it is perfectly obvious and universally admitted that my stream of consciousness is not self-supporting, is not self-sufficient, is not a closed self-determining system; it is admitted

---

[1] Paulsen, "Einleitung," p. 392.

[2] Clifford's doctrine of mind-stuff avoids this difficulty by pointing to the "small pieces of mind-stuff" of which elementary feelings are composed. Consciousness is then a composite stuff, and conscious processes are the rearrangements of the pieces of stuff. But this is to make these atoms of mind-stuff into enduring self-identical units of substance. It is substantial atomism of the most undisguised kind, a simple translation of the material atom of physics into a psychical atom; and, since these psychical atoms obey, according to the doctrine, the laws of mechanism, it is difficult to see that they differ, save in name, from the physical atom. In any case, Clifford's conception can claim neither all the merits nor all the difficulties of the "Actualistische Seele."

that each phase of the stream does not flow wholly out of the preceding phase, and that its course cannot be explained without the assumption of influences coming upon it from without. What then are these influences? The Psychical Monist must reply— they are other consciousnesses. How then about the process by which the other consciousnesses, the other streams of consciousness, influence my stream of consciousness? Is this also consciousness? (For, we are told, all process is conscious process.) If so, then it also is a stream of consciousness and it must influence my stream through the agency of yet another stream, and so on *ad infinitum*. Thus my consciousness itself, by reason of the fact that it hangs together as a stream of process relatively independent of other streams of process, implies the essence of what is meant by substantiality, namely, the continuing to have or be a numerically distinct existence, in spite of partial change.

That consciousness exists or occurs in streams, each of which is something relatively apart from, demarcated from, other parts of reality, is a fundamental fact which raises insuperable difficulties for Psychical Monism. The psychical monist cannot escape them by saying that the stream of consciousness consists of elements or atoms of consciousness or mind-stuff, and that the stream is formed by the coming together of a number of such elements; that is a psychical atomism involving the notion of "substance," so abhorrent to his fundamental principle. If any one, following Clifford and wishing to adopt the psychical monist's doctrine without his principles, takes this view of the stream of consciousness, then it must be pointed out to him that every stream has its banks which mark it off from others and give it numerical distinctness, i.e. every stream owes its existence as a stream to conditions that lie outside itself and impress upon it the character of a stream. Perhaps he will point to the Gulf Stream as a stream without banks. Then it must be answered that this is a fallacious analogy—the Gulf Stream owes its formation to external influences, and only persists as a stream so long as the momentum originally impressed upon it from without is not spent through its interaction with the waters through which it flows. The numerical distinctness of streams of consciousness is a fundamental fact with which every psychological theory and every metaphysical system must deal, and which especially demands explanation from the system which asserts that all existence is conscious-process. How then does Psychical Monism propose to deal with this fact? Merely by leaving it on one side as inexplicable. "Gentlemen, let us look this difficulty boldly in the face and pass on to the next." That justly famous proposal accurately describes the attitude of Psychical Monism when confronted with this difficulty. Thus Paulsen says, "Soul is the multiplicity of inner experiences bound together to a unity in a way of which nothing can be said."[1] (" Seele is die auf nicht weiter sagbare Weise zur Einheit verbundene Vielheit innerer Erlebnisse.") And again he writes— "It is a fact that the processes of the inner life do not occur in isolation, and that each is lived with the consciousness of belonging to the unitary whole of this individual life. How this can happen I cannot pretend to say, any more than I can say how consciousness at all is possible."[2]

Now the hanging together of a multiplicity of conscious processes in a numerically distinct or individual stream is the very essence of soul or spirit; for, if the distinguishable elements of all consciousness (sensations, feelings, ideas, presentations, or whatever we please to name them) occurred as isolated elements or complexes, or in one huge jumble in which were no coherent streams or groups, there would be nothing that could be called spirit or mind, but rather a mere chaos of mind-stuff. When, then, Paulsen tells us that there can be no stronger proof of the insufficiency of any world-view than that it should find itself compelled to declare the existence of spirit to be an insoluble riddle,[3] Psychical Monism is condemned by the mouth of its champion. For it leaves every spirit or mind as "eine auf nicht weiter sagbare Weise zur Einheit verbundene Vielheit innerer Erlebnisse."

Most of the other exponents of Psychical Monism ignore this problem or, like Paulsen, are content to call it insoluble and to pass on. F. A. Lange, for example, who would, I think, have classed himself as a Psychical Monist, speaks of "The metaphysical riddle, how out of the multiplicity of atomic movements there arises the unity of the psychical image"; and adds, "We hold this riddle, as we have often said, to be insoluble."[4] Prof. Strong leaves the problem untouched.[5] Fechner

[1] "Einleitung," p. 387.   [2] *Op. cit.*, p. 386.   [3] "Einleitung," p. 258.
[4] "History of Materialism," vol. iii. p. 213.
[5] It was interesting to me on meeting Prof. Strong recently to find that he had discovered, and was puzzling over, this problem, which he formulated in the sentence, "What holds consciousness together?"

alone, so far as I am aware, has made a resolute attempt to deal with it; but that this attempt achieved no success I hope to show in a later chapter on the unity of consciousness.

Now let us turn to another difficulty of Psychical Monism. The stream of consciousness is in part determined by influences coming from outside, which we call sense-impressions; but, when we take these fully into account, the course of the stream of consciousness remains still unexplained; that is to say, its course is not wholly determined by the two factors, consciousness itself and the sense-stimuli or sense-impressions. It is determined in a very important and, in fact, vastly predominant degree by some other real condition or conditions, which we commonly call the structure or constitution of the individual mind.[1] Quite apart, then, from any question as to what the structure of the mind may be, what stuff it may be built of, we are able to infer its presence and operation from the orderly and lawful regularity of the stream of consciousness, which cannot be explained from the nature of the stream itself and from the nature and the order of succession of the sense-impressions; and we are able to discover a number of general laws of this structure and operation, and to describe how it gradually grows, every moment of conscious life leaving it altered in such a way that its influence upon later coming parts of the stream of consciousness is modified, until its structure and its influence upon conscious life become exceedingly complex. But, as compared with consciousness itself, this conditioning factor, the structure of the mind, is relatively stable and unchanging; to its stability is due all that constancy of mode of conscious reaction which distinguishes one personality from another. The faithful retention of memories through periods of many years, manifested by their subsequent return to consciousness, implies in fact a statical or relatively unchanging condition of something, call it what we may. The psychical monist, if he is consistent, must affirm that the structure of the mind, the sum of these statical enduring conditions by which the stream of his consciousness is at every moment predominantly determined, is that of which the brain is the phenomenon, and that this enduring structure itself consists of streams of consciousness.

[1] This is admitted by the most thoroughgoing monists; thus Paulsen, for example, writes: "Im Bewusstsein ist nur ein überaus geringer Teil des gesamten Seelenlebens, das wir doch voraussetzen müssen, um die Vorgänge im Bewusstsein zu konstruieren" ("Einleitung," p. 158).

Now this supposition is quite inconsistent with all that we know of consciousness; consciousness is essentially and always a flow, a perpetual flux, a process never enduring without change for the briefest moment. And the ascription to any consciousness of the stable unchanging character of these enduring conditions of our consciousness oversteps the bounds of legitimate analogy.

Some of the psychical monists therefore shrink from this assertion and, like Professor Strong, assume that this enduring structure of the mind is a system of psychical dispositions. Writing of these as conceived by Dr Stout, Strong says, "We must therefore raise these hypothetical psychical dispositions to the rank of extra-mental realities, and a system of such realities, neither 'simple' nor 'undivided' yet quite sufficiently 'active,' will form our substitute for the soul." But this is to break with his fundamental metaphysical principles and to go over to the enemy, Animism. For such a system of psychical dispositions, neither conscious processes nor material process, yet the enduring condition of a personal consciousness, is not a substitute for the soul, but the soul itself. Parallelists are so occupied with pouring abuse on the old Cartesian metaphysical description of the soul, and in piling up the private adjectives about it, describing it as a "*Seelenatom*," a simple, undivided, inextended, immaterial, immortal atom, "ein unveränderliches, starres, absolut beharrliches Realitätspünktchen," "ein Bröckchen allgemeines Realitätsstoffes,"[1] that they have no ears for any voice that attempts to build up the conception of the soul according to the principles upon which any other scientific hypothesis is properly fashioned.

This difficulty of Psychical Monism may be briefly presented in another way, which supplements the foregoing statement. The doctrine lays it down clearly that "the existence of consciousness is our existence." Strong and Paulsen are equally explicit on this point, and it is clearly a necessary part of the doctrine. Well, then, I fall into profound dreamless sleep, or am stunned by a blow on the head, or spend an hour in deep chloroform narcosis. During this period I am unconscious and, therefore, according to this doctrine, I cease to exist. When I begin to be conscious again, this is the appearance of a new consciousness, a new self, a new "aktuelle Seele." The absurdity of this statement is manifest. My personality, my self, all that is characteristic of and essential to me as a person, survives the period of unconsciousness.

[1] Paulsen, *op. cit.*, p. 285.

Therefore my consciousness is not myself, and its existence is not essential to my existence; the continuance of my existence consists in the continuance of some other reality than my consciousness. Now, according to the doctrine, this other reality can only be some other consciousness or consciousnesses; thus it is forced to the conclusion (absurd in itself, and opposed to its fundamental proposition that my consciousness is myself) that the continuance of my personality consists in the continuance of other consciousnesses than my own, that my existence, my self, is essentially consciousness other than my own, presumably a system of the streams of consciousness of other selves.

The psychical monist, if he has ever pondered this implication of his doctrine, probably seeks to escape the difficulty by saying that when, after a period of unconsciousness, my stream of consciousness flows on again, it is not discontinuous with the stream that was cut short by chloroform; he will say that my consciousness bridges the time-gap and feels and knows itself continuous across it. I do not think that this meets the difficulty. But to establish the objection, I will point out that in some cases, when consciousness returns after being abolished by a blow on the head, it does not feel itself to be continuous with the consciousness that preceded the blow; the subject awakes like a new-born child, having no memory of his previous life, no sense of resuming or continuing it.[1] Is, then, such a case really one of a new self, a new consciousness, the inception of a new "aktuelle Seele"? Not at all; for gradually, after a longer or shorter period of conscious life, the old memories return, the old ways of thinking, feeling, and doing return, until the old personality is completely restored. All which proves that the personality, the self, does not consist in the stream of consciousness alone, but that it consists in a far greater degree in those enduring stable conditions by which the stream of consciousness is at every moment determined. Again, I insist, the consistent psychical monist is forced to the absurd conclusion that my self is not my own consciousness, but the streams of consciousness of other selves.[2]

[1] The most remarkable recorded case of this sort is that of Mr Hanna, for which see "Multiple Personality," by B. Sidis and S. Goodhart.
[2] This inconsistency of Psychical Monism can hardly be better exhibited than by the quotation side by side of two sentences from Paulsen's chapter on "Wesen der Seele." The one, which is repeated again and again with slight variations, runs: " Die Seele ist die im Bewusstsein zur Einheit zusammenge-

And here another difficulty may be touched upon, or perhaps rather the same difficulty in another form. My brain is said to be the phenomenon of which my consciousness is the reality. How, then, when I lie dead? My brain, the phenomenon, will still be present for other men, and will still be the seat of many physical and chemical processes, and for many days it will lose nothing of its complex organisation. But what has become of its reality, my consciousness? To this it may be answered: Only certain most highly specialized processes of the brain are the phenomena of which your consciousness is the reality. Then of what reality is the brain with its marvellously complex structure, and all its other processes, the appearance?

Or again, my brain, or part of it, is the appearance of my consciousness to other men. But no one has perceived my brain. Therefore, it is only a possibility of a phenomenon which has never been realized, a "permanent possibility of sensations" for other men. Suppose, then, that some one lays open my skull with the stroke of an axe; the latent possibility of the phenomenon is then actualized, my brain appears to another man: but at the moment preceding the realization of that possibility, the reality which is to appear, namely my consciousness, has disappeared, has ceased to be.

It may be noted, in passing, that these considerations present difficulties almost equally great to the other form of the identity-hypothesis, the "two-aspect-doctrine." For it is compelled to admit that that part of unknowable reality, which we are told manifests itself under the two forms of the stream of consciousness and the life of the brain of any person, continues to manifest itself as the brain-life, while its other and parallel manifestation comes and goes intermittently.

Yet another difficulty of Psychical Monism is its conception of the flowing together or composition of individual consciousnesses to form larger consciousnesses. The consciousnesses of men are held to run together into large streams of collective consciousness, civic and national consciousness, and so on; and these again are said to combine with all infra-human consciousness on earth to form an earth-consciousness; and this with the consciousness of other worlds, to form by successive stages of concurrence the all-inclusive

---

fasste Vielheit seelischer Erlebnisse" (p. 145). The other runs: "Im Bewusstsein ist nur ein überaus geringer Teil des gesamten Seelenlebens, das wir doch voraussetzen müssen, um die Vorgänge im Bewusstsein zu konstruieren" (p. 158).

divine consciousness. Not only so, but each human being's consciousness is already vastly composite, being formed by the concurrence in successive stages of the consciousnesses of his nerve centres, his cells, his molecules, the atoms, the α and β particles that compose the atoms, and so on indefinitely.

If we pass over, without insistence on it, the fact that there is forthcoming no particle of empirical evidence of any such composition of human consciousness to form greater wholes of consciousness, two difficulties remain. Each consciousness or stream of consciousness exists in and for itself of its own right, for consciousness is reality; yet each is used over and over again, first existing for itself, but also at the same time existing as an element in successively larger consciousnesses. This treatment of consciousness seems to me compatible only with the conception of it as mind-stuff, as made up of ultimate atoms of consciousness; a conception moulded upon our conception of matter, and inconsistent with the fundamental proposition of Psychical Monism that our consciousness, as we know it, is absolute reality. And how, apart from any question of the conditions that determine it, can we conceive this flowing together of consciousness? Has the phrase any meaning? For my part, I think not. Suppose my consciousness is filled with the glory of colour of a sunset sky, while yours, as you lie near by under your motor-car, is filled with a problem in mechanics. What sort of a consciousness would these two make if compounded? Presumably a gorgeously coloured problem in mechanics. This is only one of the simplest forms of the difficulty. Confining ourselves to human consciousness on the earth, let us ask how all the pain and all the pleasure of human consciousnesses are to sum together. Do all the pains run together to make one big pain, and all the pleasures to make one big pleasure, and do these co-exist in the world-consciousness? Or is it that, as in individual consciousness, the pain-producing influences and operations, and the pleasure-producing influences and operations, neutralize one another, if they are equal, or give an excess of pleasure over pain, if the one set of influences predominates? If the latter is the case, then the pleasure or pain of the world consciousness, is not the sum of the pains and pleasures of human consciousnesses, but a resultant formed by their common action, a new pain or pleasure.

The doctrine that consciousnesses flow together, each subsisting for itself and yet at the same time subsisting as a part of a larger consciousness, implies, I submit, a substantialistic and even a materialistic view of consciousness; it implies an atomistic consciousness, a mind-stuff that can be compounded in masses or scattered like powder, and still remain essentially unchanged. Such a view of consciousness is not only incompatible with the rejection of "substance," which is the strident keynote of Psychical Monism, but is inadmissible, no matter what our metaphysical views may be. It is plausible only to those who think of all consciousness and all psychical process as consisting in what we call the sensory content of consciousness; for the sensory content does seem like a patchwork. But the sensory content and the sensations and images that compose it are abstractions only, achieved by fixing our attention on one aspect of mental process. Sensations are merely incidents of the process of cognition, and no amount of compounding of sensations will result in an act of cognition, a knowing of an object; still less will it produce a judgment, an inference, a train of reasoning, or an act of will.

The foregoing discussions may be briefly resumed by saying that Psychical Monism leaves the most fundamental peculiarity of our experience entirely unexplained and unintelligible, the peculiarity namely that consciousness, as we know it, runs always and only in personal streams, the fact, in short, of personality. It describes the world as consisting of conscious processes forming one vast system of consciousness, every part of which is in functional relation with every other; a unitary whole whose unity each of us can only conceive after the pattern of that unique wholeness or unity which he discovers to be the form of his personal consciousness; and it leaves as an unrelieved mystery the fact, apparently incompatible with this conception of a world-consciousness, that the consciousness of which alone we have any knowledge occurs only in the form of personal consciousnesses, which not only do not run together, but which seem to be absolutely and completely debarred from all direct communication. It may be said at once that the alternative form of the identity-hypothesis leaves equally mysterious the fact of personality.

We find, then, that the fundamental assumption of Psychical Monism, namely, that consciousness is reality and the only reality, and its attempt to abolish as illegitimate the conception of any mode of being other than consciousness, involve it in very great difficulties, not to say absurdities; and this result will give force to the protest against any attempt to solve the psycho-physical problem by the metaphysical method, by setting out with any proposition as to the ultimate nature of reality. Without going so far as to condemn all attempts to describe the nature of reality, we may fairly protest that the powers of the human mind are so little suited to achieve knowledge of absolute reality, that our conclusions in this direction must be of a tentative character; and that it is absurd to profess to decide the question as to the existence of the soul by deduction from any assertion as to the nature of reality. To attempt to decide any question of fact by setting out from an assertion as to the nature of ultimate reality, is to practise metaphysic in the way which has brought it into disrepute with the majority of thinking men in almost all ages.

Let us now glance at certain difficulties common to all forms of Parallelism. They all alike imply universal psycho-physical Parallelism or Pan-psychism; they necessarily assume that every physical event, the mere fall of a stone to the ground, the rotation of the earth, the vibratory movements of an atom, the flight of the solar system through space, the swaying of a dead leaf on a bough, that all these and all other physical events have their psychical correlates, or aspects, or underlying realities, just as well as those obscure changes in certain restricted portions of our brains, which alone seem on the face of things to be thus accompanied. And they imply also that every psychical event has its physical correlate or manifestation, that every thought or volition of God, if there be a God who thinks and wills, manifests itself under the form of physical processes subject to mechanical laws. These implications of Parallelism are not always fully grasped by those who accept the doctrine; yet, in any form less thoroughgoing than this, it is so fragmentary and inconsistent as not to be worth a moment's consideration, and its principal exponents have, of course, fully acknowledged and insisted upon these implications. "All things," says Paulsen, "are psycho-physical beings."

If, with these implications in mind, we compare the doctrine with Animism in respect to the strain it throws upon the imagination, it must be admitted that the advantage lies with Animism, in spite of all the conundrums it raises as regards the nature, origin, and destiny of souls. But this is a point of minor importance. The serious difficulty raised by this implication of Parallelism may be stated as follows. The rich complex consciousness of man is correlated with the processes of an enormously complex and highly developed nervous system. When we survey the scale of animal life, we see that the lower down we go in the scale the simpler becomes the structure of the nervous system, until we come to simple creatures in which it consists of only a few cells but partially differentiated from the rest of the body; and finally we come to the unicellular creatures each consisting of a mere speck of nucleated protoplasm. We have good reason to believe that, if we could observe the consciousness of the animals throughout this descending scale, we should find that the stream of consciousness becomes poorer and thinner in proportion as the nervous system is less developed. Now, it is sufficiently difficult for us to conceive the nature of the psychical life of such an animal as a fish; it would seem to consist in mere sentiency and appetite. But, when we go down into the invertebrate world, the nervous system, and indeed the whole organism, becomes indefinitely simpler; to conceive of a corresponding reduction in complexity and richness of the psychical life is difficult. We can conceive the consciousness of the animalcule as at most but a mere alternation of the vaguest possible feelings of satisfaction and dissatisfaction or unrest. But when on the physical side we pass over from the animalcule to the molecule of inorganic matter, or to the gravitating atom or particle of negative electricity, or whatever the unit physical phenomenon may be, we cross an interval in the scale of complexity of organization as great as that between man and the animalcule. How, then, are we to conceive consciousness to be correspondingly reduced. To attempt any such further reduction of the concept of individual experience (inneres Erlebniss), of psychical existence or process, is to deprive it of all content, to leave the words empty of all meaning.

In order to meet this difficulty, Fechner adopted the fashion, first introduced perhaps by Leibnitz, of speaking of unconscious psychical processes, unconscious sensations and ideas (Unbewusstsein, unbewusste Empfindungen, unbewusste Vorstellungen),[1] and spoke of the assumed psychical aspect, or reality, underlying the physical processes of the inorganic world as unconscious psychical processes. Other Parallelists have used other terms in order to diminish this difficulty; Lloyd Morgan, for example, prefers to use the word 'infra-consciousness,' and Clifford, as we have seen, spoke of a mind-stuff which is not consciousness, but

[1] "Elemente der Psycho-physik," vol. ii., p. 438.

of small pieces of which the most elementary feelings are composed; but the expression most in favour is perhaps subconsciousness. Parallelism, then, involves the assumption of a vast amount of unconscious psychical process. Is this a valid conception? We start from the unity of individual experience or consciousness, and we discover the necessity of postulating existences which partially determine the course of that experience, and these we call our environment; this environment is directly apprehended by us only under the form of material objects or physical processes; we thus arrive at the conception of processes of two fundamentally different kinds, conscious process and physical process. Then the parallelist finds himself compelled, in order to carry through his scheme, to postulate a third kind of process of which, from the nature of the case, we can never have any experience, whether direct or indirect. Thus the endeavour after reduction of Dualism to Monism really results in the assumption of a third kind of existence or process which is as utterly unlike conscious process as are the processes described by physical science. But, in order to cast a veil over the questionable transaction and to create the illusion that the third kind of process is not so very unlike conscious process, the parallelist calls it unconscious psychical process. Now I do not wish to deny the propriety of the conception of unconscious, still less of subconscious, psychical process; the conception is perfectly compatible with, and perhaps even demanded by, Animism. But my point is, that the attempt to identify unconscious psychical process with consciousness is a mere play upon words. The psychical monist begins by using psychical process as synonymous with conscious process, and goes on to use psychical as a term of wider connotation than consciousness (as the animist properly and consistently may), hoping, by speaking of unconscious psychical process, to avoid the bad impression that must be made by speaking of unconscious conscious process. Psychical Monism, whose fundamental proposition is that all that exists is consciousness, is of course the variety of Monism which is hit most hard by any refusal to recognize the possibility of unconscious consciousness, or to admit the legitimacy of describing the evolution of consciousness, in the individual and in the race, as a process of aggregation of unconscious processes.

Again, the hypothesis of psycho-physical parallelism, whether it stands by itself or is supported by the identity-hypothesis in either of its two forms, is confronted by the difficulty that, while the physical processes are mechanically determined, psychical processes are essentially teleological; so that mechanical and teleological determination have to be represented as running exactly parallel and issuing always in the same results. In a later chapter I shall say something of the necessity of believing in the reality of teleological determination of mental process; but here it suffices to point out that this is not denied by most of the philosophical defenders of Parallelism. Wundt and Paulsen, for example, are agreed upon this, and Strong urges that one of the chief merits of Psychical Monism is that it satisfies our deep-rooted conviction of the real efficiency of consciousness. In fact, to give up the validity of either mechanical explanation of physical processes or the teleological explanation of mental process would be to sacrifice the claim of Monism to reconcile natural science and philosophy.

The same difficulty recurs in still more urgent form in connexion with our higher mental processes, which are not only teleological but also logical. The parallelist has to believe that purely mechanical determination runs parallel with logical process and issues in the same results. He has to believe, or at any rate assert, that every form of human activity and every product of human activity is capable of being mechanically explained. Consider, then, a page of print; the letters and words of a logical argument are impressed upon the page by a purely mechanical process. But what has determined their order? Their order is such that, when an adequately educated person reads the lines, he takes the *meaning* of the words and sentences, follows the reasoning and is led to, and forced to accept, the logical conclusion. And in ordering the words and sentences the author was conscious of their meaning, of the drift of the whole argument and of the conclusion to which it leads, and was animated by the purpose or desire of achieving the end, the demonstration in black and white of the conclusion of the argument; and throughout the period of composition his choice of words and order was determined by this purpose, by the desire to achieve an end, a result, which existed only in his consciousness. Now the parallelist necessarily maintains that all this process of ordering the words and sentences, in which the consciousness of their meaning and of their logical connexion and of the conclusion and purpose of the whole argument seem to play so important a part, that all this is in principle capable of being fully explained as the outcome of the mechanical interplay of the author's brain-processes: that a complete description of the mechanics of these processes would be a complete explanation of the ordering of the letters, words, and sentences. This is what I, in common with many others, find incredible, namely, the assertion that the meaning of the words need not be taken into account in explaining the way they were brought into their order on the page. The parallelist will assert that the author's consciousness of meaning had as its physical correlate some complex system of brain-processes, and that this was the causal mechanism that we have to conceive as ordering the words by governing the movement of the author's hand as he wrote them down. This then raises the question of empirical fact,—Is there or is there not any complete physical brain-correlate of that part of our consciousness which we call meaning?

Or suppose the printed page to bear a poem containing original and delicate similes; for example:

"Music that gentlier on the spirit lies
Than tired eye-lids upon tired eyes."

We are asked to believe that the ordering of these words can be mechanically explained. We have, then, to suppose a mechanism so delicate that it is capable of being affected by the resemblance between "tired eyelids upon tired eyes" and "gentle music," or at least of reacting in the same way to both, namely, with the production of the sound of the word "gentle"; for the meaning of the word gentle is here the essential factor in bringing these unlike things together in the consciousness of the poet. Here we come back again to the essential question—Can "meaning" be supposed to have its physical correlate in the brain? To this question I propose to return later and show reason to believe that no such correlate can be assumed. At present I merely urge the incredibility of the assumption that the "meaning" itself can be left out, when we seek to explain the ordering of our words in thinking, in writing, or in speaking.

Paulsen maintains the parallelism of the mechanically with the logically and teleologically determined series, and he illustrates his view in the following way. "An orator makes a speech; he has been attacked, he desires to defend himself and annihilate his opponent, thoughts and arguments flow in, similes and apt turns of speech, biting phrases and quotations, sarcasms against his opponent and flatterings of his hearers, seem to come of themselves. It is the link of association by which each thought drags up its successor (i.e. a mechanically operative link); but, at each moment, of thousands of possible associative links only that one which leads to the goal actually operates. Thus the whole series of processes constituting the oration is both causally and teleologically conditioned; the will gives it its general direction and feels a lively satisfaction in the successful progress."[1] The interactionist could not describe the process in terms more in accordance with his view; at every step the mechanical factor, the system of materially conditioned links of association, presents a number of rival possibilities, and at each step that one of these mechanically conditioned associations which is most suitable to the purpose of the orator is brought into operation by the psychical teleological factor, his will or purpose. On the face of it, then, the series of events is determined by the co-operation of the material mechanical factors and the psychical teleological factors. But, when Paulsen says that the whole series is both causally and teleologically conditioned, he means that the causal and the teleological processes are the same identical processes looked at in two different ways. How then does he seek to render intelligible this identity of mechanical causation and teleological determination? He achieves it by making them both purely subjective, by depriving both conceptions of all objective validity, and falling back upon Hume's doctrine that causation is merely sequence. "If one holds the right notion of causality, if one understands by it, with Hume and Leibnitz, nothing more than lawfulness, i.e. regular concomitance of the changes of many elements, then it is obvious that causality holds good of the spiritual mental world no less than of the natural."[2] Hence mechanical causation and teleological determination being alike merely subjective, i.e. applicable only within our conceptual descriptions of the real world and not operative in the real world, "there can occur no opposition between mechanical explanation and idealistic interpretation."[3] The solipsistic character of this escape is well revealed in the following passage. "I do not see what should prevent our saying, the logical operation of thought is presented physically in a brain-process, which according to the assumption is to be regarded as a part of the course of nature following physical laws. The brain would not therefore become a calculat-

[1] "Einleitung," p. 241.   [2] "Einleitung," p. 243.
[3] "Einleitung," p. 181.

ing machine, but we are led to the thought that there obtains a kind of pre-established harmony between logical and physical laws: a thought before which we do not shrink, for the material world is, according to our assumption, not something absolutely foreign to the spirit; it is after all its own creation (sein Produkt)."[1]

Wundt's reconciliation of the universal sway of mechanical causation with teleological determination is very similar. He writes—"The universality of mechanical causation is an assumption which needs to be verified by experience. The supposition that there obtain different modes of connexion, equivocal and unequivocal, in different provinces of nature, cannot therefore be rejected as logically impossible. But then for these provinces unequivocal mechanical causality does not hold good, and the assertion that both modes of connexion may be combined in one series of phenomena is inadmissible in all cases. Final causes and mechanical causes are mutually exclusive."[2] And again he writes, "the teleologically conditioned cannot be at the same time mechanically conditioned." It might be thought that in face of these explicit statements, Wundt would find it impossible to maintain Parallelism and its implication that all events must be regarded as both mechanically caused and teleologically determined. But, like Paulsen, he succeeds in maintaining Parallelism at the cost of the reality of all causation or determination by falling back upon Hume; thus—"the difference between teleological and causal conception is not an objectively valid difference (kein sachlicher) that divides the content of experience into two unlike provinces; but the two ways of conceiving things are formally different only, so that to every purposive relation there belongs a causal connexion as its complement, and conversely a teleological form can be given, if required, to every causal connexion."[3] Cause and effect, goal and effort, are nothing more than the projection, into the world of objective reality, of ground and consequence, which exist only for our thought and are connected only by a logical band; and, since the ground can be inferred from the consequence as readily as the consequence from the ground, the two ways of describing phenomenal sequences are equally valid.

Thus the parallelists seek to escape from this difficulty. They are determined to eat their cake and to hold it, to accept the

---

[1] "Einleitung," p. 100.
[2] "Physiologische Psychologie," vol. iii. p. 728.
[3] *Op. cit.*, vol. iii. p. 737.

dictum of science that all events are mechanically caused as well as the dictum of philosophy that mind operates effectively to achieve its purposes. But they can only do this at the cost of denying the applicability to reality of our conceptions both of mechanical causation and of purposive striving, at the cost, that is to say, of sinking back into Solipsism; for only by the aid of the principle of causation can each of us infer any reality other than his own consciousness.

CHAPTER XIII

IS THERE ANY WAY OF ESCAPE FROM THE DILEMMA— ANIMISM OR PARALLELISM?

IN the foregoing pages we have seen how the development of the natural sciences has led to the rejection of Animism by the greater part of the learned world of our time. In the two preceding chapters we have stated and examined the principal formulations of the psycho-physical relation proposed as substitutes for Animism; and we have found that these also are confronted with very serious difficulties, difficulties which, though they do not leap to the eye as do those of Animism, are nevertheless so great as to forbid us to accept any one of these formulations as an intelligible solution of the psycho-physical problem. We must, therefore, at this stage of our inquiry, raise the question —Are the automaton hypotheses (epiphenomenalism and the parallelistic doctrines) the only alternatives to Animism? Or, putting aside Epiphenomenalism as untenable, we may ask, Are we confronted with the dilemma—Animism or Parallelism?

This inquiry is the more necessary in an English treatise, because the lack of interest in the psycho-physical problem on the part of most of our academic philosophers seems to imply on their part the opinion that the question may be answered with a negation. I believe that, in fact, many of our idealistic philosophers hold, somewhat vaguely, no doubt, the opinion that Kant's epistemology has rendered the psycho-physical problem unreal, has shown that the problem only arises through asking a question which never should have been asked. They tell us that all thinkers of the pre-critical period and those who, since Kant, still persist in inquiring into the relations between mind and matter, between soul and body, have taken up the question from a false starting-point; that, namely, they have accepted uncritically the notions of soul and body current in popular thought; that these notions were achieved by illegitimate processes of abstraction; and that, if, instead of doing this, we begin, as Kant did, by making an impartial epistemological inquiry, we shall find that this insoluble problem never arises.

It might suffice to reply to these insinuations, as follows. We admit that, when we reflect upon the nature of experience, we find immediately given neither body nor mind, but only the duality of subject and object within the unity of experience; and we admit that the conceptions of body and mind are arrived at by abstracting from this unity of experience, on the one hand the objective and on the other hand the subjective elements. Nevertheless, we do not admit that these processes of abstraction are illegitimate; rather we affirm that they are necessary steps for each one of us, if he is to reach out in thought beyond the circle of his own experience and play a part as a member of a world of spirits, which, as you tell us, is the only real world.[1] He who refuses to make this step, a step which cannot be justified in strict logic, remains a solipsist. With the solipsist we cannot argue; but all of us are agreed that Solipsism is an impossible attitude for a sane man. We affirm that each of us can escape from Solipsism only by an act of faith or will that posits a real world, of which he is a member. This real world appears to each of us in the form of the phenomena of sense-perception; but, if he is not to remain a solipsist, he must affirm and believe that these appearances are not created by himself, but are rather due to influences or existences, not himself, yet affecting him. Or, in other words, he must believe in the validity of the category of causation; for only by believing that his perceptions are caused by some influence, some real being, other than himself, can he escape from Solipsism. Let him conceive these influences or existences how he will, and the psycho-physical problem still confronts him and

---

[1] Avenarius has described the process by which we pass from the unity of experience to the duality of subject and object, to the conception of the subjective and objective as psychical and physical worlds, and has named it the process of introjection (*Der menschliche Weltbegriff*). This doctrine of introjection seems to be regarded in some quarters as constituting a proof of the untenability of psycho-physical dualism; but, however true it may be as an abstract and generalized account of the way in which the human mind has arrived at the distinction of the physical from the psychical, it does nothing to invalidate that distinction. As Prof. A. E. Taylor has well said, "To attempt the solution of this problem by simply reverting to the standpoint of immediate experience, as it was before the creation of the concept of a physical order, would be to undo at a stroke the whole previous work of our physical scientific constructions. From the standpoint of immediate experience there can be no problem of the connexion between the physical and the psychical" ("Mind," vol. xiii. p. 481).

clamours for an answer. For among these appearances is that which he calls his body, one among many similar appearances, and this appearance points to some reality beyond it, and the psycho-physical problem is—What is the relation of my thinking self to this reality beyond? He may accept Berkeley's suggestion, to the effect that the body and all other appearances are produced in his thought by the direct action of God, a pure spirit or thinking being like himself; but, even if he brings himself seriously to believe that God has chosen to play this monstrous joke upon mankind, he is but solving the psycho-physical problem by arbitrarily choosing a peculiar and dogmatic form of Animism.

Or let him, with Herbert Spencer, affirm that this reality is unknowable; his need is then all the more urgent for some understanding of his relation to the appearances of which his body is one, since these appearances are all he can ever know.

Or, if he holds that we must be content to affirm that this reality is of the nature of mind or spirit or consciousness, without further specifying it, then he still must discover the nature of the relation between his own consciousness or mind and that other consciousness which appears to him under the form of his body.

But this preliminary inquiry is so important for the whole course of our subsequent discussion that it seems worth while to examine the modes of dealing with the psycho-physical problem followed by several eminent idealistic philosophers. And, first, we may examine Kant's own treatment of it.

According to Kant, the body belongs to the phenomenal world, which we know through the faculty of sentience and understanding; within this world of phenomena the law of mechanical causation holds unbroken sway, yet this world, the *mundus sensibilis*, has but empirical reality. The understanding, contemplating this phenomenal world, may infer the existence of some noumenon, some thing-for-itself, of which it is the appearance, but is unable to make any affirmation concerning it other than the bare affirmation of its existence. By means of a higher faculty, the practical reason, we discover the existence of a world of superior reality, the *mundus intelligibilis*; to this world belongs the soul of man, the pure ego, which is the logical nature that comprises both understanding and reason.

Now it is clear that the recognition of the truth that the physical world *as we perceive it*, or as it appears to us, is an appearance, does not abolish the psycho-physical problem, so long as, with Kant, we hold that this appearance is an appearance of something. What is the relation of my thinking self to the thing-for-itself which appears to me as the physical world in space and time? This question still presses for an answer just as urgently as if we accept the crude realist's view of the physical world. And especially, if we accept Kant's demonstration of the soul as an immortal being, we wish to know what is the relation of the soul to the thing-for-itself. Kant, in short, has left us with two kinds of reality, empirical reality and rational reality; with two real worlds, one ruled by mechanical causation, the other a world of freedom and purpose; and he has not shown us how they are related. Kant even wrote: "The separation of soul and body forms the termination of the sensible exercise of our faculty of knowledge, and the beginning of the intellectual. The body would thus be regarded, not as the cause of thought, but merely as its restrictive condition, and at the same time as promotive of the sensuous and animal, but therefore the greater hindrance to the pure and spiritual life."[1] And Kant's suggestion of phenomenalistic Parallelism as the solution of the psycho-physical problem shows that he himself was aware that the problem remained in spite of his epistemological Phenomenalism.

Kant, in fact, made an elaborate attempt to show how we may run with the hare and yet hunt with the hounds. Confronted with eighteenth-century Materialism and Hume's Scepticism on the one hand, and with the dogmatic Spiritualism of orthodox philosophy on the other hand, he boldly accepted the methods and results of

---

[1] I quote this passage from "The Discipline of Pure Reason in Relation to Hypothesis," after Paulsen, who affirms that it continued to represent Kant's view in his critical period ("Immanuel Kant, his Life and Doctrine," p. 254).

Kant wrote also, "The opinion that the thinking subject may be able to think before having any relation with bodies may be expressed as follows: that before the beginning of that kind of sense-perception through which things appear in space, the same transcendental objects, which in our present condition appear to us as bodies, may have been capable of being perceived in some quite different manner. But the opinion that the soul may continue to think after the breaking off of all relations with the bodily world may be stated in this way: that, if that kind of sensory perception through which transcendental and hitherto quite unknown objects appear to us as the material world, should cease, then nevertheless all perception of the world would not necessarily cease; and it is quite possible that these unknown objects might continue to be cognized by the thinking subject, although, of course, no longer in the guise of bodies. Now no one can adduce from speculative principles the least ground for such an assertion, not even show the possibility of it, but merely assume it; but just as little also can anyone make any valid dogmatic objection to the assertion" ("Kritik d. r. V.," Erdmann's edition, p. 338).

both—the world of mechanically determined phenomena, which is the natural issue of Materialism modified by Scepticism, and the world of pure and free Spirits which dogmatic metaphysic affirmed ; and he sought to justify our belief in the existence of both worlds by dividing our intellect into two distinct faculties. Thus he achieved a dualism of the intellect with a corresponding duality of unrelated worlds, which surely is the least defensible of all forms of dualism. Nor can Kant be given even the credit of consistent adherence to this strange doctrine ; for, in spite of his insistence on the absolute sway of mechanical principles in the phenomenal world, when he has occasion to treat of organic beings he asserts that they are not to be understood or wholly accounted for on mechanical principles. If this assertion is considered in connexion with Kant's metaphysic of the soul, it will be seen that Animism might with some plausibility be added to the long list of doctrines for which his interpreters seek to make him responsible.

It is clear, at least, that Kant did not discover any way of avoiding the necessity of accepting either Animism or one of the parallelistic formulations of the psycho-physical problem, but that he hovered uncertainly between these alternatives.

Kant's successors have made many attempts to show how the defects of his doctrine may be remedied. Three principal groups may be distinguished. On the one hand are those who, like Paulsen and Strong, have accepted the thing-for-itself and, resolutely facing the psycho-physical problem, have attempted to provide a satisfactory solution of it by developing the notion of psycho-physical Parallelism ; on the other hand are those who would purify Kant's doctrine by throwing overboard the thing-for-itself, left by him lurking behind the veil of phenomena, and would thus achieve a pure Spiritual Idealism ; while a third party, accepting, like the first, the thing-for-itself, admits all the conclusions of Materialism or its modern equivalent, Epiphenomenalism, and seeks to retain the ideal world only as the creation of human fancy, a purely imaginary world to which the human mind may withdraw itself from time to time for moral uplifting and refreshment and the enjoyment of the illusion of freedom, as a child gives itself up to the delightful illusions of fairyland. F. A. Lange, who is generally recognized as the leader of the Neo-Kantians, may be said to be the principal exponent of this last form of Idealism ; for, although he wavers unsteadily between the acceptance and the rejection of the thing-for-itself, and seems bent on combining Materialism and Solipsism in his creed, he asserts explicitly that the human spirit must soar above the vulgar real (by which he means the world of the natural sciences) into the realm of ideas which are symbols of the unknowable absolute.

Those philosophers who belong to the second class of post-Kantians mentioned above indignantly repudiate Lange's interpretation of Kant as a vulgar debasement of his teaching.[1] Let us see, then, how one of the most eminent of this school proposes to refine upon Kant's doctrine in a way which will circumvent the psycho-physical problem and avoid the necessity of choosing between Animism and Parallelism or Epiphenomenalism. Professor James Ward has recently essayed this task in his Gifford Lectures.[2]

After an elaborate destructive criticism of Naturalism and its central tenet, psycho-physical Parallelism, and after offering a refutation of Dualism, Professor Ward proceeds to set up in their place a spiritualistic Monism which shall be a pure Idealism, in the sense that it shall regard the physical world as a mere construction or figment of the mind, and which shall nevertheless escape the charge of Solipsism. By a train of lucid and irrefutable epistemological reasoning he shows "that Nature, *as we conceive it*, is neither primary nor independent and complete in itself; that it is, on the contrary, merely an abstract scheme; and that, as such, it necessarily presupposes intellectual constructiveness and motives to sustain the labours that such construction entails."[3]

Now this result of epistemological reflexion is valid as a demonstration of the illegitimacy of deducing the impotence and nullity of mind and purpose from the law of the conservation of energy or from any other generalization of the empirical sciences; but it does not justify the reduction of the physical world to the status of a figment of the imagination. The statement I have quoted is only true in virtue of the phrase which is printed in italics, namely, "as we conceive it." But Professor Ward's

---

[1] E.g the late Prof. Adamson, in his "Lectures on Kant."

[2] "Naturalism and Agnosticism," London, 1899. I am not sure whether Prof. Ward regards his doctrine as providing an escape from the dilemma—Animism or Parallelism; but it has recently been proclaimed as an alternative to them by Miss E. C. Jones ("Hibbert Journal," Oct. 1910). I imagine that Prof. Ward would admit the propriety of Animism as a working hypothesis in biological and psychological science.

[3] *Op. cit.*, vol. ii. p. 247. The italics are mine,

argument implies that it should be regarded as true though that phrase were omitted; for unless the statement is accepted in this sense, the whole argument falls to the ground. That is to say, Professor Ward, like other idealists of this school, shows that our idea of Nature is only our idea of Nature, and draws from this the conclusion that Nature itself, or the physical universe, exists only as a construction of our minds, or is altogether dependent on, and secondary to, mind. This is the fatal error of idealisms of this type. The epistemological reasoning shows not that Nature *is*, but only that it *may be*, merely a construction of our minds; that is to say, it shows that there is no strictly logical process by which we can be compelled to admit that the physical world really exists otherwise than in our thought, and that we may without logical inconsistency refuse to believe that it has any other mode of existence. Now it must be frankly recognized, as I said before, that each one of us can escape from Solipsism only by affirming the real existence of Nature, or by affirming the validity of the category of causation, which enables each of us to infer a world of existing things other than himself playing its part in the causation of his perceptions. But if anyone can discover any other mode of escape from Solipsism, he may, with perfect propriety, regard the physical world as existing only in or for thought. This is the alternative proposed by Professor Ward. He is content to deny all extra-mental existence to the physical world, because he believes he has discovered that one may escape from Solipsism by a different road, namely, by recognizing that the physical world is not merely subjective, but is trans-subjective. By calling the physical world trans-subjective, he means to imply that it exists, not only for the thought of the individual thinker, but for the thought of men in general; and that the conception of it has been achieved, not by the thought of any one human mind, but by "intersubjective intercourse," i.e., by the united efforts and converse of many minds. By recognizing this fact he escapes the grossest absurdity of the solipsist, the assumption that he alone exists; and he escapes also the solipsist's assumption that, if he himself should cease to be, the whole physical universe would also cease to be; for it would remain as the conception of other minds. This, then, is the way in which Professor Ward proposes to escape from the dilemma of choosing between Solipsism and the acceptance of the physical world as extra-mental reality. The position proposed is certainly preferable to Solipsism; but it has two fatal weaknesses: first, it retains much of the absurdity of Solipsism; secondly, it is reached only by an illegitimate step. Ward himself says of it: "Intersubjective intercourse secures us against the Solipsism into which individual experience by itself might conceivably fall, but it does not carry us beyond the wider solipsism of Kant's consciousness in general." That is to say, it involves the assumption that all the objects of the natural sciences are purely mythical; that the astronomers, who accurately foretell eclipses and the reappearance of comets after the lapse of centuries, are foretelling merely the moment at which men in general will, through some miraculous process, aided presumably by "intersubjective intercourse," agree to perceive the comet or the onset of the eclipse; that of the whole series of geological formations each one first came into being when it was discovered, or perhaps at the moment at which it was named and officially recognized by the Royal Society; that the story of the evolution of the organic world has no more objective truth than any extravagant nature-myth which has been widely entertained by any savage people; and so on and so on. Clearly, the impetus of Professor Ward's spirited attack on Naturalism has carried him too far and led him "to pour out the child with the water." An Idealism that demands the acceptance of such conclusions will always remain impotent to heal the breach between science and religion.

But, even if these conclusions were entirely acceptable, we should still have to complain of the method by which they are reached. Like Berkeley before him, Professor Ward has simply assumed the existence of other spirits than his own: and his position is less satisfactory than Berkeley's; for the great idealist did at least infer the existence of God from the evidence that our minds are the recipients of external influences. Each of us learns to recognize the existence of other human minds only through sense-perception of the manifestations of their activities in the phenomenal world; and, if we deny all extra-mental causes[1] to these sense-perceptions, we have no means of passing beyond the sphere of individual experience to the existence of other minds; we must, in short, remain solipsists pure and simple. Or does Professor Ward mean that "intersubjective intercourse" is maintained by direct action of mind on mind, and that all our sense-perceptions are induced by such direct action of one human mind on

[1] I mean causes extraneous to the mind of the percipient.

another, as in the alleged telepathic induction of hallucinations? This seems to be, in fact, the position he means to maintain; if so, it resembles Berkeley's, but with this difference, that whereas Berkeley inferred the existence of God as the cause of his own perceptions and was unable to infer the reality of other human spirits, Ward infers the existence of other human spirits, but is unable to get to God. Which position is preferable must remain a question of taste; but it is obvious that though in both cases the psycho-physical problem is in a sense transcended, yet for empirical science it is answered in the sense of Animism; for that part of the phenomenal world which appears to me as my body represents or symbolizes a certain system of influences exerted directly upon me by the divine spirit (Berkeley), or by other human spirits (Ward); and what science calls the voluntary movements of my body are changes of the appearance of myself to other spirits (or spirit) directly induced in them by that mode of activity of my soul or spirit which we call volition.

Thus we see that Idealism, consistently worked out, justifies Animism as the solution of the psycho-physical problem which must be adopted by empirical science. But, since it rejects the demand of Kant's epistemology and of Naturalism, the demand, namely, that in the physical world mechanical causation shall rule without exception, and since it involves the reduction of all the results of the natural sciences to the level of pure myth, it would seem that a sober Realism, which accepts Animism, offers a better prospect of reconciling science with the belief in the efficiency of mind and purpose. As for the Idealism which sets out with the dictum that all the phenomena and processes of nature must be explained according to purely mechanical principles (whether this dictum be maintained as an epistemological principle, as by Kant, or as a conclusion forced upon our acceptance by the successes of empirical science, as by Paulsen), nothing remains for it but the desperate attempt to save something from the wreck of religion and philosophy by the aid of the hypothesis of psycho-physical Parallelism.

I conclude, then, that there is no way of escape from the dilemma—Animism or Parallelism, and that we must accept Animism, if we find the difficulties involved in Parallelism to be fatal to it. Some of these difficulties were displayed in the foregoing chapter; in later chapters the fundamental assumption of Parallelism, namely, that the course of nature can be explained or described in terms of mechanism only, will be shown to be unwarranted and untenable.

Before going on to this refutation of Parallelism, I shall try to prepare the reader for the acceptance of its alternative by showing that neither the arguments against Animism, nor those directly supporting Parallelism, are of a nature to compel acceptance of their conclusion. And I shall deal first with the alogical arguments.

CHAPTER XIV

ARGUMENTA AD HOMINEM

WE have seen that Parallelism is urged upon our acceptance by certain *argumenta ad hominem*. In this chapter I propose to examine these and to show that arguments of a similar kind, which deserve at least as much consideration, can be adduced in favour of Animism.

Of the arguments of this kind urged in favour of Parallelism (more especially of Psychical Monism), the most important is that the hypothesis allows us to accept all the materialistic teachings of natural science, while retaining our belief in the primacy and reality of mind; that it thus would abolish all strife between science and philosophy, because, as men of science, we shall be materialists, while as philosophers we may be spiritualists or idealists; it is proposed, in short, to establish a parallelism without interaction of science and philosophy. Now we all know men who keep their science and their religion in separate "watertight compartments" of their minds, and many of us may be inclined to approve, or at least to excuse, this arrangement.[1] But what shall we say of the deliberate attempt to do the same with our scientific and our philosophical convictions; for that is the essence of Parallelism. Surely this is Dualism of a kind that is radically unsound and reprehensible. If science had finally and completely established the truth of its postulate of the universal sway of the laws of mechanism and physical causation, we might regard the efforts of the parallelists as a meritorious attempt to save something from the wreck of philosophical and religious beliefs. But so long as this postulate remains very far from empirical verification, and in fact is carried over from the inorganic world to the world of life and mind, only at the cost of flying in the face of all the many unmistakable indications that the two realms are widely different, why should the philo-

---

[1] Mr W. H. Mallock has even written a brilliant book ("Religion as a Credible Doctrine") in order to recommend this solution.

sopher or the biologist capitulate to physical science and lay himself out to give plausibility to its extortionate claim that all existence must be brought under its laws? For a capitulation it is, when the biologist, the psychologist, or the philosopher, accepts Parallelism. Paulsen assures us that physical science will never abate one jot of its claim to explain all events as purely physically caused. But that is his *ipse dixit* merely, a piece of gratuitous prophecy. There are not wanting now leaders of science who reject this claim of physical science to be the arbiter of the possible and the impossible, and to make of biology and physiology merely dependent branches of its stem.[1]

Let us put the matter in the following way. It must be, and by the more enlightened parallelists it is, admitted that it is not possible at present to establish the validity of the claim of physical science that its principles will explain all events, or to rule out psycho-physical interaction as impossible. Suppose, then, that psycho-physical interaction is a fact, that it does really occur; then the capitulation of biology and philosophy to physical science must have the effect of bringing the course of the development of human knowledge into a blind alley, in which further progress must be ever more difficult and must involve in a sense a departure from its true goal; for that goal will only be attainable by going back upon the track and picking up the true course at the point where this capitulation was made. Surely, then, it is the proper task of philosophy to keep the balance true between the great departments of science, and to show to each how far short of absolute truth its conceptions fall, to make clear their

---

[1] For a clear-sighted repudiation of this claim, see Dr J. S. Haldane's Presidential Address to the Physiological Section of the British Association ("Reports," 1908). The keynote may be indicated by the following extracts: "For Biology we must clearly and boldly claim a higher place than the purely physical sciences can claim in the hierarchy of the sciences—higher, because Biology is dealing with a deeper aspect of reality." "Since our conception of an organism is different in kind, and not merely in degree, from our conception of a material aggregate, it is clear that in tracing back life to primitive forms we are getting no nearer to what is called abiogenesis" "In Physiology, and Biology generally, we are dealing with phenomena which, so far as our present knowledge goes, not only differ in complexity, but differ in kind from physical and chemical phenomena; and the fundamental working hypothesis of Physiology must differ correspondingly from those of Physics and Chemistry. That a meeting-point between Biology and Physical Science may at some time be found, there is no reason for doubting. But we may confidently predict that if that meeting-point is found, and one of the two sciences is swallowed up, that one will not be Biology."

limits and their true relations, rather than to try to square the circle of the universe according to the prescriptions of that branch of science which happens to have made the greatest progress and to have put forward its claims with the loudest voice. To some of those who refuse to recognize the claims of physical science to apply its laws to the whole universe of existence, it seems that even now we may dimly foresee the taking up of physical science into a wider synthesis in which it will occupy an important but subordinate place; and that in this way will be effected the true reconciliation between natural science on the one hand and philosophy and religion on the other, rather than by any premature capitulation to the exorbitant demands of any one of the sciences.

We noticed that one of the advantages claimed for Parallelism is that it not only puts an end to the strife between materialistic science and spiritualistic philosophy, but that, by enabling us to accept without reserve and without the reproach of philosophical crudity the materalistic generalizations of physical science, it brings us the satisfactions that flow (for some minds) from that acceptance. To this it is added that the acceptance of Animism raises a number of perplexing questions, such as— What is the prenatal history of the soul? What becomes of it at the death of the body? What part does it play in heredity? And it is obvious that at the present time science has no means of answering these questions in any satisfactory manner.

Now, that certain temperaments find satisfaction in the doctrine that the universe is a vast mechanism all events of which, even the thoughts and acts of God (if there be a God), are in principle predictable by calculation as exactly as an eclipse of the moon, this fact goes far to explain the popularity of Parallelism, but does nothing to justify it. There are temperaments, probably equally or more numerous than the others, to which this view of the world seems little better than a nightmare; and their feelings have as much right to be considered, when we are casting our votes for the constitution of the universe.

That Parallelism naturally, if not inevitably, implies and demands a monistic conception of the universe is undoubtedly one of the grounds of its popularity; but there are two good reasons against allowing this fact to weigh against Animism.[1]

[1] And exactly the same considerations hold good of the claim of Psychical Monism, based on the ground that it implies an idealistic metaphysic.

First, the desire for a monistic or an idealistic metaphysic is usually held up by those who experience it as something peculiarly lofty and deserving of considerate treatment. But the fact that such forms of metaphysical or ontological doctrine appeal in this way to certain persons does not in any way strengthen their claim to our acceptance. Such desires are by no means universal, and it is only by ranging all those who share one's taste in metaphysic as sheep over against the goats, whose tastes are different, that the desire is made to seem, in the eyes of those who experience it, to carry with it a warrant of the truth of their views. Many worthy men have, however, preferred a pluralistic or even a materialistic metaphysic. Such tastes are merely personal idiosyncrasies, like a preference for French mustard or for music in a minor key.

Secondly, Animism is perfectly compatible with a monistic view of the universe and with an idealistic metaphysic. (Indeed we have seen that Idealism, when consistently carried through, implies Animism.) This is sufficiently shown by the fact that a number of highly competent philosophers, notably Lotze, Bradley and A. E. Taylor, combine to their own satisfaction their preference for Animism or psycho-physical Dualism with Monism and Idealism.

It is, in fact, one of the great advantages of psycho-physical Dualism that, whereas each of the rival monistic doctrines necessarily commits those who accept it to some particular ontological doctrine (Materialism, Spinozistic agnostic Monism, or Psychical Monism), we are committed by Animism to no metaphysical doctrine. We may accept it while remaining wholly on the plane of empirical science; and, in view of the strong dislike of metaphysic expressed by so many workers in the natural sciences, this fact should be for them a strong recommendation of Animism. It is true that Descartes' psycho-physical Dualism was made by him a metaphysical Dualism; for he taught that matter and soul are two ultimately different kinds of reality. But scientific Animism is under no obligation to accept Descartes' ontological dogma; it leaves open the ultimate questions, about which it is a mere piece of presumption for any man to express a decided opinion in the present state of human knowledge. For it the real natures of both body and soul remain open questions, the answers to which, we may hope, will be gradually brought nearer to the truth by the labours of after-coming generations. For the present the animist may, if he likes, suppose the body to consist of matter such as is described by physical science; or, with Kant, he may regard it as the phenomenon of an unknowable thing-for-itself; or, with Leibnitz and Lotze, as a system of real beings of like nature with the soul; or, with Berkeley, as nothing but the perpetually renewed acts of God upon our souls. In any case his ontological view, whatever it may be, so long as it is not solipsistic, need not affect, and is perfectly compatible with, his belief in psychophysical interaction.

That mechanical or parallelistic Monism seems to render a coherent account of the world in which no mysteries or fundamental problems remain, whereas Animism leaves on our hands, indeed forces upon us, a number of questions to which we can return no satisfactory answers; these facts may and do, no doubt, seem to many minds to afford good reason for rejecting Animism; but surely only to those who desire to "lay the intellect to rest on a pillow of obscure ideas." For the solutions of the deepest problems offered by such Monism are largely verbal only. Though such Monism became universally accepted, men, regardless of logic, would still speculate on the possibility of a future life, or even continue to hope for it, and would still ask whether there be not somewhere in the universe "a power not ourselves that makes for righteousness."

And this preference for an account of the universe which appears as final and complete, leaving no loose ends and no unfathomed possibilities, is neither universal nor deserving of special consideration. There are minds of another type to which Animism recommends itself just because it points to a great unknown in which great discoveries still await the intrepid explorer, a vast region at whose mysteries we can hardly guess, but to which we can look forward with wonder and awe, and towards which we may go on in a spirit of joyful adventure, confident in the knowledge that, though superstition is old, science is still young and has hardly yet learnt to spread her wings and leave the solid ground of sense-perception.[1]

As to the bearing on our problem of the fact that Animism

---

[1] "The highest philosophy of the scientific investigator is precisely this toleration of an incomplete conception of the world, and the preference for it rather than an apparently perfect, but inadequate, conception." Thus Prof. Mach in "The Science of Mechanics," p. 464.

was first excogitated by savage man, perhaps before he had learnt the use of fire, tools, or clothing, and that it has in all ages and amongst almost all peoples been the popularly accepted doctrine; I do not know that the modern animist need feel any shame on that account, or need regard the fact as affording any presumption against the truth of his view. Many an existing savage tribe and, probably, that mythical creature, primitive man himself, has agreed with the psychical monists in believing the stars to be conscious beings; and Fechner and Paulsen have not disdained to call their testimony to the support of their own view, claiming for primitive men the clear untroubled vision natural to the childhood of the world. So, in this respect, the rival doctrines may cry "quits."

Let us now glance at certain important consequences that logically follow from the acceptance of Parallelism. To many the most important consequence will seem to be the necessity of rejecting every conception of God, other than the pantheistic. Epiphenomenalism is of course not properly compatible with any religious belief or hope; it can only be so combined by those who have the "water-tight compartment" type of mind. But both forms of the identity-hypothesis are readily and usually combined with a pantheistic metaphysic, and will permit of no other form of religious belief.

I do not wish to urge this as an argument against Parallelism; but it is proper that this important implication of it should be explicitly mentioned in the course of our examination of the various theories of the relation of mind to body. It must be clearly recognized, then, that Animism, or the dualistic doctrine of soul and body reciprocally influencing one another, is the only psycho-physical theory logically compatible with Theism, with a belief in a personal God, a Divine Creator, Designer, and Ruler of the World; and that, when it is claimed for Parallelism that its acceptance will bring to an end the age-long strife between science and religion, the claim is only valid on the improbable assumption that Pantheism, which by the leaders of religion in all past ages has generally been held to be little better than Atheism, will prove in the future to be an acceptable and sufficient basis for all religious thought and feeling.

Another important implication of all forms of psycho-physical Monism is that human personality does not survive the death of the body. That Epiphenomenalism necessarily involves this implication needs no demonstration. But the implication is not perhaps so obvious and incontestable in the case of the parallelistic hypotheses. In this connexion, only the two varieties of the Identity-hypothesis need consideration; for, as we have seen, Parallelism proper logically implies one or other of these hypotheses. Fechner held, and sought with much ingenuity and ardent eloquence to show, that his psycho-physical theory was compatible with a belief in a life after death. But all unbiassed minds, I think, will admit that, if either form of the identity-hypothesis may be made to seem not to rule out the possibility of survival of human personality after death, it is only because it leaves the existence and nature of personality, of the individuality of the conscious self, an absolute mystery unrelieved by any ray of light.

Let us glance for a moment at the way in which Fechner attempted to reconcile his psycho-physical doctrine with his belief in life after death. In "Das Büchlein vom Leben nach dem Tode," he begins by ascribing immortality to men in so far as their thoughts and actions continue to affect the thoughts and lives of after-coming generations.[1]

Survival of this sort is of course undeniable; it is equally compatible with all psycho-physical theories; but it is not survival of the self-conscious personality. After this he plunges at once into poetical descriptions of the life of the souls of the departed, which, if the language is to be taken literally, show him to have shared the beliefs about the dead which are generally regarded as the exclusive property of the despised spiritists.[2] Such language alternates with passages more consistent with the pantheistic scheme. We are told that, when a man dies, his spirit pours itself freely through Nature and no longer merely senses the waves of sound and light, but itself rolls on through air and ether[3]; that the spirits of the dead will dwell in the earth as in a common body, and that all processes of Nature will be to them what the processes of our bodies are to us.[4]

Fechner himself raises the question—How can an individual consciousness retain its unity when for its physical or bodily

---

[1] "Was irgend Jemand während seines Lebens zur Schöpfung, Gestaltung oder Bewahrung der durch die Menschheit und Natur sich ziehenden Ideen beigetragen hat, das ist sein unsterblicher Teil" (p. 8).

[2] "At every festival that we make for them the dead rise up; they hover about every statue that we set up for them; they hear with us every song in which their deeds are celebrated" (p. 35).

[3] P. 53.   [4] P. 58.

aspect it has the whole earth, and has it in common with all other departed souls? But he answers the question only by asking another—"Ask first, how consciousness retains its unity in the smaller extension of the body." And we are left to infer that, because Parallelism can find no answer to this urgent question, it is absolved from the impossible task of finding an answer to the other. In another work he defines his conception of the soul in a way very difficult to reconcile with his psychophysical doctrine—" By Soul I understand the unitary being which appears to no one but itself."[1] And again—" I understand by Spirit and Soul the same being which, as opposed to the body, appears to itself"[2]; "the spirit is itself that which unites the multiplicity of the body."[3]

In short, the language used by Fechner in discussing this subject is woefully lacking in precision and consistency; the reasoning is loose to the last degree, consisting in the main of hints at analogies, suggestions of similes and metaphors; and it is only with such reasoning that he attempts to meet the essential difficulty of reconciling Parallelism with belief in any survival of personality. The difficulty may be stated as follows: According to Fechner's own teaching the consciousness of each individual is a composite resultant of the conjunction of the minor consciousnesses of the cells of the brain and body, and these again of their elements; or, strictly in terms of Psychical Monism, the spatial and functional conjunction of bodily elements is the phenomenal manifestation of the conjunction in the unitary system of personal consciousness of many minor conscious activities; or again, in terms of the two-aspect doctrine, the composition of the bodily elements is a phenomenal appearance of some composition of real elements, which in its other or psychical aspect appears as the composite stream of consciousness.[4] The dissolution of the body, then, must also be

---

[1] "Ueber die Seelenfrage" Leipzig, 1861, p. 9.
[2] *Op. cit.*, p. 15.   [3] *Op. cit.*, p. 168.
[4] Kant himself and most of his followers have admitted that the spatial relations of phenomena correspond to some system of real relations between the things-in-themselves that appear to us in perception as phenomena in space; thus Vaihinger writes ("Kant Commentar," ii. p. 143): "Kant, therefore, recognizes relations of the things-in-themselves which correspond to space, but regards them as unknowable. On the other hand Lambert's suggestion still holds good, and with all the more force, that to reason by analogy from the spatial relations of appearances to the true relations of things-in-themselves is not only allowable but required."

regarded as the phenomenal manifestation of some corresponding change in the underlying reality, and must be paralleled by a dissolution of the mental life into its elements.

The following passage will serve to illustrate the way Fechner attempts to deal with this difficulty. " How is it then with the playing of a violin? You think, if a violin, which has just been played upon, is broken up, then it is all over with its music: it dies away, never to sound again, and so also dies away the self-conscious music of the human brain, when death destroys the instrument. But at the destruction of the violin, as also at the death of the man, there is something that you neglect, in looking only at that which is most obvious. The notes of the violin resound in the wide air, and not only the last note of the music, but the whole of it. Now you suppose that, when the sound has gone by you, it has died away; but anyone standing at a greater distance can still hear it, therefore it must still exist; one who stands too far away will not hear it at all, but not because it has ceased to be; the sound merely spreads itself out too widely, becomes too feeble to be heard at a single spot; but imagine that your ear accompanies the sound and spreads itself out with the widening circle of the vibration, then you would continue to hear it. It is never extinguished; it remains for ever. The narrowly bounded violin has spread its music into infinity. You ask, who could really follow the sound and hear it whithersoever it goes? But something really follows it everywhere: the sound itself follows itself everywhere. How now, if it could hear itself? Would it not continue to hear itself for ever? Vain supposition truly in the case of the lifeless violin, but is it vain also in the case of the live instrument? The lifeless one is played upon by others, and so its music is only heard by others just where they happen to be, and does not hear itself. But the living violin of our body plays itself, and so also its music hears itself and only needs to follow after itself in order to continue to hear itself[1]."

I think it worth while to cite this passage, because it is a fair sample of the reasonings employed by Fechner throughout his many writings on this topic, and illustrates very well their attractive, fantastic, and unconvincing character.

Paulsen, who was a faithful disciple of Fechner, evidently recognized the doubtful character of Fechner's reasonings con-

[1] "Zend-Avesta," Bd. II. S. 293.

cerning the life after death; he himself dismisses the question of survival in half a page, saying —" it is unthinkable that a soul-life should be annihilated"; and suggesting that, as our past soul-life continues to exist in present memory, so the individual life may continue to exist as an enduring element of the life and consciousness of God. To which he adds, a little lamely, that nothing prevents our believing that it may continue to enjoy a certain independence and unity of consciousness within the whole.[1]

But, it may be said, Kant has settled this question once for all—Why then trouble to display the inconsequence of Fechner's fantastic reasoning? Fechner committed the error condemned by Kant in the metaphysicians who preceded him, namely, he attempted to apply his understanding to the things of the *mundus intelligibilis*, with which only the practical reason can deal.

Now I do not know that any living philosopher who is seriously to be reckoned with accepts Kant's reasoning on this matter; but the authority and prestige of Kant's name are so great that it seems necessary to consider his teaching in respect to immortality.

Kant sought to establish the immortality of the soul by setting up the *mundus intelligibilis*, which he separated from the *mundus sensibilis* or physical world by an impassable chasm, in the dark abysses of which the thing-for-itself hovered uncertainly. For he taught that, just as the world is two worlds, so man is two men, one, a phenomenal man belonging to the *mundus sensibilis* and wholly subject to mechanical law and, therefore, to dissolution; the other a pure thinking being belonging to the *mundus intelligibilis*, and therefore immortal, like all other things of that world. And Kant left the relation between these two men as completely obscure as that between the two worlds.

I have already commented upon the unacceptable character of this dualism; and here I have only to insist upon the inadmissibility of the method by which it is reached. That method was to divide the human intellect into two intellects, two disparate faculties of knowing and reasoning, the theoretical and the

---

[1] " Einleitung," S. 267. In almost the last of his published works, " A Pluralistic Universe," the late William James expressed a general adhesion to Fechner's world-view; and he certainly believed that the mind of man is not wholly destroyed on the death of the body. But he never accepted Parallelism or the mechanistic assumptions on which it is based, but held a peculiar animistic view of the psycho-physical relation, which he called the " transmission theory."

practical reasons, and to assign the two worlds to the two intellects respectively.

To maintain that the human mind comprises these two intellects, the exercise of which leads to incompatible results, to an antinomy, is to assert the inadequacy of the human mind to the tasks of philosophy, especially to the task of reconciling science with religion, which is commonly regarded as the prime function of philosophy; and, if Kant's epistemology were such as to compel our adhesion to it, we should have to resign ourselves to a radical "scepticism of the instrument." But the reasoning by which Kant attempted to establish the practical reason as a distinct faculty can hardly be seriously maintained at the present day.

He found the surest evidence of the *mundus intelligibilis* and of the faculty by aid of which we apprehend it, in man's consciousness of duty, of vocation, of the worth of spiritual and moral goods. This moral consciousness, he declared, is the expression of man's inmost nature and in it his belief in God, freedom, and immortality, may securely rest.

Thus the nature of man's moral consciousness, ascertainable as empirical fact, is made by Kant the guarantee of the *mundus intelligibilis* and of all that belongs to it, including the immortal soul of man. But modern psychology shows that what is called a man's moral consciousness is his system of moral sentiments; that he absorbs these moral sentiments in the main from the moral tradition of his social environment, which has been slowly evolved throughout the period of civilization by a process perfectly intelligible in its main outlines; that the moral sentiments are no more and no less peculiar or mysterious than the other abstract sentiments, the aesthetic or the intellectual sentiments; and that, therefore, their existence does not in the least justify the conception of the practical reason as a special faculty of an order distinct from that which we use in our ordinary commerce with the phenomenal world.

That Kant should have thought it possible to erect so great a superstructure on so fragile a basis can only be understood when we reflect upon the very peculiar circumstances of his life; how all his life long, in an age when books were comparatively rare and newspapers almost unknown, he lived in a small provincial city, hardly passing beyond sight of its steeples in all his eighty years; how in that narrow space he lived an intensely artificial life, the life of a bookish celibate recluse, remote from all the natural passions and impulses which move the mass of mankind; how, owing to these circumstances, he inevitably remained profoundly ignorant of human nature[1]; and how his conception of man and of his moral consciousness was determined by the fact that he was familiar only with the circle of earnest pietists in which he was born and bred.[2]

But, even if we could admit that the moral consciousness of mankind is as an empirical fact what Kant held it to be, the argument by which he deduces from it freedom and immortality would remain unconvincing in the last degree. In the "Critique of Pure Reason," he bases the belief in a future life on the very natural demand or desire that happiness shall be proportioned to morality. But in the "Critique of Practical Reason," he bases belief in immortality on the demand for the attainment of moral perfection which seemed to him to be implied in the moral imperative: for a finite being cannot attain to moral perfection, but is capable of infinite progress towards it; therefore, if the moral law is to be fulfilled, we must continue to progress for ever; therefore we must be immortal.

This, in brief, was the reasoning by means of which Kant sought to establish human immortality; and surely Heine's scoffing was not altogether without some slight basis in fact, when he said that Kant, having completed his scheme of things, found that the old body-servant who carried his umbrella so faithfully must have a God and a future life, and therefore gave him both. The argument has been well characterized by the late Henry Sidgwick as illustrating equally the ingenuity and the *naïveté* of Kant.[3]

Few would undertake at the present day to defend Kant's practical reason and his proof of immortality. Paulsen, for example, who must be reckoned one of the most faithful disciples, as he was one of the most able exponents of Kant, let go, as indefensible and tinged with the vices of the precritical dogmatic metaphysic, the practical reason and the moral philosophy of which it was the basis.[4]

[1] Be it said with all reverence for his great intellect and fine character.
[2] It seems that Kant had a peculiar aversion to literature of the class by aid of which he might have widened his knowledge of human nature.
[3] "The Philosophy of Kant," p. 19.
[4] "One must say that anything so internally inconsistent as the 'Critique of Practical Reason' is perhaps not to be met with again in the history of philosophical thought" (Paulsen's "Kant," Eng. trans., p. 321).

Other psycho-physical monists, more particularly Hegelians (though not all of them), prefer to dismiss the question as to the survival of personality as an unmeaning one, or at least as one of no importance if it has any meaning; thereby showing that their thought has risen to a height of philosophical abstraction at which it ceases to have any bearing upon the problems which to the rest of mankind seem of the deepest and most urgent interest.

Of contemporary authors, Prof. H. Münsterberg has adopted this attitude more boldly perhaps than any other.[1] Kant, with one of those glaring inconsistencies which abound in his writings, had treated of the future life as a progress in time, and in fact had based his proof of immortality upon the need for such moral progress, although our conception of time was in his view applicable only to the phenomenal world. Münsterberg boldly abides by the doctrine of the subjectivity of time and causation; causality is the creation of my mind merely, and time is the creation of causality and therefore equally subjective. But man is fundamentally will and purpose, and will and purpose are not causes, and therefore are not in time. Hence, "if we are really will, and thus outside of time, there is no longer any meaning in the desire for a protracted duration, this one hope in which the open and the matured materialists find themselves together." "My life as a causal system of physical and psychical processes, which lie spread out in time between the dates of my birth and of my death, will come to an end with my last breath.... But my real life as a system of inter-related will attitudes has nothing before or after, because it is beyond time.... It is not born and will not die; it is immortal, all possible thinkable time is enclosed in it; it is eternal." "There is thus no conflict between the claim of science that we are mental mechanisms bound by law and the claim of our self-consciousness that we are free personalities."

This is what Idealism of this kind offers to the mourner[2] and to him who keenly resents the great injustices of life as we know it. That this doctrine of the timeless and therefore eternal self has no value from these points of view seems obvious. And that it is Subjective Idealism and implies Solipsism seems equally clear; for it denies the validity of the conception of causation, which, as we have seen, alone enables each of us to transcend the sphere of his immediate experience. But even if we pass over

[1] It is briefly expounded in his Ingersoll Lecture, "The Eternal Life."
[2] Münsterberg's lecture is actually cast in the form of a consolatory address.

these objections, can we admit that the phrase, the timeless existence of the self, has any meaning? In common with the great majority of men of trained intelligence, I would say—none at all. Münsterberg tells us repeatedly that we are essentially will and purpose; and he repeatedly speaks of our wills as progressing or making progress, as seeking and longing, as pointing backwards. But these words, will and purpose, are deprived at once of all meaning, if we assign them to a timeless existence; the conceptions are inevitably bound up with the idea of the future, the idea of bringing to pass that which is not yet; and if we were to take away from Münsterberg's discourse every word which implies the time-reference of will, no meaning would be left to his sentences. The denier of time may object that the use of these words implying time is the inevitable result of the poverty of our language. But we have a right to assert that ideas which cannot be expressed without self-contradiction are themselves self-contradictory.

That the difficulty, defined above, of reconciling Parallelism with personal survival after death is very real and great, can hardly be denied; and that Fechner's acute mind should have been unable to do anything more towards overcoming it, than to offer such vague analogies as that of the violin, does but accentuate the difficulty, which to my mind seems insuperable. I conclude, then, that the view that the mind is dependent on the body, or that the consciousness and the body of a man are but two aspects of one thing, or that the body is merely a mode of appearance of his mental life, is strictly incompatible with belief in any survival of human personality after the death of the body.

That Animism is the only psycho-physical hypothesis which is compatible with a belief in any continuance of human personality after death, cannot, of course, be put forward as evidence of its truth; but it does justify a lively interest in the establishment of its truth; especially just now when for the first time serious attempts are being made to discover empirical evidence of such survival;[1] and the fact that these attempts seem already to justify hope of their success should at least serve to warn us against holding dogmatically, as so many now do, to Parallelism, a doctrine which is incompatible with this belief and therefore liable to be overthrown at any moment by the success of these efforts.

I do not urge as any support to Animism the fact that so

[1] See chap. xxv.

large a proportion of the human race has always believed in the life after death, nor the fact that so many ardently desire such life; nor should I do so if this belief and this desire were universal. That all men desire immortality is merely a fiction of the literary tradition;[1] but that we ought to desire a proof of the survival of our personality after death is, I think, demonstrable from moral considerations. In the first place, the great injustices of human life as we know it remain as a dark shadow that cannot be relieved if each man's personality ceases with the grave, a shadow that must darken our whole conception of the universe and of man's position in it.[2] Secondly, apart from this desire for the possibility of some readjustment of the injustices of this life, and apart altogether from the influence upon conduct of belief in the reception of rewards and punishments after death, the desire for evidence of a continuance of personality after death is justified by the influence such evidence might be expected to have upon conduct. There can be no doubt, I think, that, where a belief in a future life obtains generally among any people, it tends to maintain and to raise the standards of thought and conduct of that people. In all ages the national existence of every highly civilized people is seriously threatened by the tendency that has proved fatal to so many States, the tendency for each individual to choose to live for himself alone and to secure for himself as much enjoyment as possible, regardless of all other considerations. An effective belief in a future life seems to be the only influence capable in the long run of keeping this tendency in check, when once men have begun to reflect freely upon their position in the universe. And this belief operates in this way, even though we remain entirely in the dark as to the kind of experience that may be ours after death; for it widens our outlook, pushes back the boundaries, forbids us to regard the horizon that we see as the limit of our world, and so makes us live this life with a sense that issues are involved in it greater than any we can define or grasp; in a word, it preserves in us something of the religious attitude towards life. Now there can be no doubt that under the influence of science this belief is rapidly decaying

---

[1] See Dr F. C. S. Schiller's essay on "The Desire for Immortality," in "Humanism."

[2] It was this consideration that led the late Henry Sidgwick to devote so large a part of his energies to the search for empirical evidence of a life after death.

among all the leading nations of the world. Here is, then, not any new evidence in favour of Animism, but good reason for refusing to give it up, unless we are logically compelled to do so; good reason for subjecting the claims of Parallelism to the most severe criticism; good reason for keeping open our minds towards all the evidence that goes to prove the inadequacy of the principles of physical science to explain the whole course of the universe.

Lastly, I may properly notice in this chapter a circumstance which has exerted in recent times a very considerable influence in securing for the parallelistic interpretations the large following that they now enjoy among the students of science and philosophy; I mean the fact that so large a majority of influential writers have given their adhesion to one or other of these allied doctrines, especially among those who in recent years have explicitly discussed the psycho-physical problem. Among this large number I enumerate the following authors whose activities have fallen within the distinctly modern period—Fechner, Paulsen, Wundt, Ebbinghaus, Münsterberg, Höffding, Ribot, Huxley, Spencer, Tyndall, Romanes, Lewes, Bain, Bosanquet, Lloyd Morgan, Stout, Heymans.

It is right that these names should carry great weight. But in view of the imposing character of this array of names (which might be indefinitely prolonged), it is important that I should point out that the defenders of Animism are not confined to the ranks of authors of popular treatises and manuals of devotion, but that amongst them are a number of men whose philosophical achievements give them the right to a most respectful hearing. Among those authors who have been familiar with the achievements of modern science, and who may be reckoned on the side of Animism, because they either have explicitly defended it or have declared themselves unable to accept any one of the parallelistic doctrines, I name Lotze, Sigwart, C. Stumpf, O. Külpe, L. Busse, Bergson, James Ward, William James, Henry Sidgwick, F. H. Bradley, F. C. S. Schiller, G. T. Ladd, A. E. Taylor.[1]

---

[1] To this list of names I think I may add those of two brothers whose claims to rank high among philosophers are apt to be forgotten in a world which freely accords them the higher honours of statesmanship, I mean of course Messrs Arthur and Gerald Balfour. I add their names with some hesitation, because they have not dealt explicitly with the psycho-physical problem. Yet their keen interest in the work of the Society for Psychical Research and various passages in their published writings seem to justify the inclusion of their names in the list.

The reader may therefore approach my defense of Animism with the comforting assurance that, if he should incline towards its acceptance, he will find himself, not indeed on the popular side in the world of science and philosophy, but in highly respectable company.

CHAPTER XV

EXAMINATION OF THE ARGUMENTS AGAINST ANIMISM FROM EPISTEMOLOGY, "INCONCEIVABILITY," AND THE LAW OF CONSERVATION OF ENERGY

TWO arguments against Animism are put forward with the claim that they suffice to necessitate the rejection of that doctrine, because either one standing alone makes untenable the belief in any psychical intervention with the course of physical process. These must first be examined; for if their claims are valid, our discussion may quickly be brought to its end. It would only remain for us to choose between the rival parallelistic interpretations. If, however, they prove to be inconclusive, we must go on to examine the arguments on the same side whose claim is less absolute, and which are put forward rather as supports to these leading arguments, than as in themselves capable of deciding the issue.

These two principal arguments are that from the law of the conservation of energy, and that from the inconceivability of psycho-physical interaction. By those who accept atomistic Materialism as metaphysical truth they are combined in one great dogma, which runs—all real process consists in the movement of masses, all motion is caused by motion only, and all acceleration or change of motion of any body is caused by impact of some other body upon it. This dogma, of course, rules out psycho-physical interaction, and, if it were well established truth, there would be nothing more to be said ·in defense of Animism. But, since this dogmatic metaphysical Materialism is no longer seriously defended, we must consider the two contentions separately.

That psycho-physical interaction is impossible because we cannot conceive it or understand it, is the old argument of the Occasionalists. By them it was put in the form—We cannot conceive how things so unlike as inextended immaterial soul and material extended body can act upon one another. For they accepted Descartes' dualistic metaphysic. The premise of their argument was that action is only possible between things of like nature. This phrase, in so far as it conveys any meaning, is merely the expression of an unfounded prejudice which, like many another, has been given the dignity and importance of a metaphysical truth. The validity of the proposition is at least as doubtful as its meaning is obscure.

The various modern dressings of this argument from inconceivability, some of which we have noticed,[1] add nothing to its force. The argument was answered by Lotze for all time when he wrote—"The kernel of this error is always that we believe ourselves to possess a knowledge of the nature of the action of one thing on another which we not only do not possess, but which is in itself impossible, and that we then regard the relation between matter and soul as an exceptional case, and are astonished to find ourselves lacking in all knowledge of the nature of their interaction." "It is easy to show that in the interaction between body and soul there lies no greater riddle than in any other example of causation, and that only the false conceit that we understand something of the one case, excites our astonishment that we understand nothing of the other."[2] As Hume long ago showed, we have no insight into causal action in the physical world, even of the simplest kind. The communication of motion by impact, as of one billiard ball upon another, is the kind of causation or transitive action in the physical world with which we are most familiar; and physical science has attempted in the past to exhibit all physical causation as being of this type. In so far as we succeed in conceiving any instance of causation as of this most familiar type, we are apt to feel that we understand it or have explained it. Now, since psycho-physical interaction cannot be reduced to the same familiar type (for by the very terms of the hypothesis it is a kind of interaction *sui generis*), it is true that we cannot understand it in this sense of the word. But in no other sense than that of reduction to a familiar type of sequence, such as that of motion or impact, can we understand physical interaction; it is admitted by the philo-

[1] P. 91 and p. 122.
[2] "Medizinische Psychologie," S. 56. In a similar vein Kant wrote: "For all difficulties which concern the combination of the thinking being with matter arise without exception from the insidious dualistic idea that matter as such is not appearance, that is to say, a mere presentation of the mind to which corresponds an unknown object, but is that object itself as it exists outside us and independently of our sensory powers " ("Kritik d. r. V.," Erdmann's edition, p. 336).

sophers and physicists alike that, when we try to penetrate into the intimate nature of the process of communication of motion by impact, we find ourselves in the midst of insuperable difficulties.

It is well said by Professor Stumpf that "the unlikeness of soul and body can hardly be seriously urged (against the possibility of psycho-physical interaction) by any person of insight acquainted with the investigations of David Hume. Cause and effect are not necessarily of like nature. Only experience can show what things belong together as cause and effect. And least of all should those deny the possibility of interaction of these unlike things, who preach their substantial unity or identity; for the relation of the two worlds, the physical and the psychical, implied by this doctrine of substantial unity, is an even more intimate one than the causal relation."[1]

The following considerations make this argument from inconceivability appear not only invalid, but also a little absurd. The argument implies, as Lotze said, that we understand physical causation in some more intimate way than any other kind of causation. Now if, as Hume maintained, by causation we mean and can mean nothing more than invariable concomitance or sequence, then the invariable concomitance of consciousness and brain-process asserted by the Monists is as good a case of causation as any other. But the only alternative to this doctrine of Hume is that provided by psychology and now generally accepted; according to this view, our conception of physical causation is not arrived at only or chiefly by the observation of invariable concomitance of phenomena; for such observation can rarely be made without interruption of the series of repetitions by apparent exceptions to the rule: it is achieved rather by the projection into the material mass, which we set in movement by pushing against it and which seems to resist our push, a capacity for effort or the exercise of power such as we are immediately conscious of when we put forth our strength. That is to say our conception of causation is principally derived from our experience of volitional effort, of psychical causation, and is only secondarily applied to the explanation of physical events. Accordingly, it may be plausibly maintained, and by many philosophers has been maintained, that psychical causation is the only kind of causation of which we have any understanding. And this view is at

[1] "Leib und Seele, 1896."

least as true as that which claims that we understand physical causation only. Now, when we find, as in this case, that all the persons whose training fits them to form a judgment on a particular question are ranged in two opposite camps returning directly opposed answers to the question; the only philosophical attitude we can assume is one of suspension of judgment, and of recognition that the peculiar prejudices of individuals and the limitations of their imaginations, or even the limitation of the imagination of the whole human race at any given period of its evolution, ought not to be accepted as the criterion of what is, or is not, possible in the universe.

The other less crude way of presenting the argument fails to render it any more decisive. It is said that the spatial conceptions which we use for dealing in thought with the phenomenal world cannot legitimately be intermixed with conceptions of non-spatial influences. But this is a difficulty of our own making, which disappears if we admit that the spatial processes we perceive and conceive are but the phenomenal manifestation of some underlying real processes. And it must be admitted that, if the conceptions which we habitually use in dealing in thought with the physical world are unsuitable for dealing with the case of psycho-physical interaction, that fact cannot disprove the reality of such interaction, but merely points to our need of a more adequate system of conceptions for dealing with the psycho-physical problem. But perhaps the shortest and most effective way of meeting this argument is the following. If you deny all causation you are a solipsist (for without recognizing the validity of the principle of causation you cannot get beyond your own consciousness), and we leave you in your splendid isolation. If you are an epiphenomenalist, you believe that the brain-processes are the cause of your thoughts, that is, you believe in the action of the physical on the psychical, or causation of the psychical by the physical; and this is at least as difficult to understand as the action of the psychical on the physical. If you are a parallelist in the strict sense of the word, you leave the relation of the psychical to the physical as a perpetual mystery. If you accept either of the two remaining alternatives to Animism, you admit that matter is but phenomenal, and either you assert that the nature of reality which underlies both body and mind is unknown, or you maintain that the reality underlying physical phenomena is mental in nature; and in either case the contention that there can be no action of the mind upon the real process of which physical processes are the phenomena would be absurd.

This "inconceivability argument" and the closely allied epistemological dictum of Kant to the effect that the phenomenal world must be explained mechanically in terms of extension and motion, involve the erecting into an exclusive principle or prescription the natural tendency of our minds to conceive things under the form of matter and motion, the tendency to regard "primary qualities" of things as constituting their real nature. This we do because, as Dr Stout says, we can describe the executive order of the world better or more effectively in those terms than in any others. But that our minds work most efficiently in these terms is no guarantee that this mechanical aspect of the world is more real than other aspects.

Sense-experiences, such as odours, tastes, and sounds, and certain bodily sensations such as hunger, of which the spatial attributes are obscure and in some cases perhaps lacking, enable us to conceive a creature with intellectual powers otherwise similar to our own, but incapable of perceiving extension or position or motion, and whose sense-perceptions involve only purely qualitative and intensive changes. Such a creature might build up some conceptual account of the physical world, the world of his sense-perceptions, which might be valid in the sense that by the aid of it he would in some degree render intelligible to himself the order of those perceptions. Yet there would be nothing spatial in the world so conceived. And for such a creature, pondering the psycho-physical problem, the "inconceivability argument" would appear quite pointless. Reflexion upon the way in which such an intellect would conceive the physical world will help us to realize that the philosophers from Descartes, Locke, and Spinoza, to Kant and to many moderns,[1] who have insisted upon the necessity of conceiving the physical world in terms of extension and motion only, are merely, as was said above, erecting a peculiarity of our intellect (which is by no means

---

[1] E.g. Sir F. Pollock, who tells us with complete assurance that "we know a world of things extended in space, to the understanding of which, so far as we can understand them, the laws of matter and motion are our sole and sufficient guide" ("Spinoza: His Life and Philosophy," p. 164).

a necessary peculiarity of intellect in general) into a universal law of thought and of physical science.[1]

Of all the arguments against psycho-physical interaction, that drawn from the law of conservation of energy is regarded as the chief by many (I believe, the great majority) of those who at the present day accept Parallelism[2]; yet it may be shown to be inconclusive in so many different ways that the only difficulty with it is the difficulty of choosing a few of them for presentation here. Let us begin by admitting the law in the most rigid and thoroughgoing form in which it can be stated, and let us make the case against psycho-physical interaction as strong as possible by accepting the scheme of kinetic mechanism as a metaphysically true description of the physical universe. Then all physical energy becomes kinetic energy or the momentum of masses, and the law asserts that the kinetic energy of the universe is a constant quantity. If then any psychical influence be supposed to change the rate of motion of the least particle of matter, it must increase or diminish the existing quantity of kinetic energy; and the supposition is contrary to the law. But the course of physical events might be altered by changing the direction of the motion of particles without altering their rate; and this might be done in such a way as to produce no change in the quantity of kinetic energy. This is the conception of guidance without work foreshadowed by Descartes and rendered more definite by modern physicists.

Clerk Maxwell pointed out the possibility of applying the following principle to the explanation of the action of mind on body.

[1] The following passages written by one who is eminent as both physicist and philosopher may serve to enforce what is said above: " The French encyclopædists of the eighteenth century imagined that they were not far from a final explanation of the world by physical and mechanical principles; Laplace even conceived a mind competent to foretell the progress of nature for all eternity, if but the masses, their positions, and initial velocities were given. In the eighteenth century, this joyful overestimation of the scope of the new physico-mechanical ideas is pardonable. Indeed, it is a refreshing, noble, and elevating spectacle; and we can deeply sympathize with this expression of intellectual joy, so unique in history. But now, after a century has elapsed, after our judgment has grown more sober, the world-conception of the encyclopædists appears to us as a mechanical mythology in contrast to the animistic of the old religions." " The science of mechanics does not comprise the foundations, no, nor even a part of the world, but only an aspect of it " (Prof. Mach's " Science of Mechanics," Eng. trans., pp. 463 and 507).

[2] E.g. by Strong (*op. cit.*) and Ebbinghaus (" Grundzüge d. Psychologie ").

A force or stress applied to a moving body along a line of direction strictly at right angles to the path of its motion deflects the path of the body without doing work, without diminishing or increasing its rate of movement, and therefore without altering its kinetic energy. The spokes of a revolving wheel exert such guidance without work upon the rim. Gravitation of the planets about the sun approximates to the realization of such guidance without work, and only fails to realize it because their paths are not truly circular. If the path of the planet were truly circular, the force of gravitation acting between sun and planet would be a perfect example of guidance without work.

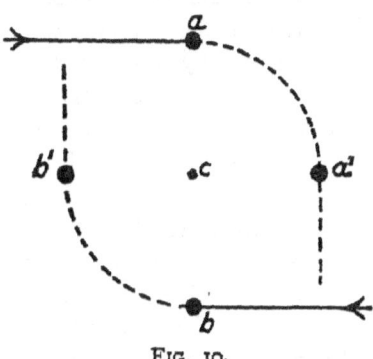

FIG. 10.

Professor Poynting, if I understand him rightly, has given greater precision to this notion in the following way.[1] Let a and b be two equal masses (atoms, molecules, or what not) in a brain, moving in opposite directions with equal velocities. Then suppose that, at the moment of greatest approximation of the two masses, mind establishes a rigid bond between them, so that they cannot recede from one another. Each must then be diverted from its path and must follow a circular path about the point c midway between them; and the two bodies must continue to rotate about this centre like a double star, so long as no change of the conditions takes place. Suppose that, at the moment when the two bodies are in the positions a^1 and b^1, mind resolves its bond as suddenly as it imposed it; then the two bodies will recede from one another along paths at right angles to their original paths, but with the same velocities as before. Thus mind would have changed the course of physical events in the brain by exerting guidance without doing work. The course of events in the physical universe would have been changed, without the sum total of kinetic energy having been diminished or increased.

This is a pleasing fancy. And it is impossible to deny that mind may act in this way on matter; and that therefore, even if the scheme of kinetic mechanism were a true picture of the

[1] "Hibbert Journal," vol. ii.

physical universe, mind might act on matter without breach of the law of conservation of kinetic energy taken in its most absolute sense.

But we need not argue the case on the assumption that atomic Materialism and kinetic Mechanism are the last words of physical science. The dogmatic uncritical belief that the physical universe was truly described in these terms was widespread in scientific circles a generation ago; but it was a faith and a hope rather than a reasonably based opinion. It seems to hold its sway in the minds of many of the older biologists, who absorbed their notions of physical science in the days of their youth when this faith was still confidently held by some physicists. But it has become clear to the more enlightened physicists that this scheme of kinetic mechanism is at best but a working hypothesis, and that it is one which, though in its day it has been of very great use, is now pretty well played out. At no time could it be accepted save by shutting one's eyes to a multitude of facts. A great many of the physical phenomena about us do not in any way suggest that they are of the nature demanded by the scheme, e.g. all the phenomena of light, of electricity and magnetism, of gravity, of chemical attraction and affinity, of latent chemical energy; and the long sustained effort of the physicists to bring these into line with the scheme was only rendered in any degree hopeful by the invention of the ether, by making it both matter and not-matter, and by assigning to it a number of properties which are quite incompatible with one another; for example, it is to be a perfect fluid, continuous, imponderable, and frictionless (which in itself is but a limiting conception achieved by taking away from the notion of fluid several of its essential features), and this perfect fluid is to be perfectly rigid and elastic. Yet even when thus described, regardless of its logical inconceivability, the ether fails to bring into the kinetic scheme of things the facts of gravitation and of chemical affinity.

Let us then replace the scheme of kinetic mechanism with that of dynamic mechanism, and, continuing to admit for the purpose of the argument that the physical energy of the universe is a quantity which never changes, let us consider another way in which psychical influence might nevertheless affect the course of physical events.

We are compelled to recognize the existence of physical energy under two very different forms, namely, the active and the potential or latent; examples of the latter are potential chemical energy (in which form the greater part of the energy contained in the body of an organism always exists) and the latent energy of position, as that of a stone when it reaches the highest point of its path after being thrown straight up from the earth. Now in the organism energy is constantly being rendered latent and constantly being liberated or converted from the latent to the active condition; and Dr Hans Driesch[1] argues that one essential peculiarity of living organisms is that in their tissues the conversion of potential into active energy is liable to be temporarily suspended or postponed by a non-mechanical agency which he calls the "entelechy" of the organism. We may see in this suggestion a possible mode in which mind might exert guidance on brain-process without doing work. The suggestion may be illustrated by the simple case of the pendulum, and the case is strictly analogous to the hypothetical case of the vibrating molecules. As the bob of the pendulum swings to and fro, its kinetic energy is wholly converted into latent energy of position at each moment in which it occupies either of the extremities of its path. Now suppose that mind could arrest it in the position of latent energy; then, if it were so held but for the briefest moment, the course of physical events would have been altered without change of the quantity of energy of the universe. And, if the mind could exert such an influence upon the atoms or molecules of the brain-substance, it might thus play a decisive part in determining the issue of brain-processes, without breach of the law of conservation of energy.

The great weight attached to the objection to psycho-physical interaction which we are now examining will perhaps excuse me to the reader if I put before him yet another possible mode of circumventing the objection, while accepting the most extended formula of the principle of conservation.

If, with most of the philosophers since Kant, we admit that the spatial ordering of physical phenomena is the work of our minds, then it follows that, though this spatial order of the things we perceive may correspond to or symbolize some system of real relations between the realities underlying the phenomena, we have no knowledge of the real nature of these relations. What, then, forbids us to believe that mind may have the power of

[1] "Science and Philosophy of the Organism," Gifford Lectures, 1908, vol. ii. p. 180.

changing these relations while leaving unchanged the quantity of energy (or capacity for influence or causation) of these realities? If mind has such power, it may influence the processes whose phenomena we conceive as brain-processes in a way which would appear to us as a spatial redistribution of energy or a transference of energy from one part of the brain to another, without intervening phenomenal medium, and without alteration of the quantity of energy.[1]

But we may meet the argument from the law of conservation of energy more boldly and, perhaps, more effectively by asserting that the "law" is merely an empirical generalization whose validity extends only to those orders of phenomena of which it has been shown to hold good by exact experiment; or that at the most it is a well-based inductive generalization which states that, whenever one form of physical energy is transformed into another, the quantity of the second form is equivalent to that of the first. In this limited and empirically justified form, the law has no bearing on our problem. It is only when it is given the form—the physical energy of the universe is a finite quantity which can be neither diminished nor increased—that the "law" rules out the possibility of the addition of energy to our organisms by extra-physical influences, if such exist. This more general statement of the law of conservation is arrived at only in the following way:—the physical universe is a closed system of energy, a system closed against psychical intervention or any intervention from without; it is empirically established that the transformations of physical energy within any closed system result in no change of the quantity of energy of the system; therefore the quantity of energy of the physical universe is constant and there can be no influx of energy from without. This it will be observed is a perfect example of an argument in a circle. The law of the conservation of energy, then, is only made to seem to rule out the possibility of the influx of psychical energy by tacitly assuming in the premise of the argument the conclusion which is drawn from it.

When authors assert that the constancy of the quantity of physical energy of the universe is an axiom, i.e. a proposition which all sane competent minds find themselves compelled to accept, as soon as they understand it, they misuse the word

[1] I owe this suggestion to Dr Percy Nunn, though I am not sure that he would approve of the way in which I have stated it. But see Dr Nunn's article, "Animism and the Doctrine of Energy," *Proc. Aristotelian Soc.*, 1911, for a correction of my inaccurate statement of his suggestion.

axiom.[1] The proposition is, if you like, a postulate, and, like every postulate, is to be used only as a working hypothesis (or for the purpose of the particular argument for which it is made), and is to be given up if it is found to conflict with empirically ascertained fact.

Twenty years ago the scientific world was oppressed by the sense of the finality of its own dicta. The indestructibility of matter, the conservation of energy and of momentum, the eternal sameness of the chemical atoms, the inevitable extinction of all life on the earth by loss of heat from the solar system, the never-ending alternation of evolution and dissolution of material systems, all these had become "axioms" whose rejection was said to be impossible for any sane mind. It was felt that little remained for science to do save the working out of equations to further decimal places. But now all that is changed,[2] the scientific atmosphere is full of the hope of new insight, the seeming boundaries of physical knowledge have proved to be spectral creations of the scientific imagination; there is a delightful uncertainty about even so fundamental a distinction as that between matter and energy; electricity, which was a wave-movement of that collection of impossible attributes, the ether, is now said to consist of corpuscles having mass; and light itself is in a fair way to become once more a rain of particles. One even hears whispered doubts about the law of the conservation of energy.

From all this the biologist should learn that he need not confine his speculations strictly within the terms prescribed by the physical science of the moment; that he should rather work out whatever explanatory principles he needs, in a certain relative independence of current physical doctrines.

The arguments against Animism from inconceivability of psycho-physical interaction, and from the law of conservation of energy, have one fundamental weakness in common. Both assume that the notion of physical things or of physical energy is perfectly clearly defined. It is necessary therefore to insist on the fact that no one has ever proposed a definition of physical energy that shall mark it off from psychical energy; although physicists and philosophers alike constantly make use of the

---

[1] See the assertion of Romanes, quoted on p. 93. Paulsen also declares it to be an axiom ("Einleitung," S. 95).

[2] See the Presidential Address of Sir J. J. Thomson to the British Association, 1909.

GENERAL ARGUMENTS AGAINST ANIMISM

phrase "physical energy" as though the term stood for a perfectly clearly defined concept.

Now there seems to be only one way of defining physical things and physical energy in a perfectly unambiguous manner and in such a way as to give any force to the two arguments we are examining, and that is the way of kinetic mechanism, according to which scheme all physical things are mass-particles, and all physical energy is their momentum. Yet, no matter how useful this scheme may have proved, and may continue to prove, it is idle in view of the present state of physical science to assert that it represents the actual nature of all physical things or processes, or that it is the only useful and therefore the only legitimate way of conceiving them.

If it be suggested that by the physical world is meant the world of things and processes that are capable of being perceived by us through the mediation of the senses, it must be pointed out that the physical world, as described by science, is quite other than this world of phenomena or appearances; nor can it be described (as Kant demanded that it should be) in terms of things and processes that are in principle capable of being objects of sense-perception. Both physical and psychological science show that such a demand cannot be complied with. If we are to escape from Solipsism, we have to believe that our sense-perceptions are in part caused by some system of external influences acting upon us; and the various conceptions of the world about us built up by the physical and biological sciences are products of the attempt to conceive this system of external influences in the manner which will most effectively increase our power of understanding, foreseeing, and controlling, the order of our sense-perceptions. Many of the most useful, and perhaps, in certain stages of the development of science, quite indispensable, conceptions employed by it are conceptions of things or processes quite incapable in principle of becoming objects of sense-perception; thus the two most essential and fundamental conceptions of present-day physical science, namely, those of energy (especially potential energy) and of the ether, are conceptions of things which are in principle incapable of being intuited, of being objects of sense-perception or of pictorial imagination.[1] Rather, like all

[1] It is instructive in this connexion to reflect upon the way we regard heat and cold. As sense-experiences heat and cold differ only as any two qualities of sensation differ; their conditions, physical, physiological, and psychological, are similar in all respects; yet heat has for long been regarded as a physical

conceptions that become current in empirical science, they are hypotheses that work in some degree, that are useful aids in the task of bringing some order and intelligibility into the chaos of individual experience. In this respect the conceptions of energy, of ether, of entropy, and all the rest of the conceptions which constitute at present the apparatus of physical science, are on a par with the conceptions of the soul, of vital force, of psychical energy, of matter, of disembodied spirits. In so far as any of these, or any other conceptions, prove themselves valuable as members of the system of conceptions by which we strive to render our experience less unintelligible and to increase our means of controlling its course, they are valid, because useful.

Energy, then, can only be defined as a capacity for exerting influence or producing change; and, unless we explicitly or (in the more usual fashion) tacitly assume that mind can exert no influence, or, in other words, that psychical energy does not exist, psychical energy is included under this definition. Here we see again on a grander scale the argument in a circle as used by those who raise these objections to Animism. It is tacitly assumed that mind can exert no influence, and this premise is implicit in the phrase " energy " or " physical energy " as it is used in the formulation of the law of the conservation of energy ; and only if that is the case, can we deduce from the law the conclusion (thus introduced as a tacit assumption into the premise of the argument) that mind cannot affect matter.

And when we are told, as by Paulsen in the passage quoted on p. 145, that physical scientists will always insist on explaining all events by the principles of physical causation and that it is right that they should do so, we must reply—What do you mean by "the physical," by "physical energy," by "physical causation " ? If you are prepared to stand by the description of the physical world given by atomic Materialism and to maintain that all physical things are hard particles and all physical processes the movements and collisions of those particles, then we understand you ; but we cannot accept your description,[1] we cannot admit

---

existent, a fluid, a thing, an energy, or a mode of energy; while cold remains a mere secondary quality of objects, or a sensation without objective reference, as when we say " I am cold." This fact may serve to bring home to us the wide difference between sense-perceptions and the conceptions of physical science.

[1] That Paulsen had constantly in mind this notion of the physical world is indicated by several passages in the " Einleitung," and the same is true probably of most of those who insist upon these arguments.

your right dogmatically to define the physical world in terms of the kinetic hypothesis; and until you can offer some satisfactory definition your assertions must remain meaningless. Let me illustrate the impossibility of defining energy in a way that excludes psychical energy. Let us suppose that Bishop Berkeley's account of our sense-perceptions is the true one, and that they are all due to the direct action of the Divine Spirit upon our spirits; then what we call the physical world is merely the sum of these divine actions, and the distinction between "the physical" and "the psychical" disappears. Now no one can prove that Berkeley's supposition is false; we can only show that, for the purpose of increasing our control over our perceptions, it is less useful than the scheme devised by physical science.[1]

[1] It seems worth while in connexion with this discussion to put before the reader the following considerations. If the theory of Animism and psychophysical interaction is true, then in a certain limited sense the double-aspect doctrine of mind and body is also true. For, if our minds are capable of influencing those processes or events that appear to us as physical phenomena, then the effects of such "action of mind on matter," if detected by us, will be detected only by inference (according to the principle of causation) from steps or changes in the sequence of phenomena or sense-perceptions; and, just as we infer from certain sense-perceptions a force or influence which, although we cannot directly perceive it, we conceive by the aid of the names magnetism or gravity, or chemical attraction, so we shall conceive more definitely by the aid of some name the force or influence which we infer as the cause of the changes in the phenomenal sequence produced by mind; and if we persist in calling "physical," all the influences that we find it necessary to conceive in order to fill our conceptual scheme of the causation of our sense-perceptions, then these activities of mind will be conceived as physical actions, or, in the loose phraseology current among us, they will appear (though indirectly inferred only) as physical processes or phenomena. And if mind exerts its influence primarily on brain-processes (or, pedantically, on those processes which appear to us in sense-perception as the phenomena of cerebral activity), then certain of the brain-processes that we conceive will be conceived under two aspects, on the one hand as the psychical activities of which each of us is directly aware, on the other hand as parts of the sequence of brain-processes our conceptions of which we build up by elaborate processes of inference from our sense-perceptions.

I may perhaps make my meaning clearer by turning again to Berkeley's supposition, and modifying it in the following way. Let us suppose with Berkeley that the Divine Spirit and our finite spirits are the only real beings; but let us suppose that not only the Divine Spirit acts directly on ours to induce our sense-perceptions, but that each of our spirits may act either in a similar way and to a limited extent directly upon other human spirits, or upon the Divine Spirit to modify in any way the influence that He exerts upon us. Then in either case, just as we build up our conception of the physical world and infer the occurrence of various physical processes from the sequence of the acts of the Divine Spirit, so these acts of human spirits, playing their minor parts in determining the sequence of our sense-perceptions, would be conceived by us as members of the

Since then, it is impossible to separate by definition, physical energy from psychical energy, and since organisms are, so far as we can see by the light of analogy, the only beings in which psychical influences directly operate, we must, if we wish to give any definite meaning to the word "physical" make it synonymous with "inorganic"; physical processes are then such as go on in the inorganic realm. And we may accept the law of the conservation of energy as a well-based generalization for the inorganic realm. But we have no warrant for extending it to the realm of organisms, of life. Men we know to be psycho-physical systems or organisms, and everything points to the view that certain of the processes of these organisms are psycho-physical processes, or processes in which psychical influences participate; and we have good warrant for believing that all animals are also psycho-physical organisms. Again all living organisms show certain peculiarities of behaviour that are not exhibited by any inorganic aggregations of matter. The peculiarities of behaviour of living organisms, especially the power of resisting the tendency to degradation of energy which seems to prevail throughout the inorganic realm, are correlated with, that is to say they constantly go together with, the presence of psycho-physical processes in them; and this fact of correlation implies causal relation between the two things.

No matter, then, how well based is the law of conservation of energy for the inorganic realm, it is quite illegitimate to extend it to the organic; indeed, as we have seen, it is only by means of an argument in a circle that this extension can be given some appearance of plausibility. The few experiments which go to show that the energy given out by an organism is equal in amount to the energy taken in,[1] are far too few and too rough to rule out the possibility that psychical effort may involve increment of energy to the organism; for increments far too small to be detected might effect very important changes in the course of the organic processes.

The issue of this too long discussion is, then, that neither the difficulty we find in conceiving or imagining the mode of action of psychical energy, nor the law of the conservation of energy, rules out the possibility of psycho-physical interaction. So far as

---

sequence of physical processes; and, in so far as we were aware of them as psychical activities, we should conceive them under this aspect also and hence as both psychical and physical.

[1] See p. 93.

they are concerned, it remains open to us to believe either that mind may exert guidance upon the brain-processes, without doing work and therefore without altering the quantity of energy; or that psychical activity may involve an influx of energy to the organism, which, even though small in amount, may exert a decisive influence. If on other grounds the reality of psychical energy or power of influence, as something of a different order from the energies of the inorganic realm, appears probable, we shall probably prefer the latter possibility; and we may believe that the essential peculiarity of living organisms is that they serve as channels of communication or of transmission of energy or influence, from the psychical to the physical sphere;[1] and we may believe also that the evolution of organisms has been essentially a process by which they have become better adapted to play this unique role.

The contentions of this chapter may be further enforced by the following considerations:—If it is impossible for science to render an intelligible account of the processes of the phenomenal world by the aid of the conception of mechanical causation alone (and that this is true of the organic realm is at least probable and may be maintained now with much greater force than when Kant recognized this probability), is science to be condemned, by the dictum of a highly disputable epistemology or by the natural prejudice of our minds in favour of mechanical and kinetic conceptions, to keep running its head for ever against a stone wall, obstinately refusing to attempt other lines of progress? If science finds that it is working with conceptions inadequate to its task, may it not cast about and attempt to develop others that may prove more fruitful?[2]

Among arguments of this group adverse to Animism there still remains to be considered that urged by Prof. Strong and stated on p. 123. It runs—the conception of the soul is reached by

---

[1] That this is true of the human organism has of course been widely believed for long ages. Prof. James has recently presented very persuasively some of the empirical evidence which gives colour to this belief ("Energies of Men," *Philosophical Review*, 1907).

[2] The reader who remains unshaken in his prejudice in favour of mechanical explanations may be urged to make himself familiar with the brilliant and seductive works of Prof. H. Bergson, especially "Évolution Créatrice." Prof. Bergson maintains that the human intellect, having been developed for the guidance of our movements among material objects, is suited only for understanding clearly spatial relations and changes, but that we possess other faculties which we must bring into play if we wish to gain any understanding of life.

inference only, we have and can have no direct knowledge of it, whereas of consciousness we have the most immediate knowledge; therefore, in assigning the soul as the ground of our consciousness, we are seeking to explain the known by the aid of the less known. This argument is only mentioned here lest it should seem that I have passed it over. It has been sufficiently answered in the course of my remarks upon the impossibility of banishing from our account of the world all notion of enduring things or beings. We saw there how Prof. Strong finds himself compelled to postulate psychical dispositions as imperfect substitutes for the soul or the body; and how his doctrine leaves on his hands the problem—"What holds consciousness together?" This may serve as an admirable illustration of the general truth that we cannot explain or render intelligible the whole, or any part, of our experience, without postulating the existence and agency of things that we have no means of knowing in any direct or immediate fashion.

This argument is but an extreme expression of a curious tendency that repeatedly crops out in the writings of many philosophers; the tendency, namely, to assume that conceptual knowledge is untrustworthy and in some sense unreal, while in sense-perception (or in the perceptions of the mythical inner sense) we attain to knowledge of a much more real or more trustworthy, because more direct, order. This assumption appears in many of the discussions directed against the thing-for-itself and the independent reality of the physical world. It is thoroughly fallacious, ignoring as it does the fact that all our perceptions are shot through and through with conceptual activity, and that, only in proportion as perception is at the same time conception, is it raised from the level of mere awareness or feeling to the level of true knowing. If this tendency were consistently carried out, it would lead to the absurd result that the ideal knower is the new-born infant, or the lowly animal whose mental life hardly rises above the level of mere sentiency and appetite.

We may conclude, then, that neither the argument from "the inconceivability of psycho-physical interaction," nor that from the law of conservation of physical energy, nor any epistemological reasoning, can rule Animism out of court[1]; that

---

[1] This is admitted by the more enlightened opponents of Animism, e.g. by Paulsen, who wrote, "Hierüber kann, als über eine Frage, die Tatsachen

GENERAL ARGUMENTS AGAINST ANIMISM

the issue between Animism and Parallelism is one that must be settled by the methods of empirical science, i.e., by the appeal to observation and experiment and the weighing of the claims of rival hypotheses; and that it is for us to-prefer the hypothesis which gives most promise of leading us nearer to an understanding of ourselves and of our environment and to a more effective control over both.

---

betrifft, allein durch Erfahrung entschieden werden. An sich sind beide denkbar. Ich betone ausdrücklich: ich halte auch die Theorie der Wechselwirkung für denkbar"; "wir konnen der Wirklichkeit nicht vorschreiben, was moglich oder nicht moglich ist: denkbar is alles, ausgenommen der Widerspruch" ("Einleitung," S. 94).

CHAPTER XVI

EXAMINATION OF THE ARGUMENTS AGAINST ANIMISM DRAWN FROM PHYSIOLOGY AND GENERAL BIOLOGY

IN this chapter we have to weigh critically the arguments against Animism provided by the biological sciences, and we will consider them in the order in which they are set forth in Chapter VIII. We saw in that chapter how the age-long search for the seat of the soul in the body seems to have been brought to a negative conclusion by modern research; how the searchers tracked the soul to the brain, and then through many generations rummaged every corner of the brain to find some one spot at which the soul might be supposed to be present, to be acted on by the sensory nerves, and to react upon the motor nerves; how the triumph of the doctrine of localization of cerebral functions in the last decades of the nineteenth century finally destroyed the hope of the discovery of such a punctual seat of the soul. We saw also how in the nineteenth century the study of those simplest actions called reflex actions showed that the bodily movement is connected with the sense-stimulus that evokes it by a chain of physical cause and effect, the transmission of a physical or chemical change through the reflex nervous arc; and how at the same time it was shown that the whole nervous system is built up on a reflex plan, and that all nervous action is of the reflex type, involving always the transmission of the nervous impulse through systems of nerve cells and fibres, in which can be found no breach of physical continuity between afferent and efferent nerves, no indication of any gap in the chain of physical causation that might be supposed to be filled by a psychical link. We saw how this disappointment of the expectation of finding a punctual seat of the soul, or some evidence of a gap in the chain of physical causation connecting sense-impression and bodily response, contributed to establish the view that all human actions may be physically explained; for, so the argument runs, if there is no seat of the soul within the body there can be no soul, and if there is no link missing from the chain of physical causation, there can be no psychical link.

Now we must accept unreservedly in their main outlines the doctrines of localization of cerebral functions and of the reflex plan of the brain structure, but we must recognize that the reasoning by which they are made to seem adverse to Animism is unsound.

The former doctrine will seem to make against interaction to those only who have accepted the scheme of kinetic mechanism as an actual and faithful picture of reality, and believe that all process is the movement of particles and all action the transmission of motion. Lotze has dealt with this point so admirably that I cannot do better than quote his words. He points out that " the root of all these difficulties seems to be a confusion in our idea of the nature of an acting force and of the relation of this force to space." " To be in one place," he says, " means nothing but to exert action and to be affected by action in that place"; there can be no other meaning attached to the phrase " being in or at a place." Again he says, " any force arises between two elements out of a relation of their qualitative natures ; a relation which makes an interaction necessary for them, but only for them and their like "; and he illustrates this by reference to the magnet, which exerts action upon, or rather is in reciprocal interaction with, bodies of certain qualities (the magnetic substances, iron, steel, nickel, and so on) in all parts of space surrounding it, but is indifferent to the great majority of substances scattered through the same space—wood, stone, organic substances generally. Just so, he says, " wherever there are elements with which the nature of the soul enables and compels it to interact, there it will be present and active ; wherever there is no such summons to action, there it will not be or will appear not to be."

If, then, other objections to the conception of interaction are not insuperable, the absence of a punctual seat of the soul in the brain may be put aside as no difficulty; and we may agree with Lotze when he says—" the soul stands in that direct interaction which has no gradation, not with the whole of the world, nor yet with the whole of the body, but with a limited number of elements ; those elements, namely, which are assigned in the order of things as the most direct links of communication in the commerce of the soul with the rest of the world. On the other hand there is nothing against the supposition that these elements, on account of other objects which they have to serve, are distributed in space, and that there are a number of separate points in the brain which form so many seats of the soul. At each of these the soul exercises one of those diverse activities which ought never to have been compressed into the formless idea of merely a single outgoing force"; [1] that is to say, it is reasonable to suppose that we shall find in the brain a number of parts of very highly specialized physico-chemical constitution, the most highly organized forms of organized matter; and that, whenever any one of these parts is thrown into activity, an action is exerted on the soul, which stimulates it to a response of which the first step is the production of a sensation of a certain quality, this quality being dependent upon the constitution of that part of the brain-substance and on the nature of the physical process which takes place in it.

Now the development of brain-physiology has shown that within each of the sensory areas of the cortex we seem to have just such elements of supremely highly organized and specific constitution; and our present knowledge enables us even to point with some plausibility to the varieties of this most highly specialized form of living matter as occupying places where the afferent neurons pass over their excitement to the efferent neurons. So at least I ventured to argue some fourteen years ago, in a paper the reasoning of which has not been refuted.[2]

Our modern and constantly increasing knowledge of the cerebral localization of mental functions is, then, not at all incompatible with the conception of psycho-physical interaction; but rather shows us a state of things in the brain just such as this conception, properly understood, seems to demand, such a state of things as is most easily reconcilable with this view. And in Chapter XXI. I shall try to show that the physiological facts of this group provide a basis for one of the strongest of the arguments that justify the conception of the soul.

The demonstration of the continuity of all nervous processes within the nervous system, of the absence of any discoverable gap in the sequence of material causation which connects sense-impres-

---

[1] This and the preceding quotations are taken from Lotze's "Metaphysic," Bk. III. chap. v. (Eng. trans.). I should like to cite many other passages, but instead will urge the reader to make himself acquainted with the whole of Book III. of that work.

[2] "Contribution towards an Improvement of Psychological Method" ("Mind," N.S., vol. vii.), and also "On the Seat of the Psycho-physical Processes" ("Brain," vol. xxiv.).

sion with muscular reaction upon it, will seem to rule out psychical intervention in the causal series only to those who take an altogether too simple view of the nature of psycho-physical interaction, the view namely that the whole causal sequence must, during some definite period of time, pass over into the psychical sphere, leaving a positive temporal gap or even a spatial and temporal gap in the sequence of nervous processes. Such a conception of psycho-physical interaction may be represented diagramatically by Fig. 11, in which, as in the diagrams of Chapter XI.,

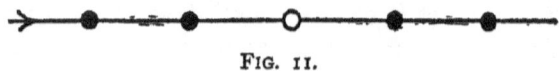

FIG. 11.

the black circles stand for brain-processes, the clear circle for psychical process, and the lines between for the causal links.

No causation is adequately represented by a sequence of this sort—no effect is determined by a single cause, but always by a conjunction of causes. It is only by a convenient convention that we commonly single out what seems to us the most prominent of the causes, and call it *the cause* of the event and all the others merely necessary conditions. The false conception of causation which is engendered by this habit, is apt to be confirmed by our common use of the phrase, "a chain of cause and effect"; for we habitually think of a chain as a series of single links, each of which is the sole connexion between its predecessor and its successor in the series. If we wish to use an illustrative analogy of this sort, we ought to speak of a *net-work* of cause and effect, rather than of a chain. As soon as we do that, this particular objection to psycho-physical interaction falls to the ground. The observable continuity of the physical sequence seems to rule out psychical links so long only as we think of the causal sequence as a chain of single links; but, clearly, it does not do so if we substitute a length, say, of chain-mail for the single strip of chain, in our pictorial imagining of the causal sequence; then the fact that, in a certain transverse section (representing any one moment of time) of such a woven chain, some links are of steel will not seem to prove that other links may not be of a different constitution.

If we would represent diagrammatically the causal relations of the brain-processes implied by the doctrine of psycho-physical interaction, the simplest figure that will serve for the purpose must have some such form as Fig. 12. Such a figure is of course hopelessly inadequate, yet it may serve to warn us against the common error we are considering.

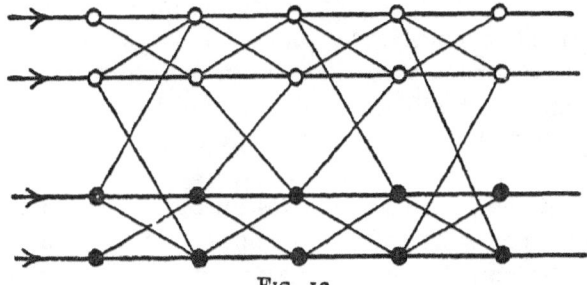

Fig. 12.

We may agree, then, with the opponents of Animism, when they tell us, as they so frequently do, that, if the brain and all its parts could be so magnified that the physiologists could wander through all its most delicate fibrils and study with the naked eye the movements of each molecule or atom, they would nowhere find any train of physical causation abruptly coming to an end without any further physical effects, and nowhere any train of physical events initiated *de novo* without physical antecedents. But we may nevertheless believe that, even if all the physical and chemical processes of the brain were perceptible by the physiologists as movements of particles, there might occur certain deflexions of the moving particles, or certain accelerations or restraints, which would remain inexplicable and unpredictable by mechanical principles.

We saw that the modern doctrine of the reflex type of all nervous functions has made for the rejection of Animism in another way also; namely, in conjunction with the doctrine of unconscious cerebration and with the physiological interpretation in terms of nervous habit of the account of mental process given by the "association-psychology," it has seemed to justify the claim that we can now understand in broad outlines the way in which all human action is mechanically determined, and that we have good evidence in support of the belief that the mechanism of the nervous system is adequate to the demands made of it by this view.

As regards one part of this evidence, that, namely, to which Huxley attached so much importance and which consists in the fact that men sometimes perform very complex trains of seemingly purposive action of which they can afterwards remember nothing, of all this class of evidence it may be said at once that the argument based on it is now known to be fallacious; it involved the assumption that all acts of which no memory can be evoked are performed unconsciously or, as it is said, automatically. Further study of such cases has shown that in many of them the loss of memory is temporary only, or that memory of the actions can be evoked by special procedures. And this shows that absence of memory of any action or train of action is not good evidence that the action was unconsciously performed, and forbids us to infer from such lack of memory that complex purposive action can be carried out unconsciously. This part of the evidence against Animism therefore falls to the ground.

This however does not dispose of the whole basis of the claim that a sufficiently detailed knowledge of the structure and function of the nervous system would provide complete explanations of human behaviour. But at this stage of our inquiry it must suffice to point out that whatever plausibility this claim may have is derived in the main from a spurious or undue simplification of the account of the nature of mental process, and from the ignoring of enormous gaps in our knowledge of, and even in our hypothetical schemes of, the physiological mechanisms which it is sought to make responsible for all the course of mental process and of bodily action; that "the association-psychology," which alone gives plausibility to this claim, is now universally admitted to have left out of account the most essential and characteristic aspect of mental process, namely its purposive selectivity; and that the assimilation of all memory to mechanical association presents difficulties which up to the present time appear to be insuperable.[1]

We shall have to consider the evidence of this class more fully when, in a later chapter, we shall approach it from the opposite point of view and shall inquire—Does not our knowledge of the bodily processes now suffice to prove that human conduct cannot be accounted for on mechanical principles?

But we must consider for a moment at this point all that class of physiological evidence which has made strongly in favour of Epiphenomenalism among the physiologists, by proving the dependence of our mental life upon the integrity of the structure and chemical constitution of the brain.

Now, it is quite illogical to hold that these facts rule out inter-

[1] See chap. xxiv.

action, or prove that the action between soul and body is a one-sided action of body on soul without reciprocal action of soul on body. For it is quite possible to match the array of facts which seem to prove the action of the body on the soul, with an equally imposing array of facts which seem to prove the influence of psychical processes, of feeling, emotion, desire, and volition, upon the body. And, if we take these two classes of facts at their face value, without attempting to explain them away by such subtleties as the identity-hypothesis, they indicate very strongly reciprocal action and reciprocal dependence of our bodily and our psychical processes.

The only form of interaction theory which may perhaps be held to be ruled out by the facts of this group, is that which assumes that the psychical processes are self contained and independent of all bodily correlates and conditions, excepting only the rise of sensation and the initiation of bodily movement. Against such a doctrine of interaction the facts of the class we are considering do tell very strongly. But they are on the other hand just such as are demanded by a doctrine of intimate interaction of soul and body all along the line of mental process; for, if our mental life is the interplay of these two factors, soul and brain, their co-operation is presumably essential to it, and the fact that the incapacity of the one (the brain) to perform its part deranges or puts a stop to the interplay, does not prove that the other (the soul) is not essential, that it plays no effective part, or that it does not exist.

Under the heading, the composite nature of the mind, we noticed in Chapter VIII. how certain facts of animal morphology and physiology on the one hand and certain pathological mental conditions on the other hand seem to force upon us the view that our individual consciousness is neither strictly unitary nor indivisible, and that such unity as it has is conditioned by the functional continuity of the parts of the nervous system. I propose to devote a later chapter to the discussion of the problem of the unity of consciousness, and here will only say that, although the facts of these two orders raise, as it seems to me, the greatest of all the difficulties in the way of Animism, they present difficulties no less great whatever view be taken of the relation between mind and body.

We have seen that the postulate of the continuity of evolution of the organic from the inorganic realm is made the basis of a general argument against Animism (p. 120) as well as of a special argument in favour of the identity-hypothesis (p. 142). We may deal with both arguments at this point; there are more ways than one in which both may be undermined. One way is totally to reject the postulate; but, if we do that, we must be ready with some alternative suggestion as to the origin of life on the earth. One such suggestion has been made by a great physicist, the late Lord Kelvin. He pointed to the fact that the earth as a material system has not been a closed system, but rather has been constantly receiving new additions of matter from outside in the form of meteorites; and he suggested that living matter was not evolved from inorganic matter upon the earth, but was perhaps brought to it in some lowly form upon a meteorite coming from some region in which life already existed, and that this organic matter was the parent of all the forms of life later evolved upon the earth.

Now this is not a very satisfactory solution of the difficulty. For, first, there is the great improbability of organic matter being conveyed upon a meteorite from some remote region, some world which had been shattered in some great disaster; it is difficult to suppose that any organism could have survived this disaster as well as the fiery ordeal of the descent upon the earth. Secondly, apart from this objection, the suggestion does but carry the difficulty one step further back and transfer it to some other material sphere, where the same problem confronts us.

The former objection applies less forcibly perhaps to the more recent suggestion of a similar kind (which comes, I believe, from another distinguished physicist, Prof. S. Arrhenius), namely that life was brought to the earth in the form of minute germs travelling through space under the driving power of "light-pressure." But the second objection applies equally to this form of the suggestion.

Let us then accept the evolution of organic forms from inorganic matter on this earth as the most probable view. There remain two possibilities of reconciliation with interactionism:

(1) We may suppose that, as Lloyd Morgan and other parallelists have argued, the inorganic matter from which organic matter was evolved had some germ or rudiment of capacity for psychical life; this supposition tells against psychophysical interaction only if we accept another supposition, namely that inorganic matter does absolutely obey purely mechanical

laws. But this cannot be admitted as completely proved. In the experiments on which the physicists rely as the inductive empirical foundation of their strict mechanical laws and their sweeping generalizations and predictions of future events, they deal in all cases according to their own teaching with immense numbers of material units, atoms, or molecules, or vortex rings, or what not. Now, if these units have any rudiment of psychical life, as the argument from continuity of evolution is held to demand, then they may be truly individuals, psychic beings of like nature with ourselves; their behaviour may be to some extent determined by purpose and psychical striving, and therefore not strictly mechanical; yet the experiments of the physicist would fail to detect the fact, just because their experiments deal always with immense numbers of units and their empirical laws are statements of statistical averages. For it is found that even the actions of human beings, if dealt with in very large numbers, seem to be capable of being stated in wide generalizations and of being predicted on the basis of such empirical statistical generalizations, e.g., it can be predicted with some confidence that a given proportion of the total population of a country will marry in each of the four seasons of the year, or will commit suicide or murder, and so on; the purposive individuality of the units is masked by this statistical mode of treatment.

Now some statisticians have argued that the possibility of stating such general laws of human behaviour proves it to be subject to the same rigid mechanical determination as is generally assumed to rule over the processes of inorganic matter. But surely a more valid inference is that, if statistical treatment can make even such undeniably purposive and teleological and individual events as marriages and suicides appear to be purely mechanically determined, it must inevitably have the same effect when applied to events in which the numbers of units dealt with are much greater, and in which the psychical operations are, by the hypothesis, of a relatively simple kind! That is to say, if we accept the argument from continuity of evolution to the animation of inorganic matter (as the parallelists do), then it is quite open to us to believe that psycho-physical interaction prevails throughout the scale, and that the process of organic evolution has been essentially the progressive organization of matter in such a way as will allow always greater and greater influence to the teleological and psychical laws, relatively to the mechanical. Or, to put the supposition in a rather different way, we may suppose that all things are monads or system of monads and that organic evolution has consisted in the parallel evolution of those systems of simple monads which appear to us as the bodies of animals and of those higher monads which, by reason of their higher powers, play a dominant role in the life of organisms, controlling the systems of subordinate simple monads.

But there remains yet another possibility. We may accept the postulate in the sense that we regard complex molecules of non-living matter as having begun gradually to exhibit the characteristic signs of life and mind; and yet we may maintain that this was due to the co-operation of a new factor. The assumption of the continuity of evolution of living things from inorganic matter, in the sense which rules out the incoming of any new factor, is a very great assumption which nothing compels us to accept; it has in fact but the slender basis of the demand for symmetry and simplicity made by our minds. The gap between the organic and the inorganic in nature is an immense one; the two kinds of material phenomena present fundamental differences, and there is every appearance of the incoming of a new factor with the first living things, a teleological factor which is capable of working against or controlling the physical law of the degradation of energy, a law which seems to rule throughout the inorganic world.

Suppose, then, that we had a full history of the evolution of organic beings from inorganic matter by slow steps of gradually increasing complexity of molecular organization; suppose that the progress of synthetic chemistry enabled us to reproduce the steps of this evolution in the chemical laboratory and to bring about the appearance of living organisms by way of *abiogenesis*; even that would not prove that the psychical did not begin to intervene in the material processes at the point at which the increasing complexity of molecular organization rendered possible or necessary the co-operation of this new factor; a factor latent or inoperative up to that point, because the conditions which permit of its co-operation were lacking. For if, as all facts indicate, certain physico-chemical conditions are necessary conditions of the co-operation of the psychical factor, then that factor will have begun to co-operate only when those necessary conditions were realized.

We saw in Chapter IX. that the triumph of the Darwinian principles is held to make against Animism, not only by compelling us to accept the principle of continuity of evolution, but also because it provides a mechanical explanation of so much in the organic world that formerly was confidently regarded as the product of teleological determination. It must be noted, however, that only the Neo-Darwinian or Weismann school maintains the all-sufficiency of the principle of natural selection to explain biological evolution, and that many eminent biologists find it impossible to accept this view. Further, we must note that, even if the Neo-Darwinian doctrine be accepted, its one great explanatory principle, natural selection, presupposes the struggle for life among organisms. And this struggle, though in its lower stages it may express merely blind craving and impulse without clear foresight of any end, is essentially teleological; and such persistent striving, which is manifested not only by all animals, but also in less degree by plants, is the most characteristic mark of organic or living beings.

It is not true, then, that Darwinism has abolished the need for teleological explanation in biology; at most it has suggested the possibility and the hope of complete mechanical explanation. In a later chapter I shall have occasion to show more fully that the hope is illusory.

CHAPTER XVII

THE INADEQUACY OF MECHANICAL CONCEPTIONS IN PHYSIOLOGY

WE have seen in an earlier chapter how, about the middle of the nineteenth century, the rapid progress of physical and chemical science gave rise to a new wave of Materialism; and how physiologists, with few exceptions, began to regard Vitalism as finally overcome and to look confidently forward to the explanation of all the processes of living organisms in terms of physics and chemistry; growth was to be explained as a mere assimilation of molecules after the manner of the growth of crystals; secretion as a mere filtration or osmosis or as a conjunction of these two processes; all regulation of movement and of other processes by the nervous system as mere reflex action.

But now, after another half-century of active physiological research, to which many hundreds of able men have devoted their lives, the achievement of the program so confidently laid down seems to have been brought no nearer. It has rather to be admitted that greater knowledge has revealed new difficulties on every hand; that no part of the program has been achieved; that no single organic function has been found to be wholly explicable on physical and chemical principles; that in every case there is manifested some power of selection, of regulation, of restitution, or of synthesis, which continues completely to elude all attempts at mechanical explanation. Even so simple a process as the secretion of fluid through a very thin membrane shows itself to be other than, and more than, a process of filtration or osmosis; and of even that most characteristic of all the animal functions, the contraction of muscle fibres, no mechanical explanation has proved acceptable to any considerable number of physiologists.[1] In the address to which I have referred

---

[1] To the best of my judgment, of all the many hypotheses put forward to explain muscular contraction, the only one that offers a complete and strictly mechanical explanation of the process is the one suggested by myself in my papers in the "Journal of Anatomy and Physiology," 1897 and 1898. Neither the hypothesis itself, nor the attempt on which it is based, namely, the attempt to make use only of strictly mechanical conceptions, has met with any general approval.

above,[1] Dr Haldane said: "If in some ways the advance of Physiology seems to have taken us nearer to a physico-chemical explanation of life, in other ways it seems to have taken us further away. On the one hand we have accumulating knowledge as to the physical and chemical sources and the ultimate destiny of the material and energy passing through the body: on the other hand an equally rapidly accumulating knowledge of an apparent teleological ordering of this material and energy; and for the teleological ordering we are at a loss for physico-chemical explanations. There was a time, about fifty years ago, when the rising generation of physiologists in their enthusiasm for the first kind of knowledge closed their eyes to the second. That time is past, and we must once more face the old problem of life."[2]

He states the case against the view that metabolic processes are nothing but physico-chemical processes in the following way. If the mechanical assumption is true, the special complex functions of each cell imply correspondingly specific and complex structural mechanism within it. "To take an example, a secreting cell in the kidney may be assumed to have a structure which responds to the stimulus of a certain percentage of urea or sodium chloride in the blood, and reacts in such a manner that energy derived from oxidation is so directed as to perform the work of taking up urea or sodium chloride from the blood and transferring it against varying osmotic pressures from one end of the cell to the other. This mechanism must also be assumed to have the property of maintaining itself in working order, and probably also of reproducing itself under appropriate stimuli, besides also perform ng various other functions. Its physico-chemical structure must thius be very definite and complex—to an extent which the older physico-chemical theories took no account of. If we look to the cells in other parts of the body we are met with the same necessity for assuming complexities of structure which seem to grow in extent with every advance in physiological knowledge, every discovery of new substances present within or around the cells, every discovery of new physiological reactions."

The assumption that all the cells of the active tissues of the

---

[1] P. 190.
[2] To the same effect Prof. E. B. Wilson—"The investigation of cell activity has on the whole rather widened than narrowed the great gulf which separates the lowest forms of life from the phenomena of the inorganic world" ("The Cell," 1900).

body have such extremely complex, definite, and specific physico-chemical structure is sufficiently difficult. But this is only the beginning of the difficulty. The difficulty is increased a thousand-fold when we try to understand in accordance with the assumption the way in which these cells, each having its perfectly specific and highly complex structure, are produced and the way in which they are arranged to form tissues and organs, reproducing with extreme faithfulness the plan of the structure of the species. "The adult organism develops from a single cell, the fertilized ovum. It is certain that this cell does not contain in a preformed condition the structure of an adult organism. The conditions of environment in which any particular ovum develops itself are doubtless indefinitely complex from the physico-chemical standpoint, as indeed is the environment of any particular portion of matter existing anywhere. But these conditions also vary almost indefinitely in the case of different ova, whereas the adult organism to which the ovum gives rise reproduces in minute detail the enormously complex characters of the parent organism. We are thus driven to the assumption that the ovum contains within itself a structure which, given certain relatively simple conditions in the environment, reacts in such a way as to build up step by step, from materials in the environment, the structure of the adult organism. To effect this the germ-cell must have a structure almost infinitely more definite and complex than that of any cell in the adult organism." In this way we are led to see that the physico-chemical doctrine of life must postulate in the germ-cell a physico-chemical mechanism of a complexity beside which that of any tissue-cell of the developed organism, wonderfully great as that must be supposed to be, seems simplicity itself. For the mechanism of that germ-cell must, if the assumption be true, somehow contain the potentiality of the specific, complex, and widely different mechanisms of all the cells of all the many different tissues of the body; and at the same time it must contain the potentiality of the exact but very complex grouping of these cells within the tissues, and of the ordering of the various tissues in relation to one another, relations which again are of extreme complexity, involving in almost all organs not merely definite juxtapositions of cells and tissues, but the most complex interpenetrations of tissues of several kinds, e.g. liver-cells, connective tissues, blood-vessels, nerves and ducts, in the case of such an organ as the liver. It must be remembered also that, according to the assumption we are examining, the mechanism of the germ-cell must contain the potentiality of determining not only the structure and functions of the organs of the vegetative life, and of the muscles, bones, skin, and hair, in short, of all that presents itself to our immediate observation in the adult organism; but also, most incredible of all, it must contain the potentiality of all that secret structure within the nervous system which is supposed to be the mechanical basis of all the inherited mental powers; all the enormously complex and precise structure which must underlie such functions as spatial perception and the various modes of instinctive behaviour that are proper to each species.

And the ovum must somehow contain (according to the assumption), in the form of precise spatial arrangements of highly complex molecules, the potentialities not only of all the characters that the individual has in common with all members of his species, but also of all the inherited peculiarities which distinguish him from his fellows, such characters as musical or mathematical genius, or those idiosyncrasies or tricks of thought and manner and feeling, whose innateness is proved by their cropping out in various members of a family who have not come into personal contact with one another.[1] Nor is this all; for, besides the specific and the individual innate characters of the adult, we have to attribute to the germ-plasm a large number of potentialities that remain latent. "Besides visible changes which it (the germ-cell) undergoes, we must believe that it is crowded with invisible characters proper to both sexes, to both the right and the left sides of the body, and to a long line of male and female ancestors separated by hundreds and even thousands of generations from the present time; and these characters, like those written on paper in invisible ink, lie ready to be evolved whenever the organism is disturbed by certain known or unknown conditions."[2]

---

[1] The close resemblance sometimes observed in twins brought up under different circumstances is especially important in this connexion. For such cases see Galton's "Inquiry into Human Faculty." Such peculiarities as the colour of hair or feathers, or the shape of the comb of fowls, may with some plausibility be attributed to the presence or absence of an atom of some element in some atom-group of the germ-plasm, or to the substitution of an atom of one element for that of another. But what difference of atoms or of atom-groups in the germ-plasm can be supposed to determine that of two men, perhaps two brothers, one shall be a musical genius, appreciating and composing difficult orchestral music at a tender age, while the other remains throughout life incapable of reproducing or even of recognizing the simplest melody?

[2] Darwin's "Variation of Animals and Plants," ii. p. 26.

Further, this viscid speck of matter, the germ-plasm, has to be supposed not only to be at any moment or period of its existence a structure of this enormous complexity, precision, and definiteness, but also to preserve this structure with extreme faithfulness through thousands and millions of years and in spite of all the vicissitudes of constantly repeated division and constant growth by assimilation of new matter.[1]

But to all the considerations of the foregoing paragraphs the convinced mechanist replies that argument of this kind, relying as it does on our ignorance of the details of cellular structure and on the limitation of our powers of constructive imagination, carries no conviction and is incapable of disproving his assumption. And in his eyes it will probably add nothing to the case against his view, to point out that we can find in inorganic nature no process remotely analogous to the growth of the complex organism out of the germ-cell, no case in which a piece of mechanism can effect the reproduction of itself by growth and division, let alone the production of a swarm of other mechanisms of various kinds each complex and definite and differing widely from all the rest.

Hence considerable importance attaches to the results of experimental interferences with the growth of organisms. Driesch and others have made many experiments which show that the development of an organism may be interfered with at various stages in the most gross mechanical manner without preventing the production of the typical form of the species, a perfect complex organism. A very few examples only of many similar cases can be noted here. Many germs pass through a stage in which they consist of a number of cells arranged in the form of a hollow sphere or other simple symmetrical solid figure. In some cases an embryo in such a stage, in which differentiation of its cells has been clearly manifested, may be subjected to such distortions as being pressed out into a flat disc or cut into two parts, and will nevertheless rectify the course of its development, thus grossly disturbed, and will grow up into the typical form. In many other cases, if a part of an organism is taken away by mechanical violence, the remaining part regenerates the lost part, and so restores the complete organism. The case of the newt's limbs is perhaps the most widely known, and is sufficiently strik-

---

[1] The necessity of attributing to the germ-plasm this astonishing stability is forcibly insisted upon by Dr Archdall Reid, "Laws of Heredity," London, 1910, p. 94.

ing and incompatible with the mechanistic assumption; for, as Driesch points out, the trans-section of the limb may be made through any plane, and in every case just so much as is lopped off grows anew from the cut surface. In other cases so much may be cut away from the body of an organism that a mere fragment of highly specialized function remains; and yet such a fragment regenerates the whole organism. A particularly striking case is that of _Clavellina_, an ascidian, that is to say, an animal organism of considerable complexity. "You first isolate the branchial apparatus from the other part of the body (which other part contains heart, stomach, and most of the intestine), and then you cut it in two in whatever direction you please. Provided they survive and do not die, as indeed many of them do, the pieces obtained by this operation will each lose its organization (becoming a mere sphere of cells devoid of specialized structure) . . . and then will each acquire another one, and this new organization is also that of a complete little _Clavellina_." [1]

In some cases again, organisms of the same species mutilated in closely similar fashion will go through two, or even three (e.g. Tubularia [2]), very different courses of restitution, all of which have the same result, namely, complete restitution of the normal form.[3]

Now the mechanistic view necessarily assumes that the course of development must be determined in large part by the spatial relations between the constituent parts of the physico-chemical mechanism; for the reciprocal influences of the parts of the mechanism are essential causes of the progressive development, and these influences must vary with every change of the spatial relations of the parts. But in experiments of the kind we are considering, the spatial relations of the parts of the "machine" are very much altered by the experimental interferences; in some cases being utterly distorted by violent dislocations, in others some of the parts being entirely removed. And

[1] "Philosophy and Science of the Organism," vol. i. p. 130.
[2] _Ibid._, vol. i. p. 160.
[3] A specially striking instance of regeneration is that of the lens of the eye of Triton. In the normal course of development, the substance of the lens is formed from the epidermal or ecto-dermal tissue; but, when the lens has been removed from the eye of the adult organism, it is regenerated by growth of tissue from the edge of the iris, a mesodermal tissue. The first description of this phenomenon was generally received with scepticism by the biologists. But it has been confirmed by several observers, and seems to have been fully established. (See T. H. Morgan's "Regeneration," p. 204.)

yet in spite of this the normal course of development and the normal structure are re-established.

This argument, which comprises Driesch's second and third proofs of Vitalism or, as he prefers to say, of the autonomy of life processes, is so important that it seems worth while to restate it in a rather different way.

According to the mechanistic view, the germ-cell must contain a number of complex constituents, presumably highly complex constituents, the reciprocal interplay between which largely determines the course of development. So long as the development consists merely in the repeated division of the germ-cell into daughter-cells, each of which resembles all the rest and occupies a similar position in the whole (which is only possible so long as the whole remains of spherical shape), we may suppose that every constituent of the germ-cell is represented in each daughter cell by a similar constituent derived by fission from that of the mother-cell (in the way that the chromatin filaments of the nucleus may be seen to undergo symmetrical division). But, as soon as the embryo becomes a-symmetrical, or its cells exhibit any degree of differentiation, we are compelled to suppose one of two things, or both of them: (1) either the divisions of the cells are no longer such as to render all the constituents of each dividing cell to each of its progeny, so that the cells become unlike one another in that they contain different constituents; or (2) while cell-divisions continue to be such in every case as to give to both daughter-cells all the constituents of the mother-cell, the cells begin to play different parts owing to the differences of their positions in the whole and the consequent differences of the incidence of the environmental influences or stimuli on the cells; e.g. if, while the cells remain of entirely similar constitution, they hang together forming a solid sphere, those forming the outer layer of the sphere will be subjected to environmental influences different from those affecting the cells that remain in the interior of the sphere. The facts of restitution of form and function after mutilation seem to compel the mechanist to adopt this second view in the case of some organisms, notably those of which (as in the case of Begonia) any small fragment or even, it is said, any one cell regenerates the complete organism. And, since all organisms are capable in some degree of restitution of parts, it would seem necessary to suppose that all cells of all organisms contain all the constituents of the germ-cell, and that all differentiation of the functions of the cells is produced by differentiation of the environmental setting of the cells. It is difficult, if not impossible, to suppose that such differentiation of the environments of the cells can suffice to determine all the differentiations of structure and function of the parts of a complex organism. But it is clear that, in so far as development depends on this differentiation and specialization of environmental setting of the cells, it must be seriously disturbed and diverted irrecoverably from its normal course by any gross mechanical distortion of the spatial relations of the cells within the whole mass, or by any change of shape forcibly impressed upon the whole from without. But experiment shows that this is not the case; therefore this form of the mechanistic view of development is false.

The alternative possibility is equally incompatible with the results of experimental interferences with development. According to this view the essential constituents of the germ cells are apportioned differently to the daughter cells in the processes of division, one cell receiving one group of constituents, another a group different in less or greater degree. In this case, then, the differentiations of environment of the cells are supplemented by the differentiations of constitution of the cells; but the preservation of the normal spatial relations of the cells must be of even more vital importance than on the previous supposition; for the cells are of varied composition, and the course of development of each cell and tissue must depend largely upon the reciprocal influences exerted between itself and its neighbours; and these influences must be largely a function of the spatial relations between the cells of different constitution; hence the slightest dislocation of the relative positions of the cells within the whole must be fatal to the development of the normal form; and still more must it be impossible for a mere fragment of the whole adult organism to regenerate the form of the whole.[1]

The building up of the structure of the organism cannot, then, be determined only by the reciprocal influences of parts of specialized constitution playing upon one another according to their spatial relations; that is to say that the building up of the structure cannot be a mechanically determined process.

The embryo seems to be resolved to acquire a certain form and structure, and to be capable of overcoming very great obstacles placed in its path. There is here something analogous to the persistence of the efforts of any creature to achieve its ends

[1] As in the case of Clavellina, mentioned above.

or purposes and the satisfaction of its needs under the driving power of instinctive impulse or craving. In both cases, mechanical obstacles turn aside the course of events from their normal or direct path; but, in whatever direction or in whatever manner the turning aside is caused, the organism adjusts itself to the changed conditions, and, in virtue of some obscure directive power, sets itself once more upon the road to its goal; which, under the altered conditions, it achieves only by means of steps that are different, sometimes extremely different, from the normal.

This power of persistently turning towards a particular end or goal, manifested in these two ways, namely, in growth and bodily movement, is the most characteristic feature of the life of organisms, objectively regarded. It seems to involve essentially teleological determination; that is to say, it seems to be essentially of the same nature as the striving towards a goal or end that runs through all our inner experience, the goal being present to consciousness with extremely different degrees of clearness and fulness. It seems to be quite impossible to explain such apparently teleological behaviour of organisms in terms of mechanism. Nothing analogous to it can be found in the inorganic realm. Perhaps it may be suggested that the behaviour of a gyroscope is analogous; it resists our attempts to turn it out of its plane of motion. But really there is no analogy here; it is merely a special case of the tendency of any mass to persist in its line of motion; when sufficient force is used and the plane of the gyroscope deflected, it persists just as blindly in the new as in the original plane of motion, showing no tendency to return to the latter; whereas, the organism, when turned aside from its natural course of growth or of movement, will not rest satisfied with the new conditions, but tries one thing after another until it regains the path towards its goal, or restores its original condition.

The development and restitution of the forms of organisms seem, then, to be utterly refractory to explanation by mechanical or physico-chemical principles; and that, from the point of view of the present argument, is the essential point. The processes seem to be essentially teleological, that is to say, they seem analogous to the behaviour of organisms; which, from analogy with our own experience of purposive striving, we believe to be prompted by psychical impulse and, in the more highly developed organisms at least, governed and guided by some prevision of the end to be achieved. And these indications cannot be set aside, though we have to confess that we cannot form any conception of the way in which this teleological guidance of morphogenesis is effected.

This seems the proper place to draw attention to a fact frequently overlooked by the mechanistic biologists. Putting aside all consideration of development, the perfected adult organism is said to be a highly complex machine. The fact of the existence of machines, the fact that aggregates of inorganic matter may be so arranged as to effect, without further human interference, purely mechanical transformations of the energy supplied to them, so as to produce highly complex products such as woven cloth, melodies, printed pages; this fact is held to show the legitimacy of the supposition that the bodies of living organisms also may produce all their seemingly designed effects according to strictly mechanical principles. But this argument overlooks a fact of fundamental importance, the fact namely that every machine, though it works according to strictly mechanical principles, is essentially a teleological structure; that is to say its genesis is due to the purpose and design of which it is the instrument only; every step of its construction, every detail of its structure, is determined by human purpose and intelligence. The man-made machine is then an embodiment of purpose and intelligence, and, if we do not beg the question in dispute by calling organisms machines, we cannot point to any machine, however simple, which does not embody human purpose and intelligence; inorganic nature produces no machines, not even of the very simplest kind.

To liken organisms to machines is, then, not to say that they and their processes can be in principle explained in terms of mechanism; it is rather to assert their teleological nature. The question remains—Are they, like machines, inert embodiments of purpose, or are they actuated by purpose?[1]

The teleological nature of organisms and their processes is then one fundamental characteristic which compels us to regard them as not wholly subject to the purely mechanical or physicochemical laws of inorganic nature; and to say that they are machines is but one way of asserting this distinction.

Organisms present a second great peculiarity that marks them off from the inorganic world. In the inorganic realm all

[1] Driesch distinguishes these two modes of manifestation of teleological control as statical and dynamical teleology respectively, and rightly insists that the latter (which alone implies true vitalism) is implied by the facts of the kind we have considered above ("Vitalismus als Geschichte u. Lehre," Leipzig, 1905).

transformations of energy involve dissipation of energy, degradation of energy of higher potential into forms of lower potential; so that, if the physical energy of the universe is a finite quantity, it is brought by all physical changes nearer to a final equilibrium in which the absence of differences of potential shall render impossible further change or work, further transformation of energy; or, in more technical language, in the inorganic world energy tends to become unavailable, entropy tends towards a maximum.

But the processes of organisms seem to be exceptions to this law; organisms seem to be capable of overcoming the tendency of energy to be degraded; the metabolic processes are in large part synthetic, and they result in the raising of energy to higher levels of potential in the form of substances peculiarly rich in energy: and in the operations of the nervous system we seem to have positive indications of a similar power of raising energy to higher levels. This power seems to be one of the essential marks that distinguish the living from the non-living, the organic from the inorganic. It is true that chemists have after long research learnt to effect some very simple examples of such synthesis, starting with non-living and in fact inorganic matter; but that fact does not diminish the significance of this peculiarity of organisms. The case is parallel to that of the machines; here again the peculiarities of organic processes are reproduced in the inorganic sphere, but only through the direction of inorganic processes by human purpose and intelligence. A simile may serve to illustrate both cases. The life processes of an organism may be likened to a river; in both cases a stream of energy undergoes successive transformations and is fed constantly by minor streams. In the case of the river, flowing always to lower levels till it reaches the sea and making heat by friction as it goes, every part or detail of the whole stream of energy-transformations involves degradation of energy; nowhere is the water raised to a higher level or the energy rendered more capable of doing work. But human purpose and intelligence may place in the course of the river an arrangement of matter, a machine, such that part of the energy of the whole stream is raised to a higher level of potential (as in certain pumps, or in the case of every watermill). So, in the course of the stream of energy-transformations that make up the physical life of any organism, part of the energy is raised to higher levels of potential in defiance of the law of degradation or entropy.

CHAPTER XVIII

INADEQUACY OF MECHANICAL PRINCIPLES TO EXPLAIN ORGANIC EVOLUTION

WE have seen how the rapid acceptance of Darwin's doctrine of the evolution of species through the operation of natural selection seemed to give Animism its death-blow; how it gave greater confidence to those who sought to show that the organic world is wholly subject to the laws of mechanism, enabling them to claim not only that organisms are machines, but also that these machines have been slowly evolved by mechanically intelligible processes.

But in this sphere also another half century of active research and controversy has shown that these confident anticipations were ill-founded. The Neo-Darwinians, under the leadership of Weismann, have attempted to show that all organic evolution can be accounted for by the principle of the natural selection of favourable variations from among a great number of small spontaneous variations of indefinite or indeterminate character. Darwin and many other biologists (a minority perhaps at the present time) have continued to accept the Lamarckian principle of the inheritance of characters acquired by use during the life of individuals. Now, such characters are in large part teleologically built up or determined; the efforts of the animal (and very possibly of plants also [1]) to satisfy its instinctive needs, and to avoid the painful, and to secure and maintain the pleasurable, influences of its environment, result in the formation of habits and in other modifications of structure and function; and these modifications, according to the Lamarckians, are in some degree inherited by the offspring, or at least, determine in the offspring variations in the direction of similar modifications.

It is obvious that, if such inheritance takes place, it is a

---

[1] That plants cannot be denied all capacity of effort or teleological striving may be maintained with great plausibility. See Mr Francis Darwin's Presidential Address to the British Association, 1908.

cause of determinate variation; that we must regard these determinate variations as important factors in organic evolution; and that in this way mind may operate teleologically as a factor of evolution to whose importance no limits can be set.[1]

The Neo-Darwinians deny that any such inheritance takes place, that any determinate variations are provided in this way for the operation of natural selection; and in denying this they deny that mind has played any such part in organic evolution.

Now, it must be noted that this denial of the Lamarckian principle is effected by way of an argument in a circle. For the principal ground for the denial of the inheritance of acquired characters is the fact that such inheritance cannot be made to seem even remotely compatible with the mechanistic interpretation of life.[2] But it was shown in the foregoing chapter that the inheritance of all the specific characters of an organism is incapable of being made to seem mechanically explicable. Therefore, in this respect, the acquired characters are no exception; and we cannot deny the transmission of them from parent to offspring on the ground that we cannot even in the vaguest way suggest the mechanics of the process. The only remaining ground for the denial is the fact that, in nearly all cases in which acquired characters seem to be inherited, a tortuous ingenuity can suggest possible, though often wildly improbable, ways in which they may have been built up by selection of indeterminate variations only.

It remains open to us, then, to believe that acquired characters are inherited in some degree, and that in this way mind has exerted teleological guidance of organic evolution, namely, by

---

[1] Prof. James Ward has sketched in masterly outline the part we may assign to "Subjective Selection" in organic evolution, if acquired characters are transmitted ("Naturalism and Agnosticism," vol. i., Lecture x.).

[2] In a recent work, "Die Mneme," R. Semon has attempted the task which I have described above as impossible; but I, for one, cannot see that, in spite of the introduction of several new words, he has achieved any success.

Prof. Ewald Hering and the late Samuel Butler proposed to regard the inheritance of acquired characters as a special case of memory. But neither of them has made clear how he conceived memory to be conditioned. If memory is conceived as conditioned by the persistence of material collocations (as most physiologists conceive it), to describe heredity as a special manifestation of memory does nothing to diminish the chief difficulty of accepting the inheritance of acquired characters. But if good reasons can be shown for regarding memory as conditioned by some immaterial mode of persistence and for holding heredity to be a function of the same immaterial principle, then a great step is made towards rendering the Lamarckian principle acceptable and the processes of heredity and evolution in some degree intelligible (see chaps xxiv. and xxvi.).

determining trends of variation, which variations natural selection has accumulated and fixed as specific characters.

But, if inheritance of acquired characters should eventually be proved to be an untenable hypothesis, we shall still be driven to look for other principles of explanation than natural selection alone. For it is now generally admitted that natural selection can exert but a negative influence; that it is, as it were, but a pruning-knife which, by constantly lopping off a bud here, a twig there, can mould the branches of the tree of life into a thousand different forms, but cannot cause it to grow or put forth new branches; that it can do nothing, in short, unless the tree puts forth of its own vitality a multitude of buds and twigs.

It has long been clear to those whose eyes were not obstinately closed to the facts, that natural selection implies the struggle for existence, and that, as was pointed out in Chapter XVII., this struggle is essentially teleological; sticks and stones, as we said, do not struggle for existence, nor, so far as we can see, do atoms, molecules, etherial vortex rings, particles of electricity, or whatever may be the ultimate element of matter fashionable just now. All inorganic things seem content to remain in whatever condition it has pleased God to assign to them.

It has long been clear also that, if natural selection be given nothing to work upon but a multitude of small indeterminate variations (i.e. fortuitous variations equally pronounced in all directions), the principle meets, as Herbert Spencer showed, immense, if not certainly insuperable, difficulties in attempting to explain the evolution of many organs and functions; especially such as in their early stages cannot be conceived to be of any use to the organism, and those which can only be of use when several other organs are simultaneously modified.[1] These difficulties are to some extent

---

[1] The inadequacy of the mechanistic principles of Neo-Darwinism to the explanation of organic evolution has lately been urged with great force by Prof. Bergson in the following way ("Évolution Créatrice," p. 81):—He points to the vertebrate eye, an organ composed of a multitude of anatomical elements and tissues, all of which are disposed with the greatest precision and harmony to subserve the function of vision. That this precise and extremely complex arrangement of a vast multitude of parts, many of which are of very highly specialised constitution, should have been achieved by the accumulation of happy accidents, is, he says, a sufficiently incredible supposition. But an eye of closely similar structure has been independently evolved in some species of mollusc. The mechanists are therefore driven to suppose that the same long series of happy accidents has occurred independently in two branches of the tree of life. This supposition, says Bergson, goes beyond the limits of legitimate

diminished by the recognition of the principle of Organic Selection[1]; according to this principle, an incipient organ or function, still so imperfectly laid down in the inherited constitution as to be of little or no value in itself, may by intelligent effort be so developed in each generation afresh as to acquire survival value for those members of each generation in which the variation occurs; and in this way, apart from any transmission of acquired characters, the purposive efforts of succeeding generations of organisms may guide or direct the course of evolution, shielding, preserving, and accumulating, the variations that make for structural changes of the same kind as they themselves produce; while other variations are weeded out, or fail to accumulate, for lack of such shielding.

But, if Neo-Darwinism accepts this principle as an aid to the surmounting of its difficulties, it renounces its mechanistic tendency; for the principle is distinctly teleological.[2]

But other difficulties in the way of Neo-Darwinism, difficulties which are not to be overcome by the aid of organic selection, have been brought to light in recent years.

Of these, one is the negative result of long-continued experiments in artificial selection directed towards the creation of new characters by the accumulation of small spontaneous indeterminate variations; that is to say, the failure of attempts to create new characters in the way in which Neo-Darwinism holds all evolution to have taken place, with this difference only that the blind exterminations of nature are replaced by the purposive selection of man. It has been found in a number of such experiments that the modifications of structure and function producible in this way seem to be strictly and narrowly limited; with each generation the amount of modification producible is less; and, as soon as strict selection is suspended, the new breed rapidly reverts to the specific type.[3]

These difficulties are inclining many biologists to look with

---

hypothesis. As another instance of the independent evolution of complex functions, Bergson cites the processes of sexual reproduction so strangely similar in plants and animals; and this function is not a necessity, but a luxury.

[1] Profs. Lloyd Morgan and J. M. Baldwin share the credit of having suggested this very important principle.

[2] See appendix to this chapter.

[3] Some of the best of these experiments are cited by H. de Vries in " Plant Breeding," London, 1907.

favour on the view (of which Professors Bateson[1] and de Vries[2] are the principal exponents) that organic evolution has proceeded in the main by discontinuous variation, i.e. by the sudden appearance, in some individuals of a species, of large modifications of structure or function which are transmitted in full to their offspring, and which, though they will be more likely to be perpetuated if they are of such a nature as to advantage the creatures in their struggle for existence, may nevertheless persist as specific characters independently of, and indeed in spite of, natural selection. It has been abundantly proved that such variations really occur, and that they sometimes appear in large numbers of individuals of a species throughout some generations. It is proposed to use the name " mutations " to distinguish variations of this kind from the small indefinite or fluctuating variations on which Darwin and the Neo-Darwinists have chiefly relied.

The supposition that mutations have been the principal factor in organic evolution certainly diminishes some of the difficulties of the theory of evolution, but it removes it further than ever from the hope of mechanistic explanation. For these mutations cannot be regarded as purely fortuitous variations, or slight accidental departures from exact transmission of the parental characters, as the fluctuating indeterminate variations fairly may be regarded. Nor are they merely monstrosities, resulting from defects of the morphogenetic process; such defects can result only in partial absence of structures, as, for example, cleft-palate, in changes of colour of parts, in duplication of organs, or in other monstrous disproportions or overgrowths of tissues of the nature of tumours, nævi, warts. Variations of these kinds could produce no new organs, no new specific characters.[3] Mutations produce

[1] "Mendel's Principles of Heredity," Cambridge, 1909.
[2] "Mutation," London, 1910.
[3] It may be said that the results of the experiments in hybridization made by the Mendelians diminish the difficulty of imagining mechanistic evolution by way of mutation; for these seem to show that certain characters of animals and plants must be regarded as units which are either fully represented in the germ or quite unrepresented; and they give some colour to the view that each organism is a bundle of such unit characters or organs, and that the whole germ is a bundle of lesser germs, each of which, the representative of one of these unit-characters, consists of some atom or molecule, or perhaps side-chain of atoms, in a complex molecule. Most, if not all, of the characters hitherto dealt with by the Mendelians are of great simplicity, e.g. coat-colour, shape of wattles or comb in birds, presence of sugar or starch in seeds, and so on; and it may be suggested with some plausibility that each such character has appeared as a mutation owing to the addition of some atom or atom group, or to the substitu-

functionally perfect organs or modifications of organs; and, if they did not do so, it would be impossible to suppose that they have played any considerable part in evolution. They demand, therefore, for their explanation some formative directive principle; and evidence of their frequent occurrence in all species, though it would make clearer to us the actual course of evolution, would do nothing to diminish the difficulties of mechanistic explanation of it, but would rather accentuate the difficulty.

Lastly, attention must be drawn to a feature of the constitution of organisms, which, as Driesch has pointed out,[1] cannot be explained by either the Darwinian or the Lamarckian principle, nor by that of organic selection; this feature is the power of restitution of functions and regeneration of organs after injury, possessed in some degree by all organisms. The power, for example, of regenerating a lost limb can have been acquired neither by use-inheritance nor by natural selection, for the simple reason that it is a power called into play in but few individuals of each generation; it is a power which, though highly advantageous to the few individuals that have occasion to manifest it, is of little importance to the species as a whole; in short, we cannot suppose all newts to be descended from ancestors that have lost their legs and have been at the same time so fortunate as to have varied or mutated in the direction of capacity for complete regeneration.

In this and in the preceding chapter we have touched upon

---

tion of one atom group for another, in the molecular constitution of the germ. If this view were tenable we should seem to see in imagination the whole course of organic evolution as consisting in successive chemical changes of this kind in the germ, each producing a new mutation. But though this naïve way of regarding evolution and inheritance may seem plausible so long as we have regard to such simple characters as the colour and shape of organs, such as combs and wattles, seed-pods and petals, it must appear to all unbiassed minds hopelessly inadequate when applied to account for complex instincts. If a complex train of instinctive action is to be accounted for mechanistically, it must be supposed that the movements making up the train of action are connected with the initiating and guiding sense-impression by a complex nervous machinery consisting of a number of compound reflex-arcs each of very great complexity, and each comprising a great number of nerve-cells connected together in complex functional series, and each connected with the others in perfectly definite manner. How, then, can such a complex structure, which is not merely a structure but a most complex and delicately working machine, be effectively represented by (i.e. its growth be determined by) some molecule or side-chain of atoms of some molecule in the germ?   [1] *Op. cit.*, vol. i. p. 286.

some of the principal difficulties that beset the attempt to explain the processes of the tissues of organisms, and especially the processes of growth, restitution, heredity, and evolution, in terms of physics and chemistry. These difficulties have appeared more and more clearly thoughout the last half century as our knowledge of the facts has increased. And so we find that, though at the beginning of this period the dominant note of biological thought was one of confident anticipation of the ultimate and indeed rapid solution of the major problems of biology in mechanical terms, and though in the earlier part of that period Vitalism was commonly spoken of as a thing of the past, a mere survival from the dark ages, to-day vitalists are again numerous amongst the biologists. The modern vitalists are no longer content to "explain" the phenomena of organic life by ascribing them to a "vital force." The notions they would introduce into biology to supplement or replace mechanical conceptions are very diverse; and many of them do not go beyond the affirmation of the belief that organic processes involve some undefined factor which cannot be described in terms of physics and chemistry. This belief, which is the essence of Vitalism, is in fact the only thing common to the "Neo-Vitalists." Owing to this diversity of view amongst vitalists, to the purely negative character of their only common tenet, and to the fact that many of them are very reserved in regard to it, abstaining from giving it any public expression; and owing, on the other hand, to the complete agreement between all the mechanists, the definite and positive nature of their doctrine, and the confident dogmatic manner in which they continue to affirm it; the latter still appear to the world as the dominant party among the biologists. But it is doubtful whether, if a census could be taken at the present time, they would prove to be more numerous than the vitalists.[1]

It is worthy of note, in this connexion, that the exclusive sway in the organic world of the principles of physical science is maintained in a more confident and dogmatic manner by the mechanistic biologists than by many of the leading physicists who have enunciated these principles and taught them to the biologists.

[1] Dr Merz, after displaying the gains that modern biology owes to the use of mechanical conceptions, remarks—"And yet it may be asked, have we come nearer an answer to the question, What is Life? At one time, for a generation which is passing away, we apparently had. But a closer scrutiny has convinced most of us that we have not. . . . The spectre of a vital principle still lurks behind all our terms." *Op. cit.*, p. 462.

MECHANISM AND ORGANIC EVOLUTION

It is perhaps worth while to enumerate here a few of these physicists of the highest standing who, since the establishment of the law of conservation of energy, have expressed or implied the opinion that physical science does not compel us to believe that the evolution and life-processes of organisms are capable of being completely described in mechanical terms; such are or were Sir G. Stokes,[1] Lord Kelvin,[2] Maxwell,[3] P. G. Tait,[4] Balfour Stewart,[4] Sir W. Crookes, Sir O. Lodge,[5] Sir J. J. Thomson, Sir J. Larmor,[6] Prof. Poynting.[7]

Finally, it is necessary to insist very strongly that, in this dispute between the mechanistic and the vitalistic biologists, the onus of proof lies with the former, and not with the vitalists, as is commonly assumed by their opponents. For it is undeniable that on the face of things living beings differ very greatly from all inorganic things, and that their processes seem to be teleologically governed rather than mechanically caused; and as we have seen, the increase of knowledge brought by the research of the last half-century has done nothing to show that this appearance is illusory, but rather has revealed the same appearance of teleological determination in a multitude of organic processes which formerly were regarded with some plausibility as purely mechanical. It may, therefore, be said to-day with even more confidence and force than in the time of Democritus or of Lucretius, of Hobbes or of Huxley, that the mechanical view of the organic world remains nothing more than a hope, a faith, a postulate, or a prejudice, in the minds of those who hold it.

[1] Presidential Address to British Association, Exeter.
[2] "On the Dissipation of Energy," Popular Lectures, II.
[3] "Life of Clerk Maxwell," by Campbell and Garnett, chap. xiv.; and in many other passages.
[4] "The Unseen Universe."
[5] "Life and Matter." In this work Sir Oliver Lodge has argued strongly in favour of the view that life involves guidance of the mechanical processes of the bodies of organisms, and that such guidance need involve no breach of the law of conservation of energy or the other generally accepted principles of physical science.
[6] "Aether and Matter," p. 288.
[7] Hibbert Journal, vol. ii.

APPENDIX TO CHAPTER XVIII

"ORGANIC SELECTION"

The principle of "Organic Selection" seems to me very important. It has been heard of, appreciated, or approved, by relatively few biologists, and experience has taught me that it is very difficult to bring some biologists to understand it. I therefore add the following appendix to this chapter:—

We may take as an example for the illustration of the principle of organic selection the instinct to lie perfectly still when suddenly confronted by an enemy, an instinct which seems to have been acquired by several species of animals of widely different groups. It seems obvious that this instinct cannot have been acquired by the accumulation of small variations; for, if this instinctive behaviour is to advantage the creature, it must be perfect from the first; any restriction of the movements of escape short of complete motionlessness would be worse than useless. But if we suppose that individuals of a species had sufficient intelligence to avoid attracting the attention of their enemies or their prey (and numerous stories imply that foxes at least display such intelligence) by remaining still in spite of their natural tendency to run away (or to dash upon their prey), then we may suppose that, if some individuals varied in the direction of lying still for a moment whenever startled, they would carry out their intelligent suppression of movement (especially in early life) more effectively than others in whom no such fortuitous variation occurred. Spontaneous variation and intelligence thus working together would secure survival more effectively than either working alone. Thus intelligence might shield or foster the accumulation of variations in this direction, until the instinct was perfected and intelligence was no longer needed to supplement the imperfect instinct. This is a very simple and perhaps not very probable example, but it may serve to illustrate the principle.

Few biologists seem to have grasped this principle, and fewer still the range of its application and the very great part it may have played in promoting and guiding teleologically the course of organic evolution. Yet, rightly considered, the principle is an essential part of the Darwinian theory; and since, if it is valid, it shows us how organic evolution may have been teleologically guided and promoted by mind, by psychical effort and subjective selection, to an extent to which we can set no limits, even though acquired characters be not inherited; and since it seems to have been impossible hitherto to find conclusive evidence of the inheritance of acquired characters, it seems worth while to dwell on it a little in the present connexion, and to attempt to show that the operation of this teleological principle is necessarily assumed by the theory of the origin of species by natural selection.

Let us try to imagine the operation of organic selection in the evolution of the prehensile paw of the monkey tribe from the forelimb of an ancestor that lived on the ground only. It seems clear that the prehensile paw must have been developed as a consequence of the animals taking to climbing trees and finding the habit advantageous. This habit was acquired, we must suppose, by some group of the ancestral species which was brought into a region in which arboreal habits were advantageous and attractive; perhaps because it abounded in trees bearing fruit that was pleasant to the taste of the species and well suited for its nourishment. At first, members of the species climbed awkwardly upon the trees to reach the fruit, their limbs being but little suited to the task; just as creatures so little adapted for tree-climbing as crabs are known to have taken to this practice in pursuit of fruit. The practice of tree-climbing constantly pursued from earliest youth would to some extent increase the facility of each animal in the execution of the necessary movements and would at the same time produce in each generation some degree of adaptation of the limbs to the task. But, if acquired characters are not inherited, these effects of practice would not be transmitted and intensified from generation to generation. Nevertheless, according to the fundamental assumption of Darwinism, the limbs of these creatures were varying constantly in all possible directions; i.e. in some individuals of each generation, variations of the limbs in the direction of better adaptation to climbing would fortuitously appear, in others, variations of different kinds which would either be adverse to climbing or indifferent from that point of view; in this respect then the individuals of each generation would fall into three classes, namely, (1) those varying in the direction of better adaptation to climbing; (2) those varying adversely; (3) those whose limbs remain unvaried from the point of view of tree-climbing. If, then, the struggle for life, in the form of competition for the food supply, the fruit of the trees, is severe, all individuals of the second class would be severely handicapped, and would suffer a higher rate of mortality; hence such variations are weeded out of the group; and of individuals of the first class a larger percentage will survive and reproduce themselves and their peculiarities than among those of the third class. In this way the whole group would achieve, generation by generation, limbs innately better adapted for climbing. But the point on which I wish to insist is that, in this progressive adaptation of the limbs by "natural selection" of fortuitous variations, teleological guidance by psychical effort and subjective selection plays an essential part without which no such evolution would have taken place. The desire of the creatures to obtain the fruit, or at least the impulse to go in search of it, leading to effort after climbing the trees on which it grows, determines that, of all variations of the limbs, those tending to better adaptation to climbing should alone be perpetuated and accumulated.[1]

This truth of fundamental importance, yet so generally overlooked,

---

[1] This hypothetical case makes it obvious that the principle of organic selection is closely allied to Prof. Ward's "subjective selection," as Prof. Ward has himself pointed out ("Naturalism and Agnosticism," i., p. 294). But in applying his principle Ward assumed the validity of the Lamarckian principle, and combined the two principles.

may be made clearer by imagining a different course of events. Suppose another group of the ancestral species to be brought into a similar region in which they find an abundance of a certain edible and nutritious root (say the yam) which is more to their taste than the fruit growing on the trees; their efforts will then be chiefly directed to finding and digging out this root, to the neglect of the fruit of the trees. The habit of digging out the root becomes established as a custom which is learnt imitatively by each generation, while, although by painful efforts the fruit might be reached, no habit and no custom of seeking it is established.[1] If, when this customary reliance upon the root as food supply has been established, times of scarcity come, or, in other words, if the "population" begins to press upon the means of subsistence, those individuals whose limbs are best adapted for discovering the roots by digging will have the best chance of survival. Hence variations of the limbs in this direction will be perpetuated and accumulated, while variations in opposite directions will be weeded out. We may then legitimately suppose that in this case the forelimbs of this group, constituting a divergent species, may become short and spade-like, like those of the mole; while those of the other group become elongated and prehensile.

We may imagine a third case in which a group of the ancestral species finds itself in a region in which the food supply most attractive to it is the fish of clear ponds or rivers, and that it secures these by swimming and diving after them. In this case again individual practice will lead in each generation to increased skill in and increased adaptation of the limbs to swimming and diving; and again, in the absence of all transmission of acquired characters, the choice and purposive efforts of the creatures in this direction will determine that, of the fortuitous variations of all possible directions, those only will be perpetuated and accumulated which are in the direction of better adaptation to swimming and diving. Thus from the one parental species we may suppose that in three different, but closely similar geographical areas, three new species are gradually differentiated, one arboreal in habit and with prehensile forelimbs, one seeking its food by digging with spade-like forelimbs, a third aquatic in habit with fin-like forelimbs; and in each case habit, arising from choice and purposive effort, will have determined the differences of bodily structure and also, it may be added, the differences of instinct which accompany the structural differences. In each case the psychical choice and effort plays an essential role, determining, guiding, or moulding the course of evolution. For suppose the ancestral species to have been one that fed on herbage only, and that it had too little intelligence and spontaneity to make experiments in feeding, when any one of the three more nutritious and abundant kinds of food were within its reach, or too conservative in taste to have appreciated these dietetic novelties; then the species would have continued unchanged in all the three environments we have imagined.

---

[1] That habits determine customs among gregarious animals, and are thus transmitted by imitation from generation to generation, is, I think, indisputable.

There seem to be hardly any bodily characters of any species the evolution of which may not be supposed to have been in this way determined teleologically, by psychical choice and effort, in absence of all transmission of acquired characters. Coat colour and marking, for example, seem to be incapable of being directly affected by the choice or any mental effort of the animal (with certain exceptions in which chromatophoric changes are controlled by the nervous system). Yet a protective colouring and marking, as, e.g., those of the leopard's skin, must be determined by the animals' choice of their environments and the way in which they apply whatever "little dose of judgment and reason" they may have to forward their success in life. If, for example, the lion and the leopard have diverged from a common stock, and if, as seems hardly deniable, their coat colours are adaptations to their environments which enable them to secure their prey more readily by rendering them inconspicuous, this divergence can only have been effected by natural selection in so far as the divergent stocks actively sought the kinds of prey that inhabit the two very different physical environments of the forest and the desert. It may be said that two groups of the ancestral stock may have been forced into geographical regions in which no choice was left them—the ancestral stock of the lion into the desert, that of the leopard into a forest region in which arboreal habits became necessary to survival. This seems improbable; but even if the supposition be admitted, it remains true that the change of habits necessitated by the new environment was in each case possible only in virtue of a certain degree of intelligent adaptation and effort on the part of successive generations; which is thus in this case also a presupposition of the operation of natural selection to produce divergence of species. If the animals had been incapable of such intelligent adaptation of their behaviour, they would have died out rapidly in the new environments.

In short, the doctrine of organic selection is but the working out in more detail of the fundamental presupposition of Darwinism, namely, the *struggle* for existence, which, as was said above, is essentially a psychical struggle in that it presupposes "the will to live."

CHAPTER XIX

INADEQUACY OF MECHANICAL CONCEPTIONS TO EXPLAIN ANIMAL AND HUMAN BEHAVIOUR

WE have seen that modern physiology regards all nervous process as of the reflex type (i.e. as similar to the reflex processes of the spinal cord by which co-ordinated and outwardly purposive movements are made in response to particular sense-stimuli); and that this doctrine, in conjunction with the "association-psychology," has played a considerable part in bringing about the rejection of Animism by biologists. It is necessary to examine this doctrine more closely and to inquire whether the conception of compound reflexes of purely mechanical nature (as elaborated especially by Herbert Spencer) is adequate to the explanation of the behaviour of men and animals.

We touch here upon the psychological problems of biology; but the facts of consciousness may with advantage be left for consideration in a later chapter, while here we consider behaviour from an objective standpoint.

If we consider the behaviour of animals of all levels of complexity of organization, we find that it is everywhere characterized by certain features that seem to present insuperable difficulties to all attempts at purely mechanical explanation. This is true even of the behaviour of the simplest of all animals, the unicellular protozoa. The mechanists have attempted to exhibit all the movements of these minute organisms as the direct results of the incidence of physical stimuli upon their substance; e.g. the protrusion of a pseudopodium by *Amœba* as the effect of a local diminution of surface tension by contact with some chemical or physical agent; the turning of flagellate or ciliate protozoa (such as *Paramœcium*) towards or away from light, or the electric current, or a bubble of carbonic acid, and their consequent congregation in the greatest possible proximity to or remoteness from such agents, as due to direct stimulation of the organs of locomotion by these agents. Movements thus directly stimulated and directed are called *tropisms*; and the mechanists attempt to show that the behaviour of these lower organisms is nothing but a series of such tropisms, direct local reactions to physical and chemical stimuli.[1]

But, when the movements of these unicellular and very simple multicellular creatures are minutely and impartially studied, it appears that, although some of their movements may be plausibly regarded as tropisms, others present features that make it impossible to regard them in this light. Thus, the progression of *Amœba*, which has been mechanically interpreted as due merely to diminution of surface tension, has been shown by the minute studies of Mr H. S. Jennings[2] to involve streaming movements of the protoplasm which are incompatible with that or any other of the suggested mechanical explanations. The same observer has shown also that the behaviour of free-swimming infusoria cannot be regarded as merely a series of tropisms; the animal responds to most of the stimuli that affect it, not merely with some local change of activity in the part on which the stimulus falls, but with a co-ordinated change of activity of all its organs of locomotion; that is, the animal behaves as an organic unity, or, as Jennings puts it, it responds to local stimulation with a "total reaction." For example, *Paramœcium* (the slipper animalcule which swims freely in water by means of the whipping movements of the hair-like threads or cilia that cover all its surface), on colliding as it swims with a hard body, suddenly reverses the movement of all its cilia and backs off; and the nature of the turning movement is independent of the point of incidence of the stimulus. So also *Amœba*, chasing or being chased, may be observed suddenly to reverse the direction of its movement and to set off in a new direction better calculated to secure its end, namely, capture or escape, and to repeat this again and again;[3] its behaviour consists in a series of "total reactions" each well adapted to secure the biological end. Or again, *Amœba* sometimes becomes detached from the solid surfaces on which it normally crawls; it then sends out long

[1] See the works of Prof. J. Loeb, especially "Die Bedeutung der Tropismen," Leipsic, 1909, and M. G. Bohn's, "Naissance de l'Intelligence." Paris, 1909.
[2] "The Behaviour of the Lower Organisms."
[3] See especially Jennings' fascinating account of the pursuit of one *Amœba* by a larger specimen (*op. cit.*). In this case the meeting of two organisms of similar constitution resulted in the persistent flight of the smaller and the persistent pursuit of it by the larger.

slender pseudopodia in all directions, until one of them comes in contact with, and adheres to, a solid body; the other pseudopodia are then quickly withdrawn, and the whole substance flows towards the point of attachment.

Observations reported by the same careful worker bring out very clearly also in the behaviour of these very lowly animals a second very important characteristic, namely, they exhibit persistent striving towards the biological end of their activity with variation of the means employed; i.e. the animal, when obstructed or checked in the pursuit of an end, neither ceases at once to strive (to continue its movements), nor persists in the same movement or attempt at movement, but rather varies the nature or direction of its movements again and again, until it hits upon a kind or a direction of movement that meets with no obstruction. In other words, it seems to work towards the biological end by the method of persistent "trial and error." Such behaviour is so commonly exhibited by these lowly creatures that Jennings asserts—" In no other group of organisms does the method of trial and error so completely dominate behaviour, perhaps, as in the infusoria."[1]

Now, this persistence of movement with variation in detail of the kind and direction of movement, while the physical environment remains unchanged, is perhaps the most distinctive feature of the behaviour of organisms; it is one to which no parallel can be found in the inorganic world. The falling stone stops dead when it strikes the earth, the clock-work stops without a struggle if you thrust a spoke into its wheel; the locomotive engine, brought up against a dead wall, continues at most to exert unavailing pressure in the same direction; and the same is true of every merely mechanical contrivance; none exhibits that most rudimentary form of self-direction which consists in spontaneously changing the direction or nature of movement.

Thus we see that, at the very bottom of the evolutionary scale, animal behaviour exhibits the two peculiarities which at all higher levels also distinguish it from the movements of inorganic things, namely, (1) the "total" or unitary nature of reaction, i.e. the reaction of the organism as a whole with co-ordination of the movements of its parts in response to a stimulus directly affecting one small part only; and (2) the persistence of the effect of the stimulus, a persistence closely analogous to that persistence of

[1] *Op. cit.*, p. 243.

varied movement which in ourselves and our fellows we recognize as the expression of a persistent effort after a desired end. And to this it must be added that these persistent and varied and total or unitary reactions of the whole organism are in the main adaptive, i.e. of such a nature as to promote the welfare of the creature.

The mechanist, of course, will argue that, if only we had intimate knowledge of the physics and chemistry of the *Amœba* or the infusorian, we could mechanically explain these peculiarities in every case. But this is merely to repeat his fundamental assumption, which, until he shall have justified it in some one single case, must remain nothing more than the expression of an ill-founded hope.

If we turn now to the middle level of the animal scale, we find behaviour characterized by the same fundamental peculiarities; and we find a further difficulty in the way of all purely mechanical explanation. Let us consider the case of a purely instinctive action, an adaptive action which is performed perfectly when the animal finds itself for the first time in a particular situation, say in the presence of an object of a particular kind. Such typical and purely instinctive actions have been widely and confidently classed as compound reflexes of purely mechanical type. It is assumed that every sensory point of the animal's surface is connected by some continuous nervous path with some muscle or group of muscles, and that, when any group of such sensory points are stimulated simultaneously, a movement is produced which is the resultant of all these simultaneously excited reflex tendencies. Some instinctive actions are evoked by simple or relatively simple sense-impressions, such as odours, simple sounds, simple impressions of touch or temperature; these differ outwardly from reflex actions only in the greater complexity of the bodily movements evoked; and they form a scale of transition from the reflex actions to the higher or more complex forms of instinctive activity. The higher or more complex instinctive activities are evoked not by simple sense-impressions, but only by the complex groups or conjunctions of sense-stimuli that are received from objects of particular kinds. Every instinctive act that depends for its initiation on the reception by the eye of an image of some object is of this kind; and that many purely instinctive actions are thus initiated is, I think, indisputable.[1]

[1] Since some authors (notably Driesch) hold the view that all instinctive actions are evoked by simple sensory stimuli, it is necessary to point to unmis-

Let us consider the case of an insect which emerges from the chrysalis fully equipped with all its organs and powers, and which, when it comes within sight of a flower of a particular species, flies to it and, by means of a series of delicately adjusted movements, deposits its eggs in just that part of the flower in which alone they can develop.[1]

Such behaviour is other than and more than a series of compound reflexes; the flower is of complex shape and its parts affect the sense-organs of the insect with a highly complex group of stimuli; i.e. the total sense-impression may be analysed by us into a complex of physical stimuli each affecting the sensory terminus of a sensory nerve. And the behaviour of the insect in response to the impression is a series of acts each of which also may be analysed by us and exhibited as the contractions of a number of muscles. Now, if it could be shown that of this complex of muscular contractions each one corresponds to and is directly evoked by one element of the complex of sensory stimuli by way of a reflex nervous arc, we should have a mechanical explanation of the action. But each step of the behaviour of the insect is more than such a complex of reflexes; it is a total complex reaction to a total complex sense-impression, and there is no point-to-point correspondence between the elements into which we analyse the reaction and those into which we analyse the impression. The total reaction, although complex, is unitary,

---

takable instances of instinctive actions evoked only by complex conjunctions of stimuli. As examples of such I would cite the behaviour of the various species of solitary wasps in presence of their prey, as described so admirably by M. Fabre ("Souvenirs entomologiques") and by Dr and Mrs Peckham ("Wasps, Social and Solitary"). The wasps of each species prey only on animals of some one kind, one species on caterpillars, another on spiders, a third on grasshoppers, and so on. It might be suggested that the wasp is led to his proper prey by a simple specific stimulus, namely by scent; but that can hardly be maintained in view of the facts, (1) that a wasp will capture caterpillars, or spiders, or grasshoppers, etc., of many different species; (2) that vision plays a great part in the direction of their behaviour. Further, even if it were possible to hold that the wasp recognizes or is led to its prey by scent, it would be impossible to regard its manipulations of its prey (in modes which are distinct, specific, and instinctive in each species) as guided only by simple stimuli. Rather the wasp's behaviour in capturing its prey depends upon its appreciation of its general shape and size and position. Instances such as that of the Yucca moth are equally decisive; it is impossible that an insect should execute delicate operations upon the parts of a flower, while guided only by simple stimuli.

[1] A beautiful example is afforded by the Yucca moth. Its behaviour is described by Lloyd Morgan in "Animal Behaviour."

while the sense-impression is a manifold of stimuli affecting a manifold of sensory nerves. Somehow the manifold of discrete impressions (say, of light-rays each affecting one of many of the facets and end-organs that make up the compound eye of the insect) has been combined or synthesized to produce a complex unitary effect, of which each element is an organic and essential part of the whole, and depends not upon any one of the elements of the complex impression, but upon all of them.

It is difficult, if not impossible, to imagine in however general and vague a manner a mechanical explanation of this synthetic process.

If now we go on to consider the behaviour of the higher insects, in which the innately prescribed modes of reaction become complicated by the results of individual experience, we find it characterized by this same peculiarity, but in a much higher degree, one which renders the difficulty of mechanical explanation correspondingly greater.

A solitary wasp, after digging a hole in the ground[1] to serve as a nest for her eggs, sets out in search of prey to be stored in the nest as food for her grubs; having found a caterpillar at any point within a radius of some hundreds of feet of her nest, she drags it over the rough ground and between the many obstacles that obscure for her all vision of the nest or its immediate surroundings; in spite of these obstacles, she takes approximately and on the whole the shortest possible course to her nest, and arrives there with her prey in virtue of a long-sustained series of varied movements all directed towards the one end, every deviation from the direct path necessitated by obstacles being rectified as soon as possible.

At every step of this prolonged journey the wasp is guided by visual impressions of the surroundings, which by many explorations she has made familiar to herself. How totally different from a series of reflexes are the movements by which she maintains and regains her true direction! A mere familiarity with, or power of recognizing, a certain number, even a very large number, of the objects that she encounters would by no means suffice to account for her behaviour. In order to guide herself she must not merely recognize objects previously seen; she must recognize objects (or the parts of the landscape immedi-

---

[1] See the admirable descriptions of Dr and Mrs Peckham in their "Wasps, Social and Solitary," 1905.

ately presented to her vision) as related in some determinate manner to the whole field of her explorations, and especially to that point of it at which her nest is situated; that is to say, each visual perception that guides her course not only involves (as in the case of the purely instinctive behaviour of the Yucca moth considered above) a synthesis of a large number of details of the field of view to a unitary whole (or a synthesis of the effects of a manifold of sense-stimuli), but also must be related in a determinate fashion to a larger whole, namely, the scheme of the whole region which in some sense and manner she carries with her. Nor is this all. Her reactions to the complex visual impressions by which her course is maintained are determined also by the nature of the task in hand at the moment; for her reactions to each part of the landscape are different according as she is looking for a spot suitable for her nest, is seeking her prey, or is carrying it back to her nest; in psychological terms, each part of the landscape has for her a meaning or significance which is dependent upon her dominant purpose at the moment she perceives it; and this meaning is a decisive factor in determining the nature of her reaction.

Even, then, if it could be admitted that the synthesis involved in the successive perceptions may be plausibly supposed to be capable of being described in chemico-physical terms as neural events, there would remain two greater difficulties: (1) that of conceiving in similar terms that essential factor in the whole process which we can only describe as the meaning or significance of that which is perceived in relation to the purpose or end of the whole train of activity; (2) that of similarly conceiving the most fundamental factor, the purpose, the conation, or will, which sustains the prolonged course of varied efforts and which determines the nature of the reaction to each complex sense-impression at each step of the process.

The higher animals, and human beings also, exhibit instinctive reactions in response to impressions that are still more remote from the simple sense-impression; these are in a still higher degree irreconcilable with the notion of compound reflex action of a mechanical type.

A clear and relatively simple instance is the instinctive cry of distress uttered by the human infant, together with the various bodily activities that normally accompany it to make up the specific expression of distress. This complex instinctive reaction may be evoked by violent stimulation of any sensory nerve; and this fact is not easily reconciled with any mechanical conception of instinctive process. For the many sensory nerve-paths do not, so far as is known, come together in the special motor centre that sends out the system of efferent nervous impulses proper to the expressions of distress. Yet somehow this centre may be brought into action through violent stimulation of any afferent nerve, with few exceptions. Two possibilities of mechanical explanation suggest themselves. One is that violent stimulation of any sensory nerve liberates in the corresponding sensory tract or centre more energy than can be led off along the normal efferent channels of the tract; that the excess of energy therefore overflows the normal channels; and that the centre for the expression of distress is connected with all other sensory centres in such a way as to receive and to be stimulated by this escaped excess of energy.

A second possibility appears if we accept a notion recently introduced by Dr Henry Head, namely, that of "specific intra-medullary receptors," i.e. afferent tracts attuned or so constituted as to take up and transmit only special modes of nervous excitation. We might suppose that violent stimulation of any afferent nerve sets up in addition to, or instead of, the excitation of the kind that is caused by more gentle stimulation, a peculiar form of excitation which is common to all nerves under the condition of excessive stimulation; that this is taken up by specific receptors (which are so arranged as to tap every afferent path) and from them is led by special paths to the "distress-centre."

Though there are special difficulties and objections in the way of both these suggestions, they seem plausible, or at any rate not impossible, so long as we consider only the expressions of distress that are caused by violent stimulation of sensory nerves. But the same expressions, the distressful cry, etc., result from other conditions, e.g. from hunger, from sensory impressions that are disagreeable without being violent, such as those made by bitter substances, from all the many situations that excite fear independently of previous experience (e.g. darkness, solitude, certain noises, the unfamiliar, the sight or contact with certain animals, etc.) and from all disappointment of expectation, all frustration of active tendencies, in short, from all the very various occasions of displeasure or disagreeable feeling. There can be no doubt that all these many different occasions of the excitement of the one instinctive response involve a great variety of nervous processes taking place in a great many different systems of nervous elements; and in face of this diversity of both type and anatomical seat of these processes, both the hypotheses suggested above seem to break down; the only factor common to all the occasions, the only invariable antecedent of the expression of distress, seems to be disagreeable feeling.

It may be pointed out that a similar problem is presented in a simpler form by some of the reflex actions of which such an animal as the dog remains capable when deprived of the whole of its brain, notably by the scratch-reflex so brilliantly studied by Prof. C. S. Sherrington.[1] In this instance the stimulus of a particular kind applied to any spot of a considerable area of the skin evokes always a particular sequence of co-ordinated movements of the hind limb, these movements being modified a little with each change of place of the stimulus. It might be argued that, since it is commonly assumed that spinal reflexes are purely mechanical processes, the analogy between the conditions of evocation of the scratch-reflex in the dog and those of the expression of distress in the infant, justify the belief that the latter is mechanically explicable. But no adequate mechanical explanation of the scratch-reflex has been suggested; and it may be argued with at least equal plausibility that the analogy between the processes shows that the scratch-reflex, like the instinctive expression of distress, involves some factor incapable of description in mechanical terms.

The same difficulty may be illustrated by reference to the instinct of curiosity as displayed by many of the higher animals and by ourselves; and here it appears even more formidable than in the previous instance. For this instinct is excited not by any simple sense-impressions, nor yet by any specific complex of sense-impressions; for there is no one class of objects to which it is especially directed or in the presence of which it is invariably displayed. The instinct seems to be brought into play in the animals by any object that resembles some object with which they are habitually interested or concerned and yet differs from it in such a degree that, while it attracts their attention, it fails to excite the ordinary response. And in ourselves the conditions of excitement of this instinct are not essentially different; it is

[1] " The Integrative Action of the Nervous System " and a long series of papers in *Proc. Roy. Soc.*

evoked by the contemplation of any object which, while sufficiently similar to familiar objects to enable the mind to play upon it, yet differs from them sufficiently to prevent our attaching the usual meaning to the complex sense-impression received from it. In short, the condition of excitement of the impulse of curiosity seems to be in all cases the presence of a strange or unfamiliar element in whatever is partially familiar, whether the object be one of sense-perception (as exclusively in the animals and very young children), or one contemplated in thought only. In either case that element of strangeness, which is the sole invariable antecedent of the awakening of the impulse of curiosity, is something that exists only for the organism and is discovered by it only by means of an intellectual operation of however rudimentary a kind. The strangeness of the object of curiosity, to which it owes its power of exciting the impulse, exists only in the mind of the organism, and is, in fact, the *meaning* of the object for the organism in so far as curiosity is awakened.

These considerations seem to establish the view that the instinctive actions which constitute the expression of curiosity cannot be regarded as reflexly excited processes; and they will, I hope, have made clear to the reader that it is impossible in the light of our present knowledge to suggest any, even the vaguest, mechanical description of the way in which this reaction is excited.

If we turn now from behaviour of these relatively simple types to that of developed human beings, we find similar difficulties in the way of all mechanical explanation; but they are raised to a still higher power.

It is usual, among those who wish to show the impossibility of mechanical interpretation of human behaviour, to seek to reduce the assumption to absurdity by pointing to particular instances of its application; to insist, for example, that, if the assumption is accepted, we have to regard the order of sequence of all the letters that make up the text of the Bible, or of a play of Shakespeare, or of any other work of literary genius, as being in principle capable of a purely mechanical explanation, one which makes no reference to the meaning of the words or sentences; or that all the movements by which the artist produces a beautiful painting or sculpture are mechanically determined, and that the appreciation of the beautiful plays no part in the control of them. And this should perhaps be a sufficient *reductio ad absurdum* of the principle. But the argument seems more capable of enforcing conviction if presented in a more special and detailed fashion. Let us consider the following case. A man receives from a friend a telegram saying—"Your son is dead." The physical agent to which the man reacts is a series of black marks on a piece of paper. The reaction outwardly considered as a series of bodily processes consists, perhaps, in a sudden, total, and final cessation of all those activities that constitute the outward signs of life ; or in complete change of the whole course of the man's behaviour throughout the rest of his life. And all this altered course of life, beginning perhaps with a series of activities that is completely novel and unprecedented in the course of his life, bears no direct relation whatever to the nature of the physical stimulus. The independence of the reaction on the nature of the physical impression is well brought out by the reflexion that the omission of a single letter, namely, the first of the series (converting the statement into—"Our son is dead "), would have determined none of this long train of bodily effects, but merely the writing of a letter of condolence or the utterance of a conventional expression of regret ; whereas, if the telegram had been written in any one of a dozen foreign languages known to the recipient, or if the same meaning had been conveyed to him by means of a series of auditory impressions or by any one of many different possible means of communication, the resulting behaviour would have been the same in all cases, in spite of the great differences between the series of sense-impressions.

The one thing common, then, to all the widely different physical impressions that produce the same physical effects, i.e. the same train of behaviour, is that they evoke the same *meaning* in the consciousness of the subject; hence this meaning is the essential link in each case between the series of physical impressions and the series of physical effects.[1]

[1] This argument has been presented independently and in rather different forms by L. Busse ("Leib und Seele") and by Dr H. Driesch (" Philosophy and Science of the Organism," vol. ii.). As presented by Busse it is sometimes called the " telegram-argument." Driesch offers it as his third proof of Vitalism ; he sums it up as follows: " In acting then, there may be no change in the specificity of the reaction when the stimulus is altered fundamentally, and again, there may be the most fundamental difference in the reaction when there is almost no change in the stimulus " (p. 70). He proposes to denote the principle of the specific correspondence between complex reaction and complex stimulus as the principle of individuality of correspondence between stimulus and effect. He further illustrates it by reference to the fact that any familiar object, such as my dog, may be seen in many positions and from many angles

It will be seen that this instance of human reaction presents just the same difficulty to all attempts at mechanical explanation as the instances of animal behaviour previously considered; but in a still higher degree. And human behaviour affords instances of the same difficulty raised to a yet higher power. We may imagine the following variant of our last example; instead of receiving a telegram saying, "Your son is dead," the man reads in the newspaper the statement that a certain ship has foundered, carrying to the bottom all its human freight. He has reason to fear that his son was a passenger on this ship. He ascertains facts which enable him to reach by a chain of reasoning the certainty that this was the case and that his son is dead. Here again a number of highly complex physical impressions of the most diverse kinds received at various times and places evoke, at the moment of conclusion of the reasoning process, the same reaction as the simple written sentence of the telegram; all these impressions have been synthesized in a higher unity which is the *meaning* of the words of the telegram and is the essential condition of the specific reaction or train of reactions. And this instance is typical of all the specifically human modes of reaction. The reaction is neither a sum nor a resultant of the elementary reactions proper to any or all of the sense-impressions received; it is a total reaction of the whole organism upon some part only of the whole field of sense-impressions, and it bears no specific relation to these, but only to the meaning which is suggested by them, or, rather, is extracted from them, by an intellectual activity excited by them.

That other great characteristic of behaviour, namely, persistency of effort with variation of means, is also exhibited by human beings in a degree far surpassing any of the animals. Consider the following example. A man receives an insult or an injury which excites his anger and the impulse to strike down the insulter. If bystanders intervene, he makes persistent and varied efforts to get at his foe, just as an angry dog may do. In that respect his behaviour differs from the animal's only in that he may evince

---

and distances, and that in each of an indefinite multitude of such cases the visual impression may evoke from me the same reaction (e.g. the calling of his name), though in each case the sum of physical stimuli constituting the impression on the sense-organ is unique. The object "is always recognized as 'the same,' though the actual retinal image differs in every case. It is absolutely impossible to understand this fact on the assumption of any kind of preformed material recipient in the brain, corresponding to the stimulus in question" (p. 73).

greater cunning or intelligence in devising various means for the attainment of the end. But it differs greatly in one respect, namely, that separation from the offender in time and place may do little or nothing to turn the man from the pursuit of his end; and in extreme cases the desire of this end, the striking down of his enemy, may dominate his behaviour for many years. Still more significant, of course, and still more remote from all possibility of mechanical explanation, is the self-control which enables another man under similar circumstances to suppress the angry impulse and, because he has learnt to value highly all nobility of conduct, to forgive the injury.

We have seen in Chapter IV. how our ignorance of the mechanical possibilities of the body seemed to Spinoza the best defence of the assumption that all human behaviour is in principle capable of mechanical explanation. And in Chapter VIII. we have seen that the modern defenders of this assumption claim to have found in modern physiology an empirical justification of it. It is true that modern physiology has shown that the nervous system consists of a vast number of material parts and that these are connected together in a vastly complex fashion; so that any one, pointing to the brain, may plausibly ask—Who can assign limits to the possible achievements of a mechanism so intricate? But the physiological doctrines on which the modern mechanist chiefly relies are, as we have seen, three: first, that the behaviour of lower organisms consists wholly of series of reflex actions or tropisms and that these are purely mechanical movements; secondly, that instinctive action is compound reflex action; thirdly, that all intellectual operations consist in the compounding of sensations and in the associative reproduction of one sensation "idea," or impression, by another; to which perhaps should be added the doctrine that volition is nothing more than the reproduction (by some other impression or idea) of an idea of movement, on which the movement follows in a mechanical fashion.

We have seen that increase of knowledge and insight has shown all of these assumptions to be illegitimate. We have seen that the behaviour of even the lowest animals presents features which defy purely mechanical explanation, and that these features become more and more prominent as we trace the modes of behaviour up the scale of life; we have seen that instinctive action is not merely compound reflex action of a mechanical type, but that it implies a synthetic activity in virtue of which a manifold of sense-stimuli becomes the occasion of a unitary reaction of the whole organism, a reaction whose nature is dependent, not merely upon the nature of the several stimuli, but upon the meaning or significance which the organism discovers in their conjunction, and upon the relation of this meaning to its own dominant purpose at the moment.

And we have seen that in human behaviour the independence of the reaction on the nature of the sense-stimuli becomes complete, so that on the one hand very diverse conjunctions of sense-stimuli evoke the same reaction, and, on the other hand, conjunctions of sense-stimuli differing only in respect to some minute detail may evoke totally different reactions; that, in fact, the dominant part in the determination of the reaction is played by the meaning which the individual discovers in the sensory presentation, by the value which he attaches to this meaning, and by the relation of this value to his settled purposes.

In short, throughout the scale of animal and human behaviour we see evidence that meaning, value, and purpose, of which we discern only doubtful traces at the bottom of the scale, play a part whose importance, relatively to the mechanical factors of reaction, constantly increases, until in human behaviour they dominate the scene. It is incumbent, then, on those who regard behaviour as mechanically explicable, to show how these factors, meaning, value, and purpose, may be mechanically conceived; yet how this demonstration is to be made, or can be at all possible, has not hitherto been even vaguely foreshadowed. In a later chapter I shall return to this question and offer a conclusive proof that such demonstration is impossible.

CHAPTER XX

THE ARGUMENT TO PSYCHO-PHYSICAL INTERACTION FROM THE "DISTRIBUTION OF CONSCIOUSNESS"

THE enunciation of the doctrine of organic evolution by natural selection was, as we have seen, a heavy blow to Animism. We have now to note that the Darwinian principle provides one strong argument against psycho-physical Parallelism in all its forms, namely, the argument from the distribution of consciousness.

Let us for the purpose of the argument use the language of Materialism, which describes the production of consciousness as one of the functions of protoplasm or of nervous substance. Now, it is a corollary of the Darwinian principle that only functions which are of service to the individual organism or to the species in the struggle for existence can undergo any evolution throughout any long period of time, or can attain any considerable degree of development or width of distribution in the organic world. If, then, any function is found to have undergone a long continued progressive evolution, and to have attained a high degree of organization in many species, we may infer that it aids effectively in the struggle for survival. Now consciousness, or the production of consciousness, is such a function. Though one cannot of course attain absolute proof of the existence of any consciousness other than one's own, yet we all believe that other men have consciousness; and all men qualified to form an opinion believe that the higher animals also enjoy consciousness (in the widest sense of the word in which it denotes sentiency and feeling of every degree, as well as the developed self-consciousness of man). And they believe also that, as higher forms of animal life were successively evolved, each higher form enjoyed a richer more varied consciousness than the forms that preceded it in the evolutionary scale. Therefore, if we accept the Darwinian principle, we must believe that consciousness (or the production of consciousness) is a function that aids in the struggle for survival, and plays some essential part in the control of the bodily processes and movements by means of which survival is achieved. The more minutely we study the distribution or occurrence of consciousness, the more certain does this inference appear.

To this argument the epiphenomenalist can, I think, find no answer; but the adherent of the two-aspect doctrine may say that all animals are conscious because all physical processes have their conscious aspect; and the psychical monist may say that all animals are necessarily conscious because all things are consciousness; and both may maintain that the richer consciousness of the higher forms of animal life is merely the expression of the greater complexity of their organization. It is necessary, therefore, to press the argument more in detail, and to say to the parallelists: If we accept for the moment your assumption that all things are conscious or are consciousness, you are bound to distinguish two varieties or modes of consciousness, namely, on the one hand, integrated or personal or true consciousness, which in human beings is that of which the other aspect or phenomenon is certain parts of the cerebrum; and, on the other hand, all that consciousness which is the inner aspect or underlying reality of the rest of the nervous system and bodily organism, which does not in our own case enter into the stream of our integrated personal consciousness, and which may be distinguished as sub-consciousness or secondary consciousness. Now, our argument applies to consciousness of the former kind only. It is the integrated consciousness (the only kind of consciousness of which we have any knowledge) which in the course of organic evolution has become ever richer and fuller, and has culminated in the personal consciousness of man. Of this form of consciousness our corollary from the Darwinian principles holds good; we infer from the progressive integration of consciousness that this integration has brought advantages in the struggle for existence, and that integrated consciousness plays some part which is impossible to the hypothetical sub-consciousness. The psychical monist may reply that progressive integration of consciousness is the essence of the evolutionary process, and that what appears to us as increasing complexity of organization throughout the evolutionary scale is the phenomenal appearance of the increasing integration of consciousness. And this reply would be satisfactory, if the degrees of integration of consciousness throughout the scale ran parallel to the degrees of complexity of bodily organization. But this is not the fact. We have good reason to believe that not only in man, but in all the vertebrate animals, the integrated consciousness is associated with the brain only, and that the integration of consciousness runs parallel throughout the scale with the degree of development of the brain and especially of the cerebrum or great brain. Now, the large brain which we find in man and many of the mammals of the present day is a product of a comparatively recent evolution. At the close of the secondary geological period there lived many species of vertebrates which, as regards their whole bodily organization (the brain alone excepted), were as complex and as highly evolved as any existing animals.[1] But their brains were, without exception, very small. The great increase of size of the brain has, in fact, been the principal feature of animal evolution since that period; it is as though Nature, having achieved perfection in merely bodily organization some millions of years ago, had then concentrated all her efforts on the further evolution of mind, of the brain and the integrated consciousness that goes with it.

Now, if the psychical monist could show that the integration of consciousness is a necessary by-product of the process of organization which appears as the evolution of the brain; or if he could offer any explanation of the fact that the organization of all the rest of the body involves no integration of consciousness such as that of the brain involves, he would escape the point of the argument; but just this he cannot do. Before the problem of the unity of personal consciousness he stands perfectly helpless, as I shall have occasion to show in the following chapter.

The foregoing argument may be resumed in a few words, as follows. The parallelists' fundamental assumption that all is consciousness, or that all things have their conscious aspect, does not enable him to escape the corollary of the Darwinian principles that consciousness aids in the struggle for life; because he is bound to recognize two forms of consciousness, namely, real consciousness and unconscious consciousness or pseudo-consciousness; and in the course of animal evolution the former has (according to this view) been developed out of the latter, and a principal feature of the later stages of evolution has been the increase of consciousness proper relatively to the hypothetical lower form of consciousness.

---

[1] It seems probable that the Pterodactyle would compare well with any existing creature in respect to complexity of organization and nicety of adaptation to its mode of life, except as regards brain and adaptability.

THE DISTRIBUTION OF CONSCIOUSNESS 275

The above discussion must, I fear, seem grotesqul and tedious to anyone who has not thoroughly grasped the paraleliest position and has not grappled with the task of thinking out its implications.

And now, having shown that the argument from the distribution of consciousness holds good against the parallelist as well as the epiphenomenalist, we may briefly complete the argument without delaying to translate the language of it into the special forms required by each variety of the parallelist doctrine.

The argument to the usefulness of consciousness from its distribution in the animal scale finds strong confirmation in the facts of its distribution in the individual organism.

In ourselves a large number of nervous processes, namely, all or most of those by which the vegetative life is controlled, normally contribute little or nothing to our personal consciousness; if they are in any sense conscious processes or are accompanied by consciousness, this consciousness normally remains shut out from the stream of personal consciousness; and we may for convenience speak of them as unconscious processes. Now there obtains a very striking and important difference between the unconscious nervous processes (which for the most part are confined to the spinal cord and lower brain) and the conscious processes (which go on wholly or chiefly in the cerebrum or upper brain). The difference is that the nervous structures in which the former occur are in the main hereditarily determined, and but little, if at all, modifiable in the course of individual experience; whereas the nervous processes of the other class occur in nervous structures which are extremely plastic, and whose development is moulded in great degree by the course of individual experience. The cerebrum of the infant seems, in fact, to consist in large part of nervous matter not innately organized, but constituting an immense mass of plastic material which gradually becomes organized under the touch of experience; and all mental acquisition, all formation of habits and associations, seems to involve the organization of this plastic tissue into fixed patterns or configurations of nervous channels. We must recognise, then, a broad difference between the two types of nervous tissue and process: the conscious are plastic, the unconscious fixed and invariable.

But more significant still are the following facts: on repetition the plastic process tends to pass over into the other class; it becomes increasingly fixed and invariable; and we have good ground for believing that this implies the formation of definite paths of connexion between the nervous elements involved, so that they form systems similar to those hereditarily fixed systems by means of which the vegetative functions are controlled. Now it is a familiar truth that the first acquisition of a habit or an association requires attentive effort and clear consciousness of the several steps of the process, and that with repetition the process goes on more "automatically," more smoothly and easily, with less attention, and with less clear consciousness of the end, or of the steps, or of the sense-impressions by which it is guided; and finally, after sufficient repetition, it seems to go on without any effort or attention and without our being conscious of it, save possibly in an extremely obscure fashion, or, in the common phrase, the process becomes secondarily automatic, mechanized, and unconscious; and at the same time it passes more or less completely out of our power of voluntary control and regulation. In other words, nervous processes are of two kinds. On the one hand are those processes which take place in organized and fixed systems of nervous elements; whether these systems are organized hereditarily or in the course of, and under the influence of, individual experience, the processes that occur in them take place without affecting personal consciousness, save perhaps in some very obscure fashion, and without any sense of effort, without attention; though there is reason to doubt whether they are ever completely mechanized or completely and finally withdrawn from the possibility of mental control.[1] On the other hand are processes which occur in nervous tissue that is still plastic, not completely organized in functional systems; these processes, and these only, are accompanied by clear consciousness, by attention, by effort, by explicit volition; and these, on repetition, pass over into the former class; the nervous elements in which they occur become more and more firmly organized, and, in proportion as this organization progresses, attentive consciousness ceases to be involved in or to accompany them. All mental growth, or at least all formation of fixed habits and associations of every kind, seems to involve such progressive organization of new nervous elements within fixed systems. Attention, which is essentially conation or will, is, as Dr Stout has well said,[2] the growing point of the mind; it is concentrated wherever the process of organization of nervous

---

[1] The facts of hypnosis and allied conditions in which the power of the mind over the body seems to be greatly increased necessitate this reservation.
[2] "Analytic Psychology."

elements is going on; and when, and in proportion as, this process approaches completion, attention (which means conation and clear consciousness) is set free to be concentrated upon other processes involving mental acquisition or growth. For it is a further distinction between the processes of these two kinds that, while the "mechanized" processes do not seriously interfere with other nervous processes, whether of the same or of the other kind, processes involving attentive consciousness interfere with one another in proportion to the degree of effort, or of concentration of attention, required by each of them.

Clear consciousness and conation are then invariable concomitants, not of nervous process in general, nor of all nervous processes occurring in the cerebral cortex or in any other part of the brain, but of those nervous processes that occur in nervous elements not yet organized in fixed systems; and wherever a new path has to be forced through the untrodden jungle of nerve cells, there and there only is conscious effort, true mental activity, involved. Without conation there is no mental growth, and the stronger the psychical impulse, the desire or effort of will, the more effectively are the difficulties of new acquisition overcome; and an effect of all such processes, an effect whose degree is proportional to the intensity of the conation and the corresponding concentration of attention involved, is the organization of the nervous elements, the combination of them in fixed functional systems.

We have, then, a perfect case of invariable concomitance and sequence; the nervous process that occurs in unorganized elements (and this only) is invariably accompanied by attentive consciousness; and such process invariably results in some degree of organization of the nervous elements, a degree which is proportional to the degree of attentive effort involved. How different, then, are the facts from the assumptions as to the relation of consciousness to nervous process necessarily implied and generally asserted by the parallelists and epiphenomenalists, namely, an invariable parallelism or concomitance in time of consciousness and of all nervous process (or all cerebral process) without distinction! The relations are such as imply that clear consciousness and conation play some real part in bringing about the organization of nervous elements, that the relation between conation or conscious mental activity and nervous organization is the causal relation.

Well founded views as to the nature of the cerebral processes enable us to go further and to form some more intimate notion of the nature of the process of nervous organization, in which consciousness and conation seem to play this essential role. The building up of neural systems seems to be essentially the establishment of paths of low resistance between the various elements or neurons concerned; the establishment of such a path seems to be the effect of the passage of a stream of nervous energy across the synapses, the places at which the neurones are in contact or close proximity with one another; for the synapses seem to be not only the places of connexion of neurones, but also the seats of the resistances by which the spread of the nervous excitation from neurone to neurone is limited and directed.

Organized systems of neurones are such as have low internal resistances; and systems of neurones and unorganized neurones are separated from others by synapses that present a high degree of resistance to the passage of the current of nervous energy. The essential feature of the process of organization is, then, the forcing of a passage across synapses of high resistance; and it would seem that for this forcing of a passage a concentration of nervous energy, resulting in a high potential of charge of nervous energy in the neurones, is an essential condition.[1] This process of concentration of nervous energy, resulting in its accumulation from places of lower potential into one system of neurones where the potential is raised to a high level and in its discharge across synapses of high resistance (and not nervous process in general) is, then, the process that is invariably and proportionally accompanied by clear consciousness and conative effort. Now this process is one that seems to be mechanically inexplicable; it involves just such antagonism of the tendency to dissipation and degradation of energy as we have seen to be characteristic of living organisms; it seems, in fact, to be the supreme manifestation of this power. It is just here, then, that we should expect to find operative any power of psychical intervention in the

[1] This is implied by the fact that in proportion to the effort required, the free nervous energy of the brain (or neurokyme) seems to be withdrawn from all other tracts of the brain, so that they are inhibited in proportion to the degree to which their activities require a high potential of energy, or, in other words, in proportion as the various systems active at the moment fall short of complete organization or "mechanization." It is implied also by many other physiological facts which cannot be detailed here (see paper by the author on "Nature of Inhibitory Processes within the Nervous System," "Brain," vol. xxvi.).

THE DISTRIBUTION OF CONSCIOUSNESS

mechanical sequence of events, and it is here that we might attempt to apply any one of those conceptions of guidance without work, which, as we saw in Chapter XIV., would permit of psychical intervention in the course of the brain-processes without breach of the law of conservation of energy in its strictest form. And it is just of this process that conation or psychical effort seems to be an invariable and necessary condition.[1]

The facts, then, point strongly to the view that conation or psychical effort really intervenes in the course of the physical processes of the brain, and that it plays an essential role in the building up of the organization of the brain. And it may be plausibly maintained that all other modes of consciousness serve but to guide or determine the incidence of conation, the primary and most fundamental form of psychical activity.

The argument from the Darwinian principles to the usefulness of consciousness to the organism may be put in a rather different way, which I will indicate very briefly only.

All the immense variety of qualities of sensation that we experience seem to be in some sense compounded from a limited number of primary or elementary qualities of sensation; and it is generally agreed that we have to regard all the primary qualities of sensation as having been differentiated step by step from some primordial germ of sensation of undifferentiated quality.

Now we are compelled to believe that to each of these primary qualities of sensation there corresponds as its invariable accompaniment a neural process of peculiar or specific quality; and there is very strong ground for believing that each such process owes its unique quality to the peculiar physico-chemical constitution of the nervous substance in which it takes place.[2] These very

[1] This argument was presented by the author in some detail in a series of papers in "Mind," N.S., vol. vii. ("A Contribution towards an Improvement of Psychological Method"), and has been elaborated in later papers, especially "Physiological Factors of the Attention-process" ("Mind," N.S., vol. x.), "The Seat of the Psycho-physical Processes" ("Brain," vol. xxiv.).

[2] I have argued in the papers referred to above that these substances of specific constitution, presumably the most highly specialized of all forms of organic matter, reside at the synapses of the cerebrum, and that the immediate occasion of sensation is the discharge of nervous energy across such substance from neuron to neuron. But this suggestion, though it harmonizes well with the argument of the foregoing pages, is not a necessary part of the present argument. It may be pointed out in passing that these highly specialized substances and their exact distribution in various parts of the cerebrum are among the innate characters of the adult organism, and that they have to be regarded as provided for, or determined by, the constitution of the germ cell, if the mechanical view of the process of heredity is accepted.

highly specialized substances have, then, been gradually evolved and differentiated in the course of evolution of the animal kingdom, and they must therefore be of value to the organisms that possess them. But, so far as we can at present see, the specific characters of these substances are without significance for the mechanical operations of the brain; they seem to subserve no other function in the life of the organism than just the production of a rich variety of qualities of sensation. If further research should prove this view to be true (and the evidence we already have strongly supports it), then we shall have in these facts another strong reason for believing in the value of consciousness to the organism and in the intervention of psychical factors in the course of the mechanical processes of the brain.

CHAPTER XXI

THE UNITY OF CONSCIOUSNESS

IN this chapter we have to consider from several points of view the fact of the unity of personal consciousness and the difficulties which this fact raises for all forms of Parallelism. The problem of the unity of consciousness has been much discussed, and the discussion has been conducted along two rather different lines; the one line of discussion, neglecting physiological considerations, has relied on purely psychological and metaphysical reasoning; the other has kept constantly in view the bearing of physiological facts. We may with advantage follow up these two lines separately; but we shall see that they converge to a common conclusion.

Every form of Parallelism necessarily assumes that the consciousness of any complex organism is in some sense composite, that it is compounded from, or made up of, elements which in principle are capable of existing in separation from the whole of which they form part, and that it is a unity only in the same sense as the bodily organism is a unity. Most of the parallelists frankly accept this corollary of their doctrine. The late Professor Ebbinghaus, for example,[1] likened the unity of human consciousness to the unity of a plant. Like the plant, he said, consciousness has many distinguishable parts, namely the various sensations, the details of imagery, and the feelings, which introspective analysis discovers in any section of its stream; between these parts or elements obtain systematic functional relations, in virtue of which they constitute an organic whole or unity, just as the leaves, flowers, stem, and roots of a plant form an organic unity in virtue of the functional relations that obtain between them.

This doctrine, that consciousness is compounded from elements, is the essence of what has been well named the atomistic psychology. The parallelists, who are logically compelled to subscribe to this atomistic doctrine, are the more ready to do so

[1] "Grundzüge d. Psychologie," Bk. I. § 2.

because the "association-psychology," which had been developed with little or no reference to this special problem, had made this doctrine the foundation of all its reasonings and had in some measure justified it by its partial success in throwing light on our mental operations. The association-psychology owed its rise to Locke's doctrine of the compounding of simple ideas to form complex ideas, and it has always retained this as its most fundamental assumption. But in one respect later exponents, notably J. S. Mill, found themselves compelled to modify it, namely by the introduction of the conception of "Mental Chemistry." For it was realized that introspection cannot always discover in the complex idea the simple ideas or elements of consciousness of which it is said to be compounded; it was assumed therefore that the elements or smaller fragments of consciousness do not merely cohere side by side to form the complex ideas, but that they *coalesce* or combine, yielding up more or less completely their original natures to form compounds whose nature is more or less different from that of each of the coalescing parts.

Thus, it is said that, when I experience a sensation of the quality purple, that sensation is produced by the compounding of two simple sensations, one of the quality red and one of the quality blue; or that, when I perceive a spot of light to be in a certain direction, my consciousness of the light-in-that-direction is a complex which is formed by the coalescence of the visual sensation with certain sensations of the "muscular sense" excited by the position or movements of the head and eyeballs; or that, when I judge one piece of bread to be larger than a second piece, my mental process is essentially the association of the idea of the one piece with the idea "larger" or with the idea of largeness, and that my state of consciousness is the complex idea produced by the compounding of these two simpler ideas. And, according to this doctrine, when I will a certain movement, my volition is merely a state of consciousness compounded of the idea of the movement that I am about to make with some obscure sensations of muscular strain in the scalp, or throat, or elsewhere, and perhaps also with the idea of myself, which in turn is a compound of many simple sensations and ideas.

On the other hand the Animist, who believes that the soul is something more than the fleeting stream of consciousness, maintains that the consciousness of any individual is or has a unity of a unique kind which has no analogue in the physical realm, and that it cannot properly be regarded as consisting of elements, units, or atoms of consciousness, put together or compounded in any way. He maintains that the unity of individual consciousness is a fundamental and primary fact, and that we are logically bound to infer some ground of this unity other than consciousness itself; he holds that each man's consciousness is a unitary whole and is separate and distinct from the consciousness of every other organism, just because it is a state or activity of a psychical subject, the ego, soul, or spirit, which is essentially a unitary and distinct being. He regards as illegitimate the conception of fragments or atoms of consciousness, particles of sensation or feeling, of mind-stuff or mind-dust of any kind, and rejects the notion that such fragments come into being or exist independently and are capable of being combined according to the laws of a "mental chemistry." He insists that no one has ever come upon such a fragment of consciousness lying about loose or unattached anywhere in the world; that each of us knows sensations and feelings only as introspectively distinguishable, but inseparable, parts of the stream of his own consciousness, and that nothing in our experience justifies us in believing that such mind-dust exists or can exist.

This doctrine of "mental chemistry" assumes that the atoms of consciousness, say two elementary sensations, come together and, fusing, yield up their own natures to form a third thing unlike both. But this is in itself an inadmissible notion; the quality of a sensation is its very being, its *esse* is truly *percipi*, and to suppose that, on being compounded with a second sensation, it ceases to be itself and becomes something else, is strictly absurd. The supposed chemical analogy of the compounding of atoms of hydrogen and oxygen to form water does not in the least justify this conception; for in this case the atoms do not change their natures on being combined; they merely appear different, because the compound affects our senses and other things in other ways than the pure substances. That the atoms retain their essential nature unchanged appears clearly, if the compound is decomposed. When, however, simultaneous stimulation by red and blue lights gives rise to sensation of the quality purple, this sensation is not merely two sensations of red and blue qualities, appearing different in virtue of their being conjoined; rather it is in itself something different from both the red and the blue qualities.

To all this it may be added that, when the psychical monist claims that his position is superior to all others because it postulates or infers no form of existence not directly known to us, he is making a false claim; for the mind-dust which he is compelled to postulate as the raw material of consciousness is, like the soul of the Animist, a hypothetical form of existence reached only by inference from immediate experience.

Most of the arguments briefly indicated in the foregoing paragraph have been presented by Lotze, the greatest modern defender of Animism, and it is impossible to state them more forcibly than in his words. "A mere sensation without a subject," he wrote, "is nowhere to be met with as a fact. It is impossible to speak of a bare movement without thinking of the mass whose movement it is; and it is just as impossible to conceive a sensation existing without the accompanying idea of that which has it, or rather of that which feels it; ... It is thus, and thus only, that the sensation is a given fact; and we have no right to abstract from its relation to its subject because the relation is puzzling, and because we wish to obtain a starting-point which looks more convenient, but is utterly unwarranted by experience."

Even if we were to admit the conception of fragments of consciousness capable of being compounded and associated together, such compounding and associating could yield at most only the content of consciousness; we could not admit the further assumption necessarily made by the parallelists, the assumption namely that we can explain in terms of such compounding and associating the processes of knowing, judging, comparing, desiring, willing, and reasoning. For these processes involve psychical activities which are more than and other than the processes of associative reproduction. Lotze made this his principal argument for the existence of the soul and for its interaction with the body. He wrote—" Any comparison of two ideas, which ends by our finding their contents like or unlike, presupposes the absolutely indivisible unity of that which compares them, and it must be one and the same thing which first forms the idea of a, then that of b, and which at the same time is conscious of the nature and extent of the difference between them. Then again the various acts of comparing ideas and referring them to one another are themselves in turn reciprocally related; and their relation brings a new activity of comparison to consciousness.

And so our whole inner world of thoughts is built up, not as a mere collection of manifold ideas existing with or after one another, but as a world in which these individual members are held together and arranged by the relating activity of this single pervading principle. This then is what we mean by the unity of consciousness, and it is this that we regard as the sufficient ground for assuming an indivisible soul."

To these two arguments from the unity of consciousness, Lotze added a third, namely that from the consciousness of the self as a unity. This argument has been much insisted upon by a class of writers who assert—" I am aware of myself as a spiritual unity, therefore I am no mere system of minor selves or of fragments of consciousness, but an immortal soul"; and some of them go so far as to assert that the consciousness of self as a unity is always present in all forms of mental process. This, of course, is merely bad psychology constructed in the interests of *a priori* speculation. But Lotze gave the argument a more subtle form. " Our belief in the soul's unity," he said, "rests not on our appearing to ourselves such a unity, but on our being able to appear to ourselves at all. Did we appear to ourselves something quite different, nay, did we seem to ourselves to be an unconnected plurality, we would from this very fact, from the bare possibility of appearing anything to ourselves, deduce the necessary unity of our being, this time in open contradiction with what self-observation set before us as our own image. What a being appears to itself to be, is not the important point; if it can appear anyhow to itself, or other things to it, it must be capable of unifying manifold phenomena in an absolute indivisibility of its nature." Again, he wrote—"What is apt to perplex us in this question is the somewhat thoughtless way in which we so often allow ourselves to play fast and loose with the notion of appearance. We are content with setting in contrast to it the being that appears, and we forget that the appearance is impossible without another being that sees it. We fancy that appearance comes forth from the hidden depths of being-in-itself, like a lustre existing before there is any eye for it to arise in, extending into reality, present to and apprehensible by him who will grasp it, but none the less continuing to exist even if known by none. We here overlook that even in the region of sensation, from which this image is borrowed, the lustre emitted by objects only seems to be emitted by them, and that it can even seem to come from them, only because our eyes are there, the receptive organ of a cognitive soul, to which appearances are possible. The lustre of light does not spread itself around us, but like all phenomena dwells only in the consciousness of him for whom it exists. And of this consciousness, of this general capacity that makes the appearance of anything possible, we maintain that it can be an attribute only of the indivisible unity of one being, and that every attempt to ascribe it to a plurality, however bound together, will, by its failure, but confirm our conviction of the supersensible unity of the soul."[1]

That, to my mind, is a beautiful piece of reasoning which carries great weight. Nevertheless it would seem that this reasoning, though it cannot be refuted, is incapable of compelling assent to its conclusion; for, since Lotze wrote these words, Parallelism has gained ground rapidly against Animism—if success be reckoned in terms of the numbers of those who accept the rival doctrines. I believe that the argument from the unity of consciousness to the real being of the soul may be made more compelling by keeping the facts of cerebral physiology closely in view, especially facts which have been discovered since Lotze wrote the passages cited above.

From the early days of speculation, physiologists have manifested a tendency to seek some unitary organ within the body the physical processes of which might be regarded as corresponding to the unity of consciousness. Aristotle postulated such an organ, ascribing to it more especially the perceptual functions that are common to the several senses. The notion of a *sensorium commune*, thus launched into the culture-tradition by Aristotle, has served many later thinkers of anti-animistic tendency as a substitute for the soul; and the search for a *sensorium commune* has been at various times confused with the search for the seat of the soul. We have seen in Chapter VIII. that the long search for a punctual or central seat of the soul has proved fruitless, and that this result has contributed to bring about the rejection of Animism. We have now to see that the search for a *sensorium commune* has proved equally fruitless, and that this result provides one of the strongest arguments in support of Animism.

The fundamental fact which requires explanation may be

[1] "Metaphysik," Bk. III. chap. i.

THE UNITY OF CONSCIOUSNESS

stated in the following concrete form :—when the eye and the ear of any person are simultaneously stimulated, the sensory effects of the stimuli applied to the two organs and of the excitations of the two nerves, the optic and the auditory, somehow cohere or belong together in the peculiar way which consists in being partial modifications of one consciousness: the stimuli and their immediate effects in the nerves are separate and distinct, yet their effects in consciousness belong together as parts of one whole. This fact has been very commonly held to imply that somewhere in the brain the two nervous excitations must become one. And, since the effects of all stimuli simultaneously applied to the senses of one organism become compounded in this way to form parts of one complex whole, the stream of consciousness, it seemed necessary to suppose that all the sensory nerves transmit their excitations to some one part of the brain, in which they are compounded to a complex physical resultant, the physical correlate of the complex psychical resultant. It was to this hypothetical common sensory centre that the name *sensorium commune* was appropriately applied.

Before the issue between Parallelism and Animism had become clearly defined, this hypothetical centre was identified in some minds with the seat of the soul. This view was, perhaps, first formulated by Descartes, but Lotze (who afterwards rejected it) has given the clearest presentation of it in his " Medizinische Psychologie."[1] He argued that we must expect to find somewhere in the brain a central chamber filled with a structureless jelly or parenchyma, as he called it, upon which all the sensory nerves abut in such a way that the excitation passing up any one of them must be communicated to the jelly. He assumed, as many others have done, that the nervous excitation is a vibration or undulation, whose form is different in the several nerves, and that, when several such vibrations are simultaneously imparted to the central jelly, it becomes the seat of a complex vibration which is the physical resultant of all the simpler waves. The jelly was thus to serve as the *sensorium commune* or physical *medium of composition* of the effects of sensory stimuli.

Other modern writers, feeling the need of such a medium of composition of the effects of sensory stimuli, have seen it in various parts of the brain; W. B. Carpenter,[2] for example, claimed the *optic thalamus* as such an organ, and Herbert Spencer the *pons*

[1] Published in 1852.   [2] " Mental Physiology."

cerebri.[1] Others have postulated, at the apex of a hierarchy of cells, a pontifical cell which might play this role.

But the progress of our knowledge of the brain has shown conclusively that there exists no one part to which all sensory paths converge, and which might be regarded as a *sensorium commune* in the sense defined above. It has been shown on the contrary that the tracts of fibres ascending to the brain from the sense-organs of different functions pass to widely separated parts of the cerebral cortex, the sensory areas, and that the various qualities of sensation depend upon or are evoked by the processes of these several areas.

Faced with these facts, some of those who have seen the necessity of postulating some medium of composition of the effects of sensory stimuli have suggested other possibilities of physical composition. E. von. Hartmann,[2] for example, suggested that, whenever any two (or more) sensory nerves are simultaneously excited, the excitation-process in the central station of each propagates itself through some intervening tract of fibres to that of the other, so that this tract becomes the seat of a complex vibration which is the physical resultant of the two processes, and that it thus serves as the medium of composition required.

One other view only of the nature of the hypothetical material medium of composition seems possible, namely the one forcibly advocated by G. H. Lewes.[3] Lewes' knowledge of the nervous system forbade him to accept the notion of any central part or pontifical cell of the brain that might serve as the *sensorium commune*; he therefore heroically proposed to identify it with the whole of the brain; he supposed that vibrations of various forms are impressed on the sensory nerves in the sense-organs, and that each such vibration propagates itself throughout the whole nervous system, which is thus pervaded in all its parts at any moment by a complex vibration, the physical resultant of the vibrations initiated at the preceding moment in the several sensory nerves.

Now all three views of the nature of the assumed physical medium of composition (and no others have been or can be suggested) are purely speculative; no particle of evidence directly supporting any one of them can be adduced. The knowledge we now have of the nervous system and its functions enables us to reject the second and third views as decisively as the first, and

---

[1] " Principles of Psychology." [2] " Philosophy of the Unconscious."
[3] " The Physical Basis of Mind."

to assert confidently that there exists in the brain no such physical medium of composition, and that the processes of the several sensory nerves simultaneously excited do not affect any common material medium to produce in it a complex physical resultant. I might substantiate this statement by showing that each of these three views is incompatible with well-established general principles of cerebral physiology, e.g. the principle that the primary qualities of sensation are determined by the specific constitutions of the nervous substances in the cerebral terminals of the sensory nerves and that these are widely scattered through the cerebral cortex and, perhaps, in part in the basal ganglia [1]; the principle, recently established, that nervous conduction is not a mere physical vibration, but involves chemical change; and the principle of localization of cerebral functions in general. These and other general considerations render it in the highest degree probable that the physical conditions or accompaniments of the complex state of sensation obtaining at any moment in the individual consciousness (and our consciousness always involves a complex of sensations more or less obscure or clear) are a number of physico-chemical processes running their courses separately in many widely scattered parts of the cerebrum.

But the strongest evidence against the view that the effects of simultaneous sense-stimuli are physically compounded may be provided by the demonstration that no such compounding occurs in one particular instance in which it has been and still is most confidently assumed, namely the instance of binocular vision. When we look at any object with both eyes, both retinæ and both optic nerves are stimulated; why then do we see one object only? The commonly accepted answer runs—Because the fibres from each pair of corresponding points of the two retinæ converge in the brain to a common path or centre. I propose to show very briefly that this answer is untrue. Let us consider the facts in their most simple and striking form, in order to appreciate as clearly as possible the nature of the problem. Two men, A and

---

[1] This is the modern form of the doctrine of specific energies of sensory nerves. Many attempts have been made to overthrow this principle, but without success. Prof. Wundt, for example, claims to have replaced it by the doctrine of the original indifference of function of cerebral centres; but his doctrine, even if tenable, only differs from the more generally accepted principle in maintaining that the specific constitutions of sensory centres are impressed upon them in the course of individual development ("Grundzüge der Phys. Psychologie").

B, are in a dark room in which is a single small illuminated area or spot of white light. A puts a red glass before his left eye and looks directly at the spot with that eye only. B puts a blue glass before his right eye and looks at the spot with that eye only. A sees a red spot, B a blue one; a sensation of quality red is experienced by A, blue by B. Then A, keeping the red glass before his left eye, puts the blue glass before his right eye, and, looking at the spot with both eyes, sees a purple spot, i.e., he experiences a sensation of which the quality is neither red nor blue, but rather blue-red, a composite quality which has affinity to both blue and red, but which is widely different from both. Why this difference between the two cases?[1]

The ordinarily accepted answer runs—In the former case the red and blue lights excite nervous processes which run their courses separately in the brains of A and B respectively; the physical causes of the red and blue sensations are separate and distinct, and therefore the sensations are distinct; but in the second case the nervous processes excited by the red and the blue lights respectively are transmitted to the same part, or same group of nervous elements, of the one brain and are there physically compounded, and therefore only one sensation is excited and this is of neither red nor blue quality, but partakes of both qualities.

I cannot display here the evidence in detail which proves that no such physical composition of effects takes place, since much of it is of a highly technical character; and I must refer the reader who wishes to study it to a separately published paper in which it is set out more fully.[2] But it seems worth while to set down here the main heads of this evidence as follows:—

(1) The spot of light seen with red and blue glasses before the two eyes respectively does not always appear purple; at moments it appears pure red, and at others pure blue, an instance of the phenomenon known as the struggle of the two visual fields, or retinal rivalry. And by voluntary effort either colour may be made to predominate over the other. It is difficult to reconcile this alternation of the two colours in consciousness with the view that the excitations of the two optic nerves become physically com-

---

[1] The problem may be presented in a form rather more striking perhaps, but more complicated, by substituting a bluish-green glass for the blue one. The subject A will then see a white spot, though his left eye is stimulated by red light and his right eye by blue-green light.

[2] "The Relations between Corresponding Retinal Points," *Brain*, vol. 34.

pounded in the visual centres of the cerebrum; and it is still more difficult to reconcile with this view the possibility of re-enforcing by voluntary effort either process to the exclusion of the other.

(2) If, instead of red and blue glasses, a single darkly-smoked glass is used before one eye (so as to diminish the intensity of the stimulus to that retina), and if then the illuminated area is looked at with the uncovered eye only, and after a few seconds the other eye is opened behind the smoked glass, the illumination of the area appears to be diminished at this moment; and, if one continues to observe it under these conditions, it may appear to become alternately brighter and darker every few seconds. This is the phenomenon known as Fechner's paradox. The fact of chief importance from our present point of view is that the opening of the eye behind the smoked glass diminishes the apparent brightness of the area; and if (according to the assumption) we regard the two eyes as the terminals of a single sense-organ, we must say that an addition to the total physical stimulus to the sense-organ diminishes the intensity of the sensation. But, if the excitations initiated in the corresponding areas of the two retinæ were transmitted to a common centre and there compounded, the effects of the two stimuli should be summed together, and the effect of opening the eye behind the smoked glass should be to increase the intensity of the sensation.

(3) Allied to the last and even more significant, though its significance is apt to be obscured by our familiarity with it, is the fact that, when we look at any illuminated surface with both eyes, it appears no brighter (or so little brighter that it is very difficult to be sure of the difference) than when looked at with one eye only; that is to say the doubling of the physical stimulus produces no increase (or only a very slight increase) in the intensity of sensation. This fact clearly is incompatible with the common view that the two optic nerves transmit their excitations to be summed in a common centre; for if that were the case, the opening of the second eye on any illuminated surface should produce the same well-marked degree of increase of brightness or of intensity of the sensation, as doubling the illumination of the surface, i.e. as doubling the intensity of stimulation of the one retina.

(4) In certain cases of hysteria the patient becomes for a time wholly blind of one eye; and a similar condition may be temporarily induced in many subjects by verbal suggestion during hypnosis. Now such functional blindness is in all pro-

bability due to an arrest of the activity of the sensory centre of the cerebral cortex; it is impossible to suppose that the verbal suggestion can paralyze the optic tract below the cortex, while leaving the cortical centre of the tract in activity; yet this would have to be supposed to occur, if the cortical centres of the two retinæ are identical.[1]

(5) In certain rare cases a lesion of the visual cortex has produced a small area of blindness in one retina only; a fact fatal to the common view.

(6) If the corresponding points of the two retinæ sent their fibres to a common cortical centre, this relation of "correspondence" should be definitely fixed and incapable of being altered; but we find that in some cases of squint there is set up a correspondence between other than the normally corresponding points, which permits of single binocular vision in spite of the squint; and further it is found that, if the squint is cured by operation, so that the normally corresponding points receive the optical images of the same object; then at first the patient sees objects double, but gradually ceases to do so, reacquiring by practice the normal system of correspondences. These facts are clearly irreconcilable with the view that single vision with the two eyes depends upon any fixed system of anatomical connexions.

(7) If the retina is stimulated intermittently, the rate of succession of the stimuli may be increased until the subject ceases to perceive any intermittence or flicker of the sensation. This rate of succession is known as flicker-point; it varies with the intensity of the stimulating light; but we may take for illustration a case in which flicker-point is reached when the stimulus is repeated twenty times a second. Now, if each retina is stimulated intermittently twenty times a second, but in such a way that the stimuli fall alternately on the two retinæ, the flicker-point is not changed; whereas, if the fibres from corresponding points converge to a common centre, flicker-point should be reached when the stimulus falls ten times a second on each retina; for then the centre would still be stimulated twenty times a second.

These are the principal facts which go to prove that the physical processes simultaneously initiated in corresponding points of the two retinæ undergo no physical compounding or fusion; and taken together they make an overwhelmingly strong proof that, in such a case as that of the fusion of the effects of red and

[1] For further discussion of the facts, see chap. xxv.

blue lights applied to the two retinæ, the fusion of effects (which undeniably occurs) is not dependent on any composition or fusion of the physical processes. The fusion of effects, therefore, takes place only in the psychical sphere. In the illustrative case we have considered, the two physical processes initiated by the red and the blue lights respectively in the two retinæ of the man A, remain as distinct as the two physical processes initiated by the red and blue lights respectively in the left eye of the man A and in the right eye of the man B ; yet in the one case the effect in consciousness produced by them is a single sensation of the quality purple in one consciousness, and in the other case they excite two sensations, one of quality red in the consciousness of A, and one of quality blue in the consciousness of B.

The fusion of effects of simultaneous sensory stimuli to a unitary resultant is, then, not a physiological or physical fusion or composition, but a purely psychical fusion ; the unitary resultant exists only in the psychical sphere. Is this fact compatible with any form of Parallelism?

Any unbiased mind must, I think, answer this question in the negative. For it is clear that these psychical fusions of effects of sensory stimuli obey, or take place according to, purely psychical laws that have no physical counterparts ; or that, if the two sensations of different quality really come into existence and afterwards fuse together producing the third quality, the fusion is a psychical process to which no physical process runs parallel. This fact appears clearly enough when we consider only the fusions that result in our complex sensations ; but it will appear still more clearly, and its full significance will be more obvious, when in a later chapter we deal with the higher mental processes.

Before going on to that part of our discussion, I wish to show that the fact we have established is not only incompatible with all forms of Parallelism and therefore indirectly an evidence of Animism, but that it affords a more direct and positive proof of the truth of Animism.

We have seen that, while most of the exponents of Parallelism meet this problem of the ground of the unity of individual consciousness with the untenable doctrine of the physical unity of the brain-processes that accompany individual consciousness, and while others ignore it completely, some of the most thorough of them recognize the existence of the problem but fail to offer any solution of it ; thus Lange and

Paulsen (Chapter XII) frankly assert that it is an insoluble problem, while Professor Strong is still pondering the problem—"What holds consciousness together?"

Only one exponent of Parallelism seems to have clearly grasped this problem and to have grappled seriously with it, namely Fechner. Fechner was a clear-sighted, as well as a boldly original, thinker and, unlike many other philosophers, he had a wide knowledge of, and a great respect for, empirical facts; and, though most of the evidence set forth above was not accessible to him, he realized clearly the fact that the brain-processes which are the physical correlates of any complex state of consciousness are a number of discrete processes taking place in various parts of the brain (a fact which curiously enough Lotze failed to recognize). In his celebrated work, "Elemente der Psychophysik," he wrote "The psychically unitary and simple are resultants of a physical manifold, the physical multiplicity gives unitary or simple resultants."[1] And Fechner saw that in this fact lies a crucial problem for his whole psycho-physical doctrine, one that urgently demands some solution. The solution he proposed was his doctrine of psycho-physical continuity and discontinuity. Surveying the types of nervous system, he regarded it as probable that in such animals as the lower arthropoda, whose nervous system consists of a chain of ganglia connected with one another only by slender bands of nerve fibres, each ganglion has its own separate consciousness; and he thought it highly probable also that the spinal cord and perhaps the basal ganglia of the higher vertebrates (including man) have their own streams of consciousness separate from the chief or cerebral consciousness. And he held that empirical facts justified the view that, if the human cerebrum could be divided by the knife into two halves, each half would enjoy its separate consciousness; and that, if the brains of two men could be effectively joined by a bridge of nervous matter, as the two halves of the human cerebrum are joined by the *corpus callosum*, the two men would have a single common consciousness. It seemed, then, to him that a condition of

[1] Vol. ii. p. 526. Again, on p. 456 we read: "Dabei haben wir uns zu erinnern, dass nicht nur unser Allgemeinbewusstsein in jedem Momente von einem Systeme von Bewegungen getragen wird, sondern dass auch alle Phanomene, die sich als besondere vom Grunde des Allgemeinbewusstseins abheben, wenn schon sie für das Bewusstsein einfach erscheinen, doch nicht an einfachen Bewegungsmomente einzelner Theile hangen sondern an dem Zusammenwirken einer Mehrheit von Theilchen und Momenten."

THE UNITY OF CONSCIOUSNESS

the unity of a consciousness is continuity in space of the nervous matter; and that a condition of separateness of consciousnesses is spatial separation of their nervous bases or material aspects. But this is not the sole and essential condition, else every intact nervous system would have one consciousness only (i.e. the conscious aspect of all its processes would run together to form a single consciousness); whereas each man's personal consciousness is (according to Fechner's doctrine) the combination of the processes of certain parts of his brain only (in their conscious aspect). The further and essential condition of the running together of lesser consciousnesses to form the larger consciousness of the individual organism is, Fechner suggests, that their material aspects shall form a spatially continuous system, every part of which in its psychical aspect rises above "the threshold of consciousness" of that individual. In a similar way Fechner would explain, or rather state, the essential condition of the flowing together of the consciousnesses of individual men to form the larger aggregations of consciousness which he assumed to exist. Such a hypothetical larger consciousness he regarded as that of an individual of a more comprehensive type than the human individual, a consciousness which is more inclusive because its "threshold" is lower, so much lower that the psycho-physical processes of the inorganic matter which connects the bodies of human beings are of sufficient intensity to rise above that "threshold."

What shall be said of this strange doctrine? In the first place it must be frankly admitted that modern studies of multiple personality seem to lend it some support. For there is some reason to believe that in these cases there exists a rupture of functional continuity between two or more parts of one nervous system, each of these parts serving as the physical basis of one of the partial personalities.

But there are many good reasons for rejecting this doctrine. (1) In the first place, the distribution in the brain of the processes that are the immediate correlates of consciousness is in all probability not such as is demanded by it; for example, the two hemispheres of the cerebrum are directly connected only by the strands of fibres that make up the *corpus callosum*, and it is highly probable that the processes in these fibres are not immediate correlates of consciousness or (in Fechner's language) that their processes do not rise above the threshold of consciousness; if this is the fact, each hemisphere is in Fechner's sense psycho-physically discontinuous with the other, and each should therefore have its separate consciousness: which is certainly not normally the case. There are also cases on record in which the *corpus callosum* was completely lacking and which nevertheless afforded no indication of "dual consciousness."[1]

(2) The doctrine involves all the objectionable features of psychical atomism and "mental chemistry," and all the difficulties of the compounding of individual consciousnesses to larger wholes which we have noted on other pages.

(3) The conception of the "threshold," which is fundamental to Fechner's whole psycho-physical scheme and especially to the doctrine of psycho-physical continuity, remains utterly obscure, a metaphor of extreme vagueness merely. The phrase "threshold of consciousness" possesses a misleading plausibility. which has secured for it a wide popularity. The consciousness, it is assumed, exists whether above or below the "threshold," and its being above the "threshold" is merely the condition of its aggregation in the complex whole of individual consciousness. The "threshold," above which consciousness is said to rise, must be then in every case the "threshold" peculiar to the individual whose consciousness is in question; yet (according to the doctrine) this individual has no existence as such apart from the "threshold"; the "threshold" is in short constitutive of the individual. It it must, I think, be admitted that a "threshold" pure and simple, regarded as the bond that holds consciousness together, is in no way superior, rather vastly inferior, to the conception of a soul as a unitary psychical being.

(4) If we could put aside all these objections and difficulties, and if it could be empirically established that the condition of the unity of consciousness is the material continuity of brain matter and of the processes in it which are the immediate correlates of consciousness; still the doctrine of psycho-physical continuity would not render in the least degree intelligible the fact that a unitary consciousness is correlated with a multitude of discrete brain-processes. The doctrine, if empirically established, would remain the statement of an absolutely unintelligible fact.

(5) If the doctrine were established, it would be incompatible with the fundamental principal of Parallelism, the principle namely that every psychical process has its physical aspect. As was pointed out above, the fusions of sensations and other elements to

[1] See paper by Dr A. Bruce in *Brain*, 1889.

form a unitary consciousness, as assumed by the doctrine, would remain purely psychical processes having no phenomenal or physical aspect; for, as Fechner himself recognized, there are no corresponding fusions of the physical processes of the brain; and the "threshold of consciousness," which is regarded as constitutive of the unitary stream of consciousness or of psychical individuality in general, would remain as a law or attribute or conditioning factor of psychical existences without parallel or counterpart in the physical world.

The demonstration that the fusion of effects of simultaneous sensory stimuli does not take place in the nervous system thus forces upon us the problem of the ground of the unity of individual consciousness in a form which brings out clearly the impossibility of finding any solution compatible with the fundamental assumption of all forms of Parallelism; and it forces us to choose between adopting the plain and straightforward solution offered by Animism and leaving this fundamental fact utterly mysterious and unintelligible. The issue is simple and direct.[1] When two stimuli are simultaneously applied to the sense-organs of any normal human being, they produce a change in his consciousness which is their combined effect or resultant. This composition or combination of their effects does not take place in the nervous system; the two nervous processes are nowhere combined or compounded; they remain throughout as distinct as if they occurred in separate brains; and yet they produce in consciousness a single effect, whose nature is jointly determined by both nervous processes. These facts can only be rendered intelligible by assuming that both processes influence or act upon some one thing or being; and, since this is not a material thing, it must be an immaterial thing. Our intellect demands this conclusion, and to refuse to accept it is to mistrust the human intellect in a way which amounts to radical Scepticism or Pyrrhonism. We cannot be content to say that each of the two processes generates or creates a sensation, which two sensations then float off to come together and join the stream of consciousness of that individual; for, even if we could admit that sensations can exist in this isolated manner, the essential problem would still remain—Why do these two sensations come together and why do they join that particular stream of consciousness, rather than any other one? The only

[1] I will ask the reader to keep in mind here the special instance of red and blue lights falling separately on corresponding areas of the two retinæ.

possible alternative to the hypothesis that this immaterial thing is an enduring psychic entity, is to assert that it is the stream of consciousness itself. Now to say that the cerebral processes act upon consciousness is a convenient and common usage; but, if the statement is to be taken seriously, it implies that the stream of consciousness is not merely the sum of the effects of, or the psychical aspects of, the brain-processes, but that it has an independent existence, that it is itself an entity or being. And this would be Animism, but Animism of a peculiarly unsatisfactory kind.[1] We should still have to assert that the stream of individual consciousness as it exists at any moment is not the whole of this immaterial being, and does not reveal its whole nature; we should have to recognize that the constancy of the effects in consciousness produced by the cerebral processes, and their relative independence of the state or content of consciousness at the moment of the incidence of the cerebral influences, are evidences that the immaterial being is more than consciousness and is the enduring possessor of capacities of reacting upon cerebral influences in a number of different ways of which some only are realized at any moment. The psychic being is then more than the stream of consciousness; and the sensory changes of consciousness produced by cerebral changes are only a partial expression of its enduring nature. And, when the effects of two or more sense-stimuli appear in consciousness combined to a common resultant, this is because the separate cerebral processes act upon this one being and stimulate it to react according to the laws of its own nature with the production of changes in the stream of consciousness. This psychic being, whose nature is thus partially expressed by the production of the unitary sensory content of consciousness in response to the manifold of cerebral influences, is that medium of composition of effects, that ground of the unity of consciousness and of psychical individuality, which the intellect demands and which cannot be found in the substance of the brain.

The facts of the relation of sensory consciousness to cerebral events thus render the conception of a unitary psychic being, call it soul or what you will, a necessary hypothesis; for the rejection of this hypothesis involves either Pyrrhonism or the acceptance of a confused tangle of obscure conceptions (conceptions of fantastic entities such as the "threshold of consciousness," or unattached fragments of consciousness, sensations flying about

[1] This variety of Animism is further discussed in chap. xxvi.

loose and coming together to yield up their own natures in creating new entities); and, even if the prejudice against the conception of a soul is so strong as to lead one to prefer to it this tangle of fantastic ideas, this still proves to be inconsistent with the fundamental principles of Parallelism.

In view of the discussion of the following chapter it is important to make clear the sense in which the phrase "the fusion or synthesis of elementary qualities of sensation or of other psychical elements" may be legitimately used and will be there used. When we speak of the fusion of sensations we mean the fusion of effects in consciousness of sensory processes in the brain. Each sensory brain-process which is the immediate correlate of a change in consciousness produces a partial affection of the soul; the nature of this effect, like that of all other effects, is determined both by the nature of that which acts and the nature of that which is acted upon. The total sensory content of consciousness at any moment is the complex reaction of the soul upon many such cerebral influences simultaneously affecting it as qualitatively distinct and spatially separate processes. The sensations or other psychical elements have no more a separate existence than have the several accelerations impressed upon a particle of matter by several simultaneously acting forces. The motion of the particle is the resultant effect of these forces upon the particle and may be analytically reduced to the sum of the several accelerations; just so the sensory content of consciousness (in so far as determined by brain-processes) is the resultant of the incidence of these influences upon the soul, and this complex resultant also may be analytically exhibited as the sum of elements which introspection discovers. But, without a particle to act upon, the several forces could produce no accelerations, and their effects are only combined in virtue of their acting upon one and the same particle; just so the brain-processes could produce no sensations except by acting upon the soul, and their effects are combined in one consciousness only in virtue of their acting upon one soul.

To some reader the question of the seat of the soul in the body may remain a difficulty. Such I would remind that to be in a place means nothing but to exert action or to be effected by action in that place; and, if he doubts this, I would ask him to attempt to attach any other clear meaning to the phrase. And, if this is agreed upon, it will be admitted that Lotze has admirably said in the following passage all that can or need be said on the question of the seat of the soul. " The soul stands in that direct interaction which has no gradation, not with the whole of the world, nor yet with the whole of the body, but with a limited number of elements; those elements, namely, which are assigned in the order of things as the most direct links of communication in the commerce of the soul with the rest of the world. There is nothing against the supposition that these elements, on account of other objects which they have to serve, are distributed in space; and that there are a number of separate points in the brain which form so many seats of the soul. Each of these would be of equal value with the rest; at each of them the soul would be present with equal completeness."[1]

Before bringing this chapter to an end, it seems necessary to revert to the problem presented by the cases of multiple personality in which there seems to be good reason to believe that two streams of consciousness accompany the processes of one brain. We seem compelled to believe that in these cases the brain, which normally is a single functional system of nervous elements, becomes divided into two systems that are functionally discontinuous, and that the cerebral processes which accompany the two streams of consciousness run their courses as two separate streams of cerebral processes in these two systems.

I shall have occasion to touch upon these cases again in a later chapter. Here I wish merely to make the following remarks. If we could prove that functional continuity of the parts of the brain is a condition of the unity of consciousness, this empirical fact would be equally compatible with Parallelism and with Animism. The parallelist would interpret the fact by saying that, when the matter of the brain is divided into two or more functionally discontinuous systems, the psychical correlates of the processes of each system form a separate stream; and the Animist would interpret it by saying that under these conditions each functional system is in relation of reciprocal action with a separate psychic being, just as the brains of any two men according to his view interact with two distinct psychic beings. And neither interpretation would in any real sense make the empirical fact intelligible; each would be merely a special application of a fundamental supposition as to the ground of unity of consciousness involved in the general psycho-physical doctrine.

[1] "Metaphysik," Bk. iii. chap. v.

CHAPTER XXII

THE PSYCHO-PHYSICS OF "MEANING"

WE are now prepared to deal with another question the careful consideration of which leads to results incompatible with Parallelism; namely, the question whether "consciousness of meaning" has any immediate correlate or counterpart among the brain-processes which might be regarded as its physical aspect, its phenomenon, or its immediate cause. This question is of crucial importance, for, as we have already seen, meaning appears as the essential link between sense-impression and action in all, save possibly the simplest, instances of animal and human behaviour. We have already touched upon the question in discussing the behaviour of animals, and have found reasons to believe that actions in the control of which appreciation of "meaning" appears to play a role are not mechanically explicable. But for the completion of the argument it is necessary to examine directly the problem of the psycho-physics of meaning.

The history of the treatment of meaning at the hands of psychologists is one of great interest; but it must suffice here to point out that the association-psychology from Locke and Hume onwards has ignored meaning as a fact of consciousness, almost completely. The simple idea of Locke was a sensation, and his complex ideas were groups or aggregates of sensations or of the images of corresponding quality, and these, it was said, are what a man is conscious of when he thinks. That in thinking a man is commonly conscious of, or means, some object which is not an idea but something existing independently of his ideas or of his thinking of it, is a fundamental fact that was obscured and neglected from the outset by the psychology of this school.

In spite of Locke's assertion that a man is conscious of his ideas, perceives them, makes them the objects of all his thought and reasoning, subsequent psychologists, guided largely by Hume, neglected more and more completely the facts of consciousness implied by this language, namely, the perceiving the idea, the thinking and reasoning about it: they made the sequence of the ideas, regarded as mere complexes of sensations and images, the whole of thought and of consciousness. It was this neglect of all that is comprised in consciousness except the sensory content that made possible association-psychology of the cruder kind, and rendered plausible the attempt to explain all mental process as consisting merely in the kaleidoscopic shifting and sorting and compounding of the sensory content by the machinery of the brain.

Yet, that, when we think or are conscious, we think of objects that are not identical with our ideas, that we mean and are conscious of meaning such objects, is an obvious and indisputable fact.[1] And it is equally clear that the thought of an object is more than the having present to consciousness a picture of it made up of sensations or images. To appreciate the fact we have only to reflect that some persons, who can think as well as others, carry on their thinking without the use of images, or at least with nothing but verbal images and, at most, fragments of representative imagery which are so irrelevant and obscure that they cannot be regarded as playing any essential part, or as constituting the thinker's consciousness of the objects of which he thinks.

When, not many years ago, psychology began to be actively cultivated as an independent empirical science, it was inevitable that these facts should be brought back to light. For some time there prevailed a tendency to regard verbal thinking as carried on with no consciousness other than that of the words, this consciousness consisting of sensory images, the revivals of sensory impressions received on hearing, seeing, or speaking words. Beyond this, pure thinking involved no consciousness, but merely the unconscious operations of the cerebral machinery.[2]

Then the late William James propounded his doctrine of the psychic fringe. He taught that the complex of sensational elements, which introspection easily seizes upon and which had been widely regarded as the whole of the consciousness involved in thinking, is, as it were, constantly surrounded by, or set upon a background of, very obscure consciousness, which in spite of its obscurity is important. But this psychic fringe seems to have been regarded by him as composed of elements or processes of

---

[1] This remains true even though the subjective idealist be in the right in affirming that such objects have no existence.

[2] This stage is well represented by M. Ribot's "Evolution of General Ideas."

the same nature as that which it fringed, namely, sensations, and to be, in fact, the sensations accompanying cerebral processes that are in process of waning from or of waxing towards their full intensity.

But, if we set aside the prejudice which arises from the fact that the sensory content is so easily seized by introspection, while all else in consciousness is so much more elusive, a prejudice which has been fostered by long tradition and countenanced by great names, it appears perfectly obvious and indisputable that on thinking of or being conscious of an object, especially an abstract or a highly general object such as virtue or ambiguity or colour or animal, the imagery is an altogether subordinate part of my total consciousness; it appears that the essential part of my consciousness is the part which eludes introspection, and which eludes it just because it is the *meaning* or reference to the object, and because, when I turn to examine my thought or my idea of the object, the object to which I now refer or which I mean is no longer the original object, but the idea or thought of that object. Such introspective examination of an "idea" thus illustrates very well the point which I wish to bring out; for the sensory content of consciousness remains unchanged or but little changed, while the object of my thought is entirely different—in the one case I mean and am conscious of the object, apple, virtue, animal, or what not; in the other case, I mean and am conscious of my idea of the object. The same point is well brought out by reflexion on the experience of hearing or reading a word whose meaning we fail for the moment to apprehend. For the moment, the word is seen as so many printed letters only, and perhaps one pronounces it aloud or mentally only; but it has no further meaning, or perhaps one is filled with a sense of the absurdity of this concatenation of visual or auditory impressions; then suddenly comes the consciousness of its meaning, something in consciousness over and above the sensory content. And it is not until this consciousness of meaning is added to the merely sensory content of consciousness that the word can play any significant part in a process of reasoning.

Again, the same point is illustrated by reflexion upon the reverse experience, namely, one thinks of an object, or means and is conscious of meaning an object, which one can neither picture nor name. And, if the object is an abstract object, one seeks the word which will embody or convey the meaning already present to consciousness, perhaps rejecting one after another, saying—No, that does not express my meaning.

These few examples may serve to illustrate the fact that meaning is the essential part of a thought or a consciousness of an object, and that the sensory content, whether vivid and rich in detail or dim and scanty, is but a subordinate part, a mere cue to the meaning. If we call the consciousness of an object an idea of it, then we must recognize that "Every idea is a concrete whole of sign and meaning, in which the meaning even when unanalysed and 'implicit' is what is essential and prominent in consciousness. The sign, on the other hand, which we saw reason to identify with certain sensational elements in this complex experience is normally subordinate."[1]

The further question arises: Is that part of consciousness which is meaning merely a complex of obscure waning or waxing sensational elements, as the doctrine of the "psychic fringe" implies? If it is admitted (and it must be admitted) that in all thought the meaning is at the focus of consciousness, then it follows that the psychic fringe of obscure sensory content, which no doubt exists, is not the meaning. It would be manifestly absurd, after recognizing that the clear imagery present to consciousness is not in itself meaning or the essential feature of conscious thought, to represent this essential part as consisting in obscure and vague sensory content which is admittedly present, if at all, only in the background of consciousness, round about, but not in, the field of attention.

That meaning is an essential feature of consciousness[2] over and above, and of a nature different from, its sensory content appears still more clearly if we consider, not merely an idea of a simple object, but our consciousness of the meaning of a sentence heard or read, especially perhaps of a long German sentence in which the essential word which determines the meaning of the whole is found at the end of the sentence. In so far as the sentence is

---

[1] The passage is taken from an article by Mr R. F. A. Hoernlé in *Mind*, N.S., No. 61, entitled, "Image, Idea, and Meaning." The reader may be referred to this article for a fuller discussion of the question.

[2] The word "meaning" may be used in a sense different from that here given it, namely, it may be said that the object of the thought is the meaning of it, that, when I think or speak of an apple, the apple itself is the meaning of my words or my thoughts. That may be a legitimate usage, but throughout these pages I use the word "meaning" to denote the consciousness of meaning, or the meaning part of consciousness or of an idea.

understood, each word, as heard, comes to consciousness not merely as a familiar sound but also as a meaning; and the meanings of the successive words qualify one another, until, as the last word is heard and its meaning comes to consciousness, the meaning of the whole sentence comes also to consciousness. When this happens, the earlier words as mere sounds, as sensory contents of consciousness, may have faded away; and a moment later the meaning conveyed by the words may remain present to consciousness, while the words themselves are no longer present; and the hearer may be unable to recall them or even, if he be a polyglot, may be unable to say in which of several languages the meaning was conveyed. And the converse of this case also is interesting; one hears sometimes a sentence spoken and perceives all the words clearly, and yet for a moment the meaning delays, the sentence remains a mere string of auditory impressions or of words each having its separate meaning, until suddenly the meaning of the whole comes to consciousness. It would be absurd to pretend that the meaning of the sentence is merely the sum or aggregate of the psychic fringes of the words, each fringe being in turn a complex of obscure sensations or images. The meaning of the sentence is present to consciousness as a unitary whole. And, as was said in connexion with the "telegram-argument" (Chapter xix. p. 268), this whole is an essential link between the sense-impressions made by the spoken words and the actions which the sentence evokes. If, then, this psychical whole, the meaning of the sentence, has not for its physical correlate in the brain a corresponding unitary whole, the fundamental principle of Parallelism is shattered.

The question is so important that I must ask the reader to bear with me while I return to processes of a simple type, in order to demonstrate still more fully that there exists no unitary neural process correlated with meaning, that in fact meaning has no immediate neural correlate which can be regarded as its immediate cause, or its phenomenon, or of which it can be regarded as the psychical aspect.

Let us consider the perception of a point of light lying in a certain direction. The ray from the point entering my pupil is brought to a focus on the retina, and there initiates a disturbance in the optic nerve, which is propagated to the cortex of the occipital or posterior pole of the cerebrum. As this excitement spreads through some chain or group of nervous elements in that part of the cortex, consciousness is affected, an element of visual sensation is added to consciousness. If no further nervous process resulted from the stimulus, there would result no further change in consciousness. But, if my attention is drawn by the impression, the effect in consciousness is more complex and constitutes what we call the perception of a spot of light in a certain direction; that is to say, the consciousness evoked is not a mere sensation, but is the sensation plus a certain relatively simple meaning which consists largely of an awareness of the spatial character and relations of the object. Of this meaning the direction of the spot is one part, and we may, for the sake of simplicity, consider this part of the meaning only. Now it is certain that the awareness of direction depends upon the appreciation in some sense of the position of the eyeball in its socket; and that this in turn depends upon afferent impulses sent up to the brain along sensory nerves of the kinæsthetic sense. The associationist account of the process of perception asserts that these afferent impulses excite kinæsthetic sensations, and that these coalesce with the visual sensations to form the resultant spot-of-light-in-the-given-direction; and a consistent Parallelist would assert also that the processes initiated in the optic nerve and in the nerves of the kinæsthetic sense respectively fuse somewhere in the brain to a complex resultant which is the physical aspect of the unitary psychical process, the perception. Now it is certain that these hypothetical kinæsthetic sensations cannot be discovered by introspection, and we have therefore no right to say that they come into existence. The spatial meaning of the percept is certainly not to be identified with any kinæsthetic sensations, and it is extremely improbable that there occurs any central fusion of the excitations of the optic and kinæsthetic nerves. Prof. Wundt (one of the very few who have made any serious attempt to work out the correlation of consciousness with brain-process) realizes this and offers a rather different account. He tells us that the kinæsthetic sensations fuse with the visual sensations, and, yielding up their own natures, impart to the resultant formed by this fusion its spatial characters. This takes place according to a principle which he calls "the principle of creative resultants"; the process is, he says, a creative synthesis, a psychical process or activity that has no parallel among the brain processes.[1] He recognizes that all but the most rudimentary mental processes

[1] "Grundzüge d. phys. Psychologie," fifth edition, vol. iii. p. 778.

involve such creative syntheses, and that the higher processes involve them on a very extended scale, in the form of higher syntheses of syntheses of lower orders; each higher synthesis involving a further remove of the content of consciousness from its physical basis. Thus, according to Wundt, only the ultimate elements of consciousness have their physical correlates or aspects among the brain-processes; and they are combined or synthesized to form new modes of consciousness by purely psychical processes and according to purely psychical laws that have no parallels or counterparts in the physical realm. And he recognizes that the unitary consciousness has for its physical correlate a multiplicity of discrete processes in the brain. This account certainly distorts the facts less crudely than does the more usual associationist account; and, coming from one who claims to be a Parallelist and is usually reckoned as one of the leading exponents of that doctrine, it is highly significant; for clearly the account is wholly inconsistent with the principles of Parallelism, and illustrates very well the fact that, when it is attempted to work out in detail the psycho-physics of even very simple mental processes, the principles of Parallelism cannot be carried through.

But there is no justification for Wundt's assertion that the excitation of the kinæsthetic nerves evokes kinæsthetic sensations which proceed to fuse or to undergo a process of synthesis. In this matter of spatial perception, all the ingenuity devoted to the problem since Lotze enunciated his doctrine of local signs has not advanced us beyond that celebrated but much misrepresented doctrine. According to that doctrine, processes of the kind which in the foregoing accounts are said to excite kinæsthetic sensations constitute the local signs of the visual sensation; but they are not said to excite kinæsthetic sensations; rather they are said to affect the soul in a way which prompts it and enables it to exert its power of spatially ordering its visual sensations within[1] the spatial system that it conceives. And this power of spatially ordering the visual and other sensations is a psychical power or faculty, which cannot be explained or reduced to a fusing of sensations that in themselves have no spatial character or attribute. In the terminology adopted in these pages, we can only say that the soul responds to or reacts upon the particular manifold of sense impressions by producing not merely a visual sensation, but also a consciousness of the spatial setting or relations of the sensation, which consciousness is the meaning, or part of the total meaning, of the perception.

Thus, in this very simple instance of perception, the content of consciousness is sensation plus a meaning, which is supplied by a psychical activity according to purely psychical laws (i.e. laws of the soul's own nature or being) in response to a given complex of cerebral influences.

But now let us complicate the case; instead of a single point of light, let there be four occupying the corners of a square. Then the perception (i.e. the consciousness of the subject at the moment of perceiving) has a richer spatial meaning; there are not merely four sensations each in a particular direction; rather the sensations with their spatial meanings are synthesized within a new whole which is the consciousness of the square; a meaning

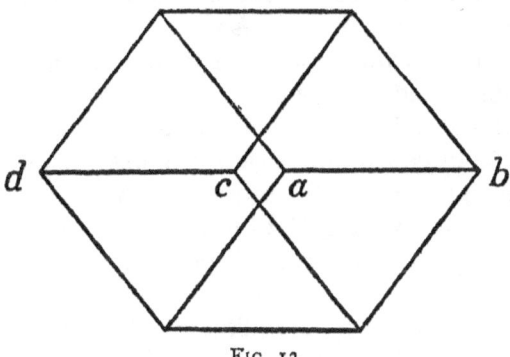

FIG. 13.

which is more or less rich according to the degree of geometrical knowledge of the subject and the degree of attention paid by him to the impressions. And it would be manifestly absurd to say that this meaning consists of the kinæsthetic sensations clustering round each of the visual sensations and coalescing into a larger mass.

Again, let there be many points of light and let them form the outline of a cube drawn on the flat like the lines of figure 13. This time the spatial meaning is still richer than before. The spatial meanings of the many points are synthesized to a still larger and more complex psychic whole, the consciousness of a cube.

The perception of an outline drawing of this sort presents three features of special interest in connexion with our topic.

First, the size or distance of the drawing and, consequently, the size of the retinal image may be varied within very wide limits;

and the drawing may be turned through any angle in the plane of the paper; and the plane of the paper may be turned through many angular degrees; and by combinations of these three changes an indefinitely great number of different combinations of retinal elements may be made the recipients of the stimuli; yet, as I perceive the drawing, my consciousness of its meaning remains unchanged, or changes only in a manner of quite subsidiary importance; the synthesis of the spatial relations or meanings of the parts still comes to consciousness as a cube.

Secondly, though no one of the sides of the cube as drawn is a square or appears as a square, if looked at in isolation from the rest of the figure, and though all the sides may be of different shapes; yet, when the figure is looked at as a whole, each side appears as a square. That is to say, the meaning of the whole, which is synthesized from the meanings of the parts, reacts upon those meanings and modifies them.

Thirdly, the drawing of the cube may be ambiguous, so that it may be interpreted in different ways, i.e. two or more meanings may be attached to it. If drawn without perspective, it may be seen as a cube of which the edge $a\,b$ is nearest to the eye, or as one of which the edge $c\,d$ is nearest. Or again, the whole figure may be seen as a system of lines drawn on the flat; and any one of these meanings may be imposed on it at will. That is to say, the system of retinal stimuli and of visual sensations evoked by them may remain unchanged, while the meaning of the whole and of all its parts is changed by the volition or intention of the observer; by a distinct act of will he holds fast one meaning of the whole, and, so long as he does so, that meaning continues to determine the meanings of all the parts; and then, at will, he calls up another meaning, which combines with the same complex of visual sensations and transforms the meanings of all the parts of the system.[1]

Suppose now that a sufficient description or definition of the figure is read by a geometer. The printed words stimulating his retina evoke a complex of sensations wholly different from those evoked by the drawing of the cube, yet they evoke in his con-

---

[1] It has been attempted to show that these changes of meaning are dependent upon changes of the innervations of the eye-muscles; but observations reported by the author ("Physiological Factors of the Attention-process," *Mind*, N.S., vol. x.) show that, though such changes of innervation may facilitate the changes of meaning, and though they tend to accompany the changes of meaning, they are nevertheless not essential conditions of these changes.

sciousness the same meaning, even though he is quite incapable of picturing the figure in representative imagery.

Suppose, further, that a written train of geometrical reasoning about the figure is read by a geometer. The words evoke in him the same meanings that were in the mind of him who wrote them down; and these meanings, interacting with one another, lead him to the same conclusion or final meaning, even though the writer reasoned with the aid of visual symbols and the reader with the aid of verbal symbols only. As regards sensory content the consciousnesses of the two men, even during the process of reasoning, were very different; yet the essential meanings were throughout the same, else the same conclusion would not have been reached.

Nothing perhaps could illustrate more forcibly than this instance the degree of independence of the sensory content possessed by the meaning, the complete difference of nature between them, and the fact that, in proportion as in mental process the meanings, the true thought-factors, predominate over the sensory content of consciousness, they are remote from the sensory basis and its nervous correlates; all this being true in the highest degree of the conclusion of the train of reasoning, which is a higher synthesis of the meanings of the various words and images used in the process.

The same facts might be illustrated by reference to musical compositions. A series of notes is struck in succession; to the unmusical hearer they may come to consciousness as a series of auditory sensations merely; but to the musical hearer they come to consciousness as a melody, a psychic whole of which the sensations are a subordinate part and the musical meaning the part of predominant importance. The melody may be transposed to other keys, or it may be written down as a series of black marks on paper, and yet in each case the very different sensations evoke in the consciousness of the musical hearer or reader the same meaning. And that here too the meaning is independent of any particular auditory or kinæsthetic sensations or imagery, is shown by the fact that one can mean a certain melody, though one may be unable to reproduce the notes or even the name of it; and, if then the notes be struck or even only some few of them, we know at once —that is the melody we meant; and under the guidance of the meaning we can reproduce the melody. Some persons accustomed to read music can appreciate the written symbols (i.e. can take the meaning of them) though they are incapable of humming, singing, whistling, or imaging the notes; they can intelligently criticize the music, and, if they afterwards hear it, can at once recognize it as the same they have read.

That thought is essentially an interplay of meanings, and that these are relatively independent of the sensory cues, whether verbal or other, by means of which meaning is conveyed or communicated or embodied, is now becoming widely recognized by psychologists; and of late years the results of a number of minute introspective studies made under experimental conditions have given a new support to this doctrine of "imageless thought."[1] It may, in fact, be regarded as established that thought is not the mere sifting and sorting of aggregates of sensational elements by the mechanical processes of the brain which evoke these elements in consciousness; and that these sensory elements and complexes are merely cues which evoke higher forms of psychical activity, which in turn bring meanings to consciousness. Meanings are, then, essential links between sense-impressions and the behaviour they evoke: not the sensations, nor any aggregate or synthesis of them, nor yet the physical correlates in the brain of the sensory content of consciousness, but these products in consciousness of a purely psychical activity are the factors which awaken within us the appropriate emotion and stir up the impulse to appropriate action, that psychic impulse or conation without which no action is initiated or sustained.

We have seen that even the sensory content of the consciousness of an object has for its physical correlate a number of discrete processes in the brain which in no sense constitute a unitary whole. How much less, then, are we justified in assuming that the unitary psychic whole of sensory-content-plus-meaning has any physical correlate in the brain which is a unitary whole and which can discharge in mechanical fashion the function of mediating between sense-impression and bodily response! Meaning, we conclude, plays an essential part in the determination of the sequence of bodily reaction on sense-impression, and meaning has no immediate physical correlate in the brain that could serve as its substitute and discharge its functions.

[1] These investigations have been concisely expounded by Prof. A. Messer, "Empfindung u. Denken," Leipsic, 1908.

CHAPTER XXIII

PLEASURE, PAIN, AND CONATION

FROM the consideration of the conditions and effects of pleasurable and painful or disagreeable feeling, conclusions may be drawn incompatible with Parallelism and directly supporting Animism. It is necessary at the outset to ask the reader to avoid a confusion that is very commonly made. The tingling, smarting, and other allied disagreeable qualities of sensation that commonly result from violent stimulation of the nerves of the skin and other parts, and are commonly called pain-sensations, must not be confused with painful-feeling, which is a mode of consciousness distinct in nature and conditions from all sensations and is in a very complete and special sense the opposite of pleasurable feeling.[1] The so-called pain-sensations have, except perhaps when at minimal intensity, painful or disagreeable feeling-tone; but the feeling-tone is distinguishable from the quality of the sensation. The sensations are the simplest conditions of feeling; we commonly say that each sensation-quality has its feeling-tone, and that this may vary from pleasurable, through a neutral point, to disagreeable, according to the intensity of the sensation. This is a crude way of stating the facts; for pleasurable or disagreeable feeling qualifies the whole of consciousness and does not attach itself exclusively to any sensation or other distinguishable element of the stream of consciousness. The statement that the feeling-tone of a particular sensation is pleasurable, means that the presence of this sensation-quality in consciousness tends to give the whole of consciousness a pleasant feeling-tone, and that, if the sensation is prominent in conscious-

---

[1] In order to avoid the ambiguity of the word pain I shall follow Stout, James, and other authorities in using the word displeasure as a technical term for painful or disagreeable feeling or feeling-tone. In common speech this word is used to imply anger as well as disagreeable feeling; but since a word is needed to denote disagreeable feeling-tone, it may justifiably be specialized for this purpose. The words pleasure and displeasure so understood are the equivalents of the German words *Lust* and *Unlust*.

ness and its feeling-tendency is not counteracted by opposed tendencies, the tone of feeling will be pleasurable. When several sensations of pleasurable tendency are present together, their tendencies re-enforce one another; and when sensations of opposed tendency are present together, the opposed tendencies partially or completely neutralize one another. Or, if the pleasurable feeling tendencies be regarded as of positive sign, and the disagreeable tendencies as of negative sign, we may express the facts by saying that the feeling-tendencies of the various sensations simultaneously present to consciousness are algebraically summed, and, according as the resultant is of positive or negative sign, the feeling-tone of consciousness is pleasurable or disagreeable, or in other words, the individual feels pleasure or displeasure. But the sensations are only one class of occasions of pleasure and displeasure. Every form of mental activity tends to affect the feeling-tone of consciousness positively or negatively, and the stronger or the more intense the activity, the stronger is its feeling-tendency. In general terms it may be said that the smooth flow of mental process towards its proper end tends to pleasure; the baffling or hindering of it by any obstruction, conflict of tendencies, or difficulty of any kind, tends to displeasure. And of all such feeling-tendencies the law of algebraic summation holds good, perhaps not absolutely, but in the main and in general.[1] The feeling-tone of consciousness at any moment is, then, the reaction of the subject as a whole upon all the many feeling-tendencies simultaneously influencing it.

These are the elementary facts of feeling broadly stated. It is obvious that they raise the problem of the unity of consciousness even more urgently than does the psycho-physic of sensation, and in a form which is, it possible, even more difficult for Parallelism to cope with. They could be reconciled with any form of Parallelism only if some physical unity corresponding to the unity of consciousness could be discovered. Failing that, how is the genesis of

---

[1] It may be objected that we commonly and properly speak of disagreeable sensations as persisting throughout periods which in the main are pleasurable. Prof. Stout, in his very admirable chapter on the feeling-tone of sensation, seems to countenance this way of speaking when he says that a total state of consciousness may be agreeably toned " in spite of the presence of this or that disagreeable item " ("Manual of Psychology," vol. i. p. 231). The more accurate statement of the facts would seem to be that, during the period of agreeably toned consciousness, there may be present in the marginal field of consciousness sensations which would determine disagreeable feeling if the attention were turned to them.

the unitary state of feeling, in the determination of which so many brain-processes play a part, to be accounted for on parallelistic principles? We have seen that no composition of brain-processes to a common physical resultant occurs. Nor will the facts allow us to postulate a special brain centre for feeling. The physical correlate of the consciousness, which, as a whole, has a certain feeling-tone, is a multiplicity of separate processes each of which plays some part in determining the nature and intensity of the feeling-tone; and these processes may occur in very many different and widely separated parts of the brain.

The impossibility of reconciling the facts with Parallelism appears most clearly if we consider some instances of psychical fusion or synthesis. Let us take first the simplest possible case, that of fusion of effects of two simple sensory stimuli; and we may take the case of the stimulation of corresponding areas of the two retinæ by red and blue lights respectively, which we discussed in the foregoing chapter. A certain subject finds, let us suppose, that, on stimulation of the right eye with the red light, the resulting sensation of red quality is pleasing, and also that, on stimulation of the left eye with blue light, the sensation of blue quality is pleasing; but on stimulation with red and blue lights simultaneously he finds the purple quality of the resulting sensation to be displeasing. We have shown in the foregoing chapter that the physical correlate of the sensation of purple quality is two separate processes in the brain; when they occur successively their sensory effects, the sensations of red and blue qualities, are pleasing; when they occur simultaneously, their common sensory effect, the sensation of purple quality, is displeasing. Hence the sensation itself, and not its two separate physical correlates, is the condition or cause of the unpleasant feeling; or, in other words, the feeling-tone is a purely psychical reaction upon the sensation of particular quality and has no immediate physical correlate.

Again, two qualities of visual sensation which, when experienced successively, are pleasing, may be found displeasing, if simultaneously present to consciousness in spatial separation; or, on the other hand, the spatial juxtaposition of two colours which in themselves are indifferent or but little pleasing may produce a very pleasing effect. In such cases the æsthetic effect depends upon our attending to both areas as parts of one whole. And it is especially significant that the same two colours in spatial juxtaposition may give a pleasing or a displeasing effect, according to the manner of their distribution; the combination may be pleasing, if the two colours are distributed in such a way as to imply a contrast and a separation of the differently coloured parts of the surface; and the same combination may be displeasing, if the colours are distributed in a way that implies their inherence in a single object. That is to say, the æsthetic effect is not determined by the parts independently, but depends upon the consciousness of the meaning of the whole.

Now let us turn to a rather more complicated instance, that of the pleasure we feel on hearing a melody, or on seeing a harmoniously coloured surface of beautifully shaped design or pattern. In such circumstances the pleasure we feel is not wholly conditioned by the qualities of the sensations; though these, if in themselves pleasing, contribute their share towards the result. It is due in chief part to the relating synthetic activity by which the parts, the successive notes (or the several areas of colour) are combined in one harmonious whole, the melody (or the pattern). That is to say, the æsthetic pleasure is not determined by the mere co-existence or sequence of sensations in themselves pleasing; for it is only in so far as we become aware of, or apprehend, the harmonious relations between the parts as parts of the whole, that the æsthetic pleasure proper is added to the purely sensuous pleasure determined by the feeling-tendencies of the several sensations. This we see clearly, if we reflect that the same tones (or the same colours) may be grouped in such orders that the apprehension of their inharmonious relations to one another, as parts of the whole, determines feeling-tone strongly in the direction of displeasure; then the feeling-tendencies of the several sensations cannot make themselves felt and the total effect is disagreeable. The æsthetic pleasure arises, then, from the synthetic psychical activity by which the sensory elements are combined to form an "object of a higher order," rather than from the mere complex or series of sensations; and, as we have seen, this synthetic activity has no immediate correlate in the physical order.

The same conclusion thrusts itself still more forcibly upon us when we consider higher forms of æsthetic appreciation, such, for example, as that of Mozart on mentally contemplating a musical composition just achieved. According to Mozart's own account, he had, at the moment of completing the composition, the whole of it present to his mind. This must have been a moment at which the synthetic activity attained a rare degree of intensity and untroubled success, bringing the musical meaning of the whole to consciousness; and, as Mozart tells us, the experience was intensely pleasurable.[1]

Or consider the conditions of the pleasure we find in reading a poem, say Wordsworth's "Solitary Reaper." For those who visualize vividly the scene depicted, the pleasing effect depends no doubt, in part, upon the pleasing imagery evoked by the words; but this source of pleasure is in itself extremely complex, and the pleasure depends far more on the meaning of the imagery than on the qualities of the sensory contents or on the harmony of their composition. How much of the charm of the whole depends upon the "loneness" of the girl, on the subtle awakening in us of a romantic interest in her personality, on the suggestion of a wealth of unknown possibilities, beauties of person and character, set upon a background of wild nature! How much, too, upon the suggestion of the intangibility, the delicateness, and the unreality, one might almost say, of the whole impression, which a single word or gesture might have marred! How much upon the sudden carrying of the mind to far-off scenes! How much to the music of the words! How much to the unity and distinctness of the whole impression! The sources of the pleasure are thousandfold, and the balance of them different for every reader. But, for all who keenly appreciate the poem, the play of meanings predominates vastly over the sensuous content of consciousness in determining the pleasure we feel. And in poems of a more reflective kind, such, for example, as the "Lines composed above Tintern Abbey," the play of highly abstract meanings predominates still more. In such cases the sensory contents, the mere words and the imagery they evoke, play a quite subordinate part.

If the conditions of pleasure and displeasure are incapable of being stated in terms of Parallelism, the consideration of their effects points just as strongly to a conclusion incompatible with that doctrine; for we find that in ourselves and throughout the scale of animal life feelings of pleasure and displeasure seem to guide and control in some degree the course of mental process

---

[1] I cite (after Prof. James) the following passage: "Even when it is a long piece . . . I can see the whole of it at a single glance in my mind, as if it were a beautiful painting or a handsome human being; in which way I do not hear it in my imagination at all as a succession—the way it must come later— but all at once, as it were. It is a rare feast! All the inventing and making goes on in me as in a beautiful, strong dream. But the best of all is the hearing of it all at once."

and, with it, the course of the brain-processes; pleasure seems to promote and sustain the mental process which it accompanies or qualifies, and seems to fix traces of it in the brain, so that it is more readily repeated; disagreeable feeling seems always to check or turn aside the course of the mental activity which it accompanies, and to diminish the tendency to repetition of the process.

Let us glance at some instances. It is generally recognized that objects which please us hold the attention more strongly than those to which we are indifferent or which are disagreeable to us; that when, for example, we perceive a melody or a design, say the pattern of a wall-paper, our attention is held by it and tends the more strongly to dwell upon it spontaneously or involuntarily the greater the pleasure or æsthetic satisfaction we derive from it. It is equally indisputable that we tend to remember the object, and to be able to reproduce or represent it, more faithfully the more pleasing it is; presumably just because of the more effective and prolonged attention given to it at the moment of perception; for example, after an evening at the opera, we remember best the melodies that we found most pleasing.

Now, we have seen in the foregoing pages that these "objects of higher orders" which yield us these æsthetic satisfactions are constructed by our mental activity; that the pleasure depends upon this synthesis of the parts to a unitary whole in consciousness; and that this synthesis and this unitary whole and the resulting pleasurable feeling-tone of consciousness are purely psychical facts that have no immediate correlates among the brain-processes. If this conclusion is valid, and I see no escape from it, then it follows that the feeling itself, and not any physical correlate, must be regarded as sustaining and intensify our attention.

Again, pleasurable or disagreeable feeling evoked by "an object of a higher order" of this kind, or in any other way, seems to play an effective part in determining the course of trains of association, more particularly the relatively passive train of associative reproduction that we call reverie. When the feeling-tone of consciousness is pleasurable, ideas of similar feeling-tone tend to predominate; and similarly, when consciousness is disagreeably toned, whether owing to organic disorder or to æsthetically displeasing surroundings or to the baffling of intellectual effort, disagreeably toned ideas tend to predominate in the train of reverie.

Feeling seems also to exert a powerful influence upon the organic functions. Music or other pleasures of the higher æsthetic and intellectual orders can drive away pain, improve digestion, and benefit the health generally. Yet the pleasurable feeling arising from these activities is a purely psychical fact without physical correlate.[1]

The consideration of the processes of acquisition of new powers of movement, of new modes of bodily reaction, and of dexterity or skill of every kind, points to the same conclusion. There can be no doubt that such processes of acquisition involve the setting up of nervous habits, and that this means the establishment of neural associations or paths of diminished resistance between groups of neurones. The nervous system contains a number of innately or hereditarily organized systems of motor neurones; such a system consists of a number of cells so intimately connected that excitement transmitted to any part at once spreads through the whole system, and connected also in such a way that the excitement of the system issues along motor nerves to a synergic group of muscles, i.e. one whose contractions produce an orderly movement of some part of the body. These innately co-ordinated movements constitute, as Lotze said, an alphabet of movement; or perhaps they are more closely analogous to a vocabulary. The contraction of each muscle corresponds to a single letter of the alphabet, that of any synergic group to a word. The processes of acquisition of new modes of bodily response to impressions are of two main types: (1) the learning to respond to a particular sense-impression with one or other of the words of the vocabulary of movement, or, in other words, the association of one of these innately co-ordinated movements with a sense-impression of a kind with which it is not innately associated; this process may be called the adaptation of movement: (2) the other mode of learning is the process of acquisition of skill, and consists in the combining of the words of the vocabulary to form sentences, i.e. in learning to combine the simple synergic contractions into more complex conjunctions and series.

[1] It seems possible to suggest a plausible account of the way in which these effects are produced. We may suppose that when for any reason the feeling-tone of consciousness is predominantly pleasurable (or disagreeable), all psycho-physical processes of opposed feeling tendency are repressed, just because their feeling tendency is incongruous with, and conflicts with, and is overpowered by, the dominating feeling-tendencies; and this repression may be supposed to affect the processes of incongruous feeling-tendency not only in so far as they are conscious, but also their cerebral concomitants.

Under the former head, that of adaptation of movement or of behaviour, fall most instances of modification of animal behaviour through experience, and notably such classical instances as the burnt child who withholds his finger from the candle-flame, and Professor Lloyd Morgan's chicks that learnt to refuse certain disagreeably-tasting caterpillars after one or two attempts to eat them. I will not dwell upon these, but will only remark in passing that it is extremely difficult, if not impossible, to suggest any satisfactory explanation of the results in terms of neural structure and processes only.

The best instances for our present purpose are such instances of animal learning as have been carefully studied by Mr Thorndike[1] and by many others who have adopted and extended his methods. A single instance, typical of many, may suffice. A hungry cat is confined in a cage, the door of which is kept closed by some latch that is liable to be opened by the cat in the course of its struggles to escape. The cat, stimulated by the sight of food placed near the cage, makes a great variety of random movements, clawing, scratching, and squeezing in all parts of the cage; it runs through its vocabulary of movement without the least indication that it appreciates the presence of a door, or of a latch by moving which the door may be opened. Sooner or later in the course of these random movements, the latch is moved by happy accident and the cat escapes to enjoy the food. Now it is found that in nearly all cases, if the cat is put back in the same cage on many successive occasions, it gradually learns to escape more and more quickly; until eventually it goes straight to the latch and makes the necessary movement. This is the process of adaptation of movement by random trial and error; by processes of this kind much of the adaptation of animal behaviour is effected.

It might seem at first sight that the slow gradual character of the process of adaptation shows it to be a purely mechanical process, namely, the setting up, by simple repetition of the liberating movement made in a certain part of the cage, of an association between that movement and the sense-impression received from that part of the cage. And this is the explanation of such processes commonly offered by unthinking physiologists. Now, it is no doubt true that a habit is gradually formed, a neural

[1] "Animal Intelligence." Monograph supplement to the "Psychological Review," vol. ii. No. 4.

association between the visual impression of one part of the cage and the appropriate movement, or rather between the neural bases of these two things.

But the essential problem remains—Why did this particular movement become associated with this particular sense-impression? The law of the formation of neural associations, as usually stated, throws no light on the problem; for it affirms merely that when two processes, a and b, occur simultaneously or in immediate succession, the recurrence of a tends to bring about the recurrence of b. Now, the cat makes many other movements than the successful one in sequence upon the sense-impressions received both from this part of the cage and from other parts; and no doubt many of these various sequences of movements on sense-impressions (especially those that were often repeated in the course of the cat's random efforts) become in some degree habitual. But if so, the fact still remains that, out of all these many sequences of movements on sense-impressions, one becomes an effective habit much more rapidly than all the others; so that it takes precedence of all others, and, after many repetitions of the escape, is called into play whenever the cat casts his glance around the walls of his cage. That is the fact which is not explained by the law of association as stated above.

Mr Thorndike, in discussing the results of his experiments, says that the pleasure of escape, attending and following upon the successful movement, stamps in this particular sensory-motor association, while the pain (or displeasure) of failure tends to stamp out all other associations. We need not lay stress on the stamping out, because that is not clearly proved; but the "stamping in" of the successful association, the more rapid increase of its effectiveness relatively to all other associations of movement with sense-impression, can only be attributed to the pleasure or satisfaction of success.

Now let us consider a simple instance of acquirement of skill, and let us take the case of the young child learning to reach out after, and to seize, seen objects.

The visual impression of an object near at hand provokes in the young child that has not yet acquired this power random movements directed very roughly only (if at all) towards the object. When in the course of these movements the palm of the hand is brought in contact with the object, the fingers close upon it and carry it to the mouth. On repetition of these efforts, success is achieved more and more rapidly and effectively; each success brings an increase of facility, which means an increase of effectiveness of the neural association between the visual impression made by an object at a particular distance and the several motor mechanisms by which the appropriate movement of the hand is carried out. If the law of association as stated above expressed fully the facts, and if the formation of the neural associations were a purely physical process consisting merely in the passage of the neural impulse from one cell-system to another, we should expect to find that all the random movements made by the hand, while the eyes are directed upon an object in a particular position, should become habitual in the same degree, or rather in proportion to the frequency of their repetition; therefore, the successful movement of the hand should become associated with that particular position of the eyes less rapidly than other of the random movements; for at each attempt to seize an object in that position, some of the random movements may be repeated several or many times, whereas the successful movement brings the series to an end and is made only once.

It is clear, therefore, that, for the explanation of the fact that the successful movement alone becomes an established habit or automatic process, some other factor must be taken into account; and this other factor seems to be the feeling-tone of consciousness, the pleasure of success and the displeasure of failure. Professor Stout has concisely expressed the facts in the following generalized statement: "Lines of action, if and so far as they are unsuccessful, tend to be discontinued or varied; and those which prove successful, to be maintained. There is a constant tendency to persist in those movements and motor attitudes which yield satisfactory experiences, and to renew them when similar conditions recur; on the other hand, those movements and attitudes which yield unsatisfactory experiences tend to be discontinued at the time of their occurrence, and to be suppressed on subsequent similar occasions." That is a more precise and guarded statement of the facts which Mr Thorndike expresses by saying that pleasure stamps in and pain stamps out the neural associations. It will be noticed that Professor Stout cautiously avoids in this passage any attribution of causal efficacy to the feelings themselves; for Professor Stout is a Parallelist, and it is wellnigh impossible to admit the efficacy of feeling in checking or promoting mental process, without admitting the influence of psychical process upon brain-process.

The late Professor James, contemplating the same facts, wrote as follows: "Let one try as one will to represent the cerebral activity in exclusively mechanical terms, I, for one, find it quite impossible to enumerate what seem to be the facts and yet to make no mention of the psychic side which they possess. However it be with other drainage currents and discharges, the drainage currents and discharges of the brain are not purely physical facts. They are psycho-physical facts, and the spiritual quality of them seems a co-determinant of their mechanical effectiveness. If the mechanical activities in a cell, as they increase, give pleasure, they seem to increase all the more rapidly for that fact; if they give displeasure, the displeasure seems to damp the activities. The psychic side of the phenomenon thus seems, somewhat like the applause or hissing at a spectacle, to be an encouraging or adverse comment on what the machinery brings forth. The soul presents nothing herself, creates nothing, is at the mercy of the material forces for all possibilities, but amongst these possibilities she selects, and by re-enforcing one and checking others, she figures not as an 'epiphenomenon,' but as something from which the play gets moral support."[1]

That pleasure and displeasure play effective parts in sustaining and repressing or diverting the course of mental activity is so clearly implied by the facts that it would be absurd to deny it;[2] but the consistent Parallelist, while admitting that a causal relation is implied, maintains that, when we consider these facts from the side of brain-processes, we have to postulate some two kinds of neural process, or some two peculiarities of nervous process in general, which are the neural correlates of pleasure and displeasure and which are the causes of those effects in the brain that seem to be due to the feelings themselves. Many attempts have been made to formulate the nature of these hypothetical neural counterparts of pleasure and displeasure, yet no one has succeeded in suggesting any tenable hypothesis of this kind.[3]

[1] "Principles of Psychology," vol. ii. p. 583.
[2] Thus, e.g. Prof. Stout affirms that "the disagreeable sensations positively disorder and enfeeble thought and action, when the endeavour is made to think or act" ("Manual of Psychology," vol. i. p. 231).
[3] It is unnecessary for me to examine here the many attempts of the kind, because Mr H. R. Marshall, in an acute and learned work ("Pain, Pleasure and Æsthetics," London, 1894), has shown that none of the suggestions previously

Without attempting to exhibit the insuperable difficulties which all such attempts must encounter, I will merely point out that this failure supports the conclusion reached in the first part of this chapter, namely, that the immediate conditions of feeling-tone are purely psychical and that feeling-tone has no immediate physical correlate in the same sense that the sensations have. If this is the case, it follows that pleasure and displeasure themselves somehow exert an influence over the course of cerebral process. But finally to establish a negative is always a matter of great difficulty, and therefore the following reasoning, which reaches the same conclusion by a different route, affords a welcome confirmation of it.

The part played by pleasure and displeasure in determining mental process, the law of subjective selection, may be concisely stated as follows. Pleasure determines appetition, displeasure determines aversion; the words appetition and aversion being used in the widest sense to denote modes of mental and bodily action that make respectively for and against the continuance and repetition of any particular experience.

The problem before us, then, is—Are these opposed forms of

---

made can be accepted, and Prof. Stout has shown ("Manual," Bk. ii., chap. viii,), conclusively as it seems to me, that Mr Marshall's own hypothesis is untenable.

More recently Prof. Max Meyer ("Psychological Review," 1908, "Pleasantness and Unpleasantness") has exhibited the unsatisfactory nature of the later suggestions, and has in turn put forward a novel one, namely, that "the correlate of pleasantness and unpleasantness is the increase or decrease of the intensity of a previously constant current [of nervous energy in the brain], if the increase or decrease is caused by a force acting at a point other than the point of sensory stimulation." I find myself in close agreement with most of Prof. Meyer's preliminary discussion, but his hypothesis seems to me, for many reasons, no more tenable than any of its predecessors. It will suffice to mention two such reasons : (1) it is incredible that a nervous current should discriminate so nicely between the remote causes of the increase or decrease of its intensity ; (2) according to the author's showing, the hypothesis involves the consequences that the more intellectual processes have more intense feeling-tone than the less intellectual, that only man and the highest of the animals are capable of pleasure and displeasure, and that adults experience pleasure and displeasure in greater intensity than children. Prof. Meyer does not hesitate to maintain that these consequences are in harmony with the facts. But general experience will surely affirm that the displeasure of such low-level experiences as toothache, sea-sickness, migraine, giddiness, and instinctive terror, vastly exceeds in intensity the displeasures of the intellect, and that the pleasures also of the organic life, in those in whom the tides of life run strongly, exceed in mere intensity those of the intellect. The superiority of the higher pleasures is to be found not in their intensity, but in moral considerations and in the fact that they are capable of rational cultivation.

bodily activity, in which appetition and aversion find expression, determined by pleasure and displeasure themselves, or by some two hypothetical specific forms of neural process which are their physical correlates?

Now, it is generally recognized that, in the main, pleasant experiences are beneficial to the organism and unpleasant experiences hurtful. The principle seems to be almost strictly true for the animals; and, though in its application to man its truth is partly obscured by the complexities of his mental life and social relations and by the frequent perversions of the tastes natural to him, yet there can be no doubt that, in the main, it holds good for man also. If, then, pleasure and displeasure are themselves the determinants of movements of appetition and avoidance, we can understand how this general agreement between the beneficial and the pleasurable and between the hurtful and the disagreeable has been brought about by natural selection. For all animals that varied in the direction of finding hurtful influences pleasant would have sought them and consequently would have been heavily handicapped in the struggle for existence; while all that varied in the direction of finding beneficial influences pleasant would have sought them and have been correspondingly benefited. And, if we adopt the parallelist assumption that two neural processes, the physical correlates of pleasure and displeasure (which we may call x and y), are the determinants of appetition and aversion, then the correlation throughout the animal world of x with the beneficial, and of y with the hurtful, bodily affections follows in the same way from the Darwinian principles. But that x should express itself in consciousness as pleasure and y as displeasure would remain an insoluble problem. For the opposition between pleasure and displeasure is the most profoundly significant we can imagine, and this correlation of pleasure with x (the neural process that determines appetition), and of displeasure with y (the process that determines avoidance), cannot be regarded as the result of happy accident. That there remains a real problem here we may see if we suppose the correlation reversed, pleasure correlated with y and displeasure with x. For then natural selection would have evolved an animal world all members of which would have constantly sought those things that were beneficial but unpleasant, would have avoided the things that were hurtful but pleasant, and would have experienced a great predominance of displeasure over pleasure. Such a state of things would seem to us profoundly irrational and absurd. If pleasure and displeasure differed only as two qualities of sensation differ, say red and blue, there would be no such problem; for it would seem just as intelligible that all animals should seek to prolong and to repeat all experience qualified by blueness, and to avoid all qualified by redness, as that the reverse should be the rule.

The parallelist assumption, then, leaves us with this problem, on which biological principles can throw no light; and we shall be driven to suppose that the correlations which obtain between pleasure and bodily appetite and between displeasure and bodily avoidance have been imposed by beneficent divine power at some stage of the process of organic evolution. But this supposition would be incompatible with the principles that Parallelism holds most dear, especially the principles of continuity of evolution and of the universal sway of mechanical principles in nature.

In short, it is only if feeling itself, and not its hypothetical neural correlates, directs bodily movement that the facts are in intelligible accordance with the principles of organic evolution. We are, in fact, compelled to choose between two alternatives, both of which are incompatible with the fundamental tenets of Parallelism. We may believe, then, that appetition and aversion are rooted in our psychical nature, and that the facts of subjective selection are the expressions of a fundamental law of that nature, a law which has no counterpart among the laws of the physical world. And if it be asked—Are we then to believe that the feelings themselves act directly upon the cerebral processes? the answer must be, I think—No; they act only indirectly, namely, by exciting conation or psychical effort, for conation is essentially the putting forth of psychical power to modify the course of physical events.

Conation or Will

A few words must be added to bring together what has been said or implied of conation on earlier pages. Following Dr Stout and other high authorities, I use the word conation as the most general term denoting all the active or striving side of our nature, as the equivalent of will in its widest sense, as comprehending desire, impulse, craving, appetite, wishing, and willing.[1] We

[1] For a statement of my views on the relation of developed volition to simpler modes of conation I may refer the reader to my "Introduction to Social Psychology," London, 1908.

arrive at the conception of conation in two ways; (1) by the observation of the outward behaviour of men and animals; (2) by introspection. In consciousness conation expresses itself in so obscure a fashion that it has long been and still is a matter of dispute whether it really constitutes a specific mode of being conscious. Dr Stout seems to me to have fully established the affirmative answer to this question [1]; but it does not seem to me one of primary importance from the point of view of the psycho-physical problem.

The principal points of importance have been indicated in Chapter XIX.; but on two heads something remains to be said; First, I would draw attention to the concentration of the energy of the whole organism in support of the conative effort, when such concentration is required. If the circumstances are such as to render the end of the conative process attainable only by long sustained effort, this concentrated output of the energies of the whole organism may go so far as to induce complete exhaustion. This we see illustrated by some of the instinctive efforts of animals; as when birds, under the driving power of the migratory impulse, continue their flight until utterly exhausted. But it is illustrated most strikingly by human behaviour in those rare instances in which circumstances and character conspire to produce the most magnificent displays of sustained volition; efforts so incredibly great and prolonged that only the adjective superhuman seems adequately to describe them; efforts which, when they cease to be demanded by the circumstances, leave the organism depleted of energy.[2] All this is utterly incompatible with the view of the animal organism necessarily held by the Parallelist, namely, the view that it is merely a bundle of cunningly contrived mechanisms bound up together, and mechanically connected in a way that effects certain co-operations and reciprocal interferences. For each of these mechanisms contains within itself its stores of potential energy in chemical form, and draws new stores of such energy from the common source of supply, the blood. But the facts of the order I refer to show that the energies of these various mechanisms are capable of being drawn upon to contribute towards the attainment of one particular end; they illustrate in the most striking manner that subordination of the parts to the

---

[1] See especially his paper on "Conation" in the *British Journal of Psychology*, vol. i.

[2] In this connexion I would refer the reader to an article by William James, on "The Energies of Men," in the *Philosophical Review*, 1907.

whole which is the essence of organic unity and which is incapable of being accounted for on purely mechanical principles.

Another aspect of conative process on which I wish to add to what has been said in Chapter XIX. is the persistence of the conative process, its persistent self-direction towards its end in spite of obstacles and deflecting forces. Psychologists have only recently begun to gain some insight into the great extent of the influence of persistent conative tendencies upon the course of mental process and of behaviour. The persistence of the effect of a resolution of the will, even though the main stream of consciousness is turned in other directions, is a fact of great importance, frequently illustrated in the course of daily life. A very simple instance is the persistent operation of the intention to go on walking. The mind may be actively engaged in thought or conversation, but, except at moments of unusual concentration of thought, the intention to go on walking continues to operate. It is commonly said that the movement of the legs goes on automatically, and by this it is usually implied that their movement is a purely reflex mechanical process; but the continuance of their movement is in reality a conative process dependent upon the initial intention. The same is true of the maintenance of particular attitudes and demeanours, of the intention or resolution to preserve a grave or a cheerful expression, to speak slowly, to hold up one's head, to read or write quickly; in all such cases we succeed in some degree (perhaps succeed eventually in modifying old habits) only in virtue of the fact that the intention once formed continues to operate in some degree when no longer present to consciousness.

The same fact is illustrated more strikingly by the long-distance cyclist who falls asleep and yet continues to pedal; by the woman who continues to knit while actively conversing or reading; by the sleeper who wakens early in virtue of a resolution taken before going to bed.

But the most striking illustrations of the persistent operation of conative tendencies, even when the subject is unaware of their existence, have been brought to light by the recent psycho-pathological investigations of the school of Prof. Freud of Vienna.[1]

[1] Prof. Freud's ideas are embodied in a number of works of which the most important are perhaps "Die Traumdeutung," "Der Witz," and "Die Psychopathologie des Alltagsleben." One only, namely "Studies of Hysteria," has been translated into English. The English reader may find several good expositions of these ideas in *American Journal of Psychology*, 1910.

The ideas of Prof. Freud are at present the subject of lively controversy, and opinions are widely divided as to their value as a contribution to medical science; but the success of Freud's therapeutic methods in his own hands and in those of a numerous and rapidly increasing band of disciples proves that there is a large basis of truth in his doctrines. The discovery to which I would draw attention in the present connexion is that strong conative tendencies, whose operation in the mind is for any reason suppressed or repressed by a voluntary effort (or by reason of their incompatibility with the organized system of conative tendencies which constitutes the character of the individual), may continue, not merely for hours and days, but for weeks, months, and years, to exert a strong influence, which manifests itself indirectly in consciousness and in behaviour. Dreams seem in some cases (Freud says in all cases) to be the indirect and perverted and partial expression of such tendencies; and the symptoms, both subjective and objective, of hysteria seem to be traceable in many cases to the subconscious operation of such repressed conative tendencies.

I have no space to dwell upon these most interesting discoveries. I wish only to insist that the peculiar nature of conative process is illustrated by a great body of facts which reveal it as something that cannot be mechanically conceived, something of an order entirely different from the working of any mechanism; a self-sustaining and self-directing activity, to which no mechanical process is even remotely analogous.

It is to be remarked also that the conditions of conation are psychical, and that in many cases these psychical conditions are such as have no immediate correlates among the brain-processes. It is generally held that pleasure excites conation; however that may be, it is at least clear that both pleasure and displeasure modify conation, pleasure sustaining and intensifying it, displeasure diverting or depressing it; and, as we have seen, these feelings (in all cases, as I have argued, but most evidently in the case of those arising out of the higher forms of æsthetic appreciation) cannot be supposed to have any immediate physical correlates.

But the great springs of conative energy are the instincts; and we have seen that, even in the case of the purely instinctive activity of animals, it seems to be impossible to describe or conceive the conditions that evoke instinctive activity in purely mechanical terms; we have seen, in fact, how an intellectual factor, namely, the consciousness of meaning, seems to be an essential link between sense impression and instinctive reaction. In man also instinctive or innate specific tendencies are the great springs of conative energy;[1] and in him they are commonly brought into play by intellectual processes of a high degree of complexity and abstraction, the essential condition of the excitement of a conative tendency being in many cases an idea of which the meaning is achieved only by a psychical synthesis of other meanings, and of which the sensory content with its physical correlates is a very subordinate part.

Now objects have value for us in proportion as they excite our conative tendencies; our consciousness of their value, positive or negative, is our consciousness of the strength of the conation they awake in us. Hence consciousness of value, like consciousness of meaning, is a mode of consciousness which has no counterpart in the physical sphere; value, like meaning, is a purely psychical fact. The impossibility of expressing values in terms of brain-processes is recognized by some Parallelists, who, therefore, like Prof. Münsterberg, propose to escape the difficulty for Parallelism by sundering the whole world known to us into two worlds that have nothing in common, a physical world of mechanical sequences and a world of values. But this method of escaping the difficulties of Parallelism cannot be admitted to be any more legitimate than any of the other ways of sundering experience into unrelated parts, some of which we have noted in earlier chapters.[2]

[1] See my "Introduction to Social Psychology."
[2] I add here a note reporting the result of experiments which are still in progress at the time of going to press, a result which illustrates in a striking manner the role of conation. The experiments consist in learning series of nonsense syllables in the manner described in the following chapter. In one series of experiments the subject maintains an attitude as completely passive as possible, consistent with regularly accentuated repetition of the syllables. In a parallel series of experiments he makes an effort of the will to learn and retain the syllable-rows as rapidly as possible. It appears that in the former series he may require ten or more times as many repetitions as in the latter series, in order to be able to repeat the syllables "by heart." Yet in all outward respects the behaviour of the subject is the same during the process of learning.

CHAPTER XXIV

MEMORY

LOOKED at broadly from the biological standpoint the essential function of mental process appears as the bringing of past experience to bear in the regulation of present behaviour. This influence of the past over the present reveals itself objectively as modification of behaviour upon the recurrence of similar conditions, and subjectively as familiarity, recognition, remembering, recollecting, and also as that anticipation or foresight of the probable course of events which enables us to prepare for them and to intervene effectively to modify their course.

If we use the phrase "the structure of the mind" to denote comprehensively the sum of those enduring internal conditions by which the play of mental process and the mode of behaviour of an organism are determined at each moment of its life, then we may say that experience modifies the structure of the mind, and that it is through the persistence of these modifications that past experience influences present behaviour and present mental process. Some part of the structure of the mind is innately determined or inherited; and all that is added to it or changed in it by the course of experience is usually and conveniently included under the term memory.

It is an implication of all forms of Parallelism that the structure of the mind may in principle be fully described in terms of cerebral structure. We have already found reason to believe that this assumption is untenable as regards the innate structure of the mind. We have now to enquire whether it is tenable in regard to the modifications of its structure induced by experience; whether, in short, all that is implied by the word "memory" can be regarded as consisting in modifications of cerebral structure.[1]

---

[1] Epiphenomenalism identifies the structure of the mind with that of the brain; Parallelism in both its principal forms maintains that it appears as, and may be adequately described as, brain-structure. In examining the problem of memory in this chapter the argument will, for the sake of brevity, be directed to Epiphenomenalism; but with some cumbrous paraphrasing it

The psychologists of the association-school were generally content to assume that each idea, or some trace of it, is deposited or stored in a single cell of the brain; that these cells become linked together by fibres in such a way that excitement of one cell spreads to another and, in doing so, brings to consciousness the idea stored within it; mental activity thus consisting in the "ringing up" of one cell after another and the appearance in consciousness of a corresponding train of ideas. At the present day no one, perhaps, would seriously defend this notion; unless "idea" be taken in the sense of element of consciousness; for we cannot form the vaguest notion of the nature of such a material trace in a single cell, nor of the way such a trace could be impressed upon it.[1] It is recognized that the physical correlate in

---

would apply equally well to the other forms of Parallelism. I have already in Chapter XII. insisted that the mere fact that the mind has a structure, or is a system of enduring capacities which is only very partially revealed in the consciousness of any moment, is one with which Psychical Monism cannot deal; and I say nothing further on that head.

[1] Prof. T. Ziehen has recently maintained the doctrine of "the memory-cell." "We assume, therefore, that the sensation of the rose is produced in certain ganglion-cells, and that these numerous sensory cells transmit their excitation further to one other ganglion-cell, a memory-cell . . . where it leaves a merely material trace or change, the image of memory" ("Introduction to Physiological Psychology," p. 158). But he does not attempt to suggest how we may conceive all this to happen. Ziehen is here writing of the visual impression of a rose. The following objections to this doctrine seem to me fatal to it: (1) We have no warrant for believing that the sensory centres that are concerned in the rise of the sensations of various qualities can propagate their specific modes of excitation to other cells. (2) But if it be admitted that this may happen and that the many sensory cells (and presumably many hundreds or thousands would be concerned in bringing to consciousness the fine gradations of colour of the petals of a tea-rose) propagate their excitations to one "memory-cell," can we suppose that, arrived in this cell, each of these peculiar excitations (mode of vibration or physico-chemical change) makes its own peculiar mark upon the "memory-cell" distinct from the mark or trace of all the rest? Yet that is implied by the doctrine. (3) If even this be admitted as possible, there remains the impossibility of conceiving what can be the nature of these enduring marks, each of which is to determine, whenever the cell is re-excited after a long interval of time, the recurrence within it of a physical or physico-chemical process identical in character with that by which the mark was impressed. (4) Lastly, there remains the still greater difficulty of conceiving how these marks are to condition not only the recurrence of the manifold of sensation qualities, but also their relative intensities and their spatial distribution in the memory-image.

Prof. Wundt writes: "Every content of consciousness, be it never so simple and regarded as isolated from all its connexions, and therefore as not capable of being further analysed, is nevertheless, physiologically regarded, always a complicated system of different neural processes, which are distributed through numerous nervous elements" ("Grundzüge d. phys. Psychologie," vol.

the brain of the perception of a relatively simple object must run its course in a large number of neurones, and that the memory-image or representation of that object must also have for its physical correlate a very complex process distributed throughout a large number of the same neurones and, perhaps, through others also. The only conception that we can form of a memory-trace in the brain as a neural disposition, the continuance of which might be the condition of the possibility of representation, is, then, that of a number of neurones intimately linked together to form a functional system; and the linking together of the members of the system must be supposed to be brought about by the spread of the excitation process or current of nervous energy from member to member throughout the system at the moment of perception.

Some such notion as this is now generally entertained by those who hold that all memory is a function of the brain.[1] Now, there can be little doubt that the linking up of neurones in this way is the basis of all that can properly be called habit; that in the course of life each of us forms a great number of habits;

---

i., p. 328). With this view, which seems to me quite indisputably correct, the doctrine of "the memory-cell" is of course wholly incompatible.

Prof. J. v. Kries ("Ueber die materiellen Grundlagen der Bewusstseins-Erscheinungen," Leipzig, 1901) has clearly shown the impossibility of finding an adequate physical basis for memories of general and abstract objects in terms of the linking together of neurones; and he rejects decisively the crude conception of a memory-cell. Of the latter he writes: "Es ist die oberflächlichste und platteste aller Vorstellungen" (p. 43). Yet he proposes to regard the retention of general ideas as "intracellulare Leistungen" (p. 45), and writes, "Soll als Spur einer optischen Wahrnehmung eine verwickelte Differenzierung einer Zelle hinterlassen werden, so müsste man diese mit dem System ihrer Ausläufer etwa durch das ganze Gebiet verzweigt und erstreckt denken, innerhalb dessen in anderen Gebilden die den Netzhautbildern direkt entsprechende Verteilung der Thatigkeits-zustände angeordnet wäre. Zellen solcher Art könnte man dann die Function einer verallgemeinernden Aufbewahrung optischer Bilder zuschreiben." Von Kries admits that his suggestion encounters great difficulties; and I think that the unprejudiced reader will find it difficult to regard it as essentially different from, or superior to, that "most superficial and banal of all notions," the memory-cell.

[1] In all my reading of physiological psychology I have nowhere found any attempt to think out the possibilities of the nature and mode of formation of a neural basis for both habit and memory which in definiteness and plausibility surpasses the scheme very briefly indicated in my little book, "A Primer of Physiological Psychology." Yet no one could be more acutely aware than myself of the inadequacy of this attempt as regards memory proper. The casual way in which most writers on these topics speak of brain-traces and memory-cells and so forth, without making any attempt to conceive the nature of these assumed traces, is to my mind astonishing.

and that the neurones of the cerebrum, a large proportion of which are not innately organized in definite systems, become so organized in systems which are the neural bases of habits. For we have to recognize not only that all the acquired dexterities of the limbs are of the nature of habits rooted in neural dispositions, but also that the education of our powers of sense perception, the co-ordination of hand and eye, and the acquirement of speech, all involve and depend upon the gradual building up of similar neural dispositions that render possible finer and more extensive co-ordinations of movements.

We have to recognize, then, that the building up of habit plays a very great part in our mental development. But Parallelism implies the assumption that all memory, all mental retention, is of the nature of habit; that conscious remembering and recollecting is but one way in which cerebral habits manifest themselves. This assumption must be carefully examined. If it should appear that there are no essential differences between the ways in which on the one hand undoubted habits and on the other hand true memory-traces are acquired, retained, and manifested, we shall have to accept the parallelistic assumption as a well-founded hypothesis; but, if it can be shown that there are fundamental differences, that habit and memory do not obey the same laws, this assumption will be discredited and we shall have gone far towards showing that memory proper is not conditioned only by material dispositions in the brain.[1]

Of recent years a large number of exact experiments have been reported as investigations into memory.[2] The experiments have in most cases consisted in committing to heart by repetition rows of words, letters, numbers, or more frequently nonsense syllables, series of syllables that convey no meaning; and in determining the laws of the association and reproduction of such

[1] The distinction between habit and true memory is urged with great force by Prof. Bergson in his fascinating work, "Matière et Mémoire," and in much of the discussion of this chapter I am following his lead and reproducing his arguments. But limitations of space and of capacity make it impossible for me to present the argument and the evidence so persuasively as he has done, and I must refer the reader to his book for the full statement of it. There is much in that book which I cannot accept, because I cannot understand it, notably the doctrine of "pure perception," which seems to me to leave the relation of sensation to perception extremely obscure.

[2] The most important and best-known are those of Ebbinghaus ("Ueber das Gedāchtniss") and of Prof. G. E. Muller (in conjunction with Prof. Schumann and Dr Pilzecker), reported in *Zeitschrift fur Psychologie*, vol. 6 and Supplem. vol. i.

series. Great refinement of method and nicety of results have been attained, and many important laws have been thus empirically established. One of the most striking of the results thus achieved is that the associations established by serial repetitions of this kind obey, in the main, in regard to their formation, operation, and decay, the laws of motor habit. It may be said, then, that here is substantial evidence justifying the identification of memory with habit. But these experiments, though generally called investigations into memory, are so conducted that the factor of true memory hardly enters into the operations. They are in the main investigations of verbal habit; for there is no reason to doubt that such a process as the repetition of the alphabet is essentially the operation of a habit; and the investigations to which I refer have dealt almost exclusively with processes closely approximating to this type.[1]

That true remembering is a process of a different type is shown clearly by the following considerations :—A written series of eight nonsense syllables is presented to me one by one by a mechanical arrangement, as rapidly as I can comfortably read them. After four repetitions of the reading, the first syllable alone is presented, and I attempt to say the series by heart and fail utterly. The presentation of the series is repeated again and again, I reading the syllables as presented. Then on trying again, perhaps after twelve repetitions, I succeed in saying them by heart without a hitch; my organs of speech seem to roll out the sounds, and all I have to do is to avoid anything that may interfere with the process; for, just as in executing any habitual series of manipulations with the hands, the process goes on best if left to itself. But now I can throw my mind back and can remember any one of the twelve readings more or less clearly as a unique event in my past history. I can remember perhaps that during the fifth reading I began to despair of ever learning the series, that I made a new effort, that someone spoke in the adjoining room and disturbed me disagreeably; I may perhaps remember what he said.

[1] The reason alleged for the choice of nonsense syllables as the material for most of this work is that they are devoid of previously formed associations. Really they are devoid of meaning, and to regard them as differing from words only in that they are devoid of associations, is to assume that *meaning* is nothing but a number of mechanical associations or reproduction-tendencies. This is the unjustified assumption which underlies the description of such experiments as investigations into the laws of memory.

If the repetition by heart of the nonsense syllables and the remembering of any one of the readings of the series are both to be called evidences of memory, it must be admitted that two very different functions, two very different modes of retention, are denoted by the one word. Let us glance at the principal differences. (1) The one depends mainly upon the formation of a habit; with each repetition I approach by a definite step towards the condition in which smooth reproduction is possible. In this process the successive readings contribute, then, to the production of a common effect, the habit, each adding a little to it. The remembering, on the other hand, depends wholly upon a single act of apprehension; the whole process and effect, the apprehension and the retention and the remembering, are absolutely unique and distinct from all other apprehensions, retentions, and rememberings.

(2) The one process of reproduction does not necessarily involve any explicit reference to the past; it involves rather a forward-looking attitude. Whereas the other is essentially retrospective and involves a reference of that which is remembered to a particular moment or position in the past series of events.

(3) The smooth reproduction of the syllables is not aided, but rather hindered, by any effort to cast back my thought to the moment of apprehension. The remembering on the other hand is aided by voluntary rummaging in the past; I can by such efforts develop more fully and vividly my remembrance of the events of the successive moments.

(4) The "learning" of the syllables involves only the linking together in serial order of eight simple impressions; and in order to accomplish this I find it necessary to repeat the series attentively some twelve times, or perhaps more, the whole process occupying the main part of my attention for some two or three minutes. The remembrance of a particular event may involve the reproduction of a vastly more complex set of sense-impressions made simultaneously or within a period of two or three seconds. These then are somehow linked together, and, though they are far more numerous and more complexly related than the row of syllables, their linking is effected in a single act of apprehension.

(5) The power of reproducing the syllable-row declines very rapidly in a way which can be accurately measured; even after five minutes or less it may have declined so far that it can only be effectively restored by reading the row again several times.

The remembrance of the particular event on the other hand, though it seems to become less vivid and trustworthy, may be effected after indefinitely long intervals.

Between the two modes of retention there are clearly great differences; and, if we ask what is the essential difference between the impressions that are retained in these very different ways, the answer cannot be in doubt: the nonsense syllables convey a minimum of meaning, the impressions truly remembered convey a more or less rich meaning. Even the row of eight syllables is not altogether meaningless. I apprehend it as meaning a row which in relation to my purpose is a unity, not merely eight impressions, but eight members of one whole each having its definite place in the whole; and, in so far as I clearly apprehend this whole and the parts of it as whole and parts, the process of "learning" is greatly aided. The importance of the meaning is well brought out by consideration of the following example. I set myself to learn a row of twenty nonsense syllables, and I find, perhaps, that one hundred or more repetitions are needed to enable me to reproduce the row. Then I take a passage of prose or verse containing twenty syllables, and I find that I can reproduce this row of twenty syllables after a single reading. How immense is the difference between the two cases! This difference is due partly to the fact that in the second case the syllables form words each of which has meaning for me; but chiefly it is due to the fact that their several meanings are synthesized to one whole in my consciousness, namely, the meaning of the whole passage. The meaning seems to bridge the series of sense-impressions and to bind them together. But, just as in the case of the reproduction of the nonsense syllables the factor of meaning is not altogether inoperative, though reproduction depends chiefly upon the links of mechanical association, so in this case the mechanical factor is not altogether lacking, though meaning plays the predominant part; for I may find after an interval that, though the meaning of the passage may return to consciousness, I am unable accurately to reproduce the words of the original.[1]

[1] I add here the results of some experiments made with the aim of bringing out this difference.

Binet and Henri set children to reproduce on the one hand rows of words conveying no connected meaning, and on the other hand rows of words constituting intelligible sentences. They found that on the average, when only seven unconnected words were presented, the children remembered five of them; whereas, when words conveying seventeen distinct notions were presented,

Everywhere in memory we find these two factors, habit and meaning, co-operating in various proportions; and always meaning is immensely more effective than habit as a condition of reproduction or remembering.[1] In an earlier chapter I have shown that we cannot with any plausibility assume that meaning has any immediate physical correlate among the brain-processes. We find here independent evidence of the truth of this view that meaning is a purely psychical product of psychical activity; for it appears as a factor in the process of remembering that is of an entirely different order from the other factor, habit; and habit is rooted in material dispositions of the brain of the only kind that we can conceive as playing any part in mental retention.

The distinction under discussion is so important that it seems worth while to illustrate it by reference to other instances of remembering. The visualization of complex scenes is perhaps the most wonderful of all forms of remembering. Consider the following simple instance. A number, say ten, points of light are thrown simultaneously, for a small fraction of a second, upon a screen, and I am required to draw a map of the spots. If the spots are irregularly distributed I find this quite impossible to achieve; and perhaps it is necessary to repeat the flash from thirty to fifty times before I can succeed in constructing a tolerably correct map of

---

fifteen of them were remembered. Ebbinghaus learnt on the average verses containing fifty-six words (and a much larger number of syllables) by six or seven readings; whereas, in spite of much practice in memorizing nonsense-syllables, he required fifty-five readings in order to be able to reproduce a series of thirty-six such syllables ("Grundzüge d. Psychologie," by H. Ebbinghaus, p. 654).

In a paper recently published ("Uber den Unterschied der logischen u. d. mechanischen Gedächtnisses," *Zeitschr. f. Psychologie*, Bd. lvi.), Herr A. Balaban reports results of experiments directed to this question. Pairs of words of two syllables were presented successively to subjects who were instructed to try to retain alternate pairs on the one hand in purely mechanical fashion (i.e. without reference to their meanings), and on the other hand by combining or connecting their meanings in some larger whole of meaning. The latter mode of learning appeared, according to the author's estimate, about twenty-five times as effective as the mechanical mode; yet in such experiments the conditions are not favourable to the development of meanings.

[1] M. Bergson speaks of habit and "pure memory" as the two kinds of memory. The "pure memory," corresponding to what I call meaning, he holds to be a purely psychical factor, and he constructs a peculiar theory of pure memory, which seems to be (if I understand him rightly) a refinement of the doctrine of the generic image of Huxley and Romanes. For my purpose it is not necessary to try to follow him in this more metaphysical part of his doctrine of memory. For the purpose of this chapter it suffices to insist upon the indisputable fact that meaning plays this great part in memory, and that it is a factor of a kind entirely different from habit.

the arrangement of the spots. But, if the spots are so arranged as to mark the principal points of any geometrical figure familiar to me, I am able to make a correct map after one or two flashes only; but only on the condition that the complex of visual sensations suggests or evokes in my consciousness the meaning of that figure.[1] In the former case, the only way to remember the arrangement of the spots is to apprehend at successive flashes the relations of sub-groups of three or four spots, each of which has some meaning for me, and at subsequent flashes to synthesize these sub-groups into a whole of some sort, which is then remembered as a whole. In the second case the complex of visual sensations serves as a cue that brings to consciousness a meaning that was latent in the memory; and this meaning of the whole group in turn serves at the moment of reproduction to bring to consciousness the spatial relations of the parts.

The experiment shows how small is our capacity for remembering the spatial relations of a number of seen points, if those relations suggest no definite meaning to our minds. Bearing this in mind, and noting also that every spot added to the group adds very greatly to the difficulty of reproducing the group, let us consider now the following case. My eye rests for a moment on a photograph or drawing of a striking face that is unknown to me. The drawing consists of a great number of points, lines, and areas, arranged in an extremely complex fashion; yet after that brief glance I am able to picture the face with considerable accuracy, perhaps even after the lapse of days or months; or I am able to single it out from among a large number of similar drawings, and my capacity to do this is not appreciably affected by considerable changes in the distance of the drawing from my eyes; yet with every change of distance the retinal points stimulated are widely different.

It may be said that my remembrance of the face is rendered possible by my familiarity with faces in general. This is true; but it does not make any more plausible the attempt to exhibit my remembrance as wholly dependent on a material disposition formed after the pattern of a habit. If we compare the two tasks, that of remembering the meaningless group of dots and that of remembering the face, and consider each as consisting in the

[1] This general description is based upon considerable experience of experiments of this kind. There are considerable differences between individuals in respect to the ease with which they achieve such a task; but those who are good visualizers do not seem to excel others.

linking together of a complex of sensations in a particular system of spatial relations, the latter task is enormously more complicated than the former, yet it is accomplished much more rapidly and certainly. The fact that I am familiar with faces does not render more plausible the assumption of a wholly material memory-trace. I have looked attentively at many thousands of faces; and, if the result of this were merely that I could produce a fairly adequate " generic image " of a face, that result would lend itself well to interpretation in terms of cerebral traces. But the fact is that, of all these many thousands of faces, I can clearly and distinctly picture some hundreds at least, and could recognize as having been seen by me on some previous occasion probably some thousands, certainly many hundreds. How, on any conceivable scheme of cerebral traces are these thousands of successive perceptions to co-operate in facilitating my perception and my remembering of a particular face, and yet to leave separate and distinct traces, each in itself an immensely complex neural disposition capable of conditioning the remembrance of a particular face?

Association-psychologists have generally adopted as their fundamental proposition some such assertion as that impressions received simultaneously or in immediate succession tend to cohere or to be associated together and to return to consciousness together or in immediate succession. And they have generally deduced from this so-called law a corresponding neural law, to the effect that the excitement, simultaneously or in immediate succession, of neural elements (nerve-cells or groups of them) results in the formation of paths of low resistance between them, by which they are put in functional association or made part of one system.[1] Now, if this deduction were correct, the assumption that all memory can be described in terms of brain-traces would be far more plausible than it actually is. But neither the premise nor the conclusion of the argument is justified by the

[1] The formation of motor habits certainly consists in the establishment of such neural associations, and, as we have seen, if all memory is conditioned by brain-traces, such neural association must be the basis of all memory. It might, then, have been expected that those who confidently assert that all facts of memory can be described in terms of neural mechanism would have some definite notions as to how such neural associations are effected. But that is by no means the case. The only plausible view of the formation of such neural associations is that indicated in my " Primer of Physiological Psychology," and based upon the hypothesis of " inhibition by drainage." Yet few physiologists or psychologists have accepted that hypothesis.

facts. Our consciousness comprises again and again complex conjunctions of sensations which show no appreciable tendency to become associated together. It is only when the attention is turned upon the objects that excite sensations, and when the sensations enter into the process of perception (serving as cues that bring some meaning to consciousness) that associations are formed. And even then, the formation of an effective neural association is by no means an immediate and invariable result; rather it may require frequent repetition of the perceptive processes; especially if the impressions to be associated belong to different sense-provinces. The fact is well illustrated by the following experience.

I began to teach one of my children his letters and numbers. The boy was six years old, bright, and fairly keen to master his tasks. He quickly learned to repeat the alphabet; and he quickly learnt also to recognize the letters printed in large type on cards; so that, the alphabet being laid out before him, he could pick out a second set of the letters and place each one without hesitation beneath its exemplar. Each letter was always named by me and generally by him, as it was taken up; and he frequently repeated the alphabet, pointing to each letter as he named it. Now the statements commonly current about association would lead one to expect that the child would be able to name the separate letters at sight (i.e. would acquire an effective association between the visual impression and the name of each letter) after a very few namings. But this was by no means the case. It was not until the naming had been repeated attentively many hundreds of times throughout some months that he acquired such effective associations. The learning to name the numbers from one to ten illustrated even more strikingly the difficulty of forming simple mechanical associations; since, though only ten visual forms and ten names were to be associated, an even larger number of repetitions of the naming were required to establish really effective associations.[1]

This experience brought home to me very vividly the great difference between memory and mechanical association. For the boy, who required so many hundred repetitions for the establishment of these simple mechanical associations, would often surprise

[1] It should be added that the naming was not repeated on any one day so often as to induce in the child a distaste for the task; also that the learning to name the numbers came first.

me by referring to scenes and events observed by him months or even years previously, sometimes describing them in a way that seemed to imply vivid and faithful representation. Yet the memory-pictures of such scenes involved far more complex conjunctions of partial impressions than did the remembering the name of a printed letter or number.[1]

The essential difference between the rememberings of these two kinds was that in the one case meaning was at a minimum, and remembering depended almost wholly upon mechanical or neural association of the nature of a habit; whereas the complex scenes and events remembered (in some instances after a single perception only) were full of meaning.

The hardened associationist will seek to reconcile these facts with his doctrine by asserting that what is here called richness of meaning of an impression consists in the existence of many associations previously formed between that impression and other impressions or sensations. But that contention will not enable him to meet the difficulty; for it has been abundantly established by the experimental investigators [2] of association that an impression which is already associated with others acquires new associations with more difficulty than one which is free from previously formed associations, and that the difficulty is greater the greater the number of the previously formed associations. Hence, if this view of the nature of meaning were true, the richer the meaning the greater should be the difficulty of combining any complex of sense impressions and of reproducing them as one memory picture; it is therefore impossible to account in this way for the fact that impressions which convey much meaning are combined and remembered with so much less difficulty than those of little meaning.[3]

---

[1] It may be that to this boy the acquirement of associations of this kind was more difficult than to most children; but even so, the significance of the facts remains.

[2] Prof. G. E. Müller, *op. cit.*

[3] It seems possible to throw light upon this question by the aid of the principle of correlation. If all memory or retention is of one type, the type of habit, and depends upon one fundamental factor, such as the plasticity of the brain-structure, then if a number of persons are tested as regards their excellence in a number of memorizing tasks, there should appear a high degree of correlation between the achievements of this group of persons under the several tests; *i.e.* if the persons are arranged in order of merit in respect to their execution of each of the tasks, there should be a considerable degree of correspondence between the several orders. If, on the other hand, memorizing involves two fundamentally different factors, namely habit and pure memory, and if these co-operate in very

We have, then, very strong grounds for maintaining that all mental retention and reproduction are conditioned in two very different ways ; one of these ways, the way of motor habit and automatism and mechanical association, is adequately accounted for by the conception of the formation of neural associations by the repeated passage of the current of nervous energy between neurone and neurone, each passage leaving the track more open for subsequent passages.[1] This is the only plausible, and in fact seems to be the only possible, conception of the way in which mental retention can be conditioned by cerebral structure or function ; but the strict limitations of this mode of retention, especially the need of many repetitions of the impressions even in very simple instances of mechanical association, show that we cannot regard it as the sole or principal condition of the higher form of retention or true memory. This we see depends upon meaning ; and meaning, as we have seen, is just that all important factor in mental process to which we can assign no immediate physical correlate among the brain-processes.

The foregoing considerations point to a view of the conditions of memory or mental retention intermediate between the two extreme views that have long been opposed to one another, the view that it is wholly conditioned by neural structure, and the view that it is conditioned wholly in some immaterial fashion. I venture to offer the following suggestion towards a theory of memory. We have regarded every perception or idea as a conjunction of sensory content with meaning. The sensory content, a complex of sensations or of images or of both, is essentially the expression of psycho-physical interaction. The

---

different proportions in different kinds of memorizing, as we have maintained, and if these two factors vary in effectiveness from one mind to another independently of one another, then we may hope to obtain evidence of the truth of this view by testing a group of persons in respect to tasks which involve predominantly habit-formation and true memory respectively. If such experiments revealed high correlation between the orders of achievement in respect to tasks of the first kind, and also between orders of achievement in respect to tasks of the second kind, but low correlation of the achievements in tasks of the one kind with those in tasks of the other kind, such a result would go far to establish the distinction between the two kinds of memory. Experiments directed along these lines are in progress, but are not yet ready for publication. The results so far achieved bear out the distinction in the way indicated.

[1] It is highly probable that the chief resistances to the passage of the current lie at the synapses, or junctions between neurons, and that the essential effect of the passage of the current is a diminution of these synaptic resistances.

idea, as a compound of sensory content and meaning, does not continue to exist as such in the interval between its acquisition and its reproduction. Neural associations or habits may so link groups of sensory elements of the brain as to lead to successive revival of the corresponding sensory complexes; something of this sort is the main condition of the predominantly mechanical reproduction of the alphabet or of rows of nonsense syllables learnt by frequent repetition. On the other hand, in so far as each sensory complex has evoked meaning in the past, it tends to revive it upon its reproduction and thus to reinstate the idea in consciousness. This is the process of evocation of an idea from the neural side. It plays only a subordinate part in the higher processes of remembering. These are determined mainly from the psychical side. What, then, is it that persists in the psychical realm? Shall we say it is the meanings themselves?[1] Clearly they do not persist as facts of consciousness. But the development of the mind from infancy onwards consists largely in the development of capacities for ideas or thoughts of richer, fuller, more abstract and more general meanings. If then meanings have no immediate physical correlates or counterparts in the brain, and if the meanings themselves do not persist, we must suppose that the persistent conditions of meanings are psychical dispositions.

We must believe, then, that there persist psychical dispositions, each of which is an enduring feature of the psychical structure and an enduring condition of the possibility of the return to consciousness of the corresponding meaning. These dispositions are elaborated in the course of experience and linked according to logical principles in processes of judgment and reasoning; whenever meanings become synthesized to larger logical wholes, the corresponding dispositions become linked as functional wholes, so that, when an appropriate sensory cue recalls one meaning to consciousness, the whole of which it is a part is also restored (under conditions otherwise favourable). And we may suppose that each meaning, as it comes into consciousness, tends to restore the sensory content which serves as its cue when the idea is evoked from the physical side. And we may suppose further that the restoration to consciousness of the sensory content

[1] The view that meanings persist in the mind as such, but in a reduced or subconscious condition, has been suggested by Mr W. M. Keatinge in chap. VIII. of his "Suggestion in Education." Although the view I am presenting differs in certain respects from his, I wish to acknowledge my indebtedness to his interesting suggestion.

involves the re-excitement of the system of neural elements, whose processes are the inseparable concomitants of the sensation elements. In this way the train of representation is determined all along the line from both the neural and the psychical sides, with constant psycho-physical interaction initiated now from this side, now from that. In thinking, judging, and in reasoning proper, the train of ideas is determined predominantly by the play of meanings, according to the principle of reproduction of similars under the guidance of the dominant purpose at the time; the images evoked may be verbal only, the neural correlate being reduced to a minimum, and habit being completely subordinated to thought.

This difficult and perhaps somewhat vague conception may perhaps be made clearer by a simile. Let the sensory brain elements of specific constitution be likened to the wires of a great piano. Each when struck gives out the tone (the quality of sensation) peculiar to itself. Habit may be likened to material connexions between the wires which bind them into groups and compel the members of each group to vibrate together. So far our simile illustrates only the conception of memory as materially conditioned. But the frame of piano wires may not only be struck from below by the hammers connected with the keyboard (the sense-organs), but may also be set vibrating in harmonious groups by action from above, namely, they may take up by resonance the notes of a melody vibrating in the air. The total system of wires vibrating at any moment will then be determined in three ways, (1) by operations on the keyboard (sense-stimuli), (2) by the nature of the mechanical ties established between the wires (habit), (3) by the air-borne chords and melodies reaching them (meanings). The simile fails of course in that, in the case of the piano, the vibrations of the air which act upon the wires are but forms of motion similar to those of the wires themselves. And, even if we try to improve it by adding a phonographic plate, which may store up the vibrations in static form and at a later time return them to the air and through it to the piano-wires, it still fails in that the trace upon the plate is merely the trace of one particular series of impressions; whereas the psychical disposition is the product of a gradual growth renewed upon many occasions.

According to this scheme, then, the sensory content of consciousness is essentially the expression of psycho-physical interaction, and can be initiated either from the neural side (in accordance with the conjunctions of sense-stimuli and preformed habits or neural associations), when it brings meanings to consciousness; or, from the psychical side, by meanings which demand specific sensory complexes for the completion of the ideas, and which thus in turn through the medium of sensation bring neural dispositions into play. Or, in other words, we may say that sensation and imagery are the medium through which the bodily processes provoke the thought activities of the soul and through which thought in turn plays back upon the brain-processes.[1]

Here, it seems to me, we have in rough outline a theory of memory which is consistent with all the empirical data, especially all those which show the dependence of sensation and imagery upon the integrity of the brain, and which yet relieves us of the impossible task of conceiving a physical basis for all memory, and allows us to believe that true memory is conditioned by the persistence of modifications of psychical structure or capacities.

This view of the twofold nature of the conditions of mental retention finds support in certain cases in which a physical shock to the brain seems to have destroyed or temporarily abolished the whole content of memory in so far as it depends on physical traces in the brain; the most notable of such cases is that of Mr Hanna.[2] A violent concussion of the brain reduced this patient to a condition which in many respects resembled that of a new-born infant. He was found to have lost all acquired facilities of movement, including those of speech and locomotion; although an educated man, he could understand neither written nor spoken language, nor could he interpret the most familiar sense-impressions; yet according to his own account, which there seems no reason to suppose is not in the main trustworthy, he puzzled over

---

[1] The most striking evidence of the determination of the sensory content of consciousness by meaning is afforded by the study of the struggle of two unlike visual fields presented to the right and left eyes respectively. If the two fields are not of very unequal brightness, attention may be directed at will to either field (*i.e.*, one may think of the objects presented in either field); the sensory content excited through the corresponding eye then predominates to the partial or complete suppression of the sensations excited through the other eye. In this way one learns to use a monocular microscope while keeping both eyes open. It is especially significant that when one's purpose is to combine the objects of the two fields, this also is possible (as when one draws an object under the microscope with the aid of the *camera lucida*); and that then the sensory contents of the two fields coexist in consciousness.

[2] "Multiple Personality," by B. Sidis and S. P. Goodhart, London, 1905.

his condition, used almost at the first moment of recovery of consciousness the category of causation,[1] and intelligently experimented in order to regain an understanding of his surroundings. He reacquired in the course of a few months almost all the stock of common facilities and knowledge that is acquired by a child in the course of many years. "He learned so rapidly in those days that it was almost miraculous." Six weeks after the accident he was able to talk freely and to give an intelligent account of his condition. Now it might be suggested that all this rapid reacquisition was not a new learning, but a mere restoration under practice of the temporarily paralysed memory-traces in his brain. But that interpretation seems to be ruled out by the fact that for a long time the content of his memory was entirely new; and, though his old memories were eventually restored, that restoration seems to have set in at a later date as a process quite distinct from the new learning. The case, then, lends itself very well to interpretation in terms of the theory of memory proposed above. If we suppose that all brain-traces of the nature of acquired habits were paralysed by the shock and remained incapable of functioning during the period of new learning, we may explain the great rapidity of the processes of acquisition by the assumption that the psychical dispositions elaborated in the course of his earlier experience remained ready to be brought into play by appropriate conjunctions of sense-stimuli, and that under their guidance the neural dispositions, whose co-operation is necessary for effective thought and expression, were rapidly organized.

Without, then, maintaining that the theory of the material conditioning of all memory can as yet be absolutely disproved, I conclude that it remains an extremely improbable hypothesis resting upon the general arguments in favour of Parallelism, rather than upon any evidence directly supporting it. And I submit that to regard the conditions of mental retention as of two disparate natures, namely, material and psychical, is more in harmony with all the empirical evidence at present available.

---

[1] He noted, for example, that when his attendants moved their lips he heard sounds, and he inferred that in this way they communicated with one another; and, after discovering that he had the power of moving the parts of his body, he noted the movement of another object (a man) and inferred that he himself had caused it to move (*op. cit.*, pp. 109, 110).

CHAPTER XXV

THE BEARING OF THE RESULTS OF "PSYCHICAL RESEARCH" ON THE PSYCHO-PHYSICAL PROBLEM

DURING the last thirty years the Society for Psychical Research has investigated in a strictly scientific manner certain obscure phenomena, the occurrence of which has been accepted by the popular mind in all ages and in all countries, but which have been rejected by the official world of modern science as merely superstitious survivals from the dark ages, reinforced by contemporary errors of observation due to the influence of these traditional superstitions.

At the present day, no one undertaking to review the psycho-physical problem can ignore the results of these investigations without laying himself open to the charge of culpable ignorance or unscientific prejudice.

The principal aim of the Society for Psychical Research has been to obtain, if possible, empirical evidence that human personality may and does survive in some sense and degree the death of the body. A considerable mass of evidence pointing in this direction has been accumulated. Its nature is such that many of those who have devoted attention to the work and have had a full and first-hand acquaintance with the investigations and their results, have become convinced that survival is a fact. And among these persons so convinced are several who, in respect to their competence to form a sane and critical judgment on this difficult question, cannot be rated inferior to any other persons.

Nevertheless, in my judgment, the evidence is not of such a nature that it can be stated in a form which should produce conviction in the mind of any impartial inquirer. Again and again the evidential character of the observations has fallen just short of perfection; the objections that stand between us and the acceptance of the conclusion seem to tremble and sway; but still they are not cast down, the critical blow has not been struck; and, perhaps, they will remain erect in spite of all efforts. This being the state of affairs, I shall not adduce any of this evidence,[1] but will merely point out that one of the advantages of the animistic solution of the psycho-physical problem is that its acceptance keeps our minds open for the impartial consideration of evidence of this sort; and that it is possible and seems even probable that Animism may receive direct and unquestionable verification through these investigations:[2] whereas Parallelism (including under

---

[1] For full accounts of the work the reader must turn to the Proceedings of the S. P. R. He will find excellent samples and discussions of the evidence in Sir O. Lodge's "Survival of Man," and in the late Mr Podmore's "The Newer Spiritualism." The former accepts, the latter rejects the evidence for survival.

[2] Some of my readers may object that empirical evidence of the survival of personality is in principle impossible. This was the opinion forcibly expressed by Kant in his "Träume eines Geister-sehers," and never abandoned by him. The question is important, and a brief discussion of it here may serve to reinforce what was said on an earlier page in criticism of Kant's arbitrary restriction of empirical science to mechanistic conceptions. The unjustified assumption implied by the objection is that conceptions based upon empirical evidence must be conceptions of objects capable in principle of being perceived through the senses. It has already been pointed out that many of the most valuable conceptions of physical science do not conform to this requirement. In order to bring home to our minds the invalidity of the assumption, let us imagine the following case. After the death of an intimate friend you seal up a pencil and a writing-block in a glass vessel. Then, whenever mentally or verbally you address questions to your deceased friend as though he were beside you, the pencil stands up and writes upon the paper, giving intelligent replies to your questions. In this way you conduct elaborate and oft-renewed conversations, in which the writing seems always perfectly to express the personality of your friend, even to revealing many facts which, as you are able afterwards to discover, must have been known to him but to no other person, facts such as the contents of a private writing-desk, or a sealed personal journal. If this occurred, it would constitute an empirical proof of the continued existence of the personality of your friend in some manner not directly perceptible by the senses, in spite of the complete dissolution of his bodily organism. You would infer his continued existence from the phenomena, though you would remain unable to imagine the mode of his existence; and to refuse to do so would be irrational and absurd. No one asserts that such phenomena have been observed; but to assert that it is impossible that they should occur is to beg the question in dispute and to argue in a circle; for the denial of its possibility could only be based on *a priori* grounds. But nothing is impossible save the self-contradictory. Now, although the phenomena we have imagined have not been observed, something similar, something constituting evidence of a similar nature, does occur. Pencils do produce what seem to be messages written by deceased persons, but in the observed cases (I leave out of account the alleged cases of "direct writing") the pencil is held and moved by the hand and arm of a living person, who, however, remains ignorant of its doings and of the thought expressed in the writing. This fact, that the pencil is moved by the hand of a living person, complicates immensely the task of evaluating the significance of the writing, but does not in principle affect the validity of the inference that may be drawn from it.

that term all forms of the anti-animistic hypotheses) closes our minds to this possibility, and is liable at any moment to be finally refuted by improvement of the quality of this empirical evidence for survival.

For if, as was argued in Chapter XIV., Animism is the only solution of the psycho-physical problem compatible with a belief in any continuance of personality after death, the empirical proof of such continuance would be the verification of Animism; it would be proof that the differences between the living human organism and the corpse are due to the presence or operation within the former of some factor or principle which is different from the body and capable of existing independently of it.

But though, in my judgment, this verification of Animism has not been furnished by "psychical research," a very important positive result has been achieved by it, namely, it has established the occurrence of phenomena that are incompatible with the mechanistic assumption. I refer especially to the phenomena of telepathy.[1]

I cannot attempt to present here the evidence for the reality of telepathy. It must suffice to say that it is of such a nature as to compel the assent of any competent person who studies it impartially. Now, so long as we consider only the evidence of telepathy between persons at no great distance from one another, it is possible to make the facts appear compatible with the mechanistic assumption by uttering the "blessed" word "brainwaves."[2] But the strain upon the mechanistic assumption becomes insupportable by it when we consider the following facts: Minute studies of automatic writings, and especially those recently reported[3] under the head of "Cross-Correspondences," have shown that such writings frequently reveal knowledge of facts which could not have been acquired by the writer by normal means, and could not have been telepathically communicated from any living person in the neighbourhood of the writer. In

---

[1] "The communication of mind with mind by means other than the recognized channels of sense." The evidence is reviewed in *Encycl. Brit.* 11th Ed. Art. "Telepathy."

[2] The explanation of telepathy at close quarters by the hypothesis of "brainwaves" transmitted through the ether cannot be absolutely rejected. But to my mind the difficulties are so great that the hypothesis is incredible. It is usual to support this hypothesis by pointing to the facts of wireless telegraphy.

[3] Proceedings of the S.P.R. from 1907 onwards.

short, the evidence is such that the keenest adverse critics[1] of the view which sees in these writings the expression of the surviving personalities of deceased persons, are driven to postulate as the only possible alternative explanation of some of them the direct communication of complex and subtle thoughts between persons separated by hundreds and even thousands of miles, thoughts of which neither is conscious or has been conscious at any time, so far as can be ascertained. There is good evidence also that in some cases three persons widely separated in space have taken part in expressing by automatic writing a single thought. Unless, then, we are prepared to adopt the supposition of a senseless and motiveless conspiracy of fraud among a number of persons who have shown themselves to be perfectly upright and earnest in every other relation,[2] we must recognize that we stand before the dilemma—survival or telepathy of this far-reaching kind. The acceptance of either horn of the dilemma is fatal to the mechanistic scheme of things. For, even if the hypothesis of "brain-waves" be regarded as affording a possible explanation of simple telepathic communication at short range, it becomes wholly incredible if it is suggested as an explanation of the co-operation of widely separated "automatic" writers in the expression of one thought. This, then, is the principal importance I attach to the results hitherto achieved by "psychical research," namely, I regard the research as having established the occurrence of phenomena which cannot be reconciled with the mechanistic scheme of things; and I adduce the results here in order to add them to the great mass of evidence to the same effect set forth in the foregoing chapters.

Besides the evidence that leads to this dilemma, so fatal to the mechanistic dogma, "psychical research" has established the reality of other phenomena very difficult to reconcile with it. Of these I will cite here only two classes. First, it has been shown that under certain conditions (especially in the hypnotic and post-hypnotic states) the mind may exert an influence over the organic processes of the body far greater than any that had been generally recognized by physiologists. Especially noteworthy are the

---

[1] This was the alternative hypothesis adopted by the late Mr F. Podmore, whose acquaintance with the facts was intimate and extensive, and who during many years had built up for himself a reputation as the keenest critic of the advanced wing of the S. P. R. (See his posthumous work, "The Newer Spiritualism.")

[2] I may add that my personal knowledge of leading members of this group of workers renders this supposition ridiculous to my mind.

production of blisters, erythemata, and ecchymoses, of the skin (the so-called stigmata) in positions and of definite shapes determined by verbal suggestions, and the rapid healing of wounds or burns with almost complete suppression of inflammation; and with these may be put the complete suppression or prevention of pain, even pain of such severity as normally accompanies a major surgical operation.[1]

Now it is true that the production of these and similar effects involves only an extension or intensification of powers normally exercised by the mind over the bodily processes. But to say that, is not to deprive the facts of the significance that I would attribute to them. Rather, these instances of hypernormal mental control over bodily processes serve merely to place in a clearer light, to bring home more forcibly to us, the impossibility of explaining these processes on mechanical principles, the impossibility of exhibiting these psycho-physical processes as purely chemico-physical or mechanical processes. By the free use of speculation I have myself carried the hypothetical account of the nervous changes involved in hypnosis as far, perhaps, as any other physiologist.[2] But it must be frankly recognized that even though my account, or any other yet proposed, be accepted as approximately true, the processes are by no means explained; the chief part of the facts remains refractory to explanation by mechanical hypotheses. Let us consider for a moment one of the simplest and most familiar instances of such control; the production of local anæsthesia or the allied process of the suppression of local neuralgic pain. I touch the left eye of a subject in hypnosis[3] as he sits with closed eyes, and tell him that he can see nothing with that eye. On opening his eyes he is then blind of the left eye,[4] and remains so until its vision is restored by a new

[1] For the evidences of such effects I refer the reader to Dr Milne Bramwell's "Hypnotism, its History, Theory, and Practice," London, 1903.

[2] "The State of the Brain during Hypnosis," *Brain*, vol. 31, and Art. "Hypnotism" in *Ency. Brit.*, 11th Ed.

[3] This and similar effects can be obtained in a considerable proportion of subjects, but the reader must not be misled into supposing that they can be readily produced in every subject.

[4] Any critically disposed reader unfamiliar with experiments of this kind, will be inclined to assume that the subject feigns blindness of the left eye, out of complaisance or obedience to the operator. But that the blindness of the left eye is genuine and involuntary may easily be shown by the following procedure. The lateral parts of the normal field of view are fields of monocular vision, the middle part only being a field of binocular vision; the ordinary working man is ignorant of the boundaries between the monocular and the binocular parts

suggestion to that effect. Or a subject who has been racked for days, or weeks, with intense neuralgic pain becomes completely free of the pain almost instantaneously upon mere verbal suggestion to that effect during hypnosis. Now it seems highly probable that in every such case the sensory path or centre of the brain concerned in the production of the sensation which is, as it were, cut out of the subject's consciousness, becomes functionally dissociated from the rest of the brain, *i.e.* circumscribed or isolated. But how is this dissociation or circumscription effected? The subject himself knows nothing of the anatomy of his brain; and, even if his brain could be so enlarged that all the members of the International Congress of Physiologists could walk about inside his nerve fibres and hold a conference in one of his "ganglion cells," their united knowledge and the resources of all their laboratories would not suffice to enable them to effect such an operation as the isolation of the sensory centres of the left eye from those of the right eye, and from the rest of the brain. If it be suggested that the anæsthesia of the left eye is produced by some paralysis of the optic nerve, comparable to the application of a ligature to it (and this of course would be within the competence of the physiologist), the case is brought no nearer to the possibility of a mechanistic explanation; for it is utterly impossible to conceive that the neural impulses initiated in the auditory nerve by the sound of the words, "Your left eye is blind," should find their way to the fibres of the left optic nerve; nor, if arrived there, could they in any conceivable fashion paralyse the conductivity of the nerve.

These processes in short remain no less mysterious and no less refractory to mechanistic explanations than the processes of growth and repair by which complex organisms develop from the germ-cells and maintain or restore the integrity of their organs. The similarity to normal processes of growth and repair of these processes of control of organic function initiated by verbal

---

of the field, and if, while his eyes are directed to a spot before him, an object is brought slowly forward from behind his head, it passes at a given moment from the monocular to the binocular part of his field of view, without affording him any indication of the fact. Now if this experiment be made with a subject whose left eye has been rendered anæsthetic by suggestion, an object being brought slowly forward on his left side and the subject being instructed to indicate the moment at which it becomes perceptible to him, he will signal his perception of the object at the moment that it crosses the boundary between the monocular and the binocular parts of his normal field of view, *i.e.* the moment at which it enters the field of the right eye.

suggestion, i.e. by mental influences (though carried out in detail by processes of which the subject remains wholly unconscious), goes far to justify the assimilation of the processes of these two types, and to justify the belief that the normal processes of growth and repair are in some sense controlled by mind, or by a teleological principle of which our conscious intelligence is but one mode of manifestation among others.

Hypnotic experiments of another class seem to me to call for special mention in the present connexion, namely those which have revealed in several subjects an astonishing power of appreciating time or duration.[1] The essence of the experiments was that the subject, having been instructed during hypnosis to make some simple written record at some future moment (generally stated in thousands of minutes), carried out the instruction in a great majority of cases with hardly appreciable error.[2] Many interesting problems are raised by these experiments; but, leaving on one side the evidence of subconscious calculations of considerable complexity, I wish to insist only on the main point, the awareness of the arrival of the prescribed moment. It is usual to seek to explain simpler cases of appreciation of the passage of time by some vague suggestion of a subconscious counting of some physiological rhythm. But in these cases, even if the ordinary means of learning the time (e.g. a reliable watch) had been used by the subject at the moment of the reception of the suggestion, this explanation would remain very far-fetched and improbable; for we know of no bodily rhythm sufficiently constant to serve as the basis of so accurate an appreciation of duration as would have enabled the subject to carry out the suggestion with the high degree of accuracy shown. And in some cases the subject had no normal means of learning the time of day for considerable periods before and after the reception of the suggestion, and yet the accuracy of the result was not diminished. What then can be made of these cases? They are too numerous, too carefully studied and reported by competent observers, to be set aside as merely in-

[1] The principal instances are those carefully studied and reported by the late Prof. Delbœuf, by Dr Milne Bramwell (*op. cit.*), and by Dr T. W. Mitchell, "A Case of Post-Hypnotic Appreciation of Time" (Proc. S. P. R., vol. xxi.). At the time of going to press I am engaged in studying a subject who seems to exhibit this power in a very striking manner, as well as the production of blisters and extravasations of blood from the skin in response to verbal suggestion.

[2] The time-errors were frequently less than one minute, seldom more than five.

stances of mal-observation. The most commonplace hypothesis that seems adequate to account for them is one of subconscious telepathy. But, whatever the true explanation may be, they must, I think, be added to the class of phenomena manifestly irreconcilable with the mechanistic dogma.

CHAPTER XXVI

CONCLUSION

IN this final chapter it remains to draw together the threads of the long discussion and to state succinctly what conclusions seem to be justified by the evidences and reasonings we have reviewed.

We have seen how the great successes of the mechanical principles of explanation in the physical sciences, and their more limited success in the biological sciences, have led the greater part of the modern world of science confidently to assume that these principles are adequate for the explanation of all biological phenomena, and to reject as unnecessary the hypothesis of the co-operation of some teleological principle in their determination. We have seen how this opinion has seemed to find support in the law of the conservation of energy, in the Darwinian principles, and in the modern developments of cerebral anatomy and physiology. We have seen that the belief thus engendered in the adequacy and the exclusive sway of mechanical principles in both the inorganic and organic realms has been and remains the principal ground of the rejection of Animism by the modern world. We saw also that the more enlightened of the opponents of Animism, recognizing the uncertain nature of this ground, have rested their case mainly upon certain metaphysical arguments that make against the acceptance of the notion of psycho-physical interaction. We then examined the chief types of the current monistic formulations of the relation of mind to body; and we found that each of them encounters great difficulties peculiar to itself, as well as others common to all of them. After ascertaining that there is no escape from the dilemma, Animism or Parallelism, we proceeded to the defense of Animism; and first, we found that none of the arguments, neither those of a metaphysical or epistemological nature, nor those drawn from the natural sciences, render impossible or untenable the notion of psycho-physical interaction. We then surveyed a mass of evidence which shows that the mechanical principles are not adequate to the explanation of biological phenomena, neither the phenomena of racial evolution nor those of the development of individual organisms, nor the behaviour of men and animals. In the psychological chapters evidence was adduced which conclusively proves that a strict parallelism between our psychical processes and the physical processes of our brains does not as a matter of empirical fact obtain; and it was shown that facts of our conscious life, especially the fact of psychical individuality, the fact of the unity of the consciousness correlated with the physical manifold of brain-processes, cannot be rendered intelligible (as admitted by leading Parallelists)[1] without the postulation of some ground of unity other than the brain or material organism.

The empirical evidence, then, seems to weigh very strongly against Parallelism and in favour of Animism. And we saw that, though the acceptance of either horn of the dilemma involves the acceptance of a number of strange consequences and leaves on our hands a number of questions to which we can return no answer, Animism has this great advantage over its rival, namely, that it remains on the plane of empirical science, and, while leaving the metaphysical questions open for independent treatment, can look forward to obtaining further light on its problems through further scientific research. It is thus a doctrine that stimulates our curiosity and stirs us to further efforts; whereas Parallelism necessarily involves the acceptance of metaphysical doctrines which claim to embody ultimate truth and which set rigid limits to the possibilities of further insight into the nature of the world, and it finds itself forced to regard certain of its problems as ultimately inexplicable.

Finally, we have seen that Parallelism rules out all religious conceptions and hopes and aspirations, save those (if there be any) which are compatible with a strictly mechanistic Pantheism, a Pantheism which differs from rigid Materialism not at all in respect to practical consequences for the life of mankind; whereas Animism in this sphere also leaves open the whole field for further speculation and inquiry, and permits us to hope and even to believe that the world is better than it seems; that the bitter injustices men suffer are not utterly irreparable; that their moral

---

[1] I remind the reader of Paulsen's dictum, "Die Seele ist eine auf nicht weiter sagbarer Weise zusammen gebundene Vielheit innerer Erlebnisse."

CONCLUSION

efforts are not wholly futile ; that the life of the human race may have a wider significance than we can demonstrate; and that the advent of a "kindly comet," or the getting out of hand of some unusually virulent tribe of microbes, would not necessarily mean the final nullity of human endeavour.

These seem to me overwhelmingly strong reasons for accepting, as the best working hypothesis of the psycho-physical relation, the animistic horn of the dilemma. I shall now very briefly consider the principal varieties of the animistic conception, and attempt to estimate the relative strengths of their claims on our acceptance.

We may consider first a peculiar view, which might be called Animism of the lowest or most meagre degree. It is not perhaps new in the history of speculation, though it was not, I think, clearly formulated until recent years.[1]

It is allied to the view of Ostwald, Bechterew, and others,[2] which regards consciousness as a form of energy that undergoes transformations to other forms and is generated by transformations of the other forms of energy. It may perhaps be most easily described by saying that, like *Epiphenomenalism*, it regards consciousness as generated by the physical processes of the brain, but (unlike Huxley's doctrine) conceives the elements of consciousness as forces that influence one another and, in turn, react upon the brain-processes. It might also be described as the combination of the notion of the "Actuelle-Seele"[3] with the belief in psycho-physical interaction. It sacrifices the advantages of Parallelism, namely, those which follow from the acceptance of a clean-cut mechanistic scheme of things, and involves many of the difficulties of Animism without bringing it important advantages. Its chief merit, and its only superiority to Epiphenomenalism, is that it finds a place, a function, and a *raison d'être*

---

[1] It was advocated in my first publication touching on the psycho-physical question ("Mind," N.S., vol. vii., 1898), and has more recently been urged by several writers, especially by Dr Archdall Reid ("Laws of Heredity," London, 1910) and by Mr E. B. M'Gilvary ("*Journ. of Phil., Psychology and Sci. Method*," 1910).

[2] See p. 130.

[3] Wundt's notion of the "Actuelle-Seele" (as consisting in the stream of consciousness composed of elements that causally interact with one another and synthesize themselves undergoing transformations in the process) differs from this view chiefly in that it denies any causal relation between the elements of the stream of consciousness and the brain-processes of which they are the invariable temporal concomitants.

for consciousness as a factor in biological evolution, and avoids the absurdity of postulating effects which have no causes.

A second type of animistic theory is that advocated by William James[1] and Prof. Bergson. It was called by James "the transmission theory" of the function of the brain in relation to consciousness. It holds that consciousness is a stuff which is capable of being divided and compounded like putty or any plastic matter, its parts enduring or retaining their identity in the various aggregations into which they enter. It is conceived as existing independently of material organisms, either "(a) in disseminated particles; and then our brains are organs of concentration, organs for combining and massing these into resultant minds of personal form. Or it may exist (b) in vaster unities (absolute 'world-soul,' or something less); and then our brains are organs for separating it into parts and giving them finite form."[2]

According to this view, then, the brain is the ground of our psychical individuality. Matter is regarded as "a mere surface-veil of phenomena, hiding and keeping back the world of genuine realities,"[3] and our brains are regarded as translucent spots or systems of pores in this veil, whereby beams of consciousness "pierce through into this sublunary world." And all the beams thus transmitted by one brain are regarded as normally cohering to form a stream of personal consciousness, which swells

---

[1] "Human Immortality," Ingersoll Lecture, 1898. The Animism of Bergson as expounded in his "Évolution Créatrice" is in many essential respects similar to James' view. But though Bergson has more fully elaborated this doctrine, I have chosen to present it in the form given it by James. Their formulations agree in the following essential points: both reject the claims of mechanism to rule in the organic world; both regard all psychical existence as of the form of consciousness only; both assume that consciousness exists independently of the physical world in some vast ocean or oceans of consciousness; both maintain that the consciousness or psychical life of each organism is a ray from this source; that the bodily organisation of each creature is that which determines individuality; that the brain is a mechanism which lets through, or brings into operation in the physical world, a stream of consciousness which is copious in proportion to the complexity of organisation of the brain.

[2] James, op. cit., note 3. James distinguished these two views as alternatives in his Ingersoll Lecture, but later ("Pluralistic Universe") he seems to have realized that they imply one another; that if consciousness can be split off from larger wholes, its fragments must also be capable of being compounded. Elsewhere he speaks of a cosmic sea or reservoir of consciousness in impersonal forms. James, in fact, recognized that the transmission theory implies the doctrine of mind-stuff, the metaphysical notion that consciousness as we know it consists of compounded or aggregated atoms of mind-stuff.

[3] James, op. cit., p. 33.

and grows rich, or contracts and grows thin and poor, according to the functional condition of the brain.

This theory seems to me very unsatisfactory for the following reasons:[1] (1) It is open to all the objections that are made against psycho-physical interaction, since it implies such interaction and the rejection of the mechanistic dogma. (2) It is open also to all the objections to the notion of the compounding of consciousness, the notion that a number of elements or fragments of consciousness can cohere together to form a logical thought, or that a thought may be formed by the chipping off of a fragment of a larger whole of consciousness, and the notion also that each fragment of consciousness functions simultaneously as an element of larger and smaller aggregates.[2] (3) Like Parallelism, it leaves the fundamental fact of psychical individuality completely obscure and unintelligible; for we can see no reason in the nature of things, or of the hypothesis, why the several beams or elements of consciousness transmitted through any one brain should normally cohere to form the thoughts of one personality, while those transmitted through separate brains should remain separate. (4) In identifying mind with consciousness (i.e. making consciousness coextensive with mind or soul and its operations) it holds out no prospect of aiding in the solution of the physiological problems that remain refractory to mechanical principles, and it would seem to necessitate the assumption of the operation in organisms of a second teleological factor other than consciousness. (5) It seems incapable of giving any intelligible account of the facts of memory.[3]

It seems, then, worth while to inquire why James, one of the most prominent exponents of this form of Animism, preferred it to what he called the soul-theory. The history of James' thought on this question, as revealed in his published works, is interesting and relevant to our discussion. James approached the study of the mind, in which he attained so pre-eminent a mastery, from the side of physiology, and, in accordance with the dominant physio-

---

[1] My very condensed statement of it inevitably fails to do justice to it, and the reader should consult the original sources. Mr Schiller's very readable "Riddles of the Sphinx" presents a psycho-physical hypothesis which in some respects is allied to the "transmission theory."

[2] See p. 169.

[3] I cannot discover that Prof. Bergson has brought the theory of memory of the "Matière et Mémoire" into intelligible relation with the psycho-physical doctrine of the "Évolution Créatrice."

logical teaching of that time, he identified thought and feeling and will with sensation; and throughout his first great book [1] he endeavoured to build up a consistent account of our mental life on a sensationalistic basis. At the same time he rejected the mechanistic dogma and affirmed the reality of psycho-physical interaction; he gave a brilliant and convincing refutation of the notion of the compounding of consciousness, and frankly recognized that the soul-theory seemed to him the necessary alternative to that doctrine. He affirmed the logical respectability of the soul-theory, gave a sympathetic statement of it, and confessed "that to posit a soul influenced in some mysterious way by the brain-states and responding to them by conscious affections of its own, seems to me the line of least logical resistance, so far as we yet have attained." [2] Nevertheless, he did not accept the soul-theory, though he gave no reasons for his hesitation, unless his characterization of it as the doctrine of Scholasticism and of common sense can be regarded as such. In his later works he showed himself more decidedly opposed to the soul-theory. In the Ingersoll Lecture of 1898 he hardly mentioned it, but advocated the "transmission theory." And, in his Oxford lectures of 1908,[3] he definitely rejected it in favour of the conception of a hierarchy of consciousnesses such as Fechner had dreamt of, the members of each level being conceived as formed by the compounding of lesser streams of consciousness of a lower level. In doing so, he recognized that he was repudiating his own demonstration of the illegitimacy of the notion of the compounding of consciousness, and explained that, after a long struggle with the problem, the magic of Prof. Bergson's attack upon the human intellect had given him courage to throw logic to the winds and to accept the notion of the compounding of consciousnesses in spite of its logical absurdity. He struggled in vain to reconcile with logical principles the notion that a consciousness can be at the same time both itself and an element or part of a different and more inclusive consciousness. "How can many consciousnesses be at the same time one consciousness? How can one and the same identical fact experience itself so diversely? The struggle was vain; I found myself in an *impasse*. I saw that I must either forswear that 'psychology without a soul' to which my whole psychological and Kantian

---

[1] "The Principles of Psychology."   [2] "Principles," p. 181.
[3] "A Pluralistic Universe."

education had committed me—I must, in short, bring back distinct spiritual agents to know the mental states, now singly and now in combination, in a word, bring back Scholasticism and common sense—or else I must squarely confess the solution of the problem impossible, and then, either give up my intellectualistic logic, the logic of identity, and adopt some higher (or lower) form of rationality, or, finally, face the fact that life is logically irrational. Sincerely, this is the actual trilemma that confronts every one of us."[1] And James chose to give up logic and the soul, and to accept the Fechnerian conception.

There can be no doubt that James, in making choice of this alternative, was greatly influenced, on the one hand, by the modern studies in psycho-pathology, which seemed to him to have shown that the normal stream of personal consciousness may be split into two or more coexistent streams, and, on the other, by his studies of those experiences of mystics in which they seem to themselves to transcend the normal limits of individuality and to become one with some larger whole of consciousness.[2] But he did not claim that these considerations compel us to this renunciation of our most fundamental logical principles. Rather he seemed driven to this renunciation by his strong objection to the soul-theory, which, as he so clearly showed, is the only alternative to it. What, then, are the grounds of this objection put forward by James? They are stated in less than two pages of large print; and for the purpose of our inquiry it is so important to have these grounds fully before us that I quote the entire passage. " It is not for idle or fantastical reasons that the notion of the substantial soul, so freely used by common men and the more popular philosophies, has fallen upon such evil days, and has no prestige in the eyes of critical thinkers. It only shares the fate of other unrepresentable substances and principles. They are, without exception all so barren that to sincere inquirers they appear as little more than names masquerading—Wo die begriffe fehlen da stellt ein wort zur rechten zeit sich ein. You see no deeper into the fact that a hundred sensations get compounded or known together by thinking that a 'soul' does the compounding than you see into a man's living eighty years by thinking of him as an octogenarian, or into our having five fingers by calling us pentadactyls. Souls have worn out both themselves and their

---

[1] " A Pluralistic Universe," p. 207.
[2] " Varieties of Religious Experience," 1902.

welcome, that is the plain truth. Philosophy ought to get the manifolds of experience unified on principles less empty. Like the word 'cause,' the word 'soul' is but a theoretic stop-gap—it marks a place and claims it for a future explanation to occupy."

"This being our post-humian and post-kantian state of mind, I will ask your permission to leave the soul wholly out of the present discussion and to consider only the residual dilemma. Some day, indeed, souls may get their innings again in philosophy—I am quite ready to admit that possibility—they form a category of thought too natural to the human mind to expire without prolonged resistance. But if the belief in the soul ever does come to life after the many funeral-discourses which humian and kantian criticism have preached over it, I am sure it will be only when some one has found in the term a pragmatic significance that has hitherto eluded observation."[1]

In spite of my profound admiration for William James, I am driven to exclaim—Could anything be more perverse! On one page he tells us that the only alternatives to the acceptance of the soul-theory are either to give up our belief in logic, or to declare that life is logically irrational.[2] On the next page he tells us that the conception of the soul is otiose, that it explains nothing, that it has no pragmatic significance and does not help us to any understanding. But surely, if any hypothesis is so logically necessary that its rejection must involve the rejection of our belief in the most fundamental logical principles, it is, *ipso facto*, justified, and bears the highest possible credentials. Has any scientific hypothesis any better justification, or can any better one be conceived? Why do we believe that the earth is round? Surely only because to deny it would involve the mistrust of logical reason! No one has directly perceived the earth as a round object. Why do we believe that the earth was at one time a fiery mass; that it is not now a hollow shell; or that the remote side of the moon, which no man has seen, is approximately spherical and is illuminated by the sun at new moon? Why do we believe in those "unrepresentable principles and substances," the ether, energy, magnetic force, electricity, atoms, electrons? These and many other things we believe in for the same good pragmatic reason, namely, that our intellect finds the conceptions of these things neces-

---

[1] "A Pluralistic Universe," p. 209.
[2] Surely these are but two ways of stating one alternative, the radical mistrust of the intellectual powers of the human race.

sary for the building up of the conceptual scheme of things by means of which we seek to render intelligible the facts of immediate experience. If we choose to resign our belief in man's powers of reason, we may believe in the flatness of the earth, in perpetual motion, in the existence of atoms of mind-stuff, in the compounding of consciousnesses, or in any other absurdity. "But I can take no comfort in such devices for making a luxury of intellectual defeat. They are but spiritual chloroform. Better live on the ragged edge, better gnaw the file forever!"[1] Or—as a less desperate alternative—retain a modest confidence in human reason, and accept the hypothesis of the soul!

In the passage quoted above (page 362), James places the notion of the soul on a level, as regards pragmatic significance, with the notion of causation. I am very willing to accept the classification; for no conception has proved of greater pragmatic value than that of cause. Wellnigh the whole of such superiority to savagery as our civilization can boast is due to our successful application of the conception of causation.

If James had belonged to that group of high and dry methodists who frown on all hypotheses, and teach that the function of science and philosophy is not to explain facts or render them intelligible, but merely to describe them with the utmost accuracy, his position would be comprehensible. But he explicitly demands explanation and intelligibility, and, in order to explain certain results of "psychical research," himself propounds the hypothesis of a cosmic reservoir of consciousness, or the existence in the universe of "a lot of diffuse mind-stuff, unable of itself to get into consistent personal form, or to take permanent possession of an organism and yet always craving to do so."[2]

I conclude, therefore, that the transmission theory, implying as it does the overthrow of human reason, encounters immense difficulties and gratuitously raises more problems than it solves, and that James' objections to the soul-theory were of the flimsiest, were in fact little more than the current prejudice in favour of that "psychology without a soul" to which, as he said, his whole psychological and Kantian education had committed him.[3]

---

[1] James, "Principles," vol. i. p. 179.

[2] Article on "Psychical Research," in the "American Magazine" for 1909, p. 588.

[3] It seems necessary to insist in this connexion that agreement with conclusions of "common sense" or even of scholastic philosophy does not in itself suffice to render an hypothesis absurd or untenable.

Those readers who prefer the soul-theory will perhaps bear with me a little longer, while I inquire how we may best conceive and describe the soul in the light of the empirical evidence now available.

First, let us see what negative assertions can be made with some confidence. We can say that the soul has not the essential attributes of matter, namely, extension (or the attribute of occupying space) and ponderability or mass; for if it had these attributes it would be subject to the laws of mechanism; and it is just because we have found that mental and vital processes cannot be completely described and explained in terms of mechanism that we are compelled to believe in the co-operation of some non-mechanical teleological factor, and to adopt the hypothesis of the soul.

The Scholastics and Cartesians have generally described the soul as an inextended immaterial substance. In doing so they meant not only to deny it the attributes of matter, which they defined as extended substance, but, in applying the term substance, they meant also to imply certain positive attributes, especially the attribute of permanence or indestructibility; and, curiously enough, they seemed to believe that, by applying this word substance in their description of the soul, they guaranteed the immortality of human personality. Now, it is hardly necessary to say that we cannot prove the immortality of the soul by this simple expedient. Nor can we accept the description of it as substance in the old scholastic sense of the word. In that old-fashioned sense of the word, substance denoted a core or substratum underlying and distinct from all the attributes of a thing; which substratum might in principle remain unchanged as the identical substance, though all its attributes were changed or stripped off it; a sort of inert lay figure that might be dressed up in many garments. That is a notion which pretty nearly all moderns are agreed to reject; for a thing can only be known through the effects or activities it exerts, and its capacities for exerting these effects are its attributes, and we can only conceive the thing as the sum of its attributes. But we may conceive the thing as possessing these capacities for action or influence, not only at the moments at which they are exerted, but also during periods in which they remain latent. A material thing or being is then a sum, not only, as J. S. Mill said, of " permanent possibilities of sensation," but also of enduring possibilities or capacities of definite kinds of action and reaction upon other material things.

In a similar way we may describe a soul as a sum of enduring capacities for thoughts, feelings, and efforts of determinate kinds. Since the word substance retains the flavour of so many controversial doctrines, we shall do well to avoid it as the name for any such sum of enduring capacities, and to use instead the word thing or being. We may then describe a soul as a being that possesses, or is, the sum of definite capacities for psychical activity and psycho-physical interaction, of which the most fundamental are (1) the capacity of producing, in response to certain physical stimuli (the sensory processes of the brain), the whole range of sensation qualities in their whole range of intensities; (2) the capacity of responding to certain sensation-complexes with the production of meanings, as, for example, spatial meanings; (3) the capacity of responding to these sensations and these meanings with feeling and conation or effort, under the spur of which further meanings may be brought to consciousness in accordance with the laws of reproduction of similars and of reasoning; (4) the capacity of reacting upon the brain-processes to modify their course in a way which we cannot clearly define, but which we may provisionally conceive as a process of guidance by which streams of nervous energy may be concentrated in a way that antagonizes the tendency of all physical energy to dissipation and degradation.

These are the fundamental capacities of conscious activity that we may assign to the soul, and we may say that in the laws or uniformities that we can discover in these processes we may discern the laws or the nature of the soul; and the view that the soul is this sum of psychical capacities we may express by saying that the soul is a psychic being.

The Cartesians described the soul as a thinking being, using thinking (cogitatio) as the most inclusive term for what in modern terminology we call being conscious. But we cannot accept this description without reservation. Our evidence at present allows us to say only that the soul thinks or is conscious (realizes its capacities or potentialities) when interacting with some bodily organism; psycho-physical interaction may be, for all we know, a necessary condition of all consciousness. For all the thinking or consciousness of which we have positive knowledge is of embodied minds or souls; and a great mass of evidence goes to show that whatever prevents the body from playing its part in this process of psycho-physical interaction arrests the flow of consciousness, i.e. brings the soul's activities also to rest, at least so far as they are conscious activities. Rather than say that the soul is a thinking being, we must then say that it is a being capable of being stimulated to conscious activities through the agency of the body or brain with which it stands in relations of reciprocal influence.

Further, we must maintain that the soul is in some sense a unitary being or entity distinct from all others; for we found that prominent among the facts which compel us to accept the animistic hypothesis are the facts of psychical individuality, the fact that consciousness, as known to us, occurs only as individual coherent streams of personal consciousness, and all the facts summed up in the phrase "the unity of consciousness." We found that these facts remain absolutely unintelligible, unless we postulate some ground of this unity and coherence and separateness of individual streams of consciousness, some ground other than the bodily organisation.

This conclusion seems to rule out the notion that the soul of man or of any complex organism may be compounded of the souls of lesser organisms, or of the cells of which the body is made up. But it does not rule out the possibility that more than one psychic being may be associated with one bodily organism. It may be that the soul that thinks in each of us is but the chief of a hierarchy of similar beings,[1] and that this one alone, owing to the favourable position it occupies (I do not mean spatial position), is able to actualize in any full measure its capacities for conscious activity; and it may be that, if the subordinated beings exercise in any degree their psychic capacities, the chief soul is able, by a direct or telepathic action, to utilize and in some measure control their activities. We may see in this possibility the explanation of those strange and bizarre phenomena which have been so zealously studied in recent years under the head of secondary or dual personality, and which constitute evidence that has seemed to many to justify the notion of a division or splitting of the mind of a human being into two minds.[2] The animistic hypothesis

---

[1] I remind the reader of the metaphysical doctrine (of Leibnitz, Lotze, and others) that the body is in its real nature an organized system of beings of like nature with the soul.

[2] The cases of alternating personality are not in question here, but only the rarer cases of seemingly concurrent dual personality or co-consciousness. Almost all those who have treated of these cases have started out from the assumption that, if the two streams of consciousness and mental activity coexist,

may seek to explain also in this way the fact that the bodily organism of certain animals may be divided into two or more parts, each of which continues to lead indefinitely an independent

they must be regarded as formed by the splitting of the normal stream of consciousness; the uncritical acceptance of this assumption renders these writers incapable of impartially weighing the evidence. Now, if we examine the very full and careful description of one of the most striking of these cases, that of Sally Beauchamp ("The Dissociation of a Personality," by Dr Morton Prince, London, 1906), we find that there were two or more alternating personalities, both of which were continuous with the original normal personality, and by the synthesis or combination of the memories of which the normal personality was restored. These alternating personalities may, therefore, properly be regarded as formed, not by the splitting of the normal stream of consciousness, but by the alternation of two phases of the empirical self, or of the organic basis of personal consciousness, each of which brings back to consciousness only memories of experiences enjoyed during former periods of its dominance.

But the most striking feature of the case was the existence of a personality (Sally by name) which dominated and controlled the whole organism at times, and claimed to be conscious, though incapable of expressing herself (save in a fragmentary manner) in bodily movement, during the periods of dominance of the other personalities. This claim was supported (1) by the fact that Sally seemed to have knowledge of all or most of the experiences, even the dreams, reflections, and emotions of the other personalities; claiming to become aware of them in some immediate fashion, though regarding them always as not her own experiences, but as those of the other personalities; (2) by the fact that during the dominance of these others, involuntary, forced, or automatic movements, sometimes speech or writing, expressing the personality of Sally, were sometimes made by the bodily organs; which movements Sally claimed to have willed, when afterwards she came into full control; (3) by the fact that the other personalities were liable to unaccountable inhibitions of the will, which also Sally claimed to have effected in some direct fashion.

Now the point I wish to insist upon is this: there is in the whole very full account no evidence to support the view that Sally, the seemingly co-conscious personality, resulted from the division of the normal personality. Rather there is positive evidence that she was not so formed; she claimed to have existed before the time of the emotional shock which led to the alternation of phases of the original personality, and (what is more important), when the normal personality was restored, this was effected by the recombination of the alternating phases, and there was no indication that Sally was in any sense synthesized within this normal and complete personality; rather she gave indications from time to time of her continuance in a repressed and relatively inactive condition.

I would put alongside this fact the following remarks of Prof. Pierre Janet, who has had a very large experience of cases of this type, and to whose statements great weight must be assigned. After expressing the opinion ("L'Automatisme psychologique," p. 343) that, if in such cases of co-consciousness as he describes a complete cure were effected, the normal personality would regain the memories of the co-conscious secondary personality, he adds, "I ought to say that I have never observed this return of the memory, and that this opinion is founded upon the examination of my schematic diagram and upon reasoning rather than upon experience. . . . *I have never seen these hysterical persons recover after their apparent cure the memory of their second existences.*" And he adds that he sup-

existence and develops all the parts and functions of the complete organism. For we may hold that, as Lotze wrote, "Section would have cleft in two, not the soul of the polyp, but the corporeal bond that held together a number of souls, so as to hinder the individual development of each."[1]

The unity of the soul does not necessarily imply that all impressions made upon it and all its activities must be combined in the stream of personal consciousness. It remains open to us to suppose that, as Prof. Pierre Janet maintains, the bringing together or synthesizing of many impressions in the unitary field of attentive self-consciousness is only effected by the expenditure of psychical energy, the available quantity of which varies from time to time, and that the quantity of this energy is deficient in those states of "psychical poverty" (la misère psychologique)[2] characterized by sub-conscious mental activities of an abnormal kind.[3]

We may, then, suppose that abnormal conditions of two distinct types are commonly confused together under the head of co-consciousness or subconscious activity. In the one type (of which Sally Beauchamp remains the best example) the co-conscious activities become so highly developed and organized that we cannot refuse to recognize them as the activities of an independent synthetic centre, a numerically distinct psychic being, which, owing to insufficient energy of control of the normally dominant

---

poses, therefore, that, though they seemed cured to his experienced eye, they were nevertheless not completely cured.

I submit, therefore, that we have no sufficient ground for the assumption that the co-conscious personality is formed by splitting off from the normal personality, that rather the facts justify the view that they are radically distinct. The facts may, therefore, be reconciled with the Animistic hypothesis by assuming that a normally subordinate psychic being obtains through the weakening of the control of the normally dominant soul an opportunity for exercising and developing its potentialities in an unusual degree.

[1] "Microcosmus" (Eng. trans.), vol. i. p. 154.
[2] *Op. cit.*, p. 444.
[3] "Comme le disaient les anciens philosophes, être c'est agir et créer, et la conscience, qui est au suprême degré une réalité, est par là même une activité agissante. Cette activité, si nous cherchons à nous représenter sa nature, est avant tout une activité de synthèse qui réunit des phénomènes donnés plus ou moins nombreux en un phénomène nouveau différent des éléments. C'est là une véritable création, car, à quelque point de vue que l'on se place, la multiplicite ne contient pas la raison de l'unité, et l'acte par lequel des éléments hétérogènes sont réunis dans une forme nouvelle n'est pas donné dans les éléments. . . La conscience est donc bien par elle-même, dès ses débuts, une activité de synthèse" (*op. cit.*, p. 484).

centre, escapes from its position of subordination and repression, and, not without a prolonged struggle,[1] actualizes and develops in an abnormal degree its latent capacities. In the other type we have to do with a mere insufficiency of synthetic energy of the one centre, from which results a temporary narrowing of the field of attentive consciousness, and the automatic or semi-mechanical functioning of parts of the psycho-physical organization. Into this class would fall all or most of the cases of functional anæsthesia and most of the instances of post-hypnotic obedience to suggestion in spite of lack of all conscious memory of the nature of the suggestion given.

The capacities and functions enumerated above seem to me the minimum that can be attributed to the soul. If we assign it these, while denying it any share in memory (regarding all mental retention as conditioned by the nervous system), we have a peculiar view of the soul, which might be concisely expressed by saying that the soul conditions the forms of mental activity, while the bodily processes (through the senses and the mechanically associated memory-traces of the brain) supply the content of consciousness. According to this view [2] the soul is to be regarded as

---

[1] The feature of the Beauchamp case which most strongly supports this view is, perhaps, the occurrence of sustained and seemingly very real conflicts of will between Sally and the alternating phases of Miss B.'s personality; these, if we accept the description given (and it is perhaps permissible to say here that the good faith and scientific competence of the reporter of the case are indisputable), were no mere conflicts of opposed impulses, such as anyone of us may experience, but conflicts of the volitions of two organized and very different personalities. Another fact brought out clearly in the description of this case, one very difficult to reconcile with the view that Sally was merely a fragment of the normal personality, is that Sally's memory was more comprehensive than that of the normal personality, since it included all or most of the latter's experiences as well as her own. Now, in what manner or under what form Sally became aware of the thoughts and emotions of Miss B. remains one of the obscurest and most interesting of the problems presented by this and similar cases. For Sally seemed to become directly aware of these thoughts and emotions and yet to know them as Miss B.'s, and to regard them in a very objective manner. I may say that, thanks to the kindness of Dr Morton Prince, I have had the opportunity of closely questioning upon this point a secondary personality very similar to Sally, and, though she seemed highly intelligent and willing to reply to the best of her ability, it was impossible to obtain any light on this problem. I have discussed the case of Sally at more length in the Proc. S. P. R., vol. xix.

[2] This is the view sympathetically presented, if not actually accepted, in James' "Principles of Psychology" and defended by myself in my "Primer of Physiological Psychology." James, after expounding the laws of association and reproduction, wrote, "The schematism we have used is, moreover, taken immediately from the analysis of objects with their elementary parts, and only extended

undergoing no development in the course of the individual's life. Rather, the soul is a system of capacities which are fully present as latent potentialities from the beginning of the individual's life; and these potentialities are realized or brought into play only in proportion as the brain-mechanisms became developed and specialized. The mental differences exhibited by any person at different stages of his life would thus be wholly due to the developmental and degenerative changes of his brain-structure. And it would follow also that the mental differences between one person and another may be, and presumably are, wholly conditioned by differences of brain-structure. It would follow also that just as we should have to conceive the soul of any human being as an unchanging system of potentialities at all stages of the individual life, mental development being purely development of the bodily mechanisms by which the psychical potentialities are brought more fully into play, so we might conceive the mental differences between man and animals of all levels as wholly due to differences of kind and degree of bodily organization; the souls of all animals, from the lowliest upward to man, would have the same potentialities, and these potentialities would be actualized in proportion to the degree of evolution of the bodily organization. Mental evolution would thus be regarded as consisting wholly in progressive evolution of bodily organization; a view which is implied also in the "transmission theory" of James and Bergson.[1]

---

by analogy to the brain. And yet it is only as incorporated in the brain that such a schematism can represent anything *causal*. This is, to my mind, the conclusive reason for saying that the order of *presentation of the mind's materials* is due to cerebral physiology alone. . . . The *effects of interested attention and volition* remain. These activities seem to hold fast to certain elements, and by emphasizing them and dwelling on them, to make their associates the only ones which are evolved. *This* is the point at which an anti-mechanical psychology must, if anywhere, make its stand in dealing with association. Everything else is pretty certainly due to cerebral laws " (" Principles," i. p. 594).

And again he wrote: "The soul *presents* nothing herself; *creates* nothing; is at the mercy of the material forces for all *possibilities*; but amongst these possibilities she selects, and by reinforcing one and checking others, she figures not as an 'epiphenomenon,' but as something from which the play gets moral support" (*op. cit.*, ii. p. 584). That this view is not consistent with James's transmission theory and later utterances seems to me clear.

[1] Lotze expressed himself as follows on this view of the essential similarity of all souls: "What causes determine the various levels of development reached by the various races of animated beings? Now here it was a possible opinion that all souls are homogeneous in nature, and that the combined influence of all external conditions, as well those whose seat is the organization of the body

This view of the soul would satisfy all the empirical evidence, except that which points to "memory" as being, in part at least, immaterially conditioned. But, though this view is compatible with the belief that the soul survives the death of the body, and even with a belief in its immortality, it signally fails to satisfy those demands of our moral and æsthetic nature which have in all ages inclined the mass of men to believe in the life-after-death. In accordance with these demands the popular view has always held that all "memory," all mental retention and reproduction, all mental and moral growth, is rooted in the soul, that, in short, the soul is the bearer of all that is essential to the developed personality of each man. For the demand for a future life has two principal sources (beyond the promptings of personal affection and the mere personal dislike of the prospect of extinction), namely, the desire that the injustices of this life may be in some way made good, and the hope that those highest products of evolution, the personalities built up by long sustained moral and intellectual effort, shall not wholly pass away at the death of the body. And the survival of a soul which bears nothing of that which distinguishes one personality from another, one which bears no marks of the experiences it has undergone in its embodied life, and enjoys no continuity of personal memory, would satisfy neither this desire nor this hope. But the popular view, though it has been maintained in modern times by Lotze, a philosopher of the first rank, cannot be reconciled with the fact that the make-up of human personality includes many habits that are unquestionably rooted in the structure of the nervous system. It conflicts also with all the large mass of evidence which indicates the dependence of all the sensory content of consciousness, all sensation and all imagery on the integrity of the brain.

If we accept the hypothesis of the dual conditions of memory set forth and defended in Chapter XXIV., we are led by it to a conception of the soul intermediate between these two extreme views, that on the one hand which denies to the soul all develop-

---

as those which supply the seat and issues of life, is the cause of the definite psychical development of each species, in one case of the inferiority of the animal kingdom, in the other of the superiority of human civilization. We did not feel ourselves justified in decidedly rejecting this opinion; on the contrary, one cannot help following its attempts at explanation with interest, for undoubtedly they are to a great extent justified" ("Microcosmus," Eng. trans., i. p. 643).

ment and therefore all that constitutes personality, and on the other hand that popular view which ascribes all development of mental power and character to the persistence of psychical modifications. For though, according to that hypothesis, all habits belong to the body, the soul does undergo a real development, an enrichment of its capacities; and, though it is not possible to say just how much of what we call personality is rooted in bodily habit and how much in psychical dispositions,[1] yet it is open to us to believe that the soul, if it survives the dissolution of the body, carries with it some large part of that which has been gained by intellectual and moral effort; and though the acceptance of the view we have suggested as to the essential part played by the body in conditioning the sensory content of consciousness, would make it impossible to suppose that the surviving soul could enjoy the exercise of thought of the kind with which alone we are familiar, yet it is not inconceivable that it might find conditions that would stimulate it to imageless thought (possibly conditions of direct or telepathic communication with other minds) or might find under other conditions (possibly in association with some other bodily organism) a sphere for the application and actualization of the capacities developed in it during its life in the body.[2]

Before bringing this long inquiry to an end, it is necessary to touch on the very obscure and difficult problem of the part played by the soul in the development of the body and the control of the organic functions. We have seen that many of the thinkers of earlier ages regarded chiefly these biological functions in considering the nature and activities of the soul; and we have seen that there has appeared and on the whole has increasingly predominated a tendency to separate these from the distinctively mental functions, and to ascribe the vital and the mental functions to distinct principles, to the soul and to the spirit respectively, or to the vital force and to the soul or mind. Among those modern writers who have continued to accept the notion of the soul, this tendency has culminated in the view, first definitely

---

[1] It must be admitted that the distinction appears especially difficult on the side of the volitional and emotional developments of personality.

[2] I venture to throw out to those who are interested in the problems of "psychical research" the suggestion that in this line of thought may be found the explanation of the fragmentariness, the seeming triviality, and the inconsistencies of so many of those "automatic movements" which claim to be expressions of surviving personalities, defects which are generally felt to be a serious difficulty in the way of accepting these expressions as what they claim to be.

propounded by Descartes and in more recent times best represented by Lotze, which regards all bodily processes, except those of the central nervous system, as wholly withdrawn from direct psychical influences, and as governed by purely mechanical principles.

But we cannot accept this position, for we have found reason to believe (Chapter XVI.) that the bodily processes, especially those of growth and repair, are not susceptible of purely mechanical explanation. If, then, we deny to the soul or thinking principle all part in these bodily processes, we shall have to postulate some second and distinct teleological factor operative in organisms. The principle of economy of hypothesis, therefore, directs us to attempt to conceive that the soul may be operative in the guidance of bodily growth, either directly or by means of a general control exercised by it over some system of subordinate psychic agents.

Lotze rejected the view we are considering for two reasons: first, because in the adult human being all the direct interactions of soul and body seem to be confined to certain parts of the brain; secondly, because we are not normally conscious of exercising any control over the body, otherwise than in the production of voluntary movements through the contractions of the skeletal muscles. These objections may be partially answered or diminished by the following considerations. The lowliest animal organisms exhibit no specialization of organs and tissues; and whatever psychic powers they enjoy must be exercised equally in or through and upon all parts of the body; and it is not until in ascending the evolutionary scale we come upon animals of very considerable complexity, that we find a centralized nervous system which we must suppose to be the organ specially concerned in psycho-physical interactions. And even in the vertebrate phylum we find good reason for believing that in the lower members the psychical functions are distributed throughout all parts of the central nervous system, at least, and that only gradually, with the increasing specialization of the brain, do they become more and more restricted to its higher levels.

It is, then, reasonable to believe that in this respect, as in so many others, the human and higher animal organisms recapitulate in their individual development the history of the evolution of the race. If we take this view, we may believe that in the early stages of bodily development, during which the main lines of the bodily structure are laid down, the direct influence of the soul makes itself felt throughout all parts of the body as a controlling power, and that only gradually, as the specialization of the tissues progresses, it becomes circumscribed and confined to higher levels of the central nervous system. These psychic operations of embryonic life may well be in some sense conscious; but we can hardly expect to have any power of recollecting them, seeing that we consciously remember little or nothing of the experiences of early childhood, although in those early years we make a greater volume of acquisitions than in any later period. And we must not forget that, even when the early years are past, and all the bodily organs have been developed to their full size, our mental life still exercises a very considerable influence upon the bodily form, moulding our features and, to a less extent, our general structure and bearing to the more adequate expression of our characters.

It is in harmony with this view that the lower vertebrates, when deprived of the brain, exhibit more spontaneity and adaptability of movement than the higher members of the group; that the lower animals exhibit a much greater power of repair and regeneration after injury or ablation of parts of their bodies, a power which is reduced to its minimum in man; and that in every species this power of repair and of rectification of disturbances of the normal growth of the body seems to be greater, the earlier the stage of development at which such disturbances are inflicted.

To the other objection to the notion of control of growth by psychical influences, namely, that we are not conscious of exerting any such control, no great importance can be attached in view of the modern demonstrations of the large range and scope of subconscious processes, processes which imply intelligence and yet find no expression in consciousness that can be introspectively seized. Lotze himself recognized in several connexions the necessity of postulating psychical activities that remain unconscious or subconscious, though forming essential links in the chain of psychical process. And, since he wrote, evidence of the great extent of such processes has accumulated rapidly. The clearest of such evidence is perhaps that afforded by automatic speech and writing; but every successful experiment in post-hypnotic suggestion affords similar evidence. Successful therapeutic suggestions and others that effect definite tissue changes are especially significant in the present connexion; for in all such cases we have definite evidence of control of bodily processes which, though unconsciously effected, must be regarded as psychical. Of the limits of this power of mental control over the organic processes of the body we are altogether ignorant, and new evidence, much of it ill-reported and therefore valueless, but much of it above suspicion, repeatedly warns us against setting up any arbitrary limit to what may be effected in this way.

The view that the soul, even in the human adult, may exercise extensive vegetative functions finds some support in the following considerations. All routine bodily functions may be regarded as habits or as closely allied in nature to habits. And, if there is any truth in what was said above as to the psychical control of the growth of the embryo, we may regard each routine function of the body as originally acquired and fixed, like the motor habit of the skeletal system, under conscious psychical guidance. Now, though our motor habits or secondarily automatic movements undoubtedly imply the existence of well-organized systems of neurones, there is some ground for saying that they never become purely mechanical processes, but that rather they always retain something of the character of psycho-physical processes. For, first, they are initiated, controlled, and sustained by volition; even so thoroughly ingrained a habit as the movements of the legs in walking continues (as was pointed out in Chapter XXIII.) not merely as the repetition of a self-sustaining mechanical sequence, but in virtue of the intention or volition to walk, which continues to be effective, even when the attention is wholly withdrawn from the process. Secondly, the least disturbance or obstruction of a habitual movement causes the process to spring back into full consciousness, thereby showing that the soul has, as it were, its hand upon the process, ready at any moment to intervene and consciously effect the adjustment of the process required by the unusual situation; at the least we feel, however obscurely, an impulse, an unrest, until the obstruction is overcome or the adjustment achieved.

The same is obviously true of those old racial habits by which our organic life is so largely regulated, e.g. our respiratory movements. Of these movements, so long as they go on gently and smoothly, we remain unconscious; they seem to be purely mechanical. But let there arise any obstruction or mal-adjustment of the processes, and we become acutely aware of them; they become conscious and distinctly volitional processes; and if the obstruction is serious, as in an attack of asthma, our whole psychical activity becomes concentrated in the effort to maintain and reinforce the process, to the almost complete exclusion from consciousness of all other things. In this respect, then, these processes closely resemble our secondarily automatic movements; and there is nothing fanciful or improbable in the view that, like these, they are habits which have been built up under psychical guidance, but at an early period of life of which no recollection is possible. These organic hereditary habits form, then, a link which connects the habits, of whose formation under psychical guidance we retain a distinct memory, with other routine processes of the body, the acquirement of which we cannot recollect; and analogy justifies us in maintaining the possibility that these also have not been established without psychical control.[1] Biologically regarded, the function of mind is the effecting of new adjustments of the bodily processes; consciousness plays its part only in the process of adjustment, and the more completely the adjustment is effected, the more completely is the process withdrawn from consciousness; hence the routine processes of our bodies normally find but very obscure expression in consciousness, contributing only to that vague background which is usually called the *coenæsthesia*.

An alternative to this view would consist in adopting the conception that each complex organism comprises (or consists of) a system of psychic beings of like nature with the soul, but subordinated to it; it might then be held that each such being is a centre of a partially independent psychical control of some part of the organic processes.

Lastly, I would maintain that if the soul is to be taken seriously as a scientific hypothesis, we shall have to face the question of its part in heredity and of its place in the scheme of organic evolution. I do not propose to attempt any speculation on these extremely difficult and obscure problems, but merely to point to them as rising above the scientific horizon. We

---

[1] It should be remembered also in this connexion that in many of the lower animals instinctive behaviour is so intimately interwoven with processes of structural development and modification, that it is impossible to draw any sharp line between them. As a single illustration of the facts I have in mind, I remind the reader of the process of "autotomy" observed among various species of arthropods; this consists in shedding a limb or appendage by means of violent muscular action.

have found reason to believe that the germ-cell, by the growth and repeated division of which the body of each organism is generated, cannot contain material dispositions that shall suffice to determine in purely mechanical fashion the course of the development of the complex organism with all its myriad specific characters and its personal and family peculiarities. How is the teleological immaterial factor, which we are driven to conceive as controlling the development, related to the parent forms, each of which contributes its share to the determination of the nature of the new organism? In face of this tremendous problem, I will only say that to me it seems easier to believe that two souls may somehow co-operate in giving origin to a new one, than that two machines of incredible complexity and delicacy of constitution should combine (in the fusion of male and female germ-plasms) to form a new one, in which half the parts of the one parent machine become intricately combined by a purely mechanical process with half the parts of the other in a structure which minutely reproduces the essential features common to both, as well as many of the individual peculiarities of either one.

As regards the evolutionary problem, I would say that, if heredity is conditioned, not mechanically by the mere structure of the germ-plasm, but by the teleological principle, it follows that the factors which have produced the evolution of species must have operated on and through this principle. Is it possible that the phrase "the soul of a race" is something more than a metaphor? That all that wonderful stability in complexity combined with gradual change through the ages, which Weismann attributes to the hypothetical germ-plasm, is in reality the attribute of an enduring psychic existent of which the lives of individual organisms are but successive manifestations.[1] However the

---

[1] Its recognition of the continuity of all life is the great merit of Prof. Bergson's theory of creative evolution; its failure to give any intelligible account of individuality is its greatest defect. I venture to think that the most urgent problem confronting the philosophic biologist is the construction of a theory of life which will harmonise the facts of individuality with the appearance of the continuity of all life, with the theory of progressive evolution, and with the facts of heredity and bi-parental reproduction. By conceiving the animating principle of each organism as but relatively individual, as a bud from the tree of life, all of whose parts draw their energies from a common stem and root, it seems possible dimly to foreshadow a synthesis of the Animism of James and Bergson with the hypothesis discussed in these concluding paragraphs. To any reader familiar with the works of Samuel Butler it will be apparent that the conception which I am attempting vaguely to foreshadow is allied to the biological doctrines

continuity of psychical constitution of succeeding generations of a species, a stock, or a family is maintained, it seems not improbable that the experience of each generation modifies in some degree the psychic constitution of its successors. The Neo-Darwinians have denied that any such modification takes place, chiefly because it seems impossible that such experiences should impress themselves upon the structure of the germ-plasm. But if the structure of the germ-plasm is not the only link between the generations, this positive objection to the Lamarckian principle disappears; and we are free to accept the mass of evidence which points to some partial transmission of the effects of experience. Such modification of the hereditary basis would be least in respect of those characters which have long been established in the race and are least susceptible to modification in the individual by psycho-physical activities; among these would be all the specific bodily characters and all the fundamental forms of psychical activity. It would be greatest in respect to those more recently acquired mental characters which are the peculiar property of man; and it is just these characters, such as mathematical, musical, and other artistic talents, and the capacity for sustained intellectual and moral effort, that seem to exhibit the clearest indications of the effects of experience and of psychical effort, cumulative from generation to generation.

I will illustrate the conception of the evolutionary process that I have in mind by reference to a single psychical capacity, namely, our capacity of spatial apprehension. Whether or no space and spatial relations be objectively real, it seems to me quite indisputable that Kant and Lotze (among many others) were in the right in regarding the capacity of spatial apprehension as an innate power of the mind, which awaits only the touch of experience to bring it into operation. Space in the terminology used in these pages, is a meaning rooted in an enduring psychical disposition,[1] a disposition which, like others that we are

---

of his earlier works, but not to the Hylozoism to which he inclined in his later years.

[1] It has been argued in Chapter XXI. that no system of neural elements, however complex, can be the sufficient ground of the capacity of spatial conception. But, even if we put aside those objections and adopted Herbert Spencer's view of the conditions of spatial conception as some immensely complex inherited system of associated nerve-cells, the impossibility of this view would force itself upon us again when we sought to conceive how this enormously complex system could be hereditarily transmitted by means of the structure of the germ-plasm.

constantly building up and extending as experience enriches the meanings that we have made our own, has been elaborated and fixed by the experience of countless generations, but which nevertheless may be capable of still further development.

According to this view then, not only conscious thinking, but also morphogenesis, heredity, and evolution, are psycho-physical processes. All alike are conditioned and governed by psychical dispositions that have been built up in the course of the experience of the race. So long as the psycho-physical processes in which they play their part proceed smoothly in the routine fashion proper to the species, they go on unconsciously or subconsciously. But whenever the circumstances of the organism demand new and more specialized adjustment of response, their smooth automatic working is disturbed, the corresponding meanings are brought to consciousness and by conscious perception and thinking and striving the required adjustment is effected.

INDEX

Abiogenesis, 233
"Actuelle Seele," 135, 357
Æsthetic feeling, 315, 331
Albertus Magnus, 33
Alcmæon, 37
Alexander of Aphrodisias, 33
Alogical arguments for Monism, 144
Amœba, 258
Anaxagoras, 15
Anaximenes, 12
Animal behaviour, 319
Animatism, 4
Animism, leading representatives, 204
——— compatible with Monism, 192
———, four types of, 357
Apollo, cult of, 11
Aquinas, 33, 35
Aristotle, 20
Arrhenius on origin of life, 231
Association-psychology, 110, 282, 301
Augustine, 32
Automatism, secondary, 276
Automaton theories, 126
Avenarius, 180
Averroes, 33

Bain, Alex., 84
Balaban on memory, 337
Baldwin, J. M., on organic selection, 249
Bateson, W., 250
Beauchamp, Sally, 367, 369
Bechterew, 130, 355
Bell, Sir C., 105
Beneke, 82
Bergson, H., 84
——— on Neo-Darwinism, 248
——— on intellect, 221
——— on memory, 333
———, his psycho-physic, 358
Berkeley, Bishop, 64, 69, 71, 181
Binet, A., on memory, 336
Binocular vision, 289
Biology and physics, 216
Biran, Maine de, 83
Blindness, functional, 291, 351
Blumenbach, 81
Boerhave, 97
Bohn, G. B., 259
Borelli, 97
Boyle, 89
Bradley, F. H., 85
Bramwell, Milne, 353
Bruno, Giordano, 38
Büchner, L., 98

Busse, L., 83, 268
Bufler, Samuel, on heredity, 247

Cabanis, 83
Capitulation of philosophy to physics, 190
Carpenter, W. B., 287
Causation and teleology, 176
Charles, R. H., on Hebrew beliefs, 7, 30
Christian theology and *pneuma*, 28
Clifford, W. K., 91, 136
Co-consciousness, 366
———, two types of, 368
Cold and heat, 217
Comte, 84
Conation and guidance, 279
——— and persistence, 326
Condillac, 74
Composite mind, 116
Compounding of consciousness, 169
Conservation of energy, 92
——— ——— not an axiom, 216
Continuity of evolution, 142, 320
——— of neural process, 217
Corresponding points, 289
Crawley, E. A., 4
Creative reason of Aristotle, 23
"Creative synthesis," 307
Crookes, Sir W., on life, 253
Cross-correspondences, 349
Curiosity, instinct of, 266

Dæmons, 10
Darwin, Charles, 119
———, Francis, 246
Deism, 89
De la Mettrie, 94
Delbœuf, 353
Delphic oracle, 10
Democritus, 15
Descartes, 49
Diogenes, 12
Dionysiac cult, 11
Discontinuous variation, 250
Dissipation of energy in organisms, 245
Dissociation, mental, 118
"Divine Assistance," doctrine of, 34
Double aspect, limited truth of, 219
Douglas, A. H., 39
Driesch, H., 81, 268
——— on restitution, 241
——— on non-mechanical agency, 214
Dualism of philosophy and science, 189

Ebbinghaus, H., on unity of consciousness, 281

Ebbinghaus, H., on memory, 332
Eidola, 16
Eleusinian mysteries, 11
Elysian fields, 9
Embryology and mechanism, 241
Empedocles, 15
Energetics, 130
Epicurus, 26
Epigenesis, 77
Epiphenomenalism, 126
—— examined, 149
Evolution, psycho-physics of, 377
—— of spacial perception, 378

FECHNER, G. T., 80, 137
—— on day-view, 142
—— on psycho-physical continuity, 294
—— on future life, 195
Feeling-tone, 313
—— and Darwinism, 324
Flournoy, Th., 118
Foster, Sir M., 45
Freud, S., 327
Fusion of sensations, 292, 299
Future life and Parallelism, 197
—— and morality, 203
—— and soul-theory, 372

GALEN, 37
Galileo, 47
Gall, 101
Gassendi, 47
Geulincx, 53
Ghost-soul, 3
God, a mechanical, 191
Gregory of Nyassa, 32
Guidance without work, 212

HABIT, law of, 110
—— and memory, 333
Hades, 8
Haldane, J. S., on mechanism, 190, 236
Haller, 9, 97, 100
Hamilton, Sir W., 84
Hanna, Mr, case of, 345
Hartley, 84, 110
Harvey, W., 49, 96
Hartmann, Ed. von, 117, 288
Head, H., 265
Hebrew Animism, 7
Hegel, 79
Helmholtz, von, 92
Helmont, van, 44, 96
Heraclitus, 13
Herbart, J. F., 81
Hering, E., on heredity, 247
Heredity, psycho-physics of, 377
Hesiod's golden age, 10
Hobbes, 59
Hodgson, Shadworth, 85, 127
Hoernlé, R. F. A., 304
Höffding, H., on Middle Ages, 28
—— on Spinoza, 59
Holbach, 74, 95

Homeric Animism, 8
Hume, 67, 71
Huxley, T. H., 110, 127, 151
Hylozoism in Greece, 15
Hypnotism, 351
Hypothesis, function of, 218

IDEALISM and materialism, 151
—— and psycho-physics, 179
Identity hypothesis, 132, 133
Immaterial substance, 32
Immortality, Greek, 11
——, collective, 40
Individuality, 163
Infra-consciousness, 172
Instinct in man, 264
Instinctive action, 262
Interaction, inconceivability of, 206, 209
Introjection, 180
Ionian philosophers, 12

JAMES, W., 85
—— on feeling, 322
—— on psychic fringe, 302
—— on transmission-theory, 358
—— on soul-theory, 370
Janet, Pierre, on dual personality, 367
Jennings, H., 259
Jerome, St, 29
Jones, E. C., 184
Joule, 92

KANT, 74
——, definition of soul, 75
—— and parallelism, 76
—— on immortality, 348, 198
——, dualism of, 183
—— on moral consciousness, 200
—— on interaction, 207
——, problem not solved by, 182
—— on inner sense, 159
Kayans, 2, 343
Keatinge, W. M., 343
Kelvin, 90, 231, 253
Kepler, 47
Knowledge and immediate awareness, 222
Kries, J. von, on memory, 332
Külpe, O., 83

LADD, G. T., 85
Lamarck, 119
Lamarckism, 246
Lang, A., 4
Lange, F. A., 26, 37, 151
—— on idealism, 184
Laplace, 90
Larmor, Sir J., 253
Leibnitz, 53
Lens of Triton regenerates, 240
Lewes, G. H., on Ionians, 12, 15
—— on psychical unity, 288
Lloyd Morgan, 120, 142, 249
Localisation of cerebral functions, 102
Locke, 61

INDEX

Locus of psychical action, 226
Lodge, Sir O., on life, 253
Loeb, J., on tropism, 259
Logic and mechanism, 175
Lotze, R. H., 82, 101
—— on interaction, 207
—— on seat of soul, 300
—— —— of interaction, 225
—— on atomism, 284
—— on unity of consciousness, 285
—— on animal division, 368
Lucretius, 36
—— and adaptation, 37

MACH, E., on mechanism, 88, 211
—— on incompleteness, 193
Machines and organisms, 244
Malebranche, 53
Mallock, W. H., 189
Marett, R. R., 4
Marshall, H. R., on feeling, 322
Materialism, Greek, 16, 59, 98, 129
——, advantages of, 144
Maxwell, Clerk, 211, 253
Mayer, R., 92
M'Gilvary, E. B., 357
M'Intyre, J. L., 42
Meaning, 175, 269, 303, 305
—— and sensation, 310
Medium of composition, 287
Memory and brain traces, 115, 330
Mendelism, 250
Mental chemistry, 282
Mercier, C., 91
Merz, T., 80, 90
—— on vitalism, 252
Meyer, M., on feeling, 323
Metaphysics and Animism, 124
Mill, J. S., 84, 282
Mind-stuff, 136
Mitchell, T. W., 353
Mohamedan philosophy, 33
Moleschott, 98
Monism, verbal solution by, 193
Monopsychism, 39
Montaigne, 41
Montesquieu, 74
Morgan, T. H., 240
Morphogenesis and mechanism, 240
Mozart, 315
Müller, G. E., 333
Müller, Joh., 98
Multiple personality, 300, 345
Münsterberg, H., 155, 201
Mutation, 250
Myers, F. W. H., 85
Mysticism, 361

NATORP on Plato, 19
Neo-Darwinism, 119, 234, 246
Neo-Platonism, 29
Neo-Vitalism, 252
Neural association, 339

Newton, 89
Nunn, P., 215

OBJECTS of higher orders, 316
Occasionalism, 53
Organic selection, 249, 254
Orphic cult, 11
Ostwald, W., 130

PAIN, 312
Pantheism, Stoic, 26
Paracelsus, 38
Paradox of Fechner, 291
Parallelism, psycho-physical, 131
—— implies Pantheism, 194
——, leading exponents of, 204
—— examined, 155
——, phenomenalistic, 132
Paramœcium, 258
Paul, St, on soul, 30
Paulsen, F., 134, 145
—— on Kant, 75
—— on future life, 200
—— on possibilities, 223
Pearson, K., 88
Peckham, Dr and Mrs, 262
Persistent effort, 270
Personality, dual, 366
Philo, 30
Physical, definition of, 217
—— science still developing, 216
Physicists on life, 253
Physiology founded, 44
—— and mechanism, 236
Plasticity of nerve, 275
Plato, 17
Pleasure and association, 320
Plotinus, 31
Pneuma, 26, 28, 30
Podmore, F., 350
Pollock, Sir F., on Spinoza, 159
Pomponazzi, 39
Pontifical cell, 288
Post-Homeric Animism, 10
Post-Kantians, three groups of, 183
Poynting on guidance, 212, 253
Pre-established harmony, 55
Pre-existence, 36
Priestley, 89
Primitive Animism, 1
Prince, Morton, 367
Protagoras, 16
Protozoa, behaviour of, 258
Psyche and pneuma, 28
Psychic fringe, 302
Psychical fusion, 297
—— monism, 133
—— —— examined, 160
—— poverty, 368
Psycho-neural correlation, 116
Psycho-physical interaction, 228
—— —— continuity, 294
Pythagoras, 14

RATIONALISM, dogmatic, 74

Reflex process, 105, 224
Reid, 84
——, Archdale, 357
Restitution of organs, 241
—— and Darwinism, 251
Rhode, Erwin, on Ionians, 12
—— on Greek Animism, 9
Ribot, T., 302
Roberts, E. J., on Plato, 18
Romanes, J. G., 93

SCEPTICISM, 27, 88
Schiller, F. C. S., 85, 203, 359
Schoolmen, early, 33
Scratch-reflex, 266
Seat of soul, search for, 99, 299
Semon, R., on Lamarckism, 247
Sensation and meaning, 345
Sensorium Commune, 25, 100, 286
Sensory qualities, evolution of, 279
"Separable forms," 35
Sheol, 7
Sherrington, C. S., 266
Sidgwick on Kant, 200, 203
Skill, acquirement of, 320
Solipsism, 134, 180, 185
Soul, vegetative functions of, 373
Spatial meaning, 307, 386
Specific energies, 289
—— receptors, 265
Speculative philosophy, 79
Spencer, H., 85, 121, 288
Spheral intelligences, 40
Spinoza, 57, 112
Spiritus, 37
—— animalis, 38
—— vitalis, 38
Stahl, G. E., 77, 95
Statistics and mechanism, 232
Stewart, J. A., on Plato, 19
——, Balfour, 253
Stigmata, 351
Stoics, 26
Stokes, Sir G., 253
Stout, G. F., 123
—— on feeling, 321
Stream of consciousness coherent, 164
Strong, C. A., 123, 135, 164, 222
Structure of the mind, 330, 166
Stumpf, C., 83, 160
—— on interaction, 208
Subconsciousness, 173, 368
Substance, 364
—— attack on, 61
—— defended, 162
Survival of death, 195
—— implies Animism, 202
—— and empirical evidence, 348
Sylvius, 96
Synthesis, mental, in instinct, 264

TAIT, P. G., 253
Taylor, A. E., 85, 180
Telegram-argument, 267
Teleology, statical and dynamical, 244
Telepathy, 349
Telesio, Bernardino, 43
Tertullian, 29
Thales, 12
Theism implies Animism, 194
Theophilus of Alexandria, 37
Thomson, Sir J. J., 210, 216, 253
Thorndike, E., 319
Thought and brain-functions, 113
—— not necessarily spatial, 210
Threshold of consciousness, 141, 295
Time, post-hypnotic appreciation of, 353
Total reactions, 260
Transmission-theory, 358
Transubjectivity of physical world, 185
Treviranus, 81
Trial and error, 260
Trichotomy, 7, 28, 30
Tropisms, 259
Truth, two forms of, 38
Tylor, E. B., 2, 4, 16
Tyndall, 121

UEBERWEG, 27, 32
Unconscious cerebration, 109, 229
—— consciousness, 172
—— psychical process, 141
Unity of consciousness, 168

VAIHINGER, 196
Values, 329
Vesalius, 44, 99
Vitalism, 78, 81
Vives, Ludovicus, 41
Vogt, K., 98
Voltaire, 74
Vries, H. de, 249

WARD, James, 85
—— —— on subjective selection, 247, 255
—— —— on idealism, 184
Wasps, 263
Weber's law, 139
Weismann, 119
Willis, 100
Wilson, E. B., on cell mechanism, 236
Wolff, Chr., 73
Wolff, C. F., 77
Wordsworth's poems, 316
Wundt, W., 154, 331
—— on primitive Animism, 5
—— on causation, 177
—— on creative synthesis, 305

ZIEHEN, T., 108, 111
—— on memory, 331

A SELECTION OF BOOKS PUBLISHED BY METHUEN AND CO. LTD. LONDON 36 ESSEX STREET W.C.

CONTENTS

	PAGE
General Literature	2
Ancient Cities	12
Antiquary's Books	12
Arden Shakespeare	13
Classics of Art	13
'Complete' Series	14
Connoisseur's Library	14
Handbooks of English Church History	15
Handbooks of Theology	15
Health Series	15
'Home Life' Series	15
Leaders of Religion	16
Library of Devotion	16
Little Books on Art	17
Little Guides	17
Little Library	18
Little Quarto Shakespeare	19
Miniature Library	19
New Library of Medicine	19
New Library of Music	20
Oxford Biographies	20
Seven Plays	20
Sport Series	20
States of Italy	20
Westminster Commentaries	20
'Young' Series	21
Shilling Library	21
Books for Travellers	22
Some Books on Art	22
Some Books on Italy	23
Fiction	24
Books for Boys and Girls	29
Shilling Novels	29
Sevenpenny Novels	30

A SELECTION OF
Messrs. Methuen's
PUBLICATIONS

In this Catalogue the order is according to authors. An asterisk denotes that the book is in the press.

Colonial Editions are published of all Messrs. METHUEN's Novels issued at a price above 2s. 6d., and similar editions are published of some works of General Literature. Colonial Editions are only for circulation in the British Colonies and India.

All books marked net are not subject to discount, and cannot be bought at less than the published price. Books not marked net are subject to the discount which the bookseller allows.

Messrs. METHUEN's books are kept in stock by all good booksellers. If there is any difficulty in seeing copies, Messrs. Methuen will be very glad to have early information, and specimen copies of any books will be sent on receipt of the published price *plus* postage for net books, and of the published price for ordinary books.

This Catalogue contains only a selection of the more important books published by Messrs. Methuen. A complete and illustrated catalogue of their publications may be obtained on application.

Andrewes (Lancelot). PRECES PRIVATAE. Translated and edited, with Notes, by F. E. BRIGHTMAN. *Cr. 8vo. 6s.*

Aristotle. THE ETHICS. Edited, with an Introduction and Notes, by JOHN BURNET. *Demy 8vo. 10s. 6d. net.*

Atkinson (T. D.). ENGLISH ARCHITECTURE. Illustrated. *Third Edition. Fcap. 8vo. 3s. 6d. net.*

A GLOSSARY OF TERMS USED IN ENGLISH ARCHITECTURE. Illustrated. *Second Edition. Fcap. 8vo. 3s. 6d. net.*

ENGLISH AND WELSH CATHEDRALS. Illustrated. *Demy 8vo. 10s. 6d. net.*

Atteridge (A. H.). FAMOUS LAND FIGHTS. Illustrated. *Cr. 8vo. 6s.*

Bain (F. W.). A DIGIT OF THE MOON: A HINDOO LOVE STORY. *Eleventh Edition. Fcap. 8vo. 3s. 6d. net.*

THE DESCENT OF THE SUN: A CYCLE OF BIRTH. *Sixth Edition. Fcap. 8vo. 3s. 6d. net.*

A HEIFER OF THE DAWN. *Eighth Edition. Fcap. 8vo. 2s. 6d. net.*

IN THE GREAT GOD'S HAIR. *Sixth Edition. Fcap. 8vo. 2s. 6d. net.*

A DRAUGHT OF THE BLUE. *Fifth Edition. Fcap. 8vo. 2s. 6d. net.*

AN ESSENCE OF THE DUSK. *Fourth Edition. Fcap. 8vo. 2s. 6d. net.*

AN INCARNATION OF THE SNOW. *Third Edition. Fcap. 8vo. 3s. 6d. net.*

A MINE OF FAULTS. *Third Edition. Fcap. 8vo. 3s. 6d. net.*

THE ASHES OF A GOD. *Second Edition. Fcap. 8vo. 3s. 6d. net.*

BUBBLES OF THE FOAM. *Second Edition. Fcap. 4to. 5s. net. Also Fcap. 8vo 3s. 6d. net.*

A SYRUP OF THE BEES. *Fcap. 4to. 5s. net. Also Fcap. 8vo. 3s. 6d. net.*

Balfour (Graham). THE LIFE OF ROBERT LOUIS STEVENSON. *Fifteenth Edition. In one Volume. Cr. 8vo. Buckram, 6s. net.*

Baring (Hon. Maurice). LANDMARKS IN RUSSIAN LITERATURE. *Third Edition. Cr. 8vo. 6s. net.*

THE RUSSIAN PEOPLE. *Second Edition. Demy 8vo. 15s. net.*

Baring-Gould (S.). THE LIFE OF NAPOLEON BONAPARTE. Illustrated. *Second and Cheaper Edition. Royal 8vo. 10s. 6d. net.*

THE TRAGEDY OF THE CÆSARS: A STUDY OF THE CHARACTERS OF THE CÆSARS OF THE JULIAN AND CLAUDIAN HOUSES. Illustrated. *Seventh Edition. Royal 8vo. 10s. 6d. net.*

General Literature

A BOOK OF CORNWALL. Illustrated. *Third Edition. Cr. 8vo. 6s.*

A BOOK OF DARTMOOR. Illustrated. *Second Edition. Cr. 8vo. 6s.*

A BOOK OF DEVON. Illustrated. *Third Edition. Cr. 8vo. 6s.*

Baring-Gould (S.) and Sheppard (H. F.). A GARLAND OF COUNTRY SONG. English Folk Songs with their Traditional Melodies. *Demy 4to. 6s.*

Baring-Gould (S.), Sheppard (H. F.), and Bussell (F. W.). SONGS OF THE WEST. Folk Songs of Devon and Cornwall. Collected from the Mouths of the People. New and Revised Edition, under the musical editorship of Cecil J. Sharp. *Large Imperial 8vo. 5s. net.*

Barker (E.). THE POLITICAL THOUGHT OF PLATO AND ARISTOTLE. *Demy 8vo. 10s. 6d. net.*

Bastable (C. F.). THE COMMERCE OF NATIONS. *Seventh Edition. Cr 8vo. 2s. 6d.*

Beckett (S. J.). THE FJORDS AND FOLK OF NORWAY. Illustrated. *Fcap. 8vo. 5s. net.*

Beckford (Peter). THOUGHTS ON HUNTING. Edited by J. Otho Paget. Illustrated. *Third Edition. Demy 8vo. 6s. net.*

Belloc (H.). PARIS. Illustrated. *Third Edition. Cr. 8vo. 6s.*
HILLS AND THE SEA. *Ninth Edition. Fcap. 8vo. 5s.*
ON NOTHING AND KINDRED SUBJECTS. *Fourth Edition. Fcap. 8vo. 5s.*
ON EVERYTHING. *Third Edition. Fcap. 8vo. 5s.*
ON SOMETHING. *Second Edition. Fcap. 8vo. 5s.*
FIRST AND LAST. *Second Edition. Fcap. 8vo. 5s.*
THIS AND THAT AND THE OTHER. *Second Edition. Fcap. 8vo. 5s.*
MARIE ANTOINETTE. Illustrated. *Third Edition. Demy 8vo. 15s. net.*
THE PYRENEES. Illustrated. *Second Edition. Demy 8vo. 7s. 6d. net.*

Bennett (Arnold). THE TRUTH ABOUT AN AUTHOR. *Second Edition. Fcap. 8vo. 2s. 6d. net.*
OVER THERE: War Scenes on the Western Front. *Fcap. 8vo. 1s. net.*

Bennett (W. H.). A PRIMER OF THE BIBLE. *Fifth Edition. Cr. 8vo. 2s. 6d.*

Bennett (W. H.) and Adeney (W. F.). A BIBLICAL INTRODUCTION. With a concise Bibliography. *Sixth Edition. Cr. 8vo. 7s. 6d. Also in Two Volumes. Cr. 8vo. Each 3s. 6d. net.*

Beresford (Admiral Lord Charles). THE MEMOIRS OF ADMIRAL LORD CHARLES BERESFORD. Illustrated. *Two Volumes. Third Edition. Demy 8vo. £1 10s. net.*

Berriman (Algernon E.). AVIATION. Illustrated. *Second Edition. Cr. 8vo. 10s. 6d. net.*
MOTORING. Illustrated. *Demy 8vo. 10s. 6d. net.*

Bicknell (Ethel E.). PARIS AND HER TREASURES. Illustrated. *Fcap. 8vo. Round corners. 5s. net.*

Blake (William). ILLUSTRATIONS OF THE BOOK OF JOB. With a General Introduction by Laurence Binyon. Illustrated. *Quarto. 21s. net.*

Bloemfontein (Bishop of). ARA CŒLI: An Essay in Mystical Theology. *Sixth Edition. Cr. 8vo. 3s. 6d. net.*
FAITH AND EXPERIENCE. *Second Edition. Cr. 8vo. 3s. 6d. net.*
THE CULT OF THE PASSING MOMENT. *Fourth Edition. Cr. 8vo. 3s. 6d. net.*

Bosanquet (Mrs. R. C.). DAYS IN ATTICA. Illustrated. *Demy 8vo. 7s. 6d. net.*

Bowden (E. M.). THE IMITATION OF BUDDHA. Quotations from Buddhist Literature for each Day in the Year. *Sixth Edition. Cr. 16mo. 2s. 6d.*

Brabant (F. G.). RAMBLES IN SUSSEX. Illustrated. *Cr. 8vo. 6s.*

Braid (James). ADVANCED GOLF. Illustrated. *Eighth Edition. Demy 8vo. 10s. 6d. net.*

Bulley (M. H.). ANCIENT AND MEDIEVAL ART. Illustrated. *Cr. 8vo. 5s. net.*

Calman (W. T.). THE LIFE OF CRUSTACEA. Illustrated. *Cr. 8vo. 6s.*

Carlyle (Thomas). THE FRENCH REVOLUTION. Edited by C. R. L. Fletcher. *Three Volumes. Cr. 8vo. 18s.*
THE LETTERS AND SPEECHES OF OLIVER CROMWELL. With an Introduction by C. H. Firth, and Notes and Appendices by S. C. Lomas. *Three Volumes. Demy 8vo. 18s. net.*

Chambers (Mrs. Lambert). LAWN TENNIS FOR LADIES. Illustrated. *Second Edition. Cr. 8vo. 2s. 6d. net.*

Chesterfield (Lord). THE LETTERS OF THE EARL OF CHESTERFIELD TO HIS SON. Edited, with an Introduction by C. Strachey, and Notes by A. Calthrop. *Two Volumes. Cr. 8vo. 12s.*

Chesterton (G. K.). CHARLES DICKENS. With two Portraits in Photogravure. *Eighth Edition. Cr. 8vo. 6s.*

THE BALLAD OF THE WHITE HORSE. *Fifth Edition. Fcap. 8vo. 5s.*

ALL THINGS CONSIDERED. *Seventh Edition. Fcap. 8vo. 5s.*

TREMENDOUS TRIFLES. *Fifth Edition. Fcap. 8vo. 5s.*

ALARMS AND DISCURSIONS. *Second Edition. Fcap. 8vo. 5s.*

A MISCELLANY OF MEN. *Second Edition. Fcap. 8vo. 5s.*

WINE, WATER, AND SONG. *Fifth Edition. Fcap. 8vo. 1s. net.*

Clausen (George). ROYAL ACADEMY LECTURES ON PAINTING. Illustrated. *Cr. 8vo. 5s. net.*

Clutton-Brock (A.). THOUGHTS ON THE WAR. *Ninth Edition. Fcap. 8vo. 1s. net.*

MORE THOUGHTS ON THE WAR. *Third Edition. Fcap. 8vo. 1s. net.*

Conrad (Joseph). THE MIRROR OF THE SEA: Memories and Impressions. *Fourth Edition. Fcap. 8vo. 5s.*

Coulton (G. G.). CHAUCER AND HIS ENGLAND. Illustrated. *Second Edition. Demy 8vo. 10s. 6d. net.*

Cowper (William). POEMS. Edited, with an Introduction and Notes, by J. C. BAILEY. Illustrated. *Demy 8vo. 10s. 6d. net.*

Cox (J. C.). RAMBLES IN SURREY. Illustrated. *Second Edition. Cr. 8vo. 6s.*

RAMBLES IN KENT. Illustrated. *Cr. 8vo. 6s.*

Davis (H. W. C.). ENGLAND UNDER THE NORMANS AND ANGEVINS: 1066-1272. *Fourth Edition. Demy 8vo. 10s. 6d. net.*

Dearmer (Mabel). A CHILD'S LIFE OF CHRIST. Illustrated. *Second and Cheaper Edition. Large Cr. 8vo. 2s. 6d. net.*

Dickinson (G. L.). THE GREEK VIEW OF LIFE. *Ninth Edition. Cr. 8vo. 2s. 6d. net.*

Dowden (J.). FURTHER STUDIES IN THE PRAYER BOOK. *Cr. 8vo. 6s.*

Driver (S. R.). SERMONS ON SUBJECTS CONNECTED WITH THE OLD TESTAMENT. *Cr. 8vo. 6s.*

Dumas (Alexandre). THE CRIMES OF THE BORGIAS AND OTHERS. With an Introduction by R. S. GARNETT. Illustrated. *Second Edition. Cr. 8vo. 6s.*

THE CRIMES OF URBAIN GRANDIER AND OTHERS. Illustrated. *Cr. 8vo. 6s.*

THE CRIMES OF THE MARQUISE DE BRINVILLIERS AND OTHERS. Illustrated. *Cr. 8vo. 6s.*

THE CRIMES OF ALI PACHA AND OTHERS. Illustrated. *Cr. 8vo. 6s.*

Durham (The Earl of). THE REPORT ON CANADA. With an Introductory Note. *Second Edition. Demy 8vo. 4s. 6d. net.*

Egerton (H. E.). A SHORT HISTORY OF BRITISH COLONIAL POLICY. *Fourth Edition. Demy 8vo. 7s. 6d. net.*

Evans (Herbert A.). CASTLES OF ENGLAND AND WALES. Illustrated. *Demy 8vo. 12s. 6d. net.*

Ewald (Carl). MY LITTLE BOY. Translated by ALEXANDER TEIXEIRA DE MATTOS. Illustrated. *Fcap. 8vo. 5s.*

Fairbrother (W. H.). THE PHILOSOPHY OF T. H. GREEN. *Second Edition. Cr. 8vo. 3s. 6d.*

ffoulkes (Charles). THE ARMOURER AND HIS CRAFT. Illustrated. *Royal 4to. £2 2s. net.*

DECORATIVE IRONWORK. From the xiith to the xviiith Century. Illustrated. *Royal 4to. £2 2s. net.*

Firth (C. H.). CROMWELL'S ARMY. A History of the English Soldier during the Civil Wars, the Commonwealth, and the Protectorate. Illustrated. *Second Edition. Cr. 8vo. 6s.*

Fisher (H. A. L.). THE REPUBLICAN TRADITION IN EUROPE. *Cr. 8vo. 6s. net.*

FitzGerald (Edward). THE RUBÁIYÁT OF OMAR KHAYYÁM. Printed from the Fifth and last Edition. With a Commentary by H. M. BATSON, and a Biographical Introduction by E. D. ROSS. *Cr. 8vo. 6s.*

Also Illustrated by E. J. SULLIVAN. *Cr. 4to. 15s. net.*

Flux (A. W.). ECONOMIC PRINCIPLES. *Demy 8vo. 7s. 6d. net.*

Fraser (E.). THE SOLDIERS WHOM WELLINGTON LED. Deeds of Daring, Chivalry, and Renown. Illustrated. *Cr. 8vo. 5s. net.*

THE SAILORS WHOM NELSON LED. Their Doings Described by Themselves. Illustrated. *Cr. 8vo. 5s. net.*

General Literature

Gibbins (H. de B.). INDUSTRY IN ENGLAND: HISTORICAL OUTLINES. With Maps and Plans. *Ninth Edition. Demy 8vo. 10s. 6d. net.*

THE INDUSTRIAL HISTORY OF ENGLAND. With 5 Maps and a Plan. *Twentieth Edition. Cr. 8vo. 3s.*

Gibbon (Edward). THE MEMOIRS OF THE LIFE OF EDWARD GIBBON. Edited by G. BIRKBECK HILL. *Cr. 8vo. 6s. net.*

THE DECLINE AND FALL OF THE ROMAN EMPIRE. Edited, with Notes, Appendices, and Maps, by J. B. BURY. Illustrated. *Seven Volumes. Demy 8vo. Illustrated. Each 10s. 6d. net. Also in Seven Volumes. Cr. 8vo. 6s. each.*

Glover (T. R.). THE CONFLICT OF RELIGIONS IN THE EARLY ROMAN EMPIRE. *Fifth Edition. Demy 8vo. 7s. 6d. net.*

POETS AND PURITANS. *Second Edition. Demy 8vo. 7s. 6d. net.*

*FROM PERICLES TO PHILIP. *Demy 8vo. 7s. 6d. net.*

VIRGIL. *Third Edition. Demy 8vo. 7s. 6d. net.*

THE CHRISTIAN TRADITION AND ITS VERIFICATION. (The Angus Lecture for 1912.) *Second Edition. Cr. 8vo. 3s. 6d. net.*

Grahame (Kenneth). THE WIND IN THE WILLOWS. *Eighth Edition. Cr. 8vo. 6s.*
Also Illustrated. *Wide Cr. 8vo. 7s. 6d. net.*

Granger (F. S.). HISTORICAL SOCIOLOGY: A TEXT-BOOK OF POLITICS. *Cr. 8vo. 3s. 6d. net.*

Griffin (W. Hall) and Minchin (H. C.). THE LIFE OF ROBERT BROWNING. Illustrated. *Second Edition. Demy 8vo. 12s. 6d. net.*

Haig (K. G.). HEALTH THROUGH DIET. *Third Edition. Cr. 8vo. 3s. 6d. net.*

Hale (J. R.). FAMOUS SEA FIGHTS: FROM SALAMIS TO TSU-SHIMA. Illustrated. *Second Edition. Cr. 8vo. 6s. net.*

Hall (H. R.). THE ANCIENT HISTORY OF THE NEAR EAST FROM THE EARLIEST TIMES TO THE BATTLE OF SALAMIS. Illustrated. *Second Edition. Demy 8vo. 15s. net.*

Hannay (D.). A SHORT HISTORY OF THE ROYAL NAVY. Vol. I., 1217-1688. *Second Edition.* Vol. II., 1689-1815. *Demy 8vo. Each 7s. 6d. net.*

Harker (Alfred). THE NATURAL HISTORY OF IGNEOUS ROCKS. With 112 Diagrams and 2 Plates. *Demy 8vo. 12s. 6d. net.*

Harper (Charles G.). THE 'AUTOCAR' ROAD-BOOK. With Maps. *Four Volumes. Cr. 8vo. Each 7s. 6d. net.*

Vol. I.—SOUTH OF THE THAMES.

Vol. II.—NORTH AND SOUTH WALES AND WEST MIDLANDS.

Vol. III.—EAST ANGLIA AND EAST MIDLANDS.

Vol. IV.—THE NORTH OF ENGLAND AND SOUTH OF SCOTLAND.

Hassall (Arthur). THE LIFE OF NAPOLEON. Illustrated. *Demy 8vo. 7s. 6d. net.*

Henley (W. E.). ENGLISH LYRICS: CHAUCER TO POE. *Second Edition. Cr. 8vo. 2s. 6d. net.*

Hill (George Francis). ONE HUNDRED MASTERPIECES OF SCULPTURE. Illustrated. *Demy 8vo. 10s. 6d. net.*

Hind (C. Lewis). DAYS IN CORNWALL. Illustrated. *Third Edition. Cr. 8vo. 6s. net.*

Hirst (W. A.). A GUIDE TO SOUTH AMERICA. With 10 Maps. *Cr. 8vo. 6s. net.*

Hobhouse (L. T.). THE THEORY OF KNOWLEDGE. *Second Edition. Demy 8vo. 10s. 6d. net.*

Hobson (J. A.). INTERNATIONAL TRADE: AN APPLICATION OF ECONOMIC THEORY. *Cr. 8vo. 2s. 6d. net.*

PROBLEMS OF POVERTY: AN INQUIRY INTO THE INDUSTRIAL CONDITION OF THE POOR. *Eighth Edition. Cr. 8vo. 2s. 6d.*

THE PROBLEM OF THE UNEMPLOYED: AN INQUIRY AND AN ECONOMIC POLICY. *Sixth Edition. Cr. 8vo. 2s. 6d.*

GOLD, PRICES AND WAGES: WITH AN EXAMINATION OF THE QUANTITY THEORY. *Second Edition. Cr. 8vo. 3s. 6d. net.*

Hodgson (Mrs. W.). HOW TO IDENTIFY OLD CHINESE PORCELAIN. Illustrated. *Third Edition. Post 8vo. 6s.*

Holdsworth (W. S.). A HISTORY OF ENGLISH LAW. *Four Volumes. Vols. I., II., III. Each Second Edition. Demy 8vo. Each 10s. 6d. net.*

Hudson (W. H.). A SHEPHERD'S LIFE: IMPRESSIONS OF THE SOUTH WILTSHIRE DOWNS. Illustrated. *Third Edition. Demy 8vo. 7s. 6d. net.*

Hutton (Edward). THE CITIES OF UMBRIA. Illustrated. *Fifth Edition. Cr. 8vo. 6s. net.*

THE CITIES OF LOMBARDY. Illustrated *Cr. 8vo. 6s. net.*

THE CITIES OF ROMAGNA AND THE MARCHES. Illustrated. *Cr. 8vo. 6s. net.*

FLORENCE AND NORTHERN TUSCANY WITH GENOA. Illustrated. *Third Edition. Cr. 8vo. 6s. net.*

SIENA AND SOUTHERN TUSCANY. Illustrated. *Second Edition. Cr. 8vo. 6s. net.*

VENICE AND VENETIA. Illustrated *Cr. 8vo. 6s. net.*

ROME. Illustrated. *Third Edition. Cr. 8vo. 6s. net.*

COUNTRY WALKS ABOUT FLORENCE. Illustrated. *Second Edition. Fcap. 8vo. 5s. net.*

THE CITIES OF SPAIN. Illustrated. *Fourth Edition. Cr. 8vo. 6s. net.*

Ibsen (Henrik). BRAND. A Dramatic Poem, translated by WILLIAM WILSON. *Fourth Edition. Cr. 8vo. 3s. 6d.*

Inge (W. R.). CHRISTIAN MYSTICISM. (The Bampton Lectures of 1899.) *Third Edition. Cr. 8vo. 5s. net.*

Innes (A. D.). A HISTORY OF THE BRITISH IN INDIA. With Maps and Plans. *Second Edition. Cr. 8vo. 6s.*

ENGLAND UNDER THE TUDORS. With Maps. *Fourth Edition. Demy 8vo. 10s. 6d. net.*

Innes (Mary). SCHOOLS OF PAINTING. Illustrated. *Second Edition. Cr. 8vo. 5s. net.*

Jenks (E.). AN OUTLINE OF ENGLISH LOCAL GOVERNMENT. *Third Edition.* Revised by R. C. K. ENSOR. *Cr. 8vo. 2s. 6d. net.*

A SHORT HISTORY OF ENGLISH LAW: FROM THE EARLIEST TIMES TO THE END OF THE YEAR 1911. *Demy 8vo. 10s. 6d. net.*

Jevons (F. B.). PERSONALITY. *Cr. 8vo. 2s. 6d. net.*

Johnston (Sir H. H.). BRITISH CENTRAL AFRICA. Illustrated. *Third Edition. Cr. 4to. 18s. net.*

THE NEGRO IN THE NEW WORLD. Illustrated. *Crown 4to. 21s. net.*

Julian (Lady) of Norwich. REVELATIONS OF DIVINE LOVE. Edited by GRACE WARRACK. *Fifth Edition. Cr. 8vo. 3s. 6d. net.*

Keats (John). POEMS. Edited, with Introduction and Notes, by E. de SÉLINCOURT. With a Frontispiece in Photogravure *Third Edition. Demy 8vo. 7s. 6d. net.*

Keble (John). THE CHRISTIAN YEAR. With an Introduction and Notes by W. LOCK. Illustrated. *Third Edition. Fcap. 8vo. 3s. 6d.*

Kempis (Thomas à). THE IMITATION OF CHRIST. From the Latin, with an Introduction by DEAN FARRAR. Illustrated. *Fourth Edition. Fcap. 8vo. 3s. 6d.*

*THOMAE A KEMPIS DE IMITATIONE CHRISTI LIBRI IV. Edited by Dr. ADRIAN FORTESCUE. *Cr. 4to. 30s. net.* Limited to 250 copies.

Kipling (Rudyard). THE POEMS. Service Edition. *In Eight Volumes. Square fcap. 8vo. Cloth, 2s. 6d. net each volume.*
 BARRACK-ROOM BALLADS. 2 *Vols.*
 THE SEVEN SEAS. 2 *Vols.*
 THE FIVE NATIONS. 2 *Vols.*
 DEPARTMENTAL DITTIES. 2 *Vols.*

BARRACK-ROOM BALLADS. 152*nd Thousand. Forty-second Edition. Cr. 8vo. Buckram, 6s. Also Fcap. 8vo. Cloth, 4s. 6d. net; leather, 5s. net.*

THE SEVEN SEAS. 116*th Thousand. Twenty-fifth Edition. Cr. 8vo. Buckram, 6s. Also Fcap. 8vo. Cloth, 4s. 6d. net; leather, 5s. net.*

THE FIVE NATIONS. 97*th Thousand. Fourteenth Edition. Cr. 8vo. Buckram, 6s. Also Fcap. 8vo. Cloth, 4s. 6d. net; leather, 5s. net.*

DEPARTMENTAL DITTIES. 68*th Thousand. Twenty-Sixth Edition. Cr. 8vo. Buckram, 6s. Also Fcap. 8vo. Cloth, 4s. 6d. net; leather, 5s. net.*

HYMN BEFORE ACTION. Illuminated. *Fcap. 4to. 1s. net.*

RECESSIONAL. Illuminated. *Fcap. 4to. 1s. net.*

*Koebel (W. H.).** THE SOUTH AMERICANS. Illustrated. *Demy 8vo. 10s. 6d. net.*

L. (E. V.) and M. (G.). SWOLLEN-HEADED WILLIAM. The Verses adapted by E V. Lucas, and the pictures by GEORGE MORROW. *Fifth Edition. Cr. 4to. 1s. net.*

Lamb (Charles and Mary). THE COMPLETE WORKS. Edited by E. V. LUCAS. A New and Revised Ed. in Six Volumes. With Frontispieces. *Fcap. 8vo. 5s. each.* The volumes are:—
 I. MISCELLANEOUS PROSE. II. ELIA AND THE LAST ESSAYS OF ELIA. III. BOOKS FOR CHILDREN. IV. PLAYS AND POEMS V. and VI. LETTERS.

General Literature

Lane-Poole (Stanley). A HISTORY OF EGYPT IN THE MIDDLE AGES. Illustrated. *Second Edition. Cr. 8vo. 6s. net.*

Lankester (Sir Ray). SCIENCE FROM AN EASY CHAIR. Illustrated. *Eighth Edition. Cr. 8vo. 6s.*
SCIENCE FROM AN EASY CHAIR. *Second Series.* Illustrated. *Second Edition. Cr. 8vo. 6s.*
DIVERSIONS OF A NATURALIST. Illustrated. *Second Edition. Cr. 8vo. 6s.*

Lewis (Edward). EDWARD CARPENTER: AN EXPOSITION AND AN APPRECIATION. *Second Edition. Cr. 8vo. 5s. net.*

Lock (Walter). ST. PAUL, THE MASTER BUILDER. *Third Edition. Cr. 8vo. 3s. 6d.*
THE BIBLE AND CHRISTIAN LIFE. *Cr. 8vo. 6s.*

Lodge (Sir Oliver). MAN AND THE UNIVERSE: A STUDY OF THE INFLUENCE OF THE ADVANCE IN SCIENTIFIC KNOWLEDGE UPON OUR UNDERSTANDING OF CHRISTIANITY. *Ninth Edition. Demy 8vo. 5s. net.*
THE SURVIVAL OF MAN: A STUDY IN UNRECOGNISED HUMAN FACULTY. *Fifth Edition. Wide Cr. 8vo. 5s. net.*
REASON AND BELIEF. *Fifth Edition. Cr. 8vo. 3s. 6d. net.*
MODERN PROBLEMS. *Cr. 8vo. 5s. net.*
THE WAR AND AFTER: SHORT CHAPTERS ON SUBJECTS OF SERIOUS PRACTICAL IMPORT FOR THE AVERAGE CITIZEN IN A.D. 1915 ONWARDS. *Sixth Edition. Fcap. 8vo. 1s. net.*

Loreburn (Earl). CAPTURE AT SEA. *Cr. 8vo. 2s. 6d. net.*

Lorimer (George Horace). LETTERS FROM A SELF-MADE MERCHANT TO HIS SON. Illustrated. *Twenty-fourth Edition. Cr. 8vo. 3s. 6d.*
OLD GORGON GRAHAM. Illustrated. *Second Edition. Cr. 8vo. 6s. Also Cr. 8vo. 2s. net.*

Lorimer (Norma). BY THE WATERS OF EGYPT. Illustrated. *Third Edition. Cr. 8vo. 6s. net.*

Lucas (E. V.). THE LIFE OF CHARLES LAMB. Illustrated. *Sixth Edition. Demy 8vo. 7s. 6d. net.*
A WANDERER IN HOLLAND. Illustrated. *Sixteenth Edition. Cr. 8vo. 6s. net.*
A WANDERER IN LONDON. Illustrated. *Seventeenth Edition, Revised. Cr. 8vo. 6s. net.*
A WANDERER IN PARIS. Illustrated. *Twelfth Edition. Cr. 8vo. 6s. net. Also Fcap. 8vo. 5s.*
A WANDERER IN FLORENCE. Illustrated. *Sixth Edition. Cr. 8vo. 6s. net.*
A WANDERER IN VENICE. Illustrated. *Second Edition. Cr. 8vo. 6s. net.*
THE OPEN ROAD: A LITTLE BOOK FOR WAYFARERS. *Twenty-fifth Edition. Fcap. 8vo. 5s. India Paper, 7s. 6d. Also Illustrated. Cr. 4to. 15s. net.*
THE FRIENDLY TOWN: A LITTLE BOOK FOR THE URBANE. *Eighth Edition. Fcap. 8vo. 2s. 6d. net.*
FIRESIDE AND SUNSHINE. *Eighth Edition. Fcap 8vo. 2s. 6d. net.*
CHARACTER AND COMEDY. *Seventh Edition. Fcap. 8vo. 2s. 6d. net.*
THE GENTLEST ART: A CHOICE OF LETTERS BY ENTERTAINING HANDS. *Eighth Edition. Fcap. 8vo. 2s. 6d. net.*
THE SECOND POST. *Fourth Edition. Fcap. 8vo. 2s. 6d. net.*
HER INFINITE VARIETY: A FEMININE PORTRAIT GALLERY. *Seventh Edition. Fcap. 8vo. 2s. 6d. net.*
GOOD COMPANY: A RALLY OF MEN. *Third Edition. Fcap. 8vo. 2s. 6d. net.*
ONE DAY AND ANOTHER. *Sixth Edition. Fcap. 8vo. 2s. 6d. net.*
OLD LAMPS FOR NEW. *Fifth Edition. Fcap. 8vo. 2s. 6d. net.*
LOITERER'S HARVEST. *Second Edition. Fcap. 8vo. 2s. 6d. net.*
LISTENER'S LURE: AN OBLIQUE NARRATION. *Eleventh Edition. Fcap. 8vo. 2s. 6d. net.*
OVER BEMERTON'S: AN EASY-GOING CHRONICLE. *Thirteenth Edition. Fcap. 8vo. 2s. 6d. net.*
MR. INGLESIDE. *Eleventh Edition. Fcap. 8vo. 2s. 6d. net.*
LONDON LAVENDER. *Eighth Edition. Fcap. 8vo. 2s. 6d. net.*
LANDMARKS. *Fifth Edition. Fcap. 8vo. 5s.*
THE BRITISH SCHOOL: AN ANECDOTAL GUIDE TO THE BRITISH PAINTERS AND PAINTINGS IN THE NATIONAL GALLERY. *Fcap. 8vo. 2s. 6d. net.*
REMEMBER LOUVAIN! A LITTLE BOOK OF LIBERTY AND WAR. With a Preface by E. V. LUCAS. *Second Edition. Fcap. 8vo. Paper Covers, 1s. net.*

Lydekker (R.). THE OX AND ITS KINDRED. Illustrated. *Cr. 8vo. 6s.*

Macaulay (Lord). CRITICAL AND HISTORICAL ESSAYS. Edited by F. C. MONTAGUE. *Three Volumes. Cr. 8vo. 18s.*

McCabe (Joseph). THE EMPRESSES OF ROME. Illustrated. *Demy 8vo.* 12s. 6d. net.

THE EMPRESSES OF CONSTANTINOPLE. Illustrated. *Demy 8vo.* 10s. 6d. net.

Macdonald (J. R. M.). A HISTORY OF FRANCE. *Three Volumes. Cr. 8vo.* £1 2s. 6d. net.

McDougall (William). AN INTRODUCTION TO SOCIAL PSYCHOLOGY. *Ninth Edition. Cr. 8vo.* 5s. net.

BODY AND MIND: A HISTORY AND A DEFENCE OF ANIMISM. *Third Edition. Demy 8vo.* 10s. 6d. net.

Maeterlinck (Maurice). THE BLUE BIRD: A FAIRY PLAY IN SIX ACTS. Translated by ALEXANDER TEIXEIRA DE MATTOS. *Fcap. 8vo. Deckle Edges.* 3s. 6d. net. An Edition, illustrated in colour by F. CAYLEY ROBINSON, is also published. *Cr. 4to.* £1 1s. net. Of the above book Thirty-six Editions in all have been issued.

MARY MAGDALENE: A PLAY IN THREE ACTS. Translated by ALEXANDER TEIXEIRA DE MATTOS. *Third Edition. Fcap. 8vo. Deckle Edges.* 3s. 6d. net.

OUR ETERNITY. Translated by ALEXANDER TEIXEIRA DE MATTOS. *Fcap. 8vo.* 5s. net.

THE UNKNOWN GUEST. Translated by ALEXANDER TEIXEIRA DE MATTOS. *Second Edition. Cr. 8vo.* 5s. net.

POEMS. Translated by BERNARD MIALL. *Second Edition. Cr. 8vo.* 5s.

Maeterlinck (Mme. M.) (Georgette Leblanc). THE CHILDREN'S BLUEBIRD. Translated by ALEXANDER TEIXEIRA DE MATTOS. Illustrated. *Fcap. 8vo.* 5s. net.

Mahaffy (J. P.). A HISTORY OF EGYPT UNDER THE PTOLEMAIC DYNASTY. Illustrated. *Second Edition. Cr. 8vo.* 6s. net.

Maitland (F. W.). ROMAN CANON LAW IN THE CHURCH OF ENGLAND. *Royal 8vo.* 7s. 6d.

Marett (R. R.). THE THRESHOLD OF RELIGION. *Third Edition. Cr. 8vo.* 5s. net.

Marriott (J. A. R.). ENGLAND SINCE WATERLOO. With Maps. *Second Edition, Revised. Demy 8vo.* 10s. 6d. net.

Masefield (John). SEA LIFE IN NELSON'S TIME. Illustrated. *Cr. 8vo.* 3s. 6d. net.

A SAILOR'S GARLAND. Selected and Edited. *Second Edition. Cr. 8vo.* 3s. 6d. net.

Masterman (C. F. G.). TENNYSON AS A RELIGIOUS TEACHER. *Second Edition. Cr. 8vo.* 6s.

THE CONDITION OF ENGLAND. *Fourth Edition. Cr. 8vo.* 6s.

Medley (D. J.). ORIGINAL ILLUSTRATIONS OF ENGLISH CONSTITUTIONAL HISTORY. *Cr. 8vo.* 7s. 6d. net.

Miles (Eustace). LIFE AFTER LIFE; OR, THE THEORY OF REINCARNATION. *Cr. 8vo.* 2s. 6d. net.

THE POWER OF CONCENTRATION: HOW TO ACQUIRE IT. *Fifth Edition. Cr. 8vo.* 3s. 6d. net.

PREVENTION AND CURE. *Second Edition. Crown 8vo.* 3s. 6d. net.

Miles (Mrs. Eustace). ECONOMY IN WAR TIME; OR, HEALTH WITHOUT MEAT. *Second Edition. Crown 8vo.* 1s. net.

Millais (J. G.). THE LIFE AND LETTERS OF SIR JOHN EVERETT MILLAIS. Illustrated. *Third Edition. Demy 8vo.* 7s. 6d. net.

Milne (J. G.). A HISTORY OF EGYPT UNDER ROMAN RULE. Illustrated. *Second Edition. Cr. 8vo.* 6s. net.

Moffat (Mary M.). QUEEN LOUISA OF PRUSSIA. Illustrated. *Fourth Edition. Cr. 8vo.* 6s.

Money (Sir Leo Chiozza). RICHES AND POVERTY, 1910. *Eleventh Edition. Demy 8vo.* 5s. net.

Montague (C. E.). DRAMATIC VALUES. *Second Edition. Fcap. 8vo.* 5s.

Morgan (C. Lloyd). INSTINCT AND EXPERIENCE. *Second Edition. Cr. 8vo.* 5s. net.

Noyes (Alfred). A SALUTE FROM THE FLEET, AND OTHER POEMS. *Second Edition. Cr. 8vo.* 5s. net.

RADA: A BELGIAN CHRISTMAS EVE. Illustrated. *Fcap. 8vo.* 4s. 6d. net.

Oman (C. W. C.). A HISTORY OF THE ART OF WAR IN THE MIDDLE AGES. Illustrated. *Demy 8vo.* 10s. 6d. net.

ENGLAND BEFORE THE NORMAN CONQUEST. With Maps. *Third Edition, Revised. Demy 8vo.* 10s. 6d. net.

Oxenham (John). BEES IN AMBER: A LITTLE BOOK OF THOUGHTFUL VERSE. *Forty-first Edition. Small Pott 8vo. Paper* 1s. net; *Cloth Boards,* 2s. net; *Velvet Persian Yapp,* 2s. 6d. net; *Full Calf, gilt top,* 7s. 6d. net.

ALL'S WELL: A COLLECTION OF WAR POEMS. *Small Pott 8vo. Paper,* 1s. net; *Velvet Persian Yapp,* 2s. 6d. net.

GENERAL LITERATURE

Oxford (M. N.). A HANDBOOK OF NURSING. *Sixth Edition, Revised. Cr. 8vo.* 3s. 6d. *net.*

Pakes (W. C. C.). THE SCIENCE OF HYGIENE. Illustrated. *Second and Cheaper Edition.* Revised by A. T. NANKIVELL. *Cr. 8vo.* 5s. *net.*

Parker (Eric). A BOOK OF THE ZOO. Illustrated. *Second Edition. Cr. 8vo.* 6s.

Petrie (W. M. Flinders.) A HISTORY OF EGYPT. Illustrated. *Six Volumes. Cr. 8vo.* 6s. *net each.*

VOL. I. FROM THE 1ST TO THE XVITH DYNASTY. *Seventh Edition.*
VOL. II. THE XVIITH AND XVIIITH DYNASTIES. *Fifth Edition.*
VOL. III. XIXTH TO XXXTH DYNASTIES.
VOL. IV. EGYPT UNDER THE PTOLEMAIC DYNASTY. J. P. MAHAFFY. *Second Edition.*
VOL V. EGYPT UNDER ROMAN RULE. J. G. MILNE. *Second Edition.*
VOL. VI. EGYPT IN THE MIDDLE AGES. STANLEY LANE POOLE. *Second Edition*

RELIGION AND CONSCIENCE IN ANCIENT EGYPT. Illustrated. *Cr. 8vo.* 2s. 6d. *net.*

SYRIA AND EGYPT, FROM THE TELL EL AMARNA LETTERS. *Cr. 8vo.* 2s. 6d. *net.*

EGYPTIAN TALES. Translated from the Papyri. First Series, IVth to XIIth Dynasty. Illustrated. *Second Edition. Cr. 8vo.* 3s. 6d. *net.*

EGYPTIAN TALES. Translated from the Papyri. Second Series, XVIIIth to XIXth Dynasty. Illustrated. *Second Edition. Cr. 8vo.* 3s. 6d. *net.*

EGYPTIAN DECORATIVE ART. Illustrated. *Cr. 8vo.* 3s. 6d. *net.*

Pollard (Alfred W.). SHAKESPEARE FOLIOS AND QUARTOS. A Study in the Bibliography of Shakespeare's Plays, 1594-1685. Illustrated. *Folio.* £1 1s. *net.*

Porter (G. R.). THE PROGRESS OF THE NATION. A New Edition. Edited by F. W. HIRST. *Demy 8vo.* £1 1s. *net.*

Power (J. O'Connor). THE MAKING OF AN ORATOR. *Cr. 8vo.* 6s.

Price (L. L.). A SHORT HISTORY OF POLITICAL ECONOMY IN ENGLAND FROM ADAM SMITH TO ARNOLD TOYNBEE. *Ninth Edition. Cr. 8vo.* 2s. 6d.

Pycraft (W. P.). A HISTORY OF BIRDS. Illustrated. *Demy 8vo.* 10s. 6d. *net.*

Rawlings (Gertrude B.). COINS AND HOW TO KNOW THEM. Illustrated. *Third Edition. Cr. 8vo.* 6s.

*****Reade (Arthur).** FINLAND AND THE FINNS. Illustrated. *Demy 8vo.* 10s. 6d. *net.*

Regan (C. Tate). THE FRESHWATER FISHES OF THE BRITISH ISLES. Illustrated. *Cr. 8vo.* 6s.

Reid (G. Archdall). THE LAWS OF HEREDITY. *Second Edition. Demy 8vo.* £1 1s. *net.*

Robertson (C. Grant). SELECT STATUTES, CASES, AND DOCUMENTS, 1660-1832. *Second, Revised and Enlarged Edition. Demy 8vo.* 10s. 6d. *net.*

ENGLAND UNDER THE HANOVERIANS. Illustrated. *Second Edition. Demy 8vo.* 10s. 6d. *net.*

Roe (Fred). OLD OAK FURNITURE. Illustrated. *Second Edition. Demy 8vo.* 10s. 6d. *net.*

Rolle (Richard). THE FIRE OF LOVE AND THE MENDING OF LIFE. Edited by FRANCES M. COMPER. *Cr. 8vo.* 3s. 6d. *net.*

Ryley (A. Beresford). OLD PASTE. Illustrated. *Royal 8vo.* £2 2s. *net.*

'Saki' (H. H. Munro). REGINALD. *Fourth Edition. Fcap. 8vo.* 2s. 6d. *net.*

REGINALD IN RUSSIA. *Fcap. 8vo.* 2s. 6d. *net.*

Schidrowitz (Philip). RUBBER. Illustrated. *Demy 8vo.* 10s. 6d. *net.*

Selous (Edmund). TOMMY SMITH'S ANIMALS. Illustrated. *Fourteenth Edition. Fcap. 8vo.* 2s. 6d.

TOMMY SMITH'S OTHER ANIMALS. Illustrated. *Seventh Edition. Fcap. 8vo.* 2s. 6d.

JACK'S INSECTS. Illustrated. *Cr. 8vo.* 6s.

Shakespeare (William).
THE FOUR FOLIOS, 1623; 1632; 1664; 1685. Each £4 4s. *net*, or a complete set, £12 12s. *net.*

THE POEMS OF WILLIAM SHAKESPEARE. With an Introduction and Notes by GEORGE WYNDHAM. *Demy 8vo.* Buckram, 10s. 6d.

Shelley (Percy Bysshe). POEMS. With an Introduction by A. CLUTTON-BROCK and notes by C. D. LOCOCK. *Two Volumes. Demy 8vo.* £1 1s. *net.*

Sladen (Douglas). SICILY: THE NEW WINTER RESORT. An Encyclopædia of Sicily. With 234 Illustrations, a Map, and a Table of the Railway System of Sicily. *Second Edition, Revised. Cr. 8vo.* 5s. *net.*

Slesser (H. H.). TRADE UNIONISM. *Cr. 8vo.* 2s. 6d.

Smith (Adam). THE WEALTH OF NATIONS. Edited by EDWIN CANNAN. *Two Volumes. Demy 8vo.* £1 1s. *net.*

Smith (G. F. Herbert). GEM-STONES AND THEIR DISTINCTIVE CHARACTERS. Illustrated. *Second Edition. Cr. 8vo.* 6s. *net.*

Stancliffe. GOLF DO'S AND DONT'S. *Sixth Edition. Fcap. 8vo.* 1s. *net.*

Stevenson (R. L.). THE LETTERS OF ROBERT LOUIS STEVENSON. Edited by Sir SIDNEY COLVIN. *A New and Enlarged Edition in four volumes. Fourth Edition. Fcap. 8vo. Each* 5s. *net. Leather, each* 6s. *net.*

Streatfeild (R. A.). MODERN MUSIC AND MUSICIANS. Illustrated. *Second Edition. Demy 8vo.* 7s. 6d. *net.*

Surtees (R. S.). HANDLEY CROSS. Illustrated. *Fifth Edition. Fcap. 8vo. Gilt top.* 3s. 6d. *net.*
MR. SPONGE'S SPORTING TOUR. Illustrated. *Second Edition. Fcap. 8vo. Gilt top.* 3s. 6d. *net.*
ASK MAMMA; OR, THE RICHEST COMMONER IN ENGLAND. Illustrated. *Fcap. 8vo. Gilt top.* 3s. 6d. *net.*
JORROCKS'S JAUNTS AND JOLLITIES. Illustrated. *Fourth Edition. Fcap. 8vo. Gilt top.* 3s. 6d. *net.*
MR. FACEY ROMFORD'S HOUNDS. Illustrated. *Fcap. 8vo. Gilt top.* 3s. 6d. *net.*
HAWBUCK GRANGE; OR, THE SPORTING ADVENTURES OF THOMAS SCOTT, ESQ. Illustrated. *Fcap. 8vo. Gilt top.* 3s. 6d. *net.*
PLAIN OR RINGLETS? Illustrated. *Fcap. 8vo. Gilt top.* 3s. 6d. *net.*

Suso (Henry). THE LIFE OF THE BLESSED HENRY SUSO. By HIMSELF. Translated by T. F. KNOX. With an Introduction by DEAN INGE. *Second Edition. Cr. 8vo.* 3s. 6d. *net.*

Swanton (E. W.). FUNGI AND HOW TO KNOW THEM. Illustrated. *Cr. 8vo.* 6s. *net.*
BRITISH PLANT-GALLS. *Cr. 8vo.* 7s. 6d. *net.*

Symes (J. E.). THE FRENCH REVOLUTION. *Second Edition. Cr. 8vo.* 2s. 6d.

Tabor (Margaret E.). THE SAINTS IN ART. With their Attributes and Symbols Alphabetically Arranged. Illustrated. *Third Edition. Fcap. 8vo.* 3s. 6d. *net.*

Taylor (A. E.). ELEMENTS OF METAPHYSICS. *Fourth Edition. Demy 8vo.* 10s. 6d. *net.*

Taylor (J. W.). THE COMING OF THE SAINTS. *Second Edition Cr. 8vo.* 5s. *net.*

Thomas (Edward). MAURICE MAETERLINCK. Illustrated. *Second Edition. Cr. 8vo.* 5s. *net.*

Thompson (Francis). SELECTED POEMS OF FRANCIS THOMPSON. With a Biographical Note by WILFRID MEYNELL. With a Portrait in Photogravure. *Twenty-eighth Thousand. Fcap. 8vo.* 5s. *net.*

Tileston (Mary W.). DAILY STRENGTH FOR DAILY NEEDS. *Twenty-second Edition. Medium 16mo.* 2s. 6d. *net. Also in black morocco,* 6s. *net.*

Topham (Anne). MEMORIES OF THE KAISER'S COURT. Illustrated. *Tenth Edition. Cr. 8vo.* 2s. 6d. *net.*

Toynbee (Paget). DANTE ALIGHIERI. HIS LIFE AND WORKS. With 16 Illustrations. *Fourth and Enlarged Edition. Cr. 8vo.* 5s. *net.*

Trevelyan (G. M.). ENGLAND UNDER THE STUARTS. With Maps and Plans. *Sixth Edition. Demy 8vo.* 10s. 6d. *net.*

Triggs (H. Inigo). TOWN PLANNING: PAST, PRESENT, AND POSSIBLE. Illustrated. *Second Edition. Wide Royal 8vo.* 15s. *net.*

Underhill (Evelyn). MYSTICISM. A Study in the Nature and Development of Man's Spiritual Consciousness. *Fifth Edition. Demy 8vo.* 15s. *net.*

Vardon (Harry). HOW TO PLAY GOLF. Illustrated. *Ninth Edition. Cr. 8vo.* 2s. 6d. *net.*

Vernon (Hon. W. Warren). READINGS ON THE INFERNO OF DANTE. With an Introduction by the Rev. Dr. MOORE. *Two Volumes. Second Edition, Rewritten. Cr. 8vo.* 15s. *net.*

General Literature

READINGS ON THE PURGATORIO OF DANTE. With an Introduction by the late DEAN CHURCH. *Two Volumes. Third Edition, Revised. Cr. 8vo.* 15s. net.

READINGS ON THE PARADISO OF DANTE. With an Introduction by the BISHOP OF RIPON. *Two Volumes. Second Edition, Revised. Cr. 8vo.* 15s. net.

Vickers (Kenneth H.). ENGLAND IN THE LATER MIDDLE AGES. With Maps. *Second Edition, Revised. Demy 8vo.* 10s. 6d. net.

Waddell (L. A.). LHASA AND ITS MYSTERIES. With a Record of the Expedition of 1903-1904. Illustrated. *Third and Cheaper Edition. Medium 8vo.* 7s. 6d. net.

Wade (G. W. and J. H.). RAMBLES IN SOMERSET. Illustrated. *Cr. 8vo.* 6s.

Wagner (Richard). RICHARD WAGNER'S MUSIC DRAMAS. Interpretations, embodying Wagner's own explanations. By ALICE LEIGHTON CLEATHER and BASIL CRUMP. *Fcap. 8vo.* 2s. 6d. each.
THE RING OF THE NIBELUNG.
  Sixth Edition.
LOHENGRIN AND PARSIFAL.
  Third Edition.
TRISTAN AND ISOLDE.
  Second Edition.
TANNHÄUSER AND THE MASTERSINGERS OF NUREMBURG.

Waterhouse (Elizabeth). WITH THE SIMPLE-HEARTED. Little Homilies to Women in Country Places. *Third Edition. Small Pott 8vo.* 2s. net.
THE HOUSE BY THE CHERRY TREE. A Second Series of Little Homilies to Women in Country Places. *Small Pott 8vo.* 2s. net.
COMPANIONS OF THE WAY. Being Selections for Morning and Evening Reading. Chosen and arranged by ELIZABETH WATERHOUSE. *Large Cr. 8vo.* 5s. net.
THOUGHTS OF A TERTIARY. *Second Edition. Small Pott 8vo.* 1s. net.
VERSES. *Second Edition, Enlarged. Fcap. 8vo.* 2s. net.
A LITTLE BOOK OF LIFE AND DEATH. Selected and Arranged. *Seventeenth Edition. Small Pott 8vo. Cloth,* 1s. 6d. net; *Velvet Persian Yapp,* 2s. 6d. net.

Waters (W. G.). ITALIAN SCULPTORS. Illustrated. *Cr. 8vo.* 7s. 6d. net.

Weigall (Arthur E. P.). A GUIDE TO THE ANTIQUITIES OF UPPER EGYPT: FROM ABYDOS TO THE SUDAN FRONTIER. Illustrated. *Second Edition. Cr. 8vo.* 7s. 6d. net.

Wells (J.). OXFORD AND OXFORD LIFE. *Third Edition. Cr. 8vo.* 3s. 6d.
A SHORT HISTORY OF ROME. *Fourteenth Edition.* With 3 Maps. *Cr. 8vo.* 3s. 6d.

Wheeler (Owen). A PRIMER OF PHOTOGRAPHY. With 17 Illustrations. *Cr. 8vo.* 2s. 6d. net.

Whitten (Wilfred). A LONDONER'S LONDON. Illustrated. *Second Edition. Cr. 8vo.* 6s.

Wilde (Oscar). THE WORKS OF OSCAR WILDE. *Twelve Volumes. Fcap. 8vo.* 5s. net each volume.

  I. LORD ARTHUR SAVILE'S CRIME AND THE PORTRAIT OF MR. W. H. II. THE DUCHESS OF PADUA. III. POEMS. IV. LADY WINDERMERE'S FAN. V. A WOMAN OF NO IMPORTANCE. VI. AN IDEAL HUSBAND. VII. THE IMPORTANCE OF BEING EARNEST. VIII. A HOUSE OF POMEGRANATES. IX. INTENTIONS. X. DE PROFUNDIS AND PRISON LETTERS. XI. ESSAYS. XII. SALOMÉ, A FLORENTINE TRAGEDY, and LA SAINTE COURTISANE. XIII. THE CRITIC IN PALL MALL. XIV. SELECTED PROSE OF OSCAR WILDE.

A HOUSE OF POMEGRANATES. Illustrated. *Cr. 4to.* 12s. 6d. net.

Wilding (Anthony F.). ON THE COURT AND OFF. With 58 Illustrations. *Seventh Edition. Cr. 8vo.* 5s. net.

Wilson (Ernest H.). A NATURALIST IN WESTERN CHINA. Illustrated. *Second Edition.* 2 Vols. *Demy 8vo.* £1 10s. net.

Wood (Sir Evelyn). FROM MIDSHIPMAN TO FIELD-MARSHAL. Illustrated. *Fifth Edition. Demy 8vo.* 7s. 6d. net.
THE REVOLT IN HINDUSTAN (1857-59). Illustrated. *Second Edition. Cr. 8vo.* 6s.

Wood (Lieut. W. B.) and Edmonds (Col. J. E.). A HISTORY OF THE CIVIL WAR IN THE UNITED STATES (1861-65). With an Introduction by SPENSER WILKINSON. With 24 Maps and Plans. *Third Edition. Demy 8vo.* 12s. 6d. net.

Wordsworth (W.). POEMS. With an Introduction and Notes by NOWELL C. SMITH. *Three Volumes. Demy 8vo.* 15s. net.

Yeats (W. B.). A BOOK OF IRISH VERSE. *Third Edition. Cr. 8vo.* 3s. 6d.

PART II.—A SELECTION OF SERIES

Ancient Cities

General Editor, SIR B. C. A. WINDLE

Cr. 8vo.   4s. 6d. net each volume

With Illustrations by E. H. NEW, and other Artists

BRISTOL. Alfred Harvey.
CANTERBURY. J. C. Cox.
CHESTER. Sir B. C. A. Windle.
DUBLIN. S. A. O. Fitzpatrick.

EDINBURGH. M. G. Williamson.
LINCOLN. E. Mansel Sympson.
SHREWSBURY. T. Auden.
WELLS and GLASTONBURY. T. S. Holmes.

The Antiquary's Books

General Editor, J. CHARLES COX

Demy 8vo.   7s. 6d. net each volume

With Numerous Illustrations

ANCIENT PAINTED GLASS IN ENGLAND. Philip Nelson.

ARCHÆOLOGY AND FALSE ANTIQUITIES. R. Munro.

BELLS OF ENGLAND, THE. Canon J. J. Raven. *Second Edition.*

BRASSES OF ENGLAND, THE. Herbert W. Macklin. *Third Edition.*

CASTLES AND WALLED TOWNS OF ENGLAND, THE. A. Harvey.

CELTIC ART IN PAGAN AND CHRISTIAN TIMES. J. Romilly Allen. *Second Edition.*

CHURCHWARDENS' ACCOUNTS. J. C. Cox.

DOMESDAY INQUEST, THE. Adolphus Ballard.

ENGLISH CHURCH FURNITURE. J. C. Cox and A. Harvey. *Second Edition.*

ENGLISH COSTUME. From Prehistoric Times to the End of the Eighteenth Century. George Clinch.

ENGLISH MONASTIC LIFE. Cardinal Gasquet. *Fourth Edition.*

ENGLISH SEALS. J. Harvey Bloom.

FOLK-LORE AS AN HISTORICAL SCIENCE. Sir G. L. Gomme.

GILDS AND COMPANIES OF LONDON, THE. George Unwin.

HERMITS AND ANCHORITES OF ENGLAND, THE. Rotha Mary Clay.

MANOR AND MANORIAL RECORDS, THE. Nathaniel J. Hone. *Second Edition.*

MEDIÆVAL HOSPITALS OF ENGLAND, THE. Rotha Mary Clay.

OLD ENGLISH INSTRUMENTS OF MUSIC. F. W. Galpin. *Second Edition.*

GENERAL LITERATURE 13

The Antiquary's Books—*continued*

OLD ENGLISH LIBRARIES. Ernest A. Savage.

OLD SERVICE BOOKS OF THE ENGLISH CHURCH. Christopher Wordsworth, and Henry Littlehales. *Second Edition.*

PARISH LIFE IN MEDIÆVAL ENGLAND. Cardinal Gasquet. *Fourth Edition.*

PARISH REGISTERS OF ENGLAND, THE. J. C. Cox.

REMAINS OF THE PREHISTORIC AGE IN ENGLAND. Sir B. C. A. Windle. *Second Edition.*

ROMAN ERA IN BRITAIN, THE. J. Ward.

ROMANO-BRITISH BUILDINGS AND EARTHWORKS. J. Ward.

ROYAL FORESTS OF ENGLAND, THE. J. C. Cox.

SCHOOLS OF MEDIEVAL ENGLAND, THE. A. F. Leach.

SHRINES OF BRITISH SAINTS. J. C. Wall.

The Arden Shakespeare

Demy 8vo. 2s. 6d. net each volume

An edition of Shakespeare in Single Plays; each edited with a full Introduction, Textual Notes, and a Commentary at the foot of the page

ALL'S WELL THAT ENDS WELL.
ANTONY AND CLEOPATRA. *Second Edition.*
AS YOU LIKE IT.
CYMBELINE. *Second Edition.*
COMEDY OF ERRORS, THE.
HAMLET. *Fourth Edition.*
JULIUS CAESAR.
KING HENRY IV. PT. I.
KING HENRY V.
KING HENRY VI. PT. I
KING HENRY VI. PT. II.
KING HENRY VI. PT. III.
KING HENRY VIII.
KING LEAR.
KING RICHARD II.
KING RICHARD III.
LIFE AND DEATH OF KING JOHN, THE.
LOVE'S LABOUR'S LOST. *Second Edition.*

MACBETH.
MEASURE FOR MEASURE.
MERCHANT OF VENICE, THE. *Second Edition.*
MERRY WIVES OF WINDSOR, THE.
MIDSUMMER NIGHT'S DREAM, A.
OTHELLO.
PERICLES.
ROMEO AND JULIET.
SONNETS AND A LOVER'S COMPLAINT.
TAMING OF THE SHREW, THE.
TEMPEST, THE.
TIMON OF ATHENS.
TITUS ANDRONICUS.
TROILUS AND CRESSIDA.
TWELFTH NIGHT.
TWO GENTLEMEN OF VERONA, THE.
VENUS AND ADONIS.
WINTER'S TALE, THE.

Classics of Art

Edited by DR. J. H. W. LAING

With numerous Illustrations. Wide Royal 8vo

ART OF THE GREEKS, THE. H. B. Walters. 12s. 6d. *net.*

ART OF THE ROMANS, THE. H. B. Walters. 15s. *net.*

CHARDIN. H. E. A. Furst. 12s. 6d. *net.*

DONATELLO. Maud Cruttwell. 15s. *net.*

FLORENTINE SCULPTORS OF THE RENAISSANCE. Wilhelm Bode. Translated by Jessie Haynes. 12s. 6d. *net.*

GEORGE ROMNEY. Arthur B. Chamberlain. 12s. 6d. *net.*

Classics of Art—continued

GHIRLANDAIO. Gerald S. Davies. *Second Edition.* 10s. 6d. *net.*
LAWRENCE. Sir Walter Armstrong. £1 1s. *net.*
MICHELANGELO. Gerald S. Davies. 12s. 6d. *net.*
RAPHAEL. A. P. Oppé. 12s. 6d. *net.*
REMBRANDT'S ETCHINGS. A. M. Hind. Two Volumes. 21s. *net.*

RUBENS. Edward Dillon. 25s. *net.*
TINTORETTO. Evelyn March Phillipps. 15s. *net.*
TITIAN. Charles Ricketts. 15s. *net.*
TURNER'S SKETCHES AND DRAWINGS. A. J. Finberg. *Second Edition.* 12s. 6d. *net.*
VELAZQUEZ. A. de Beruete. 10s. 6d. *net.*

The 'Complete' Series

Fully Illustrated. Demy 8vo

COMPLETE AMATEUR BOXER, THE. J. G. Bohun Lynch. 5s. *net.*
COMPLETE ASSOCIATION FOOTBALLER, THE. B. S. Evers and C. E. Hughes-Davies. 5s. *net.*
COMPLETE ATHLETIC TRAINER, THE. S. A. Mussabini. 5s. *net.*
COMPLETE BILLIARD PLAYER, THE. Charles Roberts. 10s. 6d. *net.*
COMPLETE COOK, THE. Lilian Whitling. 7s. 6d. *net.*
COMPLETE CRICKETER, THE. Albert E. Knight. 7s. 6d. *net. Second Edition.*
COMPLETE FOXHUNTER, THE. Charles Richardson. 12s. 6d. *net. Second Edition.*
COMPLETE GOLFER, THE. Harry Vardon. 10s. 6d. *net. Fourteenth Edition, Revised.*
COMPLETE HOCKEY-PLAYER, THE. Eustace E. White. 5s. *net. Second Edition.*
COMPLETE HORSEMAN, THE. W. Scarth Dixon. *Second Edition.* 10s. 6d. *net.*
COMPLETE JUJITSUAN, THE. W. H. Garrud. 5s. *net.*

COMPLETE LAWN TENNIS PLAYER, THE. A. Wallis Myers. 10s. 6d. *net. Fourth Edition.*
COMPLETE MOTORIST, THE. Filson Young and W. G. Aston. 5s. *net. Revised Edition.*
COMPLETE MOUNTAINEER, THE. G. D. Abraham. 15s. *net. Second Edition.*
COMPLETE OARSMAN, THE. R. C. Lehmann. 10s. 6d. *net.*
COMPLETE PHOTOGRAPHER, THE. R. Child Bayley. 10s. 6d. *net. Fifth Edition, Revised.*
COMPLETE RUGBY FOOTBALLER, ON THE NEW ZEALAND SYSTEM, THE. D. Gallaher and W. J. Stead. 10s. 6d. *net. Second Edition.*
COMPLETE SHOT, THE. G. T. Teasdale-Buckell. 12s. 6d. *net. Third Edition.*
COMPLETE SWIMMER, THE. F. Sachs. 7s. 6d. *net.*
COMPLETE YACHTSMAN, THE. B. Heckstall-Smith and E. du Boulay. *Second Edition, Revised.* 15s. *net.*

The Connoisseur's Library

With numerous Illustrations. Wide Royal 8vo. 25s. net each volume

ENGLISH COLOURED BOOKS. Martin Hardie.
ENGLISH FURNITURE. F. S. Robinson.
ETCHINGS. Sir F. Wedmore. *Second Edition.*
EUROPEAN ENAMELS. Henry H. Cunynghame.
FINE BOOKS. A. W. Pollard.
GLASS. Edward Dillon.
GOLDSMITHS' AND SILVERSMITHS' WORK. Nelson Dawson. *Second Edition.*
ILLUMINATED MANUSCRIPTS. J. A. Herbert. *Second Edition.*

IVORIES. Alfred Maskell.
JEWELLERY. H. Clifford Smith. *Second Edition.*
MEZZOTINTS. Cyril Davenport.
MINIATURES. Dudley Heath.
PORCELAIN. Edward Dillon.
SEALS. Walter de Gray Birch.
WOOD SCULPTURE. Alfred Maskell. *Second Edition.*

Handbooks of English Church History

Edited by J. H. BURN. *Crown 8vo. 2s. 6d. net each volume*

FOUNDATIONS OF THE ENGLISH CHURCH, THE. J. H. Maude.

SAXON CHURCH AND THE NORMAN CONQUEST, THE. C. T. Cruttwell.

MEDIÆVAL CHURCH AND THE PAPACY, THE. A. C. Jennings.

REFORMATION PERIOD, THE. Henry Gee.

STRUGGLE WITH PURITANISM, THE. Bruce Blaxland.

CHURCH OF ENGLAND IN THE EIGHTEENTH CENTURY, THE. Alfred Plummer.

Handbooks of Theology

DOCTRINE OF THE INCARNATION, THE. R. L. Ottley. *Fifth Edition. Demy 8vo. 12s. 6d. net.*

HISTORY OF EARLY CHRISTIAN DOCTRINE, A. J. F. Bethune-Baker. *Demy 8vo. 10s. 6d. net.*

INTRODUCTION TO THE HISTORY OF RELIGION, AN. F. B. Jevons. *Sixth Edition. Demy 8vo. 10s. 6d. net.*

INTRODUCTION TO THE HISTORY OF THE CREEDS, AN. A. E. Burn. *Demy 8vo. 10s. 6d. net.*

PHILOSOPHY OF RELIGION IN ENGLAND AND AMERICA, THE. Alfred Caldecott. *Demy 8vo. 10s. 6d. net.*

XXXIX ARTICLES OF THE CHURCH OF ENGLAND, THE. Edited by E. C. S. Gibson. *Ninth Edition. Demy 8vo. 12s. 6d. net.*

Health Series

Fcap. 8vo. 1s. net

CARE OF THE BODY, THE. F. Cavanagh.

CARE OF THE TEETH, THE. A. T. Pitts.

*EYES OF OUR CHILDREN, THE. N. Bishop Harman.

HEALTH FOR THE MIDDLE-AGED. Seymour Taylor.

*HEALTH OF A WOMAN, THE. H. J. F. Simpson.

*HOW TO LIVE LONG. W. Carr.

*HYGIENE OF THE SKIN, THE. G. Pernet.

*PREVENTION OF THE COMMON COLD, THE. O. K. Williamson.

THROAT AND EAR TROUBLES. Macleod Yearsley.

HEALTH OF THE CHILD, THE. O. Hildesheim.

The 'Home Life' Series

Illustrated. Demy 8vo. 6s. to 10s. 6d. net

HOME LIFE IN AMERICA. Katherine G. Busbey. *Second Edition.*

HOME LIFE IN CHINA. I. Taylor Headland.

HOME LIFE IN FRANCE. Miss Betham-Edwards. *Sixth Edition.*

HOME LIFE IN GERMANY. Mrs. A. Sidgwick. *Third Edition.*

HOME LIFE IN HOLLAND. D. S. Meldrum. *Second Edition.*

HOME LIFE IN ITALY. Lina Duff Gordon. *Third Edition.*

HOME LIFE IN NORWAY. H. K. Daniels. *Second Edition.*

HOME LIFE IN RUSSIA. A. S. Rappoport.

HOME LIFE IN SPAIN. S. L. Bensusan. *Second Edition.*

Leaders of Religion

Edited by H. C. BEECHING. *With Portraits*

Crown 8vo. 2s. net each volume

CARDINAL NEWMAN. R. H. Hutton. *Second Edition.*
JOHN WESLEY. J. H. Overton.
BISHOP WILBERFORCE. G. W. Daniell.
CARDINAL MANNING. A. W. Hutton. *Second Edition.*
CHARLES SIMEON. H. C. G. Moule.
JOHN KNOX. F. MacCunn. *Second Edition.*
JOHN HOWE. R. F. Horton.
THOMAS KEN. F. A. Clarke.
GEORGE FOX, THE QUAKER. T. Hodgkin. *Third Edition.*

JOHN KEBLE. Walter Lock. *Seventh Edition.*
THOMAS CHALMERS. Mrs. Oliphant. *Second Edition.*
LANCELOT ANDREWES. R. L. Ottley. *Second Edition.*
AUGUSTINE OF CANTERBURY. E. L. Cutts.
WILLIAM LAUD. W. H. Hutton. *Fourth Edition.*
JOHN DONNE. Augustus Jessop.
THOMAS CRANMER. A. J. Mason.
LATIMER. R. M. and A. J. Carlyle.
BISHOP BUTLER W. A. Spooner.

The Library of Devotion

With Introductions and (where necessary) Notes

Small Pott 8vo, cloth, 2s.; leather, 2s. 6d. net each volume

CONFESSIONS OF ST. AUGUSTINE, THE. *Ninth Edition.*
IMITATION OF CHRIST, THE. *Eighth Edition.*
CHRISTIAN YEAR, THE. *Fifth Edition.*
LYRA INNOCENTIUM. *Third Edition.*
TEMPLE, THE. *Second Edition.*
BOOK OF DEVOTIONS, A. *Second Edition.*
SERIOUS CALL TO A DEVOUT AND HOLY LIFE, A. *Fifth Edition.*
GUIDE TO ETERNITY, A.
INNER WAY, THE. *Third Edition.*
ON THE LOVE OF GOD.
PSALMS OF DAVID, THE.
LYRA APOSTOLICA.
SONG OF SONGS, THE.
THOUGHTS OF PASCAL, THE. *Second Edition.*
MANUAL OF CONSOLATION FROM THE SAINTS AND FATHERS, A.
DEVOTIONS FROM THE APOCRYPHA.
SPIRITUAL COMBAT, THE.

DEVOTIONS OF ST. ANSELM, THE.
BISHOP WILSON'S SACRA PRIVATA.
GRACE ABOUNDING TO THE CHIEF OF SINNERS.
LYRA SACRA. A Book of Sacred Verse. *Second Edition.*
DAY BOOK FROM THE SAINTS AND FATHERS, A.
LITTLE BOOK OF HEAVENLY WISDOM, A. A Selection from the English Mystics.
LIGHT, LIFE, and LOVE. A Selection from the German Mystics.
INTRODUCTION TO THE DEVOUT LIFE, AN.
LITTLE FLOWERS OF THE GLORIOUS MESSER ST. FRANCIS AND OF HIS FRIARS, THE.
DEATH AND IMMORTALITY.
SPIRITUAL GUIDE, THE. *Third Edition.*
DEVOTIONS FOR EVERY DAY IN THE WEEK AND THE GREAT FESTIVALS.
PRECES PRIVATAE.
HORAE MYSTICAE. A Day Book from the Writings of Mystics of Many Nations.

Little Books on Art

With many Illustrations. Demy 16mo. 2s. 6d. net each volume

Each volume consists of about 200 pages, and contains from 30 to 40 Illustrations, including a Frontispiece in Photogravure

ALBRECHT DÜRER. L. J Allen.
ARTS OF JAPAN, THE. E. Dillon. *Third Edition.*
BOOKPLATES. E. Almack.
BOTTICELLI. Mary L. Bonnor.
BURNE-JONES. F. de Lisle. *Third Edition.*
CELLINI. R. H. H. Cust.
CHRISTIAN SYMBOLISM. Mrs. H. Jenner.
CHRIST IN ART. Mrs. H. Jenner.
CLAUDE. E. Dillon.
CONSTABLE. H. W. Tompkins. *Second Edition.*
COROT. A. Pollard and E. Birnstingl.
EARLY ENGLISH WATER-COLOUR. C. E. Hughes.
ENAMELS. Mrs. N. Dawson. *Second Edition.*
FREDERIC LEIGHTON. A. Corkran.
GEORGE ROMNEY. G. Paston.
GREEK ART. H. B. Walters. *Fifth Edition.*
GREUZE AND BOUCHER. E. F. Pollard.
HOLBEIN. Mrs. G. Fortescue.
ILLUMINATED MANUSCRIPTS. J. W. Bradley.
JEWELLERY. C. Davenport. *Second Edition.*
JOHN HOPPNER. H. P. K. Skipton.
SIR JOSHUA REYNOLDS. J. Sime. *Second Edition.*
MILLET. N. Peacock. *Second Edition.*
MINIATURES. C. Davenport, V.D., F.S.A. *Second Edition.*
OUR LADY IN ART. Mrs. H. Jenner.
RAPHAEL. A. R. Dryhurst. *Second Edition.*
RODIN. Muriel Ciolkowska.
TURNER. F. Tyrrell-Gill.
VANDYCK. M. G. Smallwood.
VELAZQUEZ. W. Wilberforce and A. R. Gilbert.
WATTS. R. E. D. Sketchley. *Second Edition.*

The Little Guides

With many Illustrations by E. H. NEW and other artists, and from photographs

Small Pott 8vo. 2s. 6d. net each volume

The main features of these Guides are (1) a handy and charming form; (2) illustrations from photographs and by well-known artists; (3) good plans and maps; (4) an adequate but compact presentation of everything that is interesting in the natural features, history, archæology, and architecture of the town or district treated.

CAMBRIDGE AND ITS COLLEGES. A. H. Thompson. *Third Edition, Revised.*
CHANNEL ISLANDS, THE. E. E. Bicknell.
ENGLISH LAKES, THE. F. G. Brabant.
ISLE OF WIGHT, THE. G. Clinch.
LONDON. G. Clinch.
MALVERN COUNTRY, THE. Sir B.C.A.Windle *Second Edition.*
NORTH WALES. A. T. Story.
OXFORD AND ITS COLLEGES. J. Wells. *Tenth Edition.*
ST. PAUL'S CATHEDRAL. G. Clinch.
SHAKESPEARE'S COUNTRY. Sir B. C. A. Windle. *Fifth Edition.*
SOUTH WALES. G. W. and J. H. Wade.
TEMPLE, THE. H. H. L. Bellot.
WESTMINSTER ABBEY. G. E. Troutbeck. *Second Edition.*

The Little Guides—continued

BERKSHIRE. F. G. Brabant.
BUCKINGHAMSHIRE. E. S. Roscoe. *Second Edition, Revised.*
CAMBRIDGESHIRE. J. C. Cox.
CHESHIRE. W. M. Gallichan.
CORNWALL. A. L. Salmon. *Second Edition.*
DERBYSHIRE. J. C. Cox. *Second Edition.*
DEVON. S. Baring-Gould. *Third Edition.*
DORSET. F. R. Heath. *Fourth Edition.*
DURHAM. J. E. Hodgkin.
ESSEX. J. C. Cox. *Second Edition.*
GLOUCESTERSHIRE. J. C. Cox.
HAMPSHIRE. J. C. Cox. *Second Edition.*
HERTFORDSHIRE. H. W. Tompkins.
KENT. J. C. Cox. *Second Edition, Re-written.*
KERRY. C. P. Crane. *Second Edition.*
LEICESTERSHIRE AND RUTLAND. A. Harvey and V. B. Crowther-Beynon.
MIDDLESEX. J. B. Firth.
MONMOUTHSHIRE. G. W. and J. H. Wade.
NORFOLK. W. A. Dutt. *Third Edition, Revised.*
NORTHAMPTONSHIRE. W. Dry. *Second Edition, Revised.*
*NORTHUMBERLAND. J. E. Morris.
NOTTINGHAMSHIRE. L. Guilford.
OXFORDSHIRE. F. G. Brabant. *Second Edition.*
SHROPSHIRE. J. E. Auden.
SOMERSET. G. W. and J. H. Wade. *Third Edition.*
STAFFORDSHIRE. C. Masefield.
SUFFOLK. W. A. Dutt.
SURREY. J. C. Cox. *Second Edition, Re-written.*
SUSSEX. F. G. Brabant. *Fourth Edition.*
WARWICKSHIRE. J. C. Cox.
WILTSHIRE. F. R. Heath. *Second Edition.*
YORKSHIRE, THE EAST RIDING. J. E. Morris.
YORKSHIRE, THE NORTH RIDING. J. E. Morris.
YORKSHIRE, THE WEST RIDING. J. E. Morris. 3s. 6d. net.

BRITTANY. S. Baring-Gould. *Second Edition.*
NORMANDY. C. Scudamore. *Second Edition.*
ROME. C. G. Ellaby.
SICILY. F. H. Jackson.

The Little Library

With Introduction, Notes, and Photogravure Frontispieces

Small Pott 8vo. Each Volume, cloth, 1s. 6d. net

Anon. A LITTLE BOOK OF ENGLISH LYRICS. *Second Edition.*

Austen (Jane). PRIDE AND PREJUDICE. *Two Volumes.*
NORTHANGER ABBEY.

Bacon (Francis). THE ESSAYS OF LORD BACON.

Barham (R. H.). THE INGOLDSBY LEGENDS. *Two Volumes.*

Barnett (Annie). A LITTLE BOOK OF ENGLISH PROSE. *Third Edition.*

Beckford (William). THE HISTORY OF THE CALIPH VATHEK.

Blake (William). SELECTIONS FROM THE WORKS OF WILLIAM BLAKE.

Borrow (George). LAVENGRO. *Two Volumes.*
THE ROMANY RYE.

Browning (Robert). SELECTIONS FROM THE EARLY POEMS OF ROBERT BROWNING.

Canning (George). SELECTIONS FROM THE ANTI-JACOBIN: With some later Poems by GEORGE CANNING.

Cowley (Abraham). THE ESSAYS OF ABRAHAM COWLEY.

General Literature

The Little Library—continued

Crabbe (George). SELECTIONS FROM THE POEMS OF GEORGE CRABBE.

Crashaw (Richard). THE ENGLISH POEMS OF RICHARD CRASHAW.

Dante Alighieri. PURGATORY. PARADISE.

Darley (George). SELECTIONS FROM THE POEMS OF GEORGE DARLEY.

Dickens (Charles). CHRISTMAS BOOKS. *Two Volumes.*

Gaskell (Mrs.). CRANFORD. *Second Edition.*

Hawthorne (Nathaniel). THE SCARLET LETTER.

Kinglake (A. W.). EOTHEN. *Second Edition.*

Locker (F.). LONDON LYRICS.

Marvell (Andrew). THE POEMS OF ANDREW MARVELL.

Milton (John). THE MINOR POEMS OF JOHN MILTON.

Moir (D. M.). MANSIE WAUCH.

Nichols (Bowyer). A LITTLE BOOK OF ENGLISH SONNETS.

Smith (Horace and James). REJECTED ADDRESSES.

Sterne (Laurence). A SENTIMENTAL JOURNEY.

Tennyson (Alfred, Lord). THE EARLY POEMS OF ALFRED, LORD TENNYSON.
IN MEMORIAM.
THE PRINCESS.
MAUD.

Vaughan (Henry). THE POEMS OF HENRY VAUGHAN.

Waterhouse (Elizabeth). A LITTLE BOOK OF LIFE AND DEATH. *Seventeenth Edition.*

Wordsworth (W.). SELECTIONS FROM THE POEMS OF WILLIAM WORDSWORTH.

Wordsworth (W.) and Coleridge (S. T.). LYRICAL BALLADS. *Third Edition.*

The Little Quarto Shakespeare

Edited by W. J. CRAIG. With Introductions and Notes

Pott 16mo. 40 *Volumes. Leather, price* 1s. *net each volume*
Mahogany Revolving Book Case. 10s. *net*

Miniature Library

Demy 32mo. *Leather,* 2s. *net each volume*

EUPHRANOR: A Dialogue on Youth. Edward FitzGerald.

EDWARD, LORD HERBERT OF CHERBURY, THE LIFE OF. Written by himself.

POLONIUS; or, Wise Saws and Modern Instances. Edward FitzGerald.

THE RUBÁIYÁT OF OMAR KHAYYÁM. Edward FitzGerald. *Fifth Edition.* 1s. *net.*

The New Library of Medicine

Edited by C. W. SALEEBY. *Demy* 8vo

AIR AND HEALTH. Ronald C. Macfie. 7s. 6d. *net. Second Edition.*

CARE OF THE BODY, THE. F. Cavanagh. *Second Edition.* 7s. 6d. *net.*

CHILDREN OF THE NATION, THE. The Right Hon. Sir John Gorst. *Second Edition.* 7s. 6d. *net.*

DISEASES OF OCCUPATION. Sir Thos. Oliver. 10s. 6d. *net. Second Edition.*

DRUGS AND THE DRUG HABIT. H. Sainsbury. 7s. 6d. *net.*

FUNCTIONAL NERVE DISEASES. A. T. Schofield. 7s. 6d. *net.*

HYGIENE OF MIND, THE. Sir T. S. Clouston. *Sixth Edition.* 7s. 6d. *net.*

INFANT MORTALITY. Sir George Newman. 7s. 6d. *net.*

PREVENTION OF TUBERCULOSIS (CONSUMPTION), THE. Arthur Newsholme. 10s. 6d. *net. Second Edition.*

The New Library of Music

Edited by ERNEST NEWMAN. *Illustrated. Demy 8vo. 7s. 6d. net*

BRAHMS. J. A. Fuller-Maitland. *Second Edition.*

HANDEL. R. A. Streatfeild. *Second Edition.*

HUGO WOLF. Ernest Newman.

Oxford Biographies

Illustrated. Fcap. 8vo. Each volume, cloth, 2s. 6d. net; leather, 3s. 6d. net

DANTE ALIGHIERI. Paget Toynbee. *Fifth Edition.*

GIROLAMO SAVONAROLA. E. L. S. Horsburgh. *Sixth Edition.*

JOHN HOWARD. E. C. S. Gibson.

SIR WALTER RALEIGH. I. A. Taylor.

ERASMUS. E. F. H. Capey.

CHATHAM. A. S. McDowall.

CANNING. W. Alison Phillips.

FRANÇOIS DE FÉNELON. Viscount St. Cyres.

Seven Plays

Fcap. 8vo. 2s. net

HONEYMOON, THE. A Comedy in Three Acts. Arnold Bennett. *Third Edition.*

GREAT ADVENTURE, THE. A Play of Fancy in Four Acts. Arnold Bennett. *Fourth Edition.*

MILESTONES. Arnold Bennett and Edward Knoblauch. *Seventh Edition.*

WARE CASE, THE. George Playdell.

IDEAL HUSBAND, AN. Oscar Wilde. *Acting Edition.*

KISMET. Edward Knoblauch. *Third Edition.*

TYPHOON. A Play in Four Acts. Melchior Lengyel. English Version by Laurence Irving. *Second Edition.*

Sport Series

Illustrated. Fcap. 8vo. 1s. net

FLYING, ALL ABOUT. Gertrude Bacon.

GOLFING SWING, THE. Burnham Hare. *Fourth Edition.*

*GYMNASTICS. D. Scott.

SKATING. A. E. Crawley.

SWIM, HOW TO. H. R. Austin.

WRESTLING. P. Longhurst.

The States of Italy

Edited by E. ARMSTRONG and R. LANGTON DOUGLAS

Illustrated. Demy 8vo

MILAN UNDER THE SFORZA, A HISTORY OF. Cecilia M. Ady. 10s. 6d. net.

PERUGIA, A HISTORY OF. W. Heywood. 12s. 6d. net.

VERONA, A HISTORY OF. A. M. Allen. 12s. 6d. net.

The Westminster Commentaries

General Editor, WALTER LOCK

Demy 8vo

ACTS OF THE APOSTLES, THE. Edited by R. B. Rackham. *Seventh Edition.* 10s. 6d. net.

FIRST EPISTLE OF PAUL THE APOSTLE TO THE CORINTHIANS, THE. Edited by H. L. Goudge. *Fourth Edition.* 6s. net.

BOOK OF AMOS, THE. Edited by E. A. Edghill. With an Introduction by G. A. Cooke. 6s. net.

BOOK OF EXODUS, THE. Edited by A. H. M'Neile. With a Map and 3 Plans. 10s. 6d. net.

BOOK OF EZEKIEL, THE. Edited by H. A. Redpath. 10s. 6d. net.

BOOK OF GENESIS, THE. Edited, with Introduction and Notes, by S. R. Driver. *Tenth Edition.* 10s. 6d. net.

ADDITIONS AND CORRECTIONS IN THE SEVENTH AND EIGHTH EDITIONS OF THE BOOK OF GENESIS. S. R. Driver. 1s. net.

BOOK OF THE PROPHET ISAIAH, THE. Edited by G. W. Wade. 10s. 6d. net.

BOOK OF JOB, THE. Edited by E. C. S. Gibson. *Second Edition.* 6s. net.

EPISTLE OF ST. JAMES, THE. Edited, with Introduction and Notes, by R. J. Knowling. *Second Edition.* 6s. net.

General Literature

The 'Young' Series
Illustrated. Crown 8vo

YOUNG BOTANIST, THE. W. P. Westell and C. S. Cooper. 3s. 6d. net.

YOUNG CARPENTER, THE. Cyril Hall. 5s.

YOUNG ELECTRICIAN, THE. Hammond Hall. *Second Edition.* 5s.

YOUNG ENGINEER, THE. Hammond Hall. *Third Edition.* 5s.

YOUNG NATURALIST, THE. W. P. Westell. 6s.

YOUNG ORNITHOLOGIST, THE. W. P. Westell. 5s.

Methuen's Shilling Library
Fcap. 8vo. 1s. net

ALL THINGS CONSIDERED. G. K. Chesterton.

BEST OF LAMB, THE. Edited by E. V. Lucas.

BLUE BIRD, THE. Maurice Maeterlinck.

CHARLES DICKENS. G. K. Chesterton.

CHARMIDES, AND OTHER POEMS. Oscar Wilde.

CHITRÀL: The Story of a Minor Siege. Sir G. S. Robertson.

CONDITION OF ENGLAND, THE. G. F. G. Masterman.

DE PROFUNDIS. Oscar Wilde.

FAMOUS WITS, A BOOK OF. W. Jerrold.

FROM MIDSHIPMAN TO FIELD-MARSHAL. Sir Evelyn Wood, F.M., V.C.

HARVEST HOME. E. V. Lucas.

HILLS AND THE SEA. Hilaire Belloc.

HOME LIFE IN FRANCE. M. Betham-Edwards.

HUXLEY, THOMAS HENRY. P. Chalmers-Mitchell.

IDEAL HUSBAND, AN. Oscar Wilde.

IMPORTANCE OF BEING EARNEST, THE. Oscar Wilde.

INTENTIONS. Oscar Wilde.

JOHN BOYES, KING OF THE WA-KIKUYU. John Boyes.

LADY WINDERMERE'S FAN. Oscar Wilde.

LETTERS FROM A SELF-MADE MERCHANT TO HIS SON. George Horace Lorimer.

LIFE OF JOHN RUSKIN, THE. W. G. Collingwood.

LIFE OF ROBERT LOUIS STEVENSON, THE. Graham Balfour.

LITTLE OF EVERYTHING, A. E. V. Lucas.

LORD ARTHUR SAVILE'S CRIME. Oscar Wilde.

LORE OF THE HONEY-BEE, THE. Tickner Edwardes.

MAN AND THE UNIVERSE. Sir Oliver Lodge.

MARY MAGDALENE. Maurice Maeterlinck.

MIRROR OF THE SEA, THE. J. Conrad.

OLD COUNTRY LIFE. S. Baring-Gould.

OSCAR WILDE: A Critical Study. Arthur Ransome.

PARISH CLERK, THE. P. H. Ditchfield.

PICKED COMPANY, A. Hilaire Belloc.

REASON AND BELIEF. Sir Oliver Lodge.

SELECTED POEMS. Oscar Wilde.

SEVASTOPOL, AND OTHER STORIES. Leo Tolstoy.

SOCIAL EVILS AND THEIR REMEDY. Leo Tolstoy.

SOME LETTERS OF R. L. STEVENSON. Selected by Lloyd Osbourne.

SUBSTANCE OF FAITH, THE. Sir Oliver Lodge.

TENNYSON. A. C. Benson.

TOWER OF LONDON, THE. R. Davey.

TWO ADMIRALS. Admiral John Moresby.

UNDER FIVE REIGNS. Lady Dorothy Nevill.

VAILIMA LETTERS. Robert Louis Stevenson.

VICAR OF MORWENSTOW, THE. S. Baring-Gould.

Books for Travellers

Crown 8vo. 6s. net each

Each volume contains a number of Illustrations in Colour

AVON AND SHAKESPEARE'S COUNTRY, THE. A. G. Bradley.

BLACK FOREST, A BOOK OF THE. C. E. Hughes.

BRETONS AT HOME, THE. F. M. Gostling.

CITIES OF LOMBARDY, THE. Edward Hutton.

CITIES OF ROMAGNA AND THE MARCHES, THE. Edward Hutton.

CITIES OF SPAIN, THE. Edward Hutton.

CITIES OF UMBRIA, THE. Edward Hutton.

DAYS IN CORNWALL. C. Lewis Hind.

EGYPT, BY THE WATERS OF. N. Lorimer.

FLORENCE AND NORTHERN TUSCANY, WITH GENOA. Edward Hutton.

LAND OF PARDONS, THE (Brittany). Anatole Le Braz.

NAPLES. Arthur H. Norway.

NAPLES RIVIERA, THE. H. M. Vaughan.

NEW FOREST, THE. Horace G. Hutchinson.

NORFOLK BROADS, THE. W. A. Dutt.

NORWAY AND ITS FJORDS. M. A. Wyllie.

RHINE, A BOOK OF THE. S. Baring-Gould.

ROME. Edward Hutton.

ROUND ABOUT WILTSHIRE. A. G. Bradley.

SCOTLAND OF TO-DAY. T. F. Henderson and Francis Watt.

SIENA AND SOUTHERN TUSCANY. Edward Hutton.

SKIRTS OF THE GREAT CITY, THE. Mrs. A. G. Bell.

THROUGH EAST ANGLIA IN A MOTOR CAR. J. E. Vincent.

VENICE AND VENETIA. Edward Hutton.

WANDERER IN FLORENCE, A. E. V. Lucas.

WANDERER IN PARIS, A. E. V. Lucas.

WANDERER IN HOLLAND, A. E. V. Lucas.

WANDERER IN LONDON, A. E. V. Lucas.

WANDERER IN VENICE, A. E. V. Lucas.

Some Books on Art

ARMOURER AND HIS CRAFT, THE. Charles ffoulkes. Illustrated. *Royal 4to.* £2 2s. net.

ART, ANCIENT AND MEDIEVAL. M. H. Bulley. Illustrated. *Crown 8vo.* 5s. net.

BRITISH SCHOOL, THE. An Anecdotal Guide to the British Painters and Paintings in the National Gallery. E. V. Lucas. Illustrated. *Fcap. 8vo.* 2s. 6d. net.

DECORATIVE IRON WORK. From the XIth to the XVIIIth Century. Charles ffoulkes. *Royal 4to.* £2 2s. net.

FRANCESCO GUARDI, 1712-1793. G. A. Simonson. Illustrated. *Imperial 4to.* £2 2s. net.

ILLUSTRATIONS OF THE BOOK OF JOB. William Blake. *Quarto.* £1 1s. net.

ITALIAN SCULPTORS. W. G. Waters. Illustrated. *Crown 8vo.* 7s. 6d. net.

OLD PASTE. A. Beresford Ryley. Illustrated. *Royal 4to.* £2 2s. net.

ONE HUNDRED MASTERPIECES OF PAINTING. With an Introduction by R. C. Witt. Illustrated. *Second Edition. Demy 8vo.* 10s. 6d. net.

ONE HUNDRED MASTERPIECES OF SCULPTURE. With an Introduction by G. F. Hill. Illustrated. *Demy 8vo.* 10s. 6d. net.

ROMNEY FOLIO, A. With an Essay by A. B. Chamberlain. *Imperial Folio.* £15 15s. net.

ROYAL ACADEMY LECTURES ON PAINTING. George Clausen. Illustrated. *Crown 8vo.* 5s. net.

SAINTS IN ART, THE. Margaret E. Tabor. Illustrated. *Third Edition. Fcap. 8vo.* 3s. 6d. net.

SCHOOLS OF PAINTING. Mary Innes. Illustrated. *Cr. 8vo.* 5s. net.

CELTIC ART IN PAGAN AND CHRISTIAN TIMES. J. R. Allen. Illustrated. *Second Edition. Demy 8vo.* 7s. 6d. net.

'CLASSICS OF ART.' See page 13.

'THE CONNOISSEUR'S LIBRARY.' See page 14.

'LITTLE BOOKS ON ART.' See page 17.

Some Books on Italy

ETRURIA AND MODERN TUSCANY, OLD. Mary L. Cameron. Illustrated. *Second Edition. Cr. 8vo. 6s. net.*

FLORENCE: Her History and Art to the Fall of the Republic. F. A. Hyett. *Demy 8vo. 7s. 6d. net.*

FLORENCE, A WANDERER IN. E. V. Lucas. Illustrated. *Sixth Edition. Cr. 8vo. 6s. net.*

FLORENCE AND HER TREASURES. H. M. Vaughan. Illustrated. *Fcap. 8vo. 5s. net.*

FLORENCE, COUNTRY WALKS ABOUT. Edward Hutton. Illustrated. *Second Edition. Fcap. 8vo. 5s. net.*

FLORENCE AND THE CITIES OF NORTHERN TUSCANY, WITH GENOA. Edward Hutton. Illustrated. *Third Edition. Cr. 8vo. 6s. net.*

LOMBARDY, THE CITIES OF. Edward Hutton. Illustrated. *Cr. 8vo. 6s. net.*

MILAN UNDER THE SFORZA, A HISTORY OF. Cecilia M. Ady. Illustrated. *Demy 8vo. 10s. 6d. net.*

NAPLES: Past and Present. A. H. Norway. Illustrated. *Fourth Edition. Cr. 8vo. 6s. net.*

NAPLES RIVIERA, THE. H. M. Vaughan. Illustrated. *Second Edition. Cr. 8vo. 6s. net.*

NAPLES AND SOUTHERN ITALY. E. Hutton. Illustrated. *Cr. 8vo. 6s. net.*

PERUGIA, A HISTORY OF. William Heywood. Illustrated. *Demy 8vo. 12s. 6d. net.*

ROME. Edward Hutton. Illustrated. *Third Edition. Cr. 8vo. 6s. net.*

ROMAGNA AND THE MARCHES, THE CITIES OF. Edward Hutton. *Cr. 8vo. 6s. net.*

ROME OF THE PILGRIMS AND MARTYRS. Ethel Ross Barker. *Demy 8vo. 12s. 6d. net.*

ROME. C. G. Ellaby. Illustrated. *Small Pott 8vo. Cloth, 2s. 6d. net; leather, 3s. 6d. net.*

SICILY. F. H. Jackson. Illustrated. *Small Pott 8vo. Cloth, 2s. 6d. net; leather, 3s. 6d. net.*

SICILY: The New Winter Resort. Douglas Sladen. Illustrated. *Second Edition. Cr. 8vo. 5s. net.*

SIENA AND SOUTHERN TUSCANY. Edward Hutton. Illustrated. *Second Edition. Cr. 8vo. 6s. net.*

UMBRIA, THE CITIES OF. Edward Hutton. Illustrated. *Fifth Edition. Cr. 8vo. 6s. net.*

VENICE AND VENETIA. Edward Hutton. Illustrated. *Cr. 8vo. 6s. net*

VENICE ON FOOT. H. A. Douglas. Illustrated. *Second Edition. Fcap. 8vo. 5s. net.*

VENICE AND HER TREASURES. H. A. Douglas. Illustrated. *Fcap. 8vo. 5s. net.*

VERONA, A HISTORY OF. A. M. Allen. Illustrated. *Demy 8vo. 12s. 6d. net.*

DANTE AND HIS ITALY. Lonsdale Ragg. Illustrated. *Demy 8vo. 12s. 6d. net.*

DANTE ALIGHIERI: His Life and Works. Paget Toynbee. Illustrated. *Fourth Edition. Cr. 8vo. 5s. net.*

HOME LIFE IN ITALY. Lina Duff Gordon. Illustrated. *Third Edition. Demy 8vo. 10s. 6d. net.*

LAKES OF NORTHERN ITALY, THE. Richard Bagot. Illustrated. *Second Edition. Fcap. 8vo. 5s. net.*

LORENZO THE MAGNIFICENT. E. L. S. Horsburgh. Illustrated. *Second Edition. Demy 8vo. 15s. net.*

MEDICI POPES, THE. H. M. Vaughan. Illustrated. *Demy 8vo. 15s. net.*

ST. CATHERINE OF SIENA AND HER TIMES. By the Author of 'Mdlle. Mori.' Illustrated. *Second Edition. Demy 8vo. 7s. 6d. net.*

S. FRANCIS OF ASSISI, THE LIVES OF. Brother Thomas of Celano. *Cr. 8vo. 5s. net.*

SAVONAROLA, GIROLAMO. E. L. S. Horsburgh. Illustrated. *Fourth Edition. Cr. 8vo. 5s. net.*

SKIES ITALIAN: A Little Breviary for Travellers in Italy. Ruth S. Phelps. *Fcap. 8vo. 5s. net.*

UNITED ITALY. F. M. Underwood. *Demy 8vo. 10s. 6d. net.*

Part III.—A Selection of Works of Fiction

Albanesi (E. Maria). SUSANNAH AND ONE OTHER. *Fourth Edition. Cr. 8vo. 6s.*
I KNOW A MAIDEN. *Third Edition. Cr. 8vo. 6s.*
THE INVINCIBLE AMELIA; or, The Polite Adventuress. *Third Edition. Cr. 8vo. 3s. 6d.*
THE GLAD HEART. *Fifth Edition. Cr. 8vo. 6s.*
OLIVIA MARY. *Fourth Edition. Cr. 8vo. 6s.*
THE BELOVED ENEMY. *Second Edition. Cr. 8vo. 6s.*

Bagot (Richard). A ROMAN MYSTERY. *Third Edition Cr. 8vo. 6s.*
THE PASSPORT. *Fourth Edition. Cr. 8vo. 6s.*
ANTHONY CUTHBERT. *Fourth Edition. Cr. 8vo. 6s.*
LOVE'S PROXY. *Cr. 8vo. 6s.*
THE HOUSE OF SERRAVALLE. *Third Edition. Cr. 8vo. 6s.*
DARNELEY PLACE. *Second Edition. Cr. 8vo. 6s.*

Bailey (H. C.). THE LONELY QUEEN. *Third Edition. Cr. 8vo. 6s.*
THE SEA CAPTAIN. *Third Edition. Cr. 8vo. 6s.*
THE GENTLEMAN ADVENTURER. *Third Edition Cr. 8vo. 6s.*
THE HIGHWAYMAN. *Third Edition. Cr. 8vo. 6s.*

Baring-Gould (S.). THE BROOM-SQUIRE. Illustrated. *Fifth Edition. Cr. 8vo. 6s.*
PABO THE PRIEST. *Cr. 8vo. 6s.*
WINEFRED. Illustrated. *Second Edition. Cr. 8vo. 6s.*

Barr (Robert). IN THE MIDST OF ALARMS. *Third Edition. Cr. 8vo. 6s.*
THE COUNTESS TEKLA. *Fifth Edition. Cr. 8vo. 6s.*

THE MUTABLE MANY. *Third Edition. Cr. 8vo. 6s.*

Begbie (Harold). THE CURIOUS AND DIVERTING ADVENTURES OF SIR JOHN SPARROW, Bart.; or, The Progress of an Open Mind. *Second Edition. Cr. 8vo. 6s.*

Belloc (H.). EMMANUEL BURDEN, MERCHANT. Illustrated. *Second Edition. Cr. 8vo. 6s.*
A CHANGE IN THE CABINET. *Third Edition. Cr. 8vo. 6s.*

Bennett (Arnold). CLAYHANGER. *Twelfth Edition. Cr. 8vo. 6s.*
HILDA LESSWAYS. *Eighth Edition. Cr. 8vo. 6s.*
*THESE TWAIN. *Third Edition. Cr. 8vo. 6s.*
THE CARD. *Thirteenth Edition. Cr. 8vo. 6s.*
BURIED ALIVE. *Sixth Edition. Cr. 8vo. 6s.*
A MAN FROM THE NORTH. *Third Edition. Cr. 8vo. 6s.*
THE MATADOR OF THE FIVE TOWNS. *Second Edition. Cr. 8vo. 6s.*
THE REGENT: A Five Towns Story of Adventure in London. *Fourth Edition. Cr. 8vo. 6s.*
THE PRICE OF LOVE. *Fourth Edition. Cr. 8vo. 6s.*
WHOM GOD HATH JOINED. *A New Edition. Cr. 8vo. 6s.*
A GREAT MAN: A Frolic. *Sixth Edition. Cr. 8vo. 6s.*

Benson (E. F.). DODO: A Detail of the Day. *Seventeenth Edition. Cr. 8vo. 6s.*

Birmingham (George A.). SPANISH GOLD. *Seventeenth Edition. Cr. 8vo. 6s.*
THE SEARCH PARTY. *Tenth Edition. Cr. 8vo. 6s.*

Fiction

LALAGE'S LOVERS. *Third Edition. Cr. 8vo. 6s.*
THE ADVENTURES OF DR. WHITTY. *Fourth Edition. Cr. 8vo. 6s.*
GOSSAMER. *Third Edition. Cr. 8vo. 6s.*

Bowen (Marjorie). I WILL MAINTAIN. *Ninth Edition. Cr. 8vo. 6s.*
DEFENDER OF THE FAITH. *Seventh Edition. Cr. 8vo. 6s.*
A KNIGHT OF SPAIN. *Third Edition. Cr. 8vo. 6s.*
THE QUEST OF GLORY. *Third Edition. Cr. 8vo. 6s.*
GOD AND THE KING. *Sixth Edition. Cr. 8vo. 6s.*
THE GOVERNOR OF ENGLAND. *Third Edition. Cr. 8vo. 6s.*
PRINCE AND HERETIC. *Third Edition. Cr. 8vo. 6s.*
THE CARNIVAL OF FLORENCE. *Fifth Edition. Cr. 8vo. 6s.*
MR. WASHINGTON. *Third Edition. Cr. 8vo. 6s.*
BECAUSE OF THESE THINGS. *Third Edition. Cr. 8vo. 6s.*

Castle (Agnes and Egerton). THE GOLDEN BARRIER. *Third Edition. Cr. 8vo. 6s.*
FORLORN ADVENTURERS. *Second Edition. Cr. 8vo. 6s.*

Chesterton (G. K.). THE FLYING INN. *Fourth Edition. Cr. 8vo. 6s.*

Conrad (Joseph). THE SECRET AGENT: A SIMPLE TALE. *Fourth Edition. Cr. 8vo. 6s.*
A SET OF SIX. *Fourth Edition. Cr. 8vo. 6s.*
UNDER WESTERN EYES. *Second Edition. Cr. 8vo. 6s.*
VICTORY: AN ISLAND TALE. *Fifth Edition. Cr. 8vo. 6s.*
CHANCE. *Ninth Edition. Cr. 8vo. 6s.*

Conyers (Dorothea). SALLY. *Fourth Edition. Cr. 8vo. 6s.*
SANDY MARRIED. *Fifth Edition. Cr. 8vo. 6s.*
OLD ANDY. *Fourth Edition. Cr. 8vo. 6s.*

Corelli (Marie). A ROMANCE OF TWO WORLDS. *Thirty-Second Edition. Cr. 8vo. 6s.*
VENDETTA; OR, THE STORY OF ONE FORGOTTEN. *Thirty-second Edition. Cr. 8vo. 6s.*
THELMA: A NORWEGIAN PRINCESS. *Forty-sixth Edition. Cr. 8vo. 6s.*
ARDATH: THE STORY OF A DEAD SELF. *Twenty-second Edition. Cr. 8vo. 6s.*
THE SOUL OF LILITH. *Eighteenth Edition. Cr. 8vo. 6s.*
WORMWOOD: A DRAMA OF PARIS. *Twentieth Edition. Cr. 8vo. 6s.*
BARABBAS: A DREAM OF THE WORLD'S TRAGEDY. *Forty-eighth Edition. Cr. 8vo. 6s.*
THE SORROWS OF SATAN. *Sixtieth Edition. Cr. 8vo. 6s.*
THE MASTER-CHRISTIAN. *Fifteenth Edition. 181st Thousand. Cr. 8vo. 6s.*
TEMPORAL POWER: A STUDY IN SUPREMACY. *Second Edition. 150th Thousand. Cr. 8vo. 6s.*
GOD'S GOOD MAN: A SIMPLE LOVE STORY. *Seventeenth Edition. 156th Thousand. Cr. 8vo. 6s.*
HOLY ORDERS: THE TRAGEDY OF A QUIET LIFE. *Second Edition. 120th Thousand. Cr. 8vo. 6s.*
THE MIGHTY ATOM. *Thirty-second Edition. Cr. 8vo. 6s.*
BOY: A SKETCH. *Thirteenth Edition. Cr. 8vo. 6s.*
CAMEOS. *Fifteenth Edition. Cr. 8vo. 6s.*
THE LIFE EVERLASTING. *Sixth Edition. Cr. 8vo. 6s.*

Crockett (S. R.). LOCHINVAR. *Illustrated. Fourth Edition. Cr. 8vo. 6s.*
THE STANDARD BEARER. *Second Edition. Cr. 8vo. 6s.*

Doyle (Sir A. Conan). ROUND THE RED LAMP. *Twelfth Edition. Cr. 8vo. 6s.*

Findlater (J. H.). THE GREEN GRAVES OF BALGOWRIE. *Fifth Edition. Cr. 8vo. 6s.*

Fry (B. and C. B.). A MOTHER'S SON. *Fifth Edition. Cr. 8vo. 6s.*

Harraden (Beatrice). IN VARYING MOODS. *Fourteenth Edition. Cr. 8vo. 6s.*
HILDA STRAFFORD and THE REMITTANCE MAN. *Twelfth Edition. Cr. 8vo. 6s.*
INTERPLAY. *Fifth Edition. Cr. 8vo. 6s.*

Hichens (Robert). THE PROPHET OF BERKELEY SQUARE. *Second Edition. Cr. 8vo. 6s.*

TONGUES OF CONSCIENCE. *Fourth Edition. Cr. 8vo. 6s.*

FELIX: THREE YEARS IN A LIFE. *Seventh Edition. Cr. 8vo. 6s.*

THE WOMAN WITH THE FAN. *Eighth Edition. Cr. 8vo. 6s.*

BYEWAYS. *Cr. 8vo. 6s.*

THE GARDEN OF ALLAH. *Twenty-fifth Edition.* Illustrated. *Cr. 8vo. 6s.*

THE CALL OF THE BLOOD. *Ninth Edition. Cr. 8vo. 6s.*

BARBARY SHEEP. *Second Edition. Cr. 8vo. 3s. 6d.*

THE DWELLER ON THE THRESHOLD. *Cr. 8vo. 6s.*

THE WAY OF AMBITION. *Fifth Edition. Cr. 8vo. 6s.*

Hope (Anthony). A CHANGE OF AIR. *Sixth Edition. Cr. 8vo. 6s.*

A MAN OF MARK. *Seventh Edition. Cr. 8vo. 6s.*

THE CHRONICLES OF COUNT ANTONIO. *Sixth Edition. Cr. 8vo. 6s.*

PHROSO. Illustrated. *Ninth Edition. Cr. 8vo. 6s.*

SIMON DALE. Illustrated. *Ninth Edition. Cr. 8vo. 6s.*

THE KING'S MIRROR. *Fifth Edition. Cr. 8vo. 6s.*

QUISANTÉ. *Fourth Edition. Cr. 8vo. 6s.*

THE DOLLY DIALOGUES. *Cr. 8vo. 6s.*

TALES OF TWO PEOPLE. *Third Edition. Cr. 8vo. 6s.*

A SERVANT OF THE PUBLIC. Illustrated. *Fourth Edition. Cr. 8vo. 6s.*

THE GREAT MISS DRIVER. *Fourth Edition. Cr. 8vo. 6s.*

MRS. MAXON PROTESTS. *Third Edition. Cr. 8vo. 6s.*

A YOUNG MAN'S YEAR. *Second Edition. Cr. 8vo. 6s.*

Jacobs (W. W.). MANY CARGOES. *Thirty-third Edition. Cr. 8vo. 3s. 6d.* Also Illustrated in colour. *Demy 8vo. 7s. 6d. net.*

SEA URCHINS. *Seventeenth Edition. Cr. 8vo. 3s. 6d.*

A MASTER OF CRAFT. Illustrated. *Tenth Edition. Cr. 8vo. 3s. 6d.*

LIGHT FREIGHTS. Illustrated. *Eleventh Edition. Cr. 8vo. 3s. 6d.*

THE SKIPPER'S WOOING. *Twelfth Edition. Cr. 8vo. 3s. 6d.*

AT SUNWICH PORT. Illustrated. *Eleventh Edition. Cr. 8vo. 3s. 6d.*

DIALSTONE LANE. Illustrated. *Eighth Edition. Cr. 8vo. 3s. 6d.*

ODD CRAFT. Illustrated. *Fifth Edition. Cr. 8vo. 3s. 6d.*

THE LADY OF THE BARGE. Illustrated. *Ninth Edition. Cr. 8vo. 3s. 6d.*

SALTHAVEN. Illustrated. *Third Edition. Cr. 8vo. 3s. 6d.*

SAILORS' KNOTS. Illustrated. *Fifth Edition. Cr. 8vo. 3s. 6d.*

SHORT CRUISES. *Third Edition. Cr. 8vo. 3s. 6d.*

King (Basil). THE WILD OLIVE. *Third Edition. Cr. 8vo. 6s.*

THE STREET CALLED STRAIGHT. *Fourth Edition. Cr. 8vo. 6s.*

THE WAY HOME. *Second Edition. Cr. 8vo. 6s.*

THE LETTER OF THE CONTRACT. *Cr. 8vo. 6s.*

London (Jack). WHITE FANG. *Ninth Edition. Cr. 8vo. 6s.*

Lowndes (Mrs. Belloc). MARY PECHELL. *Second Edition. Cr. 8vo. 6s.*

STUDIES IN LOVE AND IN TERROR. *Second Edition. Cr. 8vo. 6s.*

THE END OF HER HONEYMOON. *Third Edition. Cr. 8vo. 6s.*

THE LODGER. *Third Edition. Crown 8vo. 6s.*

Lucas (E. V.). LISTENER'S LURE: AN OBLIQUE NARRATION. *Tenth Edition. Fcap. 8vo. 5s.*

OVER BEMERTON'S: AN EASY-GOING CHRONICLE. *Twelfth Edition. Fcap. 8vo. 5s.*

MR. INGLESIDE. *Tenth Edition. Fcap. 8vo. 5s.*

LONDON LAVENDER. *Eighth Edition. Fcap. 8vo. 5s.*

LANDMARKS. *Fourth Edition. Cr. 8vo. 6s.*

Fiction

Lyall (Edna). DERRICK VAUGHAN, NOVELIST. *44th Thousand. Cr. 8vo. 3s. 6d.*

Macnaughtan (S.). THE FORTUNE OF CHRISTINA M'NAB. *Fifth Edition. Cr. 8vo. 6s.*
PETER AND JANE. *Fourth Edition. Cr. 8vo. 6s.*

Malet (Lucas). A COUNSEL OF PERFECTION. *Second Edition. Cr. 8vo. 6s.*
COLONEL ENDERBY'S WIFE. *Fourth Edition. Cr. 8vo. 6s.*
THE HISTORY OF SIR RICHARD CALMADY: A ROMANCE. *Seventh Edition. Cr. 8vo. 6s.*
THE WAGES OF SIN. *Sixteenth Edition. Cr. 8vo. 6s.*
THE CARISSIMA. *Fifth Edition. Cr. 8vo. 6s.*
THE GATELESS BARRIER. *Fifth Edition. Cr. 8vo. 6s.*

Mason (A. E. W.). CLEMENTINA. Illustrated. *Ninth Edition. Cr. 8vo. 6s.*

Maxwell (W. B.). THE RAGGED MESSENGER. *Third Edition. Cr. 8vo. 6s.*
VIVIEN. *Thirteenth Edition. Cr. 8vo. 6s.*
THE GUARDED FLAME. *Seventh Edition. Cr. 8vo. 6s.*
ODD LENGTHS. *Second Edition. Cr. 8vo. 6s.*
HILL RISE. *Fourth Edition. Cr. 8vo. 6s.*
THE COUNTESS OF MAYBURY: BETWEEN YOU AND I *Fourth Edition. Cr. 8vo. 6s.*
THE REST CURE. *Fourth Edition. Cr. 8vo. 6s.*

Milne (A. A.). THE DAY'S PLAY. *Sixth Edition. Cr. 8vo. 6s.*
THE HOLIDAY ROUND. *Second Edition. Cr. 8vo. 6s.*
ONCE A WEEK. *Cr. 8vo. 6s.*

Montague (C. E.). A HIND LET LOOSE. *Third Edition. Cr. 8vo. 6s.*
THE MORNING'S WAR. *Second Edition. Cr. 8vo. 6s.*

Morrison (Arthur). TALES OF MEAN STREETS. *Seventh Edition. Cr. 8vo. 6s.*
A CHILD OF THE JAGO. *Sixth Edition. Cr. 8vo. 6s.*
THE HOLE IN THE WALL. *Fourth Edition. Cr. 8vo. 6s.*
DIVERS VANITIES. *Cr. 8vo. 6s.*

Ollivant (Alfred). OWD BOB, THE GREY DOG OF KENMUIR. With a Frontispiece. *Twelfth Edition. Cr. 8vo. 6s.*
THE TAMING OF JOHN BLUNT. *Second Edition. Cr. 8vo. 6s.*
THE ROYAL ROAD. *Second Edition. Cr. 8vo. 6s.*

Oppenheim (E. Phillips). MASTER OF MEN. *Fifth Edition. Cr. 8vo. 6s.*
THE MISSING DELORA. Illustrated. *Fourth Edition. Cr. 8vo. 6s.*
THE WAY OF THESE WOMEN. *Third Edition. Cr. 8vo. 6s.*
THE DOUBLE LIFE OF MR. ALFRED BURTON. *Second Edition. Cr. 8vo. 6s.*
A PEOPLE'S MAN. *Third Edition. Cr. 8vo. 6s.*
MR. GREX OF MONTE CARLO. *Third Edition. Cr. 8vo. 6s.*
*THE VANISHED MESSENGER. *Second Edition. Cr. 8vo. 6s.*

Oxenham (John). A WEAVER OF WEBS. Illustrated. *Fifth Edition. Cr. 8vo. 6s.*
PROFIT AND LOSS. *Sixth Edition. Cr. 8vo. 6s.*
THE LONG ROAD. *Fourth Edition. Cr. 8vo. 6s.*
THE SONG OF HYACINTH, AND OTHER STORIES. *Second Edition. Cr. 8vo. 6s.*
MY LADY OF SHADOWS. *Fourth Edition. Cr. 8vo. 6s.*
LAURISTONS. *Fourth Edition. Cr. 8vo. 6s.*
THE COIL OF CARNE. *Sixth Edition. Cr. 8vo. 6s.*
THE QUEST OF THE GOLDEN ROSE. *Fourth Edition. Cr. 8vo. 6s.*
MARY ALL-ALONE. *Third Edition. Cr. 8vo. 6s.*
BROKEN SHACKLES. *Fourth Edition. Cr. 8vo. 6s.*

Parker (Gilbert). PIERRE AND HIS PEOPLE. *Seventh Edition. Cr. 8vo. 6s.*
MRS. FALCHION. *Fifth Edition. Cr. 8vo. 6s.*

THE TRANSLATION OF A SAVAGE. *Fourth Edition. Cr. 8vo. 6s.*

THE TRAIL OF THE SWORD. Illustrated. *Tenth Edition. Cr. 8vo. 6s.*

WHEN VALMOND CAME TO PONTIAC: THE STORY OF A LOST NAPOLEON. *Seventh Edition. Cr. 8vo. 6s.*

AN ADVENTURER OF THE NORTH: THE LAST ADVENTURES OF 'PRETTY PIERRE.' *Fifth Edition. Cr. 8vo. 6s.*

THE SEATS OF THE MIGHTY. Illustrated. *Nineteenth Edition. Cr. 8vo. 6s.*

THE BATTLE OF THE STRONG: A ROMANCE OF TWO KINGDOMS. Illustrated. *Seventh Edition. Cr. 8vo. 6s.*

THE POMP OF THE LAVILETTES. *Third Edition. Cr. 8vo. 3s. 6d.*

NORTHERN LIGHTS. *Fourth Edition. Cr. 8vo. 6s.*

THE JUDGMENT HOUSE. *Fourth Edition. Cr. 8vo. 6s.*

Pemberton (Max). THE FOOTSTEPS OF A THRONE. Illustrated. *Fourth Edition. Cr. 8vo. 6s.*

I CROWN THEE KING. Illustrated. *Cr. 8vo. 6s.*

Perrin (Alice). THE CHARM. *Fifth Edition. Cr. 8vo. 6s.*

THE ANGLO-INDIANS. *Fifth Edition. Cr. 8vo. 6s.*

THE HAPPY HUNTING GROUND. *Third Edition. Cr. 8vo. 6s.*

Phillpotts (Eden). LYING PROPHETS. *Third Edition. Cr. 8vo. 6s.*

CHILDREN OF THE MIST. *Sixth Edition. Cr. 8vo. 6s.*

THE HUMAN BOY. With a Frontispiece. *Seventh Edition. Cr. 8vo. 6s.*

SONS OF THE MORNING. *Second Edition. Cr. 8vo. 6s.*

THE RIVER. *Fourth Edition. Cr. 8vo. 6s.*

THE AMERICAN PRISONER. *Fourth Edition. Cr. 8vo. 6s.*

THE PORTREEVE. *Fourth Edition. Cr. 8vo. 6s.*

THE STRIKING HOURS. *Second Edition. Cr. 8vo. 6s.*

DEMETER'S DAUGHTER. *Third Edition. Cr. 8vo. 6s.*

Pickthall (Marmaduke). SAID, THE FISHERMAN. *Tenth Edition. Cr. 8vo. 6s.*

Pleydell (George). THE WARE CASE. *Fcap. 8vo. 1s. net.*

'Q' (A. T. Quiller-Couch). MERRY-GARDEN AND OTHER STORIES. *Cr. 8vo. 6s.*

MAJOR VIGOUREUX. *Third Edition. Cr. 8vo. 6s.*

Reed (Myrtle). LAVENDER AND OLD LACE. *Fcap. 8vo. 1s. net.*

Ridge (W. Pett). A SON OF THE STATE. *Third Edition. Cr. 8vo. 3s. 6d.*

SPLENDID BROTHER. *Fourth Edition. Cr. 8vo. 6s.*

THANKS TO SANDERSON. *Second Edition. Cr. 8vo. 6s.*

THE REMINGTON SENTENCE. *Third Edition. Cr. 8vo. 6s.*

THE HAPPY RECRUIT. *Second Edition. Cr. 8vo. 6s.*

THE KENNEDY PEOPLE. *Second Edition. Cr. 8vo. 6s.*

Sidgwick (Mrs. Alfred). THE LANTERN-BEARERS. *Third Edition. Cr. 8vo. 6s.*

ANTHEA'S GUEST. *Fourth Edition. Cr. 8vo. 6s.*

LAMORNA. *Third Edition. Cr. 8vo. 6s.*

BELOW STAIRS. *Second Edition. Cr. 8vo. 6s.*

IN OTHER DAYS. *Third Edition. Cr. 8vo. 6s.*

Somerville (E. Œ.) and Ross (Martin). DAN RUSSEL THE FOX. Illustrated. *Seventh Edition. Cr. 8vo. 6s.*

Swinnerton (F.). ON THE STAIRCASE. *Second Edition. Cr. 8vo. 6s.*

Watson (F.). THE VOICE OF THE TURTLE. *Second Edition. Cr. 8vo. 6s.*

Wells (H. G.). BEALBY. *Third Edition. Cr. 8vo. 6s.*

Weyman (Stanley). UNDER THE RED ROBE. Illustrated. *Thirtieth Edition. Cr. 8vo. 6s.*

FICTION

Williamson (C. N. and A. M.). THE LIGHTNING CONDUCTOR: THE STRANGE ADVENTURES OF A MOTOR CAR. Illustrated. *Twenty-second Edition. Cr. 8vo. 6s.*

THE PRINCESS PASSES: A ROMANCE OF A MOTOR. Illustrated. *Ninth Edition. Cr. 8vo. 6s.*

LADY BETTY ACROSS THE WATER. *Eleventh Edition. Cr. 8vo. 6s.*

THE BOTOR CHAPERON. Illustrated *Tenth Edition. Cr. 8vo. 6s.*

THE CAR OF DESTINY. Illustrated. *Fifth Edition. Cr. 8vo. 6s.*

MY FRIEND THE CHAUFFEUR. Illustrated. *Thirteenth Edition. Cr. 8vo. 6s.*

SCARLET RUNNER. Illustrated. *Third Edition. Cr. 8vo. 6s.*

SET IN SILVER. Illustrated. *Fifth Edition. Cr. 8vo. 6s.*

LORD LOVELAND DISCOVERS AMERICA. Illustrated. *Second Edition. Cr. 8vo. 6s.*

THE GOLDEN SILENCE. Illustrated. *Seventh Edition. Cr. 8vo. 6s.*

THE GUESTS OF HERCULES. Illustrated. *Fourth Edition. Cr. 8vo. 6s.*

THE HEATHER MOON. Illustrated. *Fifth Edition. Cr. 8vo. 6s.*

IT HAPPENED IN EGYPT. Illustrated. *Seventh Edition. Cr. 8vo. 6s.*

THE SOLDIER OF THE LEGION. *Second Edition. Cr. 8vo. 6s.*

SECRET HISTORY. *Cr. 8vo. 6s.*

THE LOVE PIRATE. Illustrated. *Second Edition. Cr. 8vo. 6s.*

Books for Boys and Girls

Illustrated. Crown 8vo. 3s. 6d.

GETTING WELL OF DOROTHY, THE. Mrs. W. K. Clifford.

GIRL OF THE PEOPLE, A. L. T. Meade.

HONOURABLE MISS, THE. L. T. Meade.

MASTER ROCKAFELLAR'S VOYAGE. W. Clark Russell.

ONLY A GUARD-ROOM DOG. Edith E. Cuthell.

RED GRANGE, THE. Mrs. Molesworth.

SYD BELTON: The Boy who would not go to Sea. G. Manville Fenn.

THERE WAS ONCE A PRINCE. Mrs. M. E. Mann.

Methuen's Shilling Novels

Fcap. 8vo. 1s. net

ADVENTURES OF DR. WHITTY, THE. G. A. Birmingham.

ANGLO-INDIANS, THE. Alice Perrin.

ANNA OF THE FIVE TOWNS. Arnold Bennett.

*BABES IN THE WOOD. B. M. Croker.

BAD TIMES, THE. G. A. Birmingham.

BARBARY SHEEP. Robert Hichens.

BELOVED ENEMY, THE. E. Maria Albanesi.

BOTOR CHAPERON, THE. C. N and A. M. Williamson.

BOY. Marie Corelli.

CARD, THE. Arnold Bennett.

CHANGE IN THE CABINET, A. Hilaire Belloc.

CHINK IN THE ARMOUR, THE. Mrs. Belloc Lowndes.

CHRONICLES OF A GERMAN TOWN. The Author of "Mercia in Germany."

COIL OF CARNE, THE. John Oxenham.

COUNSEL OF PERFECTION, A. Lucas Malet.

DAN RUSSEL THE FOX. E. Œ. Somerville and Martin Ross.

Methuen's Shilling Novels—*continued.*

DEMON, THE. C. N. and A. M. Williamson.
DUKE'S MOTTO, THE. J. H. McCarthy.
FIRE IN STUBBLE. Baroness Orczy.
GATE OF DESERT, THE. John Oxenham.
GATES OF WRATH, THE. Arnold Bennett.
GUARDED FLAME, THE. W. B. Maxwell.
HALO, THE. Baroness von Hutten.
HEART OF THE ANCIENT WOOD, THE. Charles G. D. Roberts.
HILL RISE. W. B. Maxwell.
JANE. Marie Corelli.
JOSEPH. Frank Danby.
LADY BETTY ACROSS THE WATER. C. N. and A. M. Williamson.
LALAGE'S LOVERS. G. A. Birmingham.
LANTERN BEARERS, THE. Mrs. Alfred Sidgwick.
LIGHT FREIGHTS. W. W. Jacobs.
LONG ROAD, THE. John Oxenham.
MESS DECK, THE. W. F. Shannon.
MIGHTY ATOM, THE. Marie Corelli.
MIRAGE. E. Temple Thurston.
MISSING DELORA, THE. E. Phillips Oppenheim.
MY DANISH SWEETHEART. W. Clark Russell.
NINE DAYS' WONDER, A. B. M. Croker.
PATHWAY OF THE PIONEER, THE. Dolf Wyllarde.

PETER AND JANE. S. Macnaughtan.
QUEST OF THE GOLDEN ROSE, THE. John Oxenham.
ROUND THE RED LAMP. Sir A. Conan Doyle.
SAÏD, THE FISHERMAN. Marmaduke Pickthall.
SEA CAPTAIN, THE. H. C. Bailey.
SEA LADY, THE. H. G. Wells.
SEARCH PARTY, THE. G. A. Birmingham.
SECRET WOMAN, THE. Eden Phillpotts.
SHORT CRUISES. W. W. Jacobs.
SPANISH GOLD. G. A. Birmingham.
STREET CALLED STRAIGHT, THE. Basil King.
TALES OF MEAN STREETS. Arthur Morrison.
TERESA OF WATLING STREET. Arnold Bennett.
TYRANT, THE. Mrs. Henry de la Pasture.
UNDER THE RED ROBE. Stanley J. Weyman.
UNOFFICIAL HONEYMOON, THE. Dolf Wyllarde.
VIRGINIA PERFECT. Peggy Webling.
WALLET OF KAI LUNG. Ernest Bramah.
WEDDING DAY, THE. C. N. and A. M. Williamson.
WHITE FANG. Jack London.
WILD OLIVE, THE. Basil King.
WOMAN WITH THE FAN, THE. Robert Hichens.

Methuen's Sevenpenny Novels

Fcap. 8vo. 7d. net

ANGEL. B. M. Croker.
BARBARA REBELL. Mrs. Belloc Lowndes.
BLUNDER OF AN INNOCENT, THE. E. Maria Albanesi.
BROOM SQUIRE, THE. S. Baring-Gould.
BY STROKE OF SWORD. Andrew Balfour.

COUNT'S CHAUFFEUR, THE. William le Queux.
DERRICK VAUGHAN, NOVELIST. Edna Lyall.
DODO. E. F. Benson.
DRAMA IN SUNSHINE, A. H. A. Vachell.
DRIFT. L. T. Meade.

Methuen's Sevenpenny Novels—*continued*.

GOLDEN CENTIPEDE, THE. Louise Gerard.
GREEN GRAVES OF BALGOWRIE, THE. Jane H. Findlater.
HOUSE OF WHISPERS, THE. William le Queux.
HUMAN BOY, THE. Eden Phillpotts.
I CROWN THEE KING. Max Pemberton.
INCA'S TREASURE, THE. E. Glanville.
IN THE ROAR OF THE SEA. S. Baring-Gould.
INTO TEMPTATION. Alice Perrin.
KATHERINE THE ARROGANT. Mrs. B. M. Croker.
LADY IN THE CAR, THE. William le Queux.
LATE IN LIFE. Alice Perrin.
LONE PINE. R. B. Townshend.
LOVE PIRATE, THE. C. N. and A. M. Williamson.
MASTER OF MEN. E. Phillips Oppenheim.

MISER HOADLEY'S SECRET. A. W. Marchmont.
MIXED MARRIAGE, A. Mrs. F. E. Penny.
MOMENT'S ERROR, A. A. W. Marchmont.
MOTHER'S SON, A. B. and C. B. Fry.
PETER, A PARASITE. E. Maria Albanesi.
POMP OF THE LAVILETTES, THE. Sir Gilbert Parker.
PRINCE RUPERT THE BUCCANEER. C. J. Cutcliffe Hyne.
PRINCESS VIRGINIA, THE. C. N. and A. M. Williamson.
PROFIT AND LOSS. John Oxenham.
RED DERELICT, THE. Bertram Mitford.
RED HOUSE, THE. E. Nesbit.
SIGN OF THE SPIDER, THE. Bertram Mitford.
SON OF THE STATE, A. W. Pett Ridge.

Printed by MORRISON & GIBB LIMITED, *Edinburgh*

www.ingramcontent.com/pod-product-compliance
Lightning Source LLC
Chambersburg PA
CBHW031248230426
43670CB00005B/89